RA, ZETSUBOU-SENSEI

The Power of Negative Thinking (4)

Koji Kumeta

Translated and adapted by Joyce Aurino
Lettered by Foltz Design

BALLANTINE BOOKS • NEW YORK

Sayonara, Zetsubou-sensei: The Power of Negative Thinking volume 4 is a work of fiction. Names, characters, places, and incidents are the products of the author's imagination or are used fictitiously. Any resemblance to actual events, locales, or persons, living or dead, is entirely coincidental.

A Del Rey Manga/Kodansha Trade Paperback Original

Published in the United States by Del Rey, an imprint of The Random House Publishing Group, a division of Random House, Inc., New York.

Del Rey is a registered trademark and the Del Rey colophon is a trademark of Random House, Inc.

Publication rights arranged through Kodansha Ltd.

First published in Japan in 2006 by Kodansha Ltd., Tokyo

ISBN 978-0-345-51025-9

Printed in the United States of America

www.delreymanga.com

2 3 4 5 6 7 8 9

Translator/Adapter: Joyce Aurino
Lettering: Foltz Design

SAYONARA, ZETSUBOU-SENSEI

The Power of Negative Thinking ④

CONTENTS

Sayonara, Zetsubou-sensei: The Power of Negative Thinking

Koji Kumeta

Volume 4
Shônen Magazine Comics

SUMMARY OF PREVIOUS VOLUME

Nozomu, a man who loves peace and Stalin, is a veterinarian specializing in the care of carrier pigeons. One day, due to an injury, one of the carrier pigeons is unable to fly and Nozomu decides to become a carrier human in its place. He flies (on foot) to an address at Higashi-Jûjô but he throws in a dance for the addressee, a young executive with the Wind Underworld Dance Master, and his delivery is rejected.

Nozomu is told that if he holds his breath and does an underwater yoga position, the guy will receive the message, so there seems to be a smell of religion about this. When Nozomu tries to back out of it, saying it's a bit much, he's forced to take ten quizzes. The guy tells him to say the phrase "I'll do ascetic training" ten times, so it does, in fact, smell of religion. When Nozomu hurriedly runs out and jumps into a taxi, the driver asks him, "Dai Sakkai is a copy of Tenchûsatsu, isn't it? Isn't it?" While the driver is trying to get Nozomu to agree with him, and Nozomu is at a loss as to what to do, a Century with a black paint job rear-ends them.

Honorifics Explained

Throughout the Del Rey Manga books, you will find Japanese honorifics left intact in the translations. For those not familiar with how the Japanese use honorifics and, more important, how they differ from American honorifics, we present this brief overview.

Politeness has always been a critical facet of Japanese culture. Ever since the feudal era, when Japan was a highly stratified society, use of honorifics—which can be defined as polite speech that indicates relationship or status—has played an essential role in the Japanese language. When addressing someone in Japanese, an honorific usually takes the form of a suffix attached to one's name (example: "Asuna-san"), is used as a title at the end of one's name, or appears in place of the name itself (example: "Negi-sensei," or simply "Sensei").

Honorifics can be expressions of respect or endearment. In the context of manga and anime, honorifics give insight into the nature of the relationship between characters. Many English translations leave out these important honorifics and therefore distort the feel of the original Japanese. Because Japanese honorifics contain nuances that English honorifics lack, it is our policy at Del Rey not to translate them. Here, instead, is a guide to some of the honorifics you may encounter in Del Rey Manga.

-san: This is the most common honorific and is equivalent to Mr., Miss, Ms., or Mrs. It is the all-purpose honorific and can be used in any situation where politeness is required.

-sama: This is one level higher than "-san" and is used to confer great respect.

-dono: This comes from the word "tono," which means "lord." It is an even higher level than "-sama" and confers utmost respect.

-kun: This suffix is used at the end of boys' names to express familiarity or endearment. It is also sometimes used by men among friends, or when addressing someone younger or of a lower station.

-chan: This is used to express endearment, mostly toward girls. It is also used for little boys, pets, and even among lovers. It gives a sense of childish cuteness.

Bozu: This is an informal way to refer to a boy, similar to the English terms "kid" and "squirt."

Sempai/

Senpai: This title suggests that the addressee is one's senior in a group or organization. It is most often used in a school setting, where underclassmen refer to their upperclassmen as "sempai." It can also be used in the workplace, such as when a newer employee addresses an employee who has seniority in the company.

Kohai: This is the opposite of "sempai" and is used toward underclassmen in school or newcomers in the workplace. It connotes that the addressee is of a lower station.

Sensei: Literally meaning "one who has come before," this title is used for teachers, doctors, or masters of any profession or art.

-[blank]: This is usually forgotten in these lists, but it is perhaps the most significant difference between Japanese and English. The lack of honorific means that the speaker has permission to address the person in a very intimate way. Usually, only family, spouses, or very close friends have this kind of per- mission. Known as *yobisute,* it can be gratifying when some- one who has earned the intimacy starts to call one by one's name without an honorific. But when that intimacy hasn't been earned, it can be very insulting.

Koji Kumeta

SAYONARA, ZETSUBOU-SENSEI 4

The Power of Negative Thinking

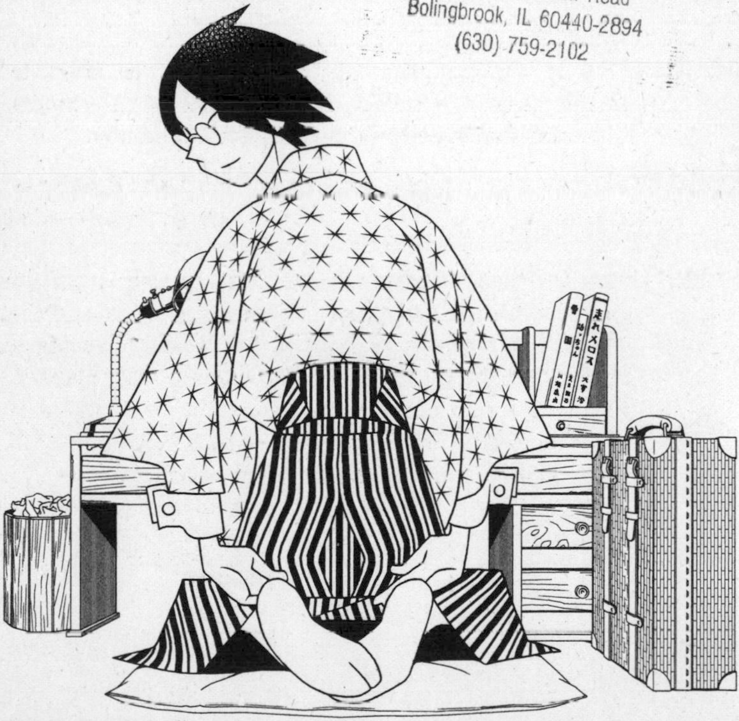

Contents

Originally published in 2006 in *Weekly Shōnen Magazine* #1 to #13 (no story was printed in #12).

Cast of Characters

ATTENDANCE LIST
CLASS 2-F

KAGER USAI
CLASS CHAIRMAN

TEACHER-IN-CHARGE
NOZOMU ITOSHIKI
SUPER-NEGATIVE MAN

NAMI HITOU
ORDINARY GIRL

ABIRU KOBUSHI
TAIL FETISH GIRL ; THOUGHT TO BE
VICTIM OF DOMESTIC VIOLENCE

MERU OTONASHI
POISON EMAIL GIRL

JUN KUTOU
MASTER STORYTELLER

HARUMI FUJIYOSHI
EAR FETISH,
ADDICTED TO COUPLING

KIRI KOMORI
HIKIKOMORI GIRL

CHIRI KITSU
METHODICAL AND PRECISE GIRL

**TARO MARIA
SEKIUTSU**
ILLEGAL IMMIGRANT; REFUGEE GIRL

KOTONON
NET IDOL

MATOI TSUNETSUKI
SUPER-LOVE-OBSESSED
STALKER GIRL

KAERE KIMURA
(ALSO KAEDE)
BILINGUAL GIRL

KAFUKA FUURA
SUPER-POSITIVE GIRL

THE THROWAWAY BRONZE

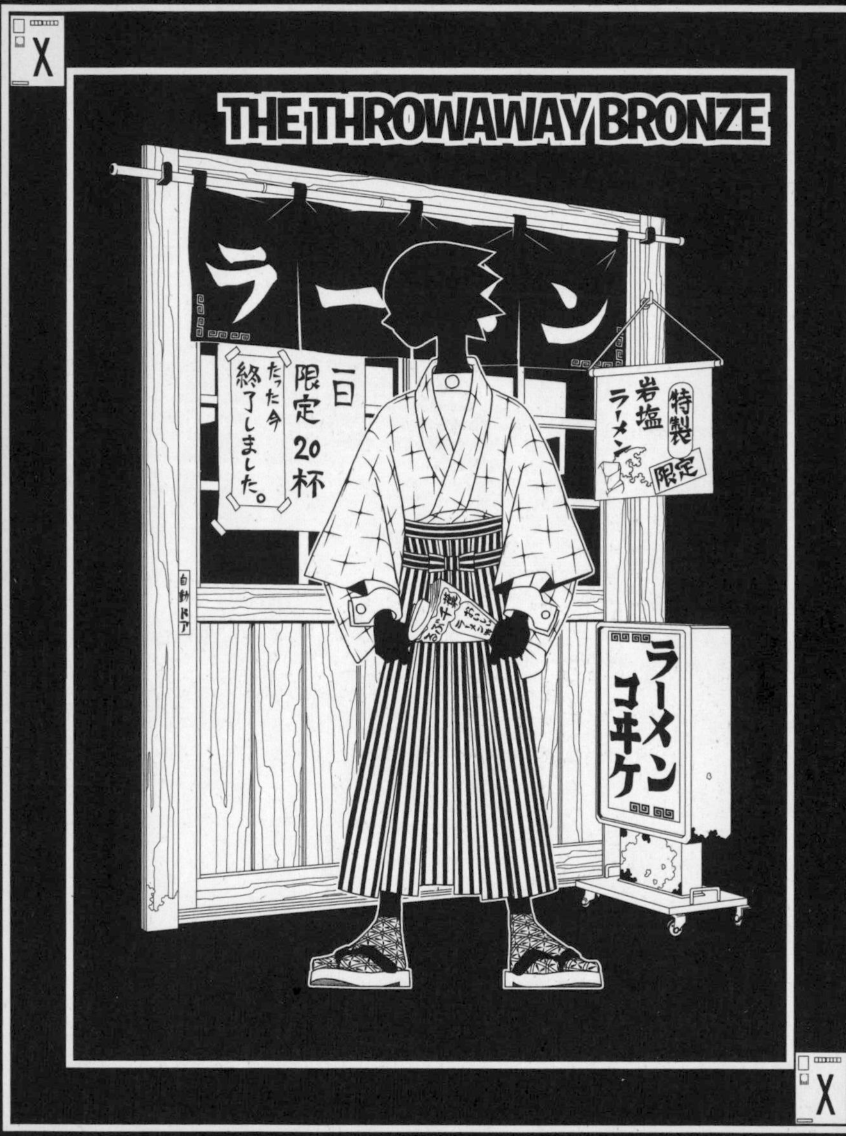
ラーメン
一日限定20杯
たった今終了しました。
自動ドア
特製
岩塩ラーメン
限定
ラーメン
コヰケ

CHAPTER 31

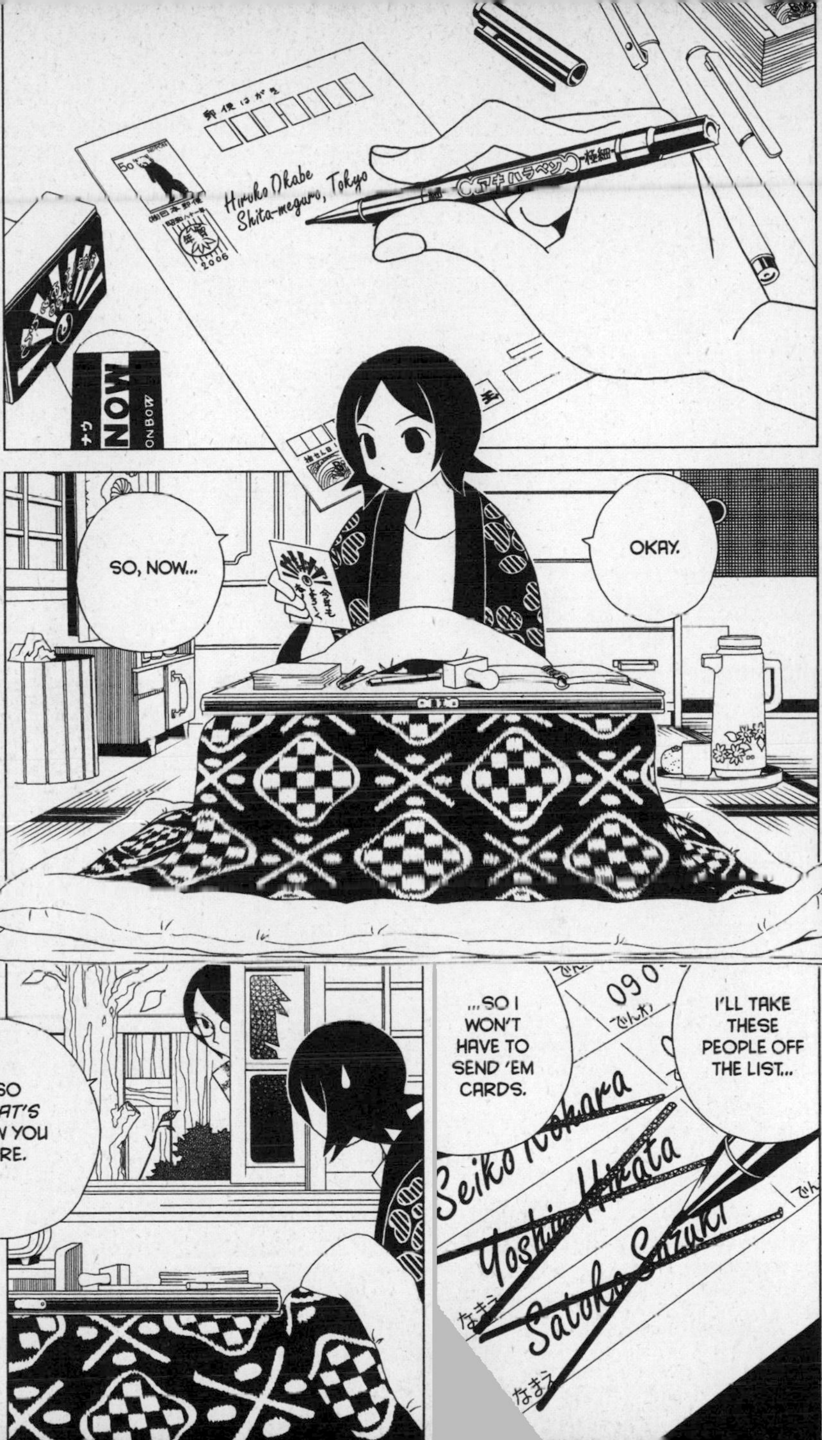
郵便はがき
Hiruko Okabe
Shita-megaro, Tokyo
2006
アキハラペン
極細
NOW
OKAY.
SO, NOW...
I'LL TAKE THESE PEOPLE OFF THE LIST...
...SO I WON'T HAVE TO SEND 'EM CARDS.
Satoko Suzuki
SO THAT'S HOW YOU ARE.

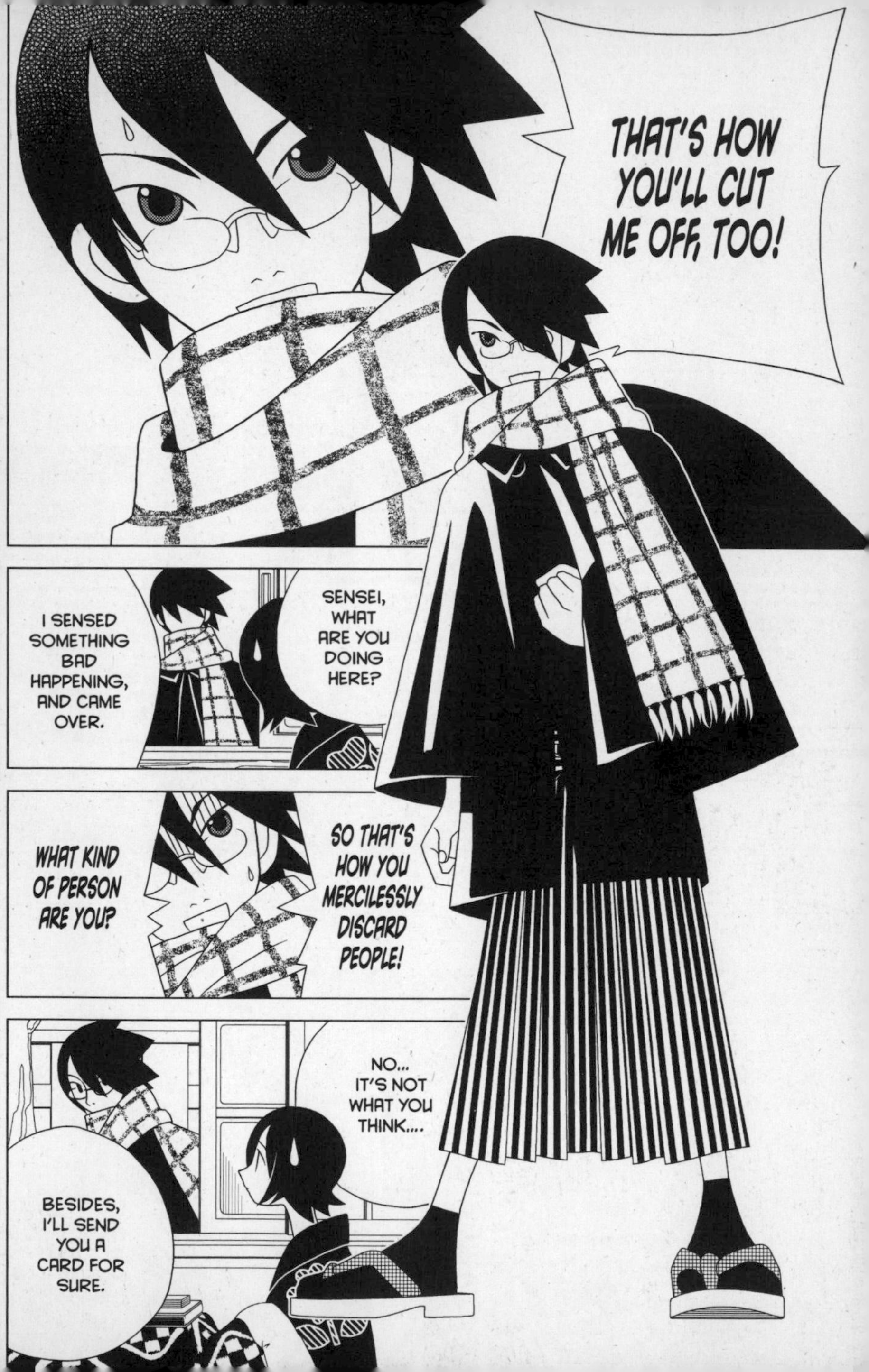
THAT'S HOW YOU'LL CUT ME OFF, TOO!
SENSEI, WHAT ARE YOU DOING HERE?
I SENSED SOMETHING BAD HAPPENING, AND CAME OVER.
SO THAT'S HOW YOU MERCILESSLY DISCARD PEOPLE!
WHAT KIND OF PERSON ARE YOU?
NO... IT'S NOT WHAT YOU THINK....
BESIDES, I'LL SEND YOU A CARD FOR SURE.

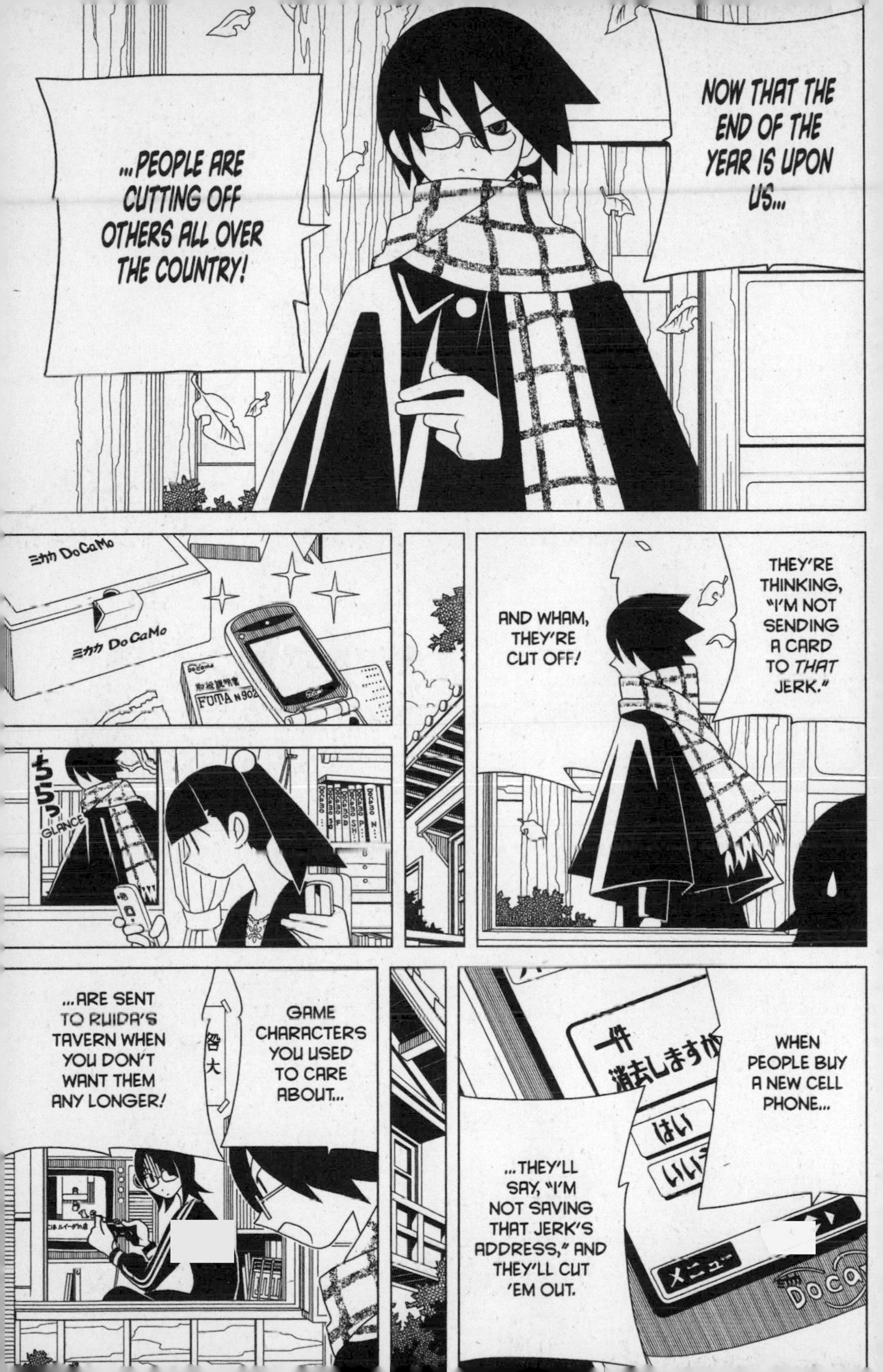
NOW THAT THE END OF THE YEAR IS UPON US...
...PEOPLE ARE CUTTING OFF OTHERS ALL OVER THE COUNTRY!
THEY'RE THINKING, "I'M NOT SENDING A CARD TO *THAT* JERK."
AND WHAM, THEY'RE CUT OFF!
ミカカ DoCaMo
ミカカ DoCaMo
FUTA N902
ちらっ
GLANCE
WHEN PEOPLE BUY A NEW CELL PHONE...
...THEY'LL SAY, "I'M NOT SAVING THAT JERK'S ADDRESS," AND THEY'LL CUT 'EM OUT.
一件
はい
メニュー
GAME CHARACTERS YOU USED TO CARE ABOUT...
...ARE SENT TO RUIDA'S TAVERN WHEN YOU DON'T WANT THEM ANY LONGER!

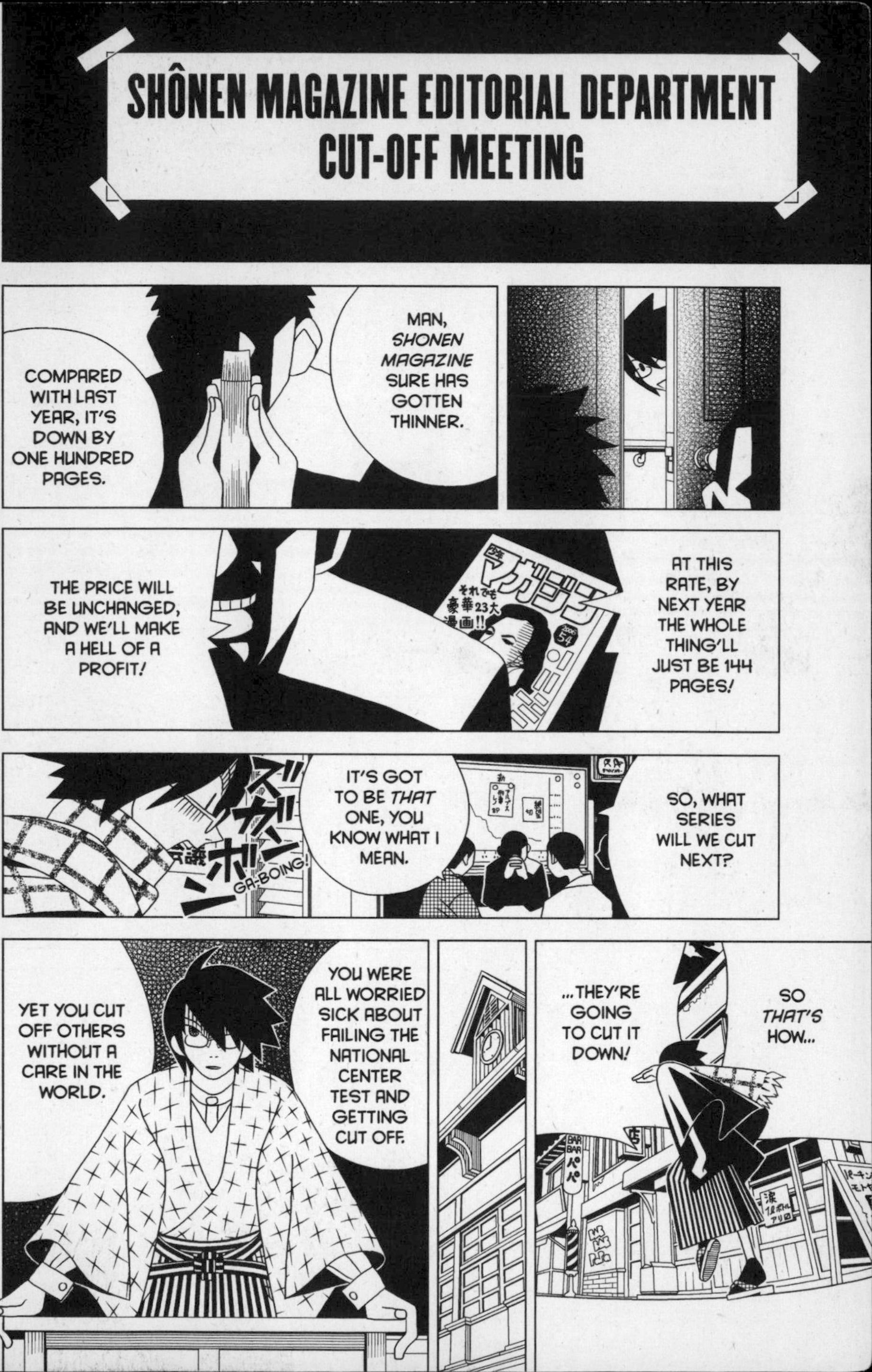
SHÔNEN MAGAZINE EDITORIAL DEPARTMENT
CUT-OFF MEETING
MAN, *SHONEN MAGAZINE* SURE HAS GOTTEN THINNER.
COMPARED WITH LAST YEAR, IT'S DOWN BY ONE HUNDRED PAGES.
AT THIS RATE, BY NEXT YEAR THE WHOLE THING'LL JUST BE 144 PAGES!
それでも豪華23大漫画!!
THE PRICE WILL BE UNCHANGED, AND WE'LL MAKE A HELL OF A PROFIT!
SO, WHAT SERIES WILL WE CUT NEXT?
IT'S GOT TO BE *THAT* ONE, YOU KNOW WHAT I MEAN.
GA-BOING!
SO *THAT'S* HOW...
...THEY'RE GOING TO CUT IT DOWN!
YOU WERE ALL WORRIED SICK ABOUT FAILING THE NATIONAL CENTER TEST AND GETTING CUT OFF.
YET YOU CUT OFF OTHERS WITHOUT A CARE IN THE WORLD.

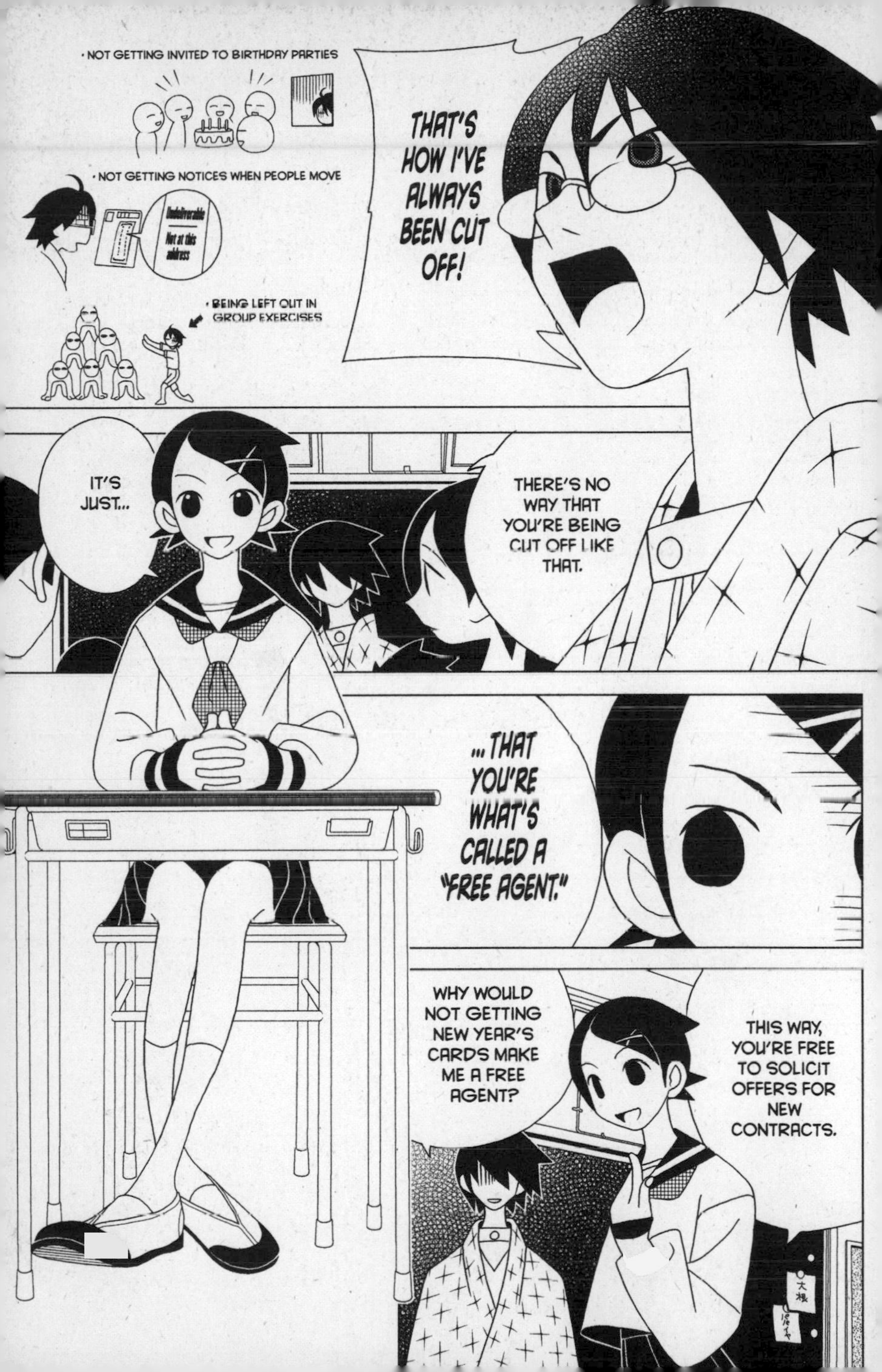
THAT'S HOW I'VE ALWAYS BEEN CUT OFF!
• NOT GETTING INVITED TO BIRTHDAY PARTIES
• NOT GETTING NOTICES WHEN PEOPLE MOVE
Undeliverable
Not at this address
• BEING LEFT OUT IN GROUP EXERCISES
THERE'S NO WAY THAT YOU'RE BEING CUT OFF LIKE THAT.
IT'S JUST...
...THAT YOU'RE WHAT'S CALLED A "FREE AGENT."
THIS WAY, YOU'RE FREE TO SOLICIT OFFERS FOR NEW CONTRACTS.
WHY WOULD NOT GETTING NEW YEAR'S CARDS MAKE ME A FREE AGENT?

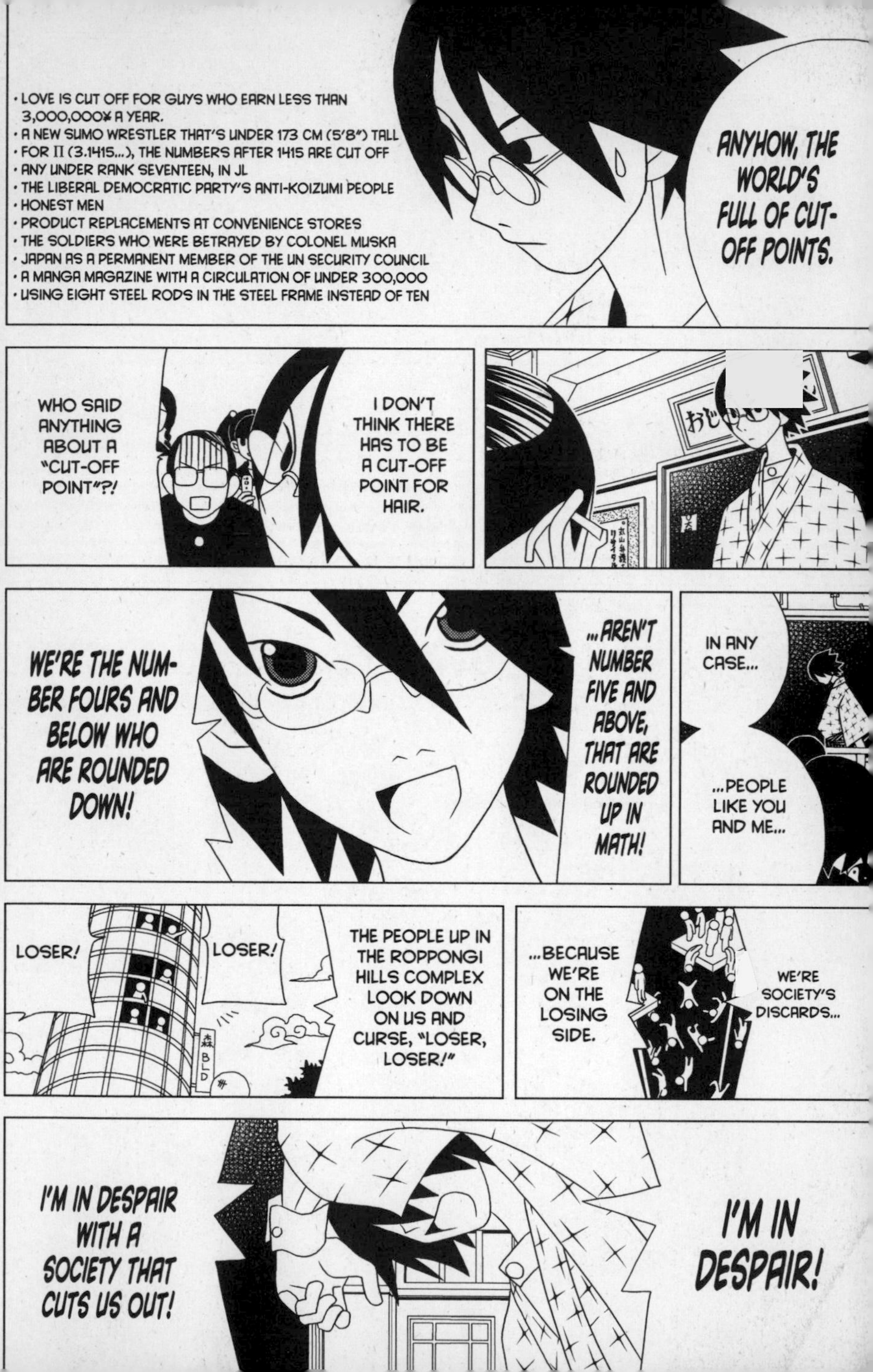
ANYHOW, THE WORLD'S FULL OF CUT-OFF POINTS.
• LOVE IS CUT OFF FOR GUYS WHO EARN LESS THAN 3,000,000¥ A YEAR.
• A NEW SUMO WRESTLER THAT'S UNDER 173 CM (5'8") TALL
• FOR Π (3.1415...), THE NUMBERS AFTER 1415 ARE CUT OFF
• ANY UNDER RANK SEVENTEEN, IN JL
• THE LIBERAL DEMOCRATIC PARTY'S ANTI-KOIZUMI PEOPLE
• HONEST MEN
• PRODUCT REPLACEMENTS AT CONVENIENCE STORES
• THE SOLDIERS WHO WERE BETRAYED BY COLONEL MUSKA
• JAPAN AS A PERMANENT MEMBER OF THE UN SECURITY COUNCIL
• A MANGA MAGAZINE WITH A CIRCULATION OF UNDER 300,000
• USING EIGHT STEEL RODS IN THE STEEL FRAME INSTEAD OF TEN
I DON'T THINK THERE HAS TO BE A CUT-OFF POINT FOR HAIR.
WHO SAID ANYTHING ABOUT A "CUT-OFF POINT"?!
IN ANY CASE...
...PEOPLE LIKE YOU AND ME...
...AREN'T NUMBER FIVE AND ABOVE, THAT ARE ROUNDED UP IN MATH!
WE'RE THE NUMBER FOURS AND BELOW WHO ARE ROUNDED DOWN!
WE'RE SOCIETY'S DISCARDS...
...BECAUSE WE'RE ON THE LOSING SIDE.
THE PEOPLE UP IN THE ROPPONGI HILLS COMPLEX LOOK DOWN ON US AND CURSE, "LOSER, LOSER!"
LOSER!
LOSER!
森 BLD
I'M IN DESPAIR!
I'M IN DESPAIR WITH A SOCIETY THAT CUTS US OUT!

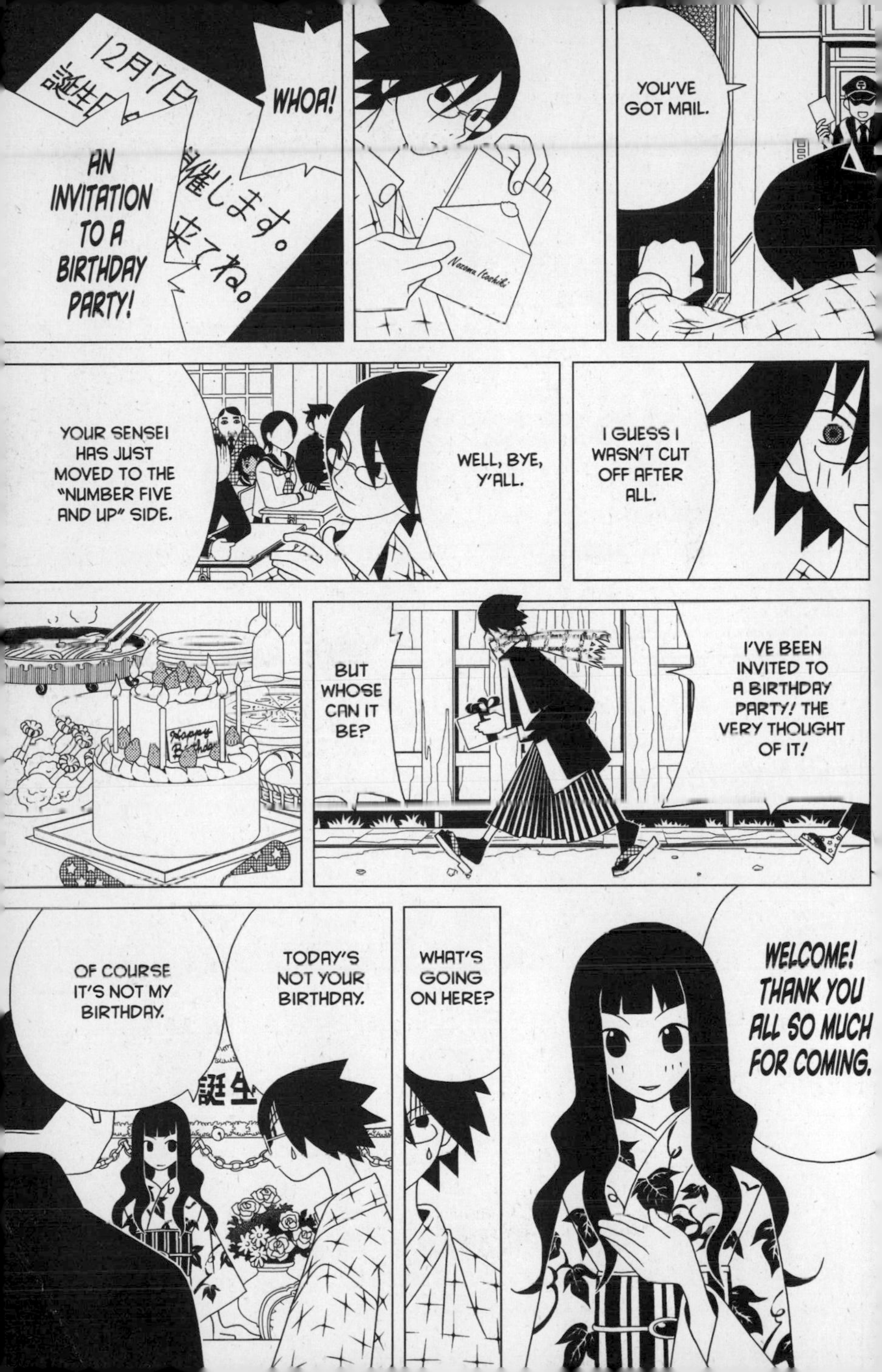
YOU'VE GOT MAIL.
WHOA!
Nozomu Itoshiki
12月7日
誕生日
催します。
来てね。
AN INVITATION TO A BIRTHDAY PARTY!
I GUESS I WASN'T CUT OFF AFTER ALL.
WELL, BYE, Y'ALL.
YOUR SENSEI HAS JUST MOVED TO THE "NUMBER FIVE AND UP" SIDE.
I'VE BEEN INVITED TO A BIRTHDAY PARTY! THE VERY THOUGHT OF IT!
BUT WHOSE CAN IT BE?
Happy Birthday
WELCOME! THANK YOU ALL SO MUCH FOR COMING.
WHAT'S GOING ON HERE?
TODAY'S NOT YOUR BIRTHDAY.
誕生
OF COURSE IT'S NOT MY BIRTHDAY.

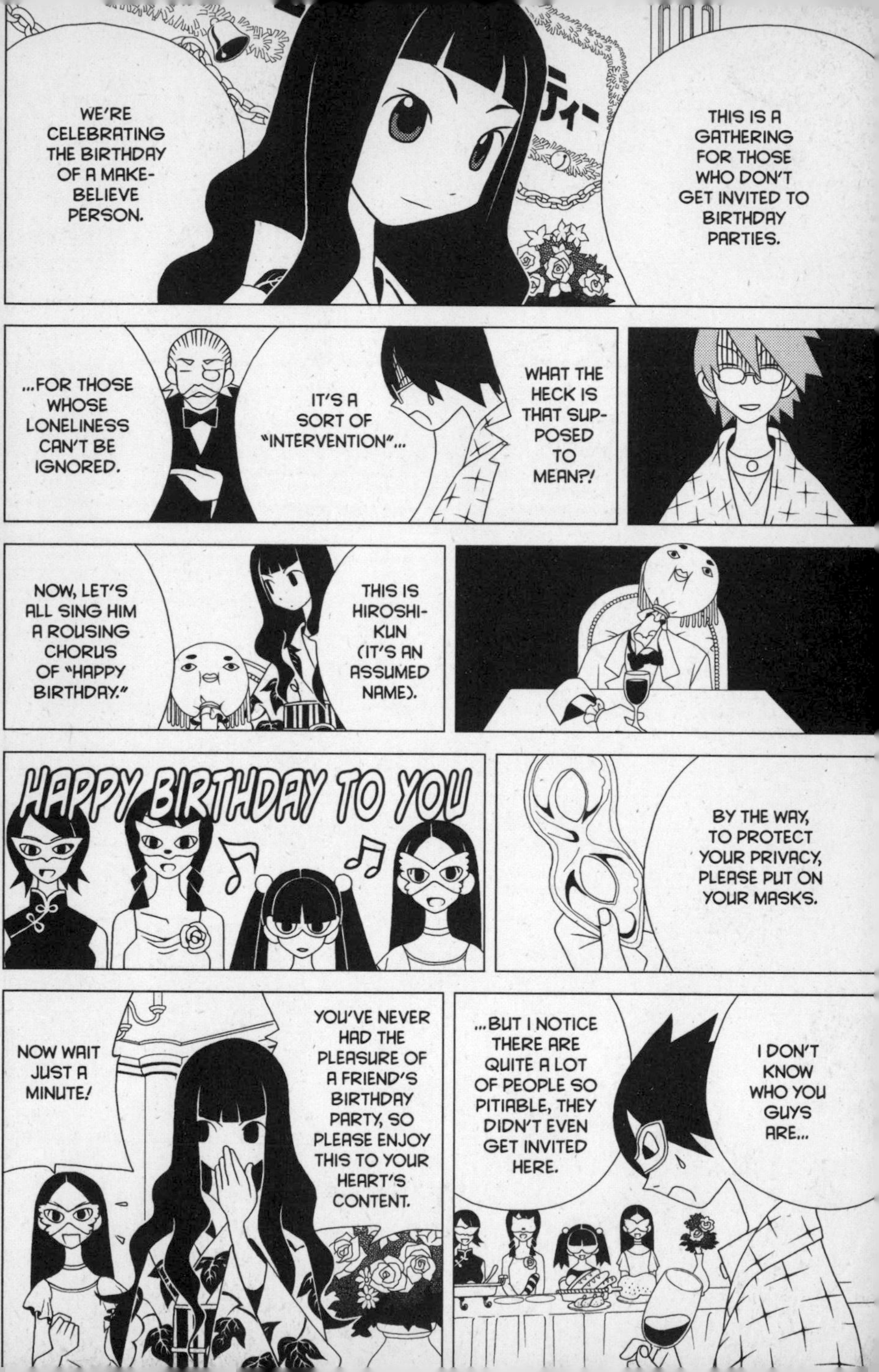
THIS IS A GATHERING FOR THOSE WHO DON'T GET INVITED TO BIRTHDAY PARTIES.
ティー
WE'RE CELEBRATING THE BIRTHDAY OF A MAKE-BELIEVE PERSON.
WHAT THE HECK IS THAT SUP-POSED TO MEAN?!
IT'S A SORT OF "INTERVENTION"...
...FOR THOSE WHOSE LONELINESS CAN'T BE IGNORED.
THIS IS HIROSHI-KUN (IT'S AN ASSUMED NAME).
NOW, LET'S ALL SING HIM A ROUSING CHORUS OF "HAPPY BIRTHDAY."
BY THE WAY, TO PROTECT YOUR PRIVACY, PLEASE PUT ON YOUR MASKS.
HAPPY BIRTHDAY TO YOU
I DON'T KNOW WHO YOU GUYS ARE...
...BUT I NOTICE THERE ARE QUITE A LOT OF PEOPLE SO PITIABLE, THEY DIDN'T EVEN GET INVITED HERE.
YOU'VE NEVER HAD THE PLEASURE OF A FRIEND'S BIRTHDAY PARTY, SO PLEASE ENJOY THIS TO YOUR HEART'S CONTENT.
NOW WAIT JUST A MINUTE!

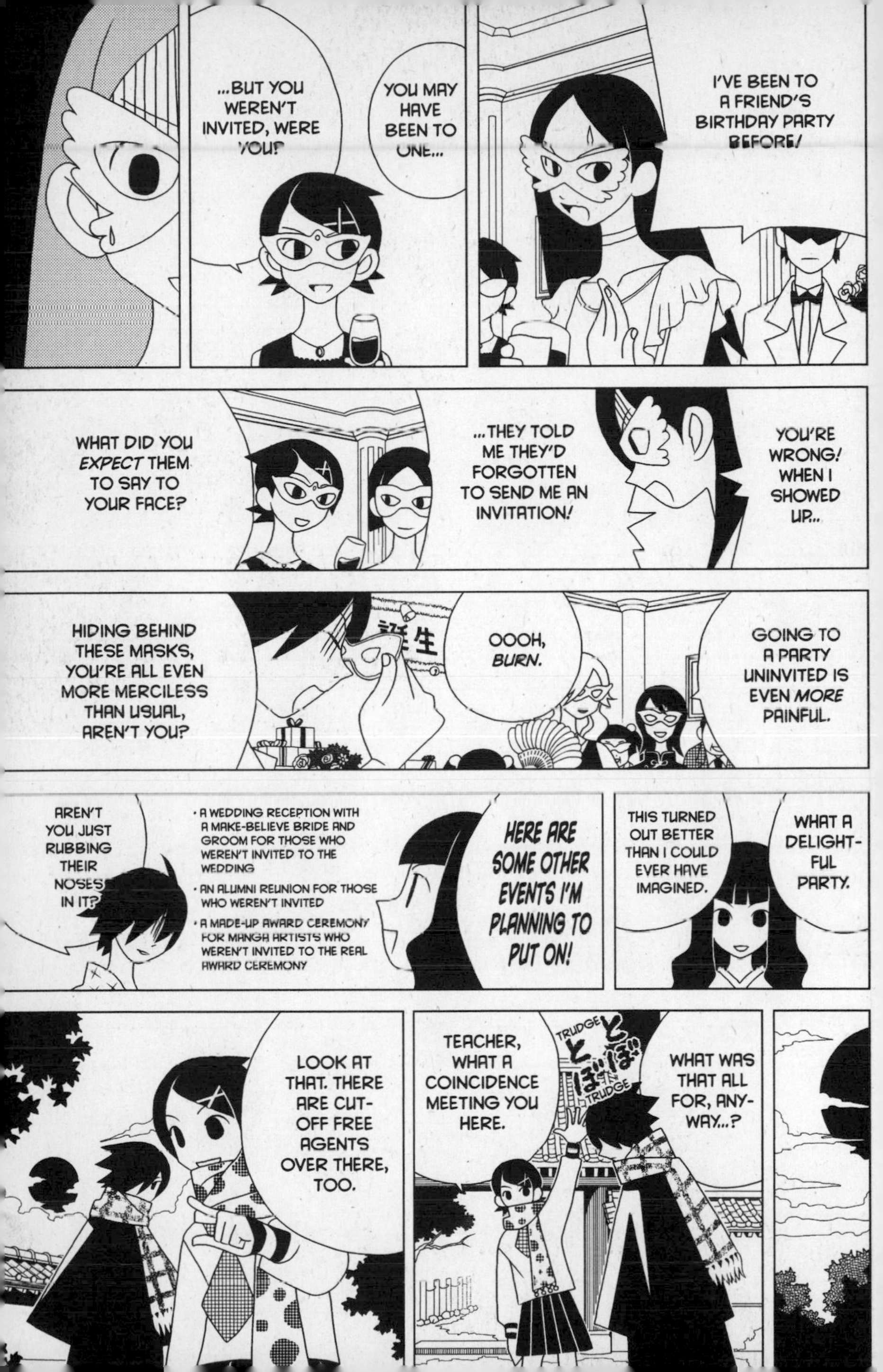
I'VE BEEN TO A FRIEND'S BIRTHDAY PARTY BEFORE!
YOU MAY HAVE BEEN TO ONE...
...BUT YOU WEREN'T INVITED, WERE YOU?
YOU'RE WRONG! WHEN I SHOWED UP...
...THEY TOLD ME THEY'D FORGOTTEN TO SEND ME AN INVITATION!
WHAT DID YOU *EXPECT* THEM TO SAY TO YOUR FACE?
GOING TO A PARTY UNINVITED IS EVEN *MORE* PAINFUL.
OOOH, *BURN.*
誕生
HIDING BEHIND THESE MASKS, YOU'RE ALL EVEN MORE MERCILESS THAN USUAL, AREN'T YOU?
WHAT A DELIGHTFUL PARTY.
THIS TURNED OUT BETTER THAN I COULD EVER HAVE IMAGINED.
HERE ARE SOME OTHER EVENTS I'M PLANNING TO PUT ON!
• A WEDDING RECEPTION WITH A MAKE-BELIEVE BRIDE AND GROOM FOR THOSE WHO WEREN'T INVITED TO THE WEDDING
• AN ALUMNI REUNION FOR THOSE WHO WEREN'T INVITED
• A MADE-UP AWARD CEREMONY FOR MANGA ARTISTS WHO WEREN'T INVITED TO THE REAL AWARD CEREMONY
AREN'T YOU JUST RUBBING THEIR NOSES IN IT?
WHAT WAS THAT ALL FOR, ANYWAY...?
とぼとぼ TRUDGE TRUDGE
TEACHER, WHAT A COINCIDENCE MEETING YOU HERE.
LOOK AT THAT. THERE ARE CUT-OFF FREE AGENTS OVER THERE, TOO.

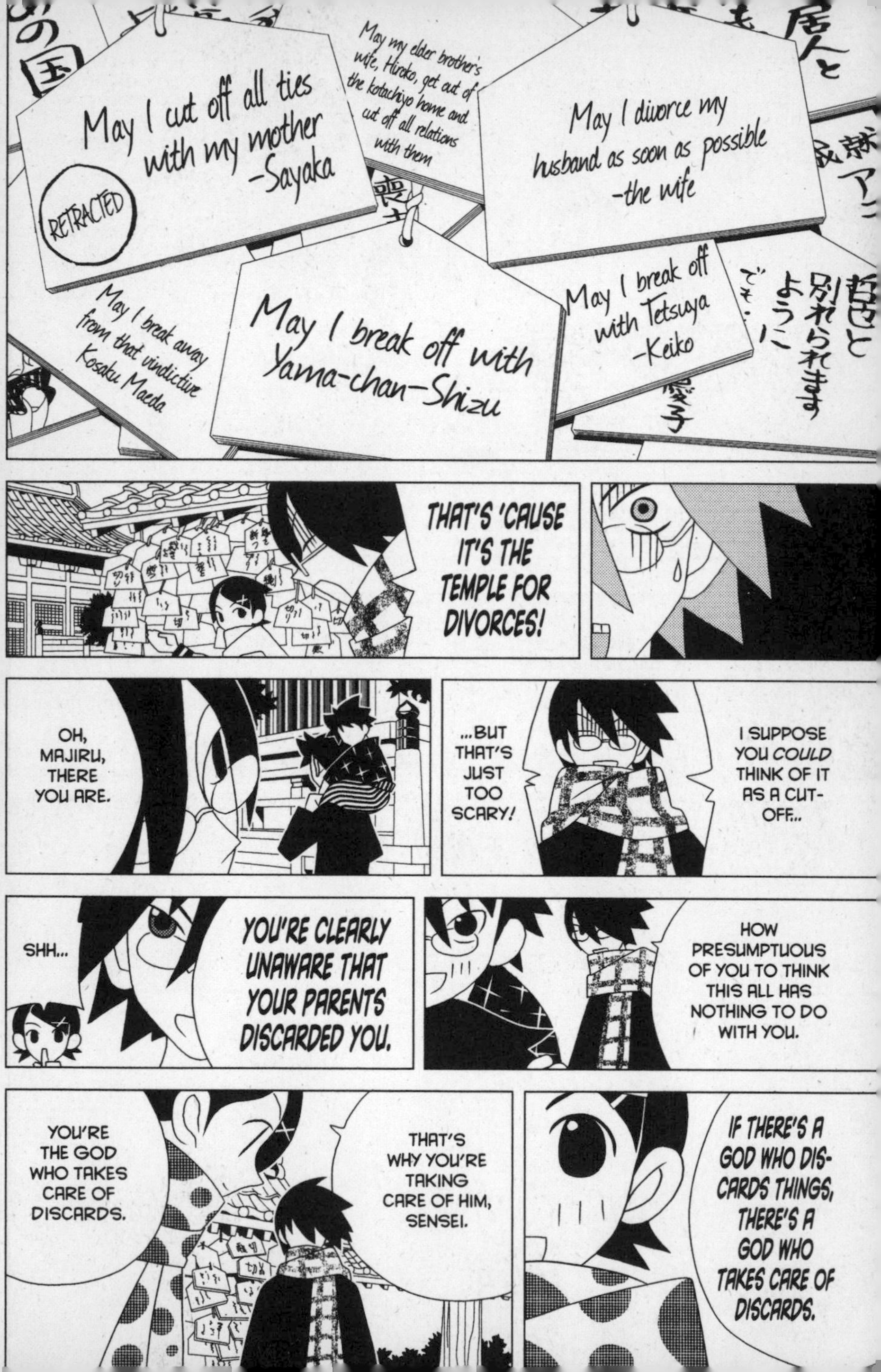
May I divorce my husband as soon as possible -the wife
May my elder brother's wife, Hiroko, get out of the kotachiyo home and cut off all relations with them
May I cut off all ties with my mother -Sayaka
RETRACTED
May I break off with Tetsuya -Keiko
May I break off with Yama-chan-Shizu
May I break away from that vindictive Kosaku Maeda
THAT'S 'CAUSE IT'S THE TEMPLE FOR DIVORCES!
I SUPPOSE YOU COULD THINK OF IT AS A CUT-OFF...
...BUT THAT'S JUST TOO SCARY!
OH, MAJIRU, THERE YOU ARE.
HOW PRESUMPTUOUS OF YOU TO THINK THIS ALL HAS NOTHING TO DO WITH YOU.
YOU'RE CLEARLY UNAWARE THAT YOUR PARENTS DISCARDED YOU.
SHH...
IF THERE'S A GOD WHO DISCARDS THINGS, THERE'S A GOD WHO TAKES CARE OF DISCARDS.
THAT'S WHY YOU'RE TAKING CARE OF HIM, SENSEI.
YOU'RE THE GOD WHO TAKES CARE OF DISCARDS.

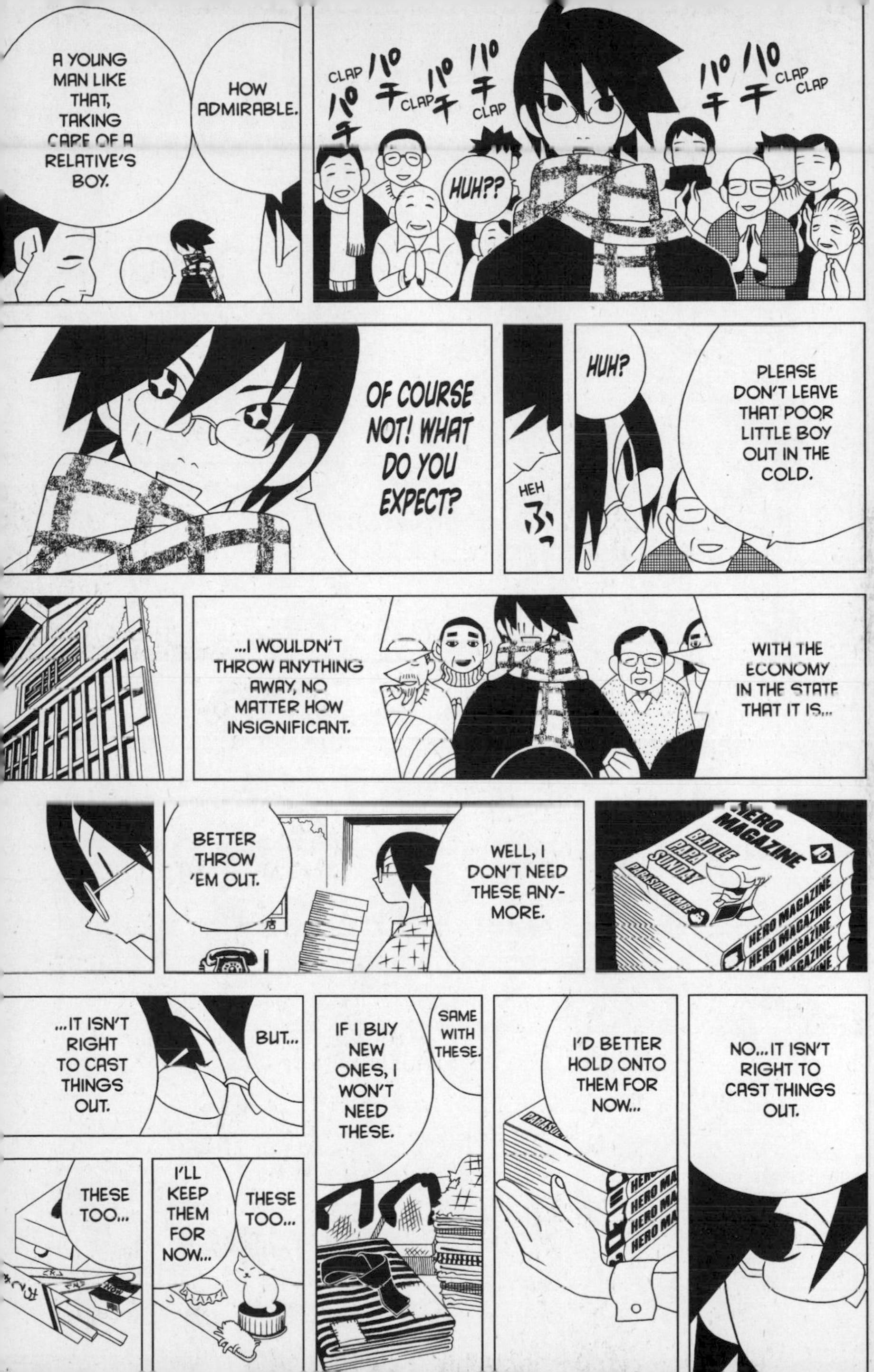
パチ パチ CLAP CLAP
パチ パチ CLAP CLAP CLAP パチ CLAP
HUH??
HOW ADMIRABLE.
A YOUNG MAN LIKE THAT, TAKING CARE OF A RELATIVE'S BOY.
PLEASE DON'T LEAVE THAT POOR LITTLE BOY OUT IN THE COLD.
HUH?
HEH ふっ
OF COURSE NOT! WHAT DO YOU EXPECT?
WITH THE ECONOMY IN THE STATE THAT IT IS...
...I WOULDN'T THROW ANYTHING AWAY, NO MATTER HOW INSIGNIFICANT.
HERO MAGAZINE
BATTLE PAPA SUNDAY
HERO MAGAZINE
HERO MAGAZINE
WELL, I DON'T NEED THESE ANYMORE.
BETTER THROW 'EM OUT.
NO...IT ISN'T RIGHT TO CAST THINGS OUT.
I'D BETTER HOLD ONTO THEM FOR NOW...
SAME WITH THESE.
IF I BUY NEW ONES, I WON'T NEED THESE.
BUT...
...IT ISN'T RIGHT TO CAST THINGS OUT.
THESE TOO...
I'LL KEEP THEM FOR NOW...
THESE TOO...

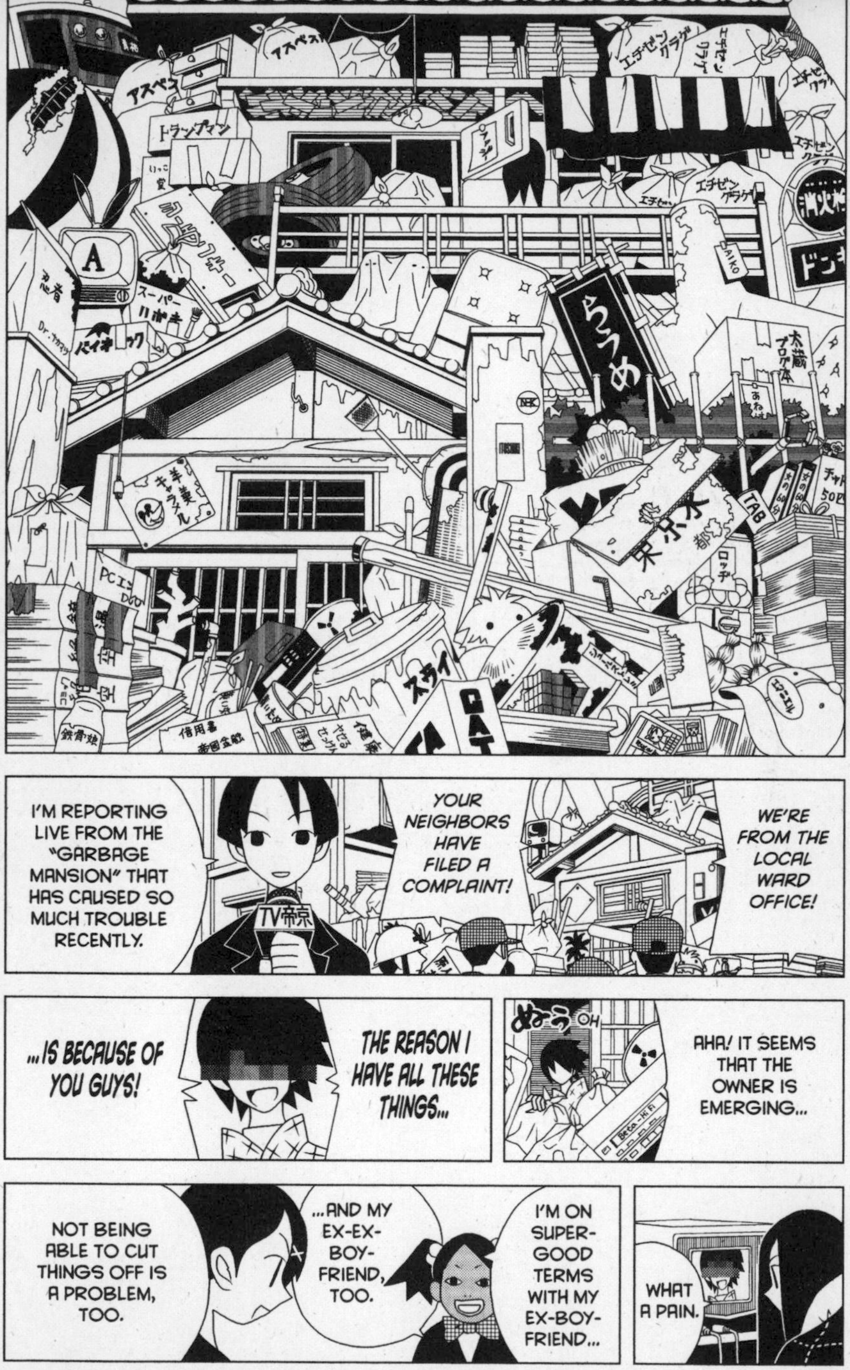
WE'RE FROM THE LOCAL WARD OFFICE!
YOUR NEIGHBORS HAVE FILED A COMPLAINT!
I'M REPORTING LIVE FROM THE "GARBAGE MANSION" THAT HAS CAUSED SO MUCH TROUBLE RECENTLY.
TV帝京
ぬうっ OH
AHA! IT SEEMS THAT THE OWNER IS EMERGING...
THE REASON I HAVE ALL THESE THINGS...
...IS BECAUSE OF YOU GUYS!
WHAT A PAIN.
I'M ON SUPER-GOOD TERMS WITH MY EX-BOY-FRIEND...
...AND MY EX-EX-BOY-FRIEND, TOO.
NOT BEING ABLE TO CUT THINGS OFF IS A PROBLEM, TOO.

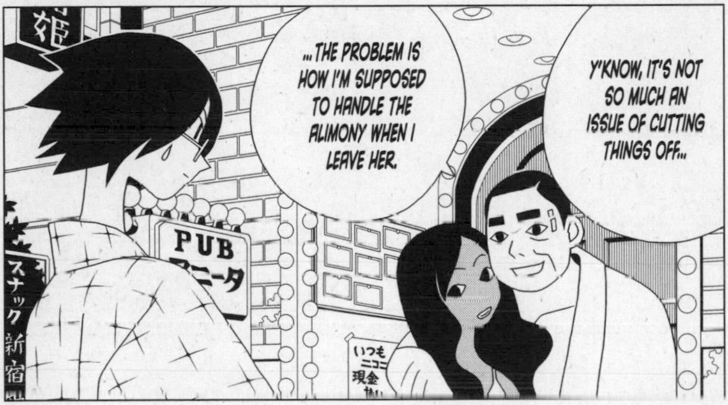
Y'KNOW, IT'S NOT SO MUCH AN ISSUE OF CUTTING THINGS OFF...
...THE PROBLEM IS HOW I'M SUPPOSED TO HANDLE THE ALIMONY WHEN I LEAVE HER.
PUB

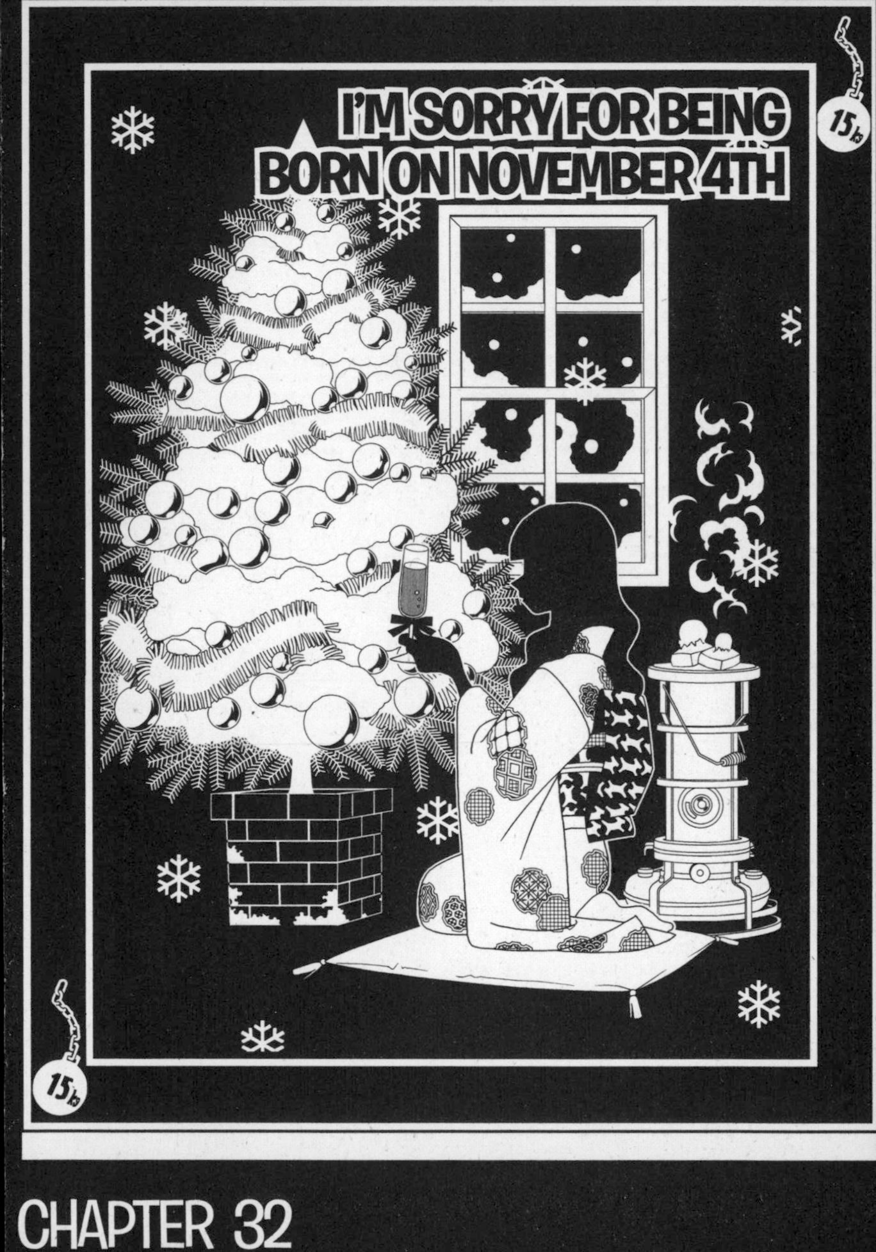
I'M SORRY FOR BEING
BORN ON NOVEMBER 4TH
15kg
15kg

CHAPTER 32

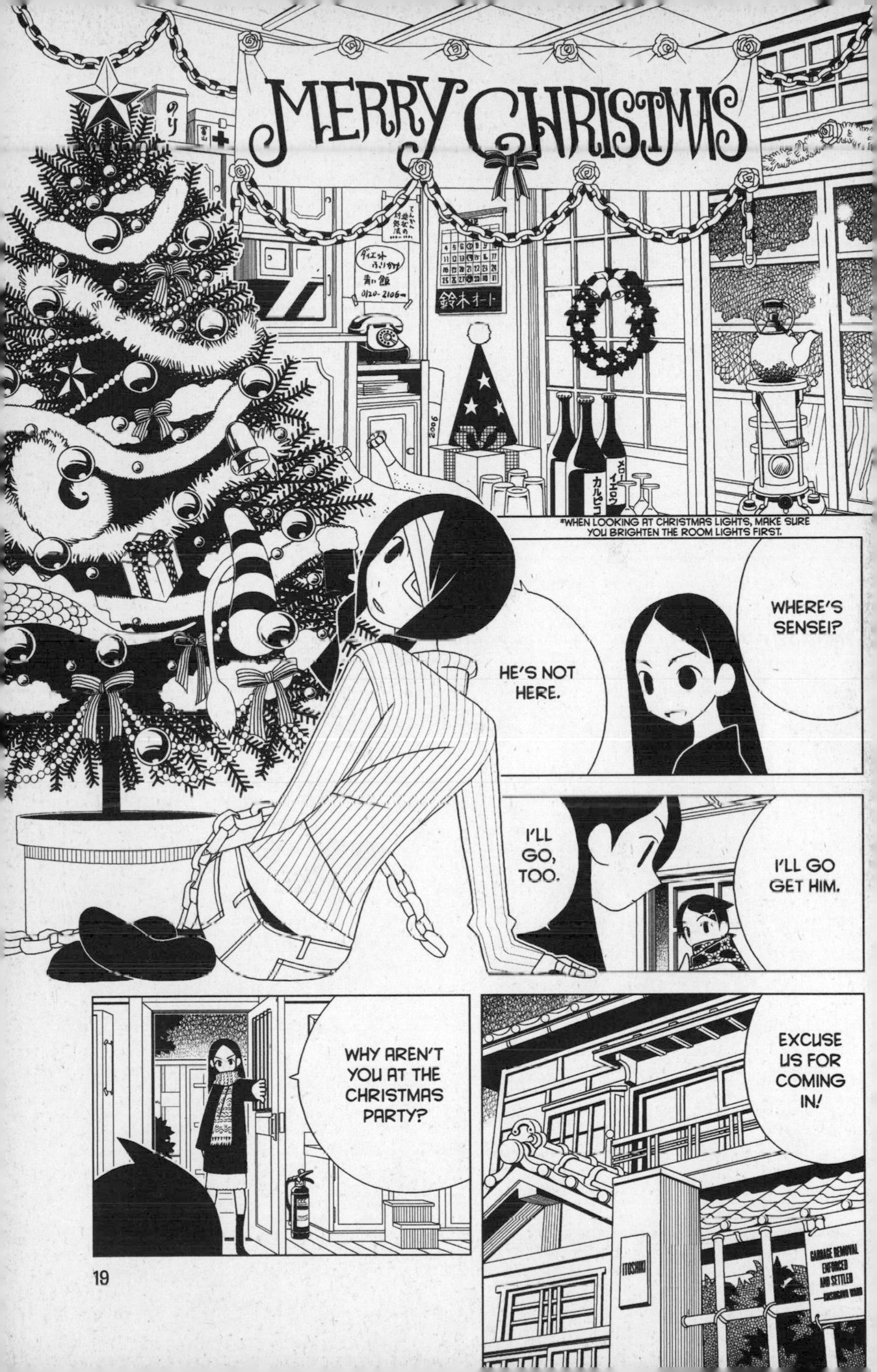
MERRY CHRISTMAS
*WHEN LOOKING AT CHRISTMAS LIGHTS, MAKE SURE YOU BRIGHTEN THE ROOM LIGHTS FIRST.
鈴木オート
WHERE'S SENSEI?
HE'S NOT HERE.
I'LL GO GET HIM.
I'LL GO, TOO.
EXCUSE US FOR COMING IN!
ITOSHIKI
GARBAGE REMOVAL ENFORCED AND SETTLED
WHY AREN'T YOU AT THE CHRISTMAS PARTY?

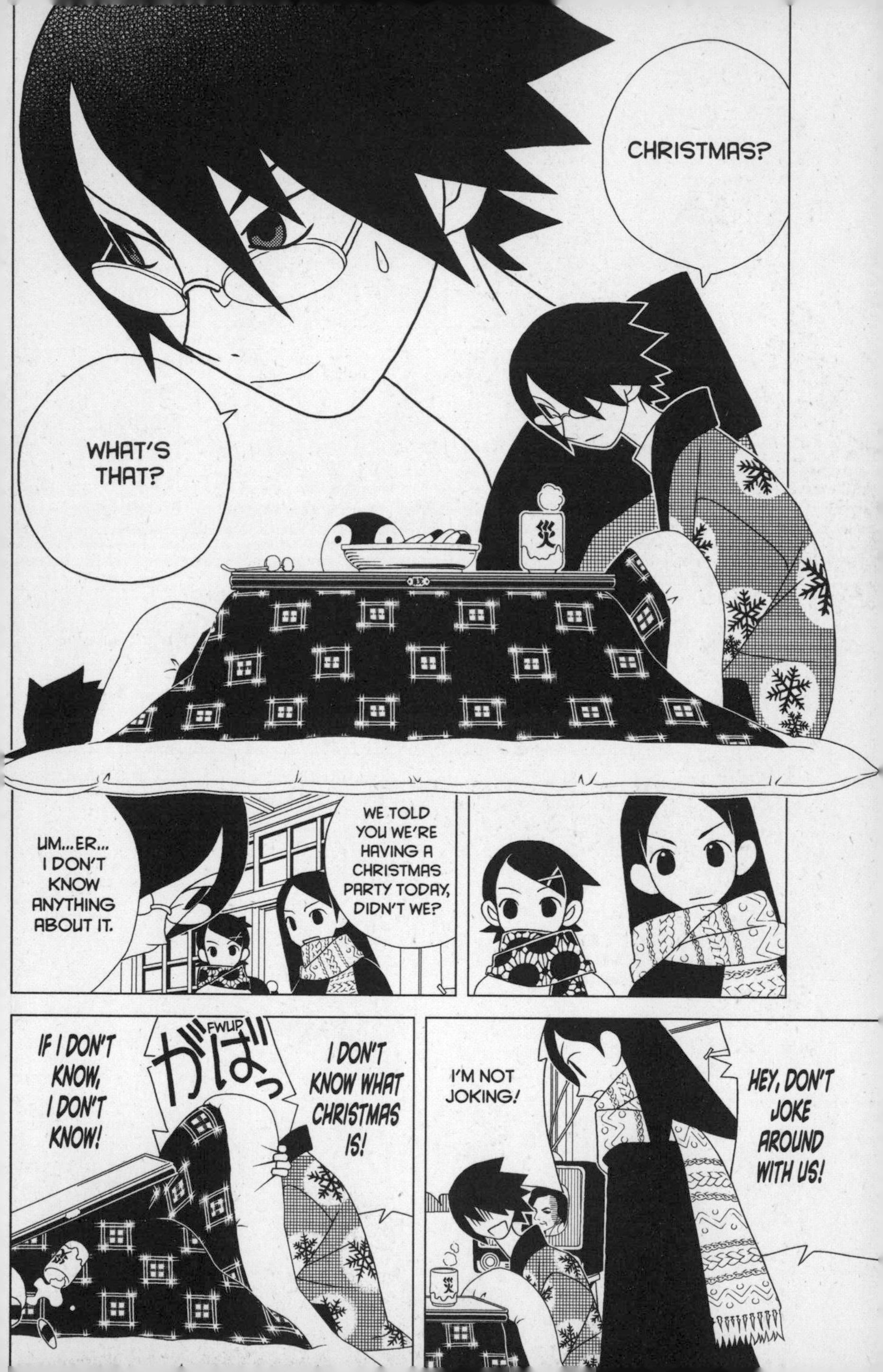
CHRISTMAS?
WHAT'S THAT?
WE TOLD YOU WE'RE HAVING A CHRISTMAS PARTY TODAY, DIDN'T WE?
UM...ER... I DON'T KNOW ANYTHING ABOUT IT.
HEY, DON'T JOKE AROUND WITH US!
I'M NOT JOKING!
I DON'T KNOW WHAT CHRISTMAS IS!
がばっ
FWUP
IF I DON'T KNOW, I DON'T KNOW!

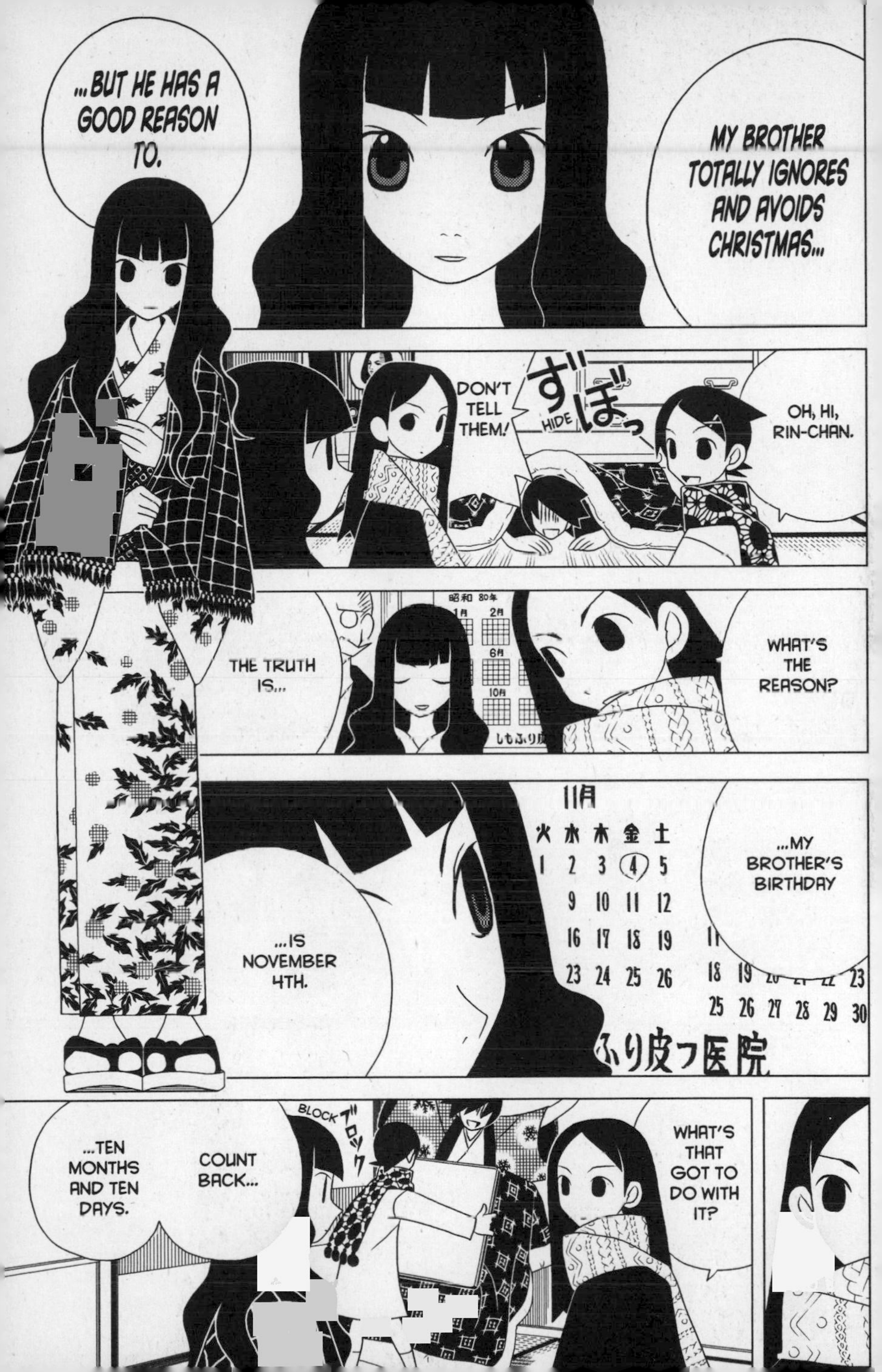
MY BROTHER TOTALLY IGNORES AND AVOIDS CHRISTMAS...
...BUT HE HAS A GOOD REASON TO.
OH, HI, RIN-CHAN.
ずぼっ
HIDE
DON'T TELL THEM!
WHAT'S THE REASON?
THE TRUTH IS...
昭和 80年
しもふり皮
...MY BROTHER'S BIRTHDAY
...IS NOVEMBER 4TH.
11月
ふり皮っ医院
WHAT'S THAT GOT TO DO WITH IT?
ブロック
BLOCK
COUNT BACK...
...TEN MONTHS AND TEN DAYS.

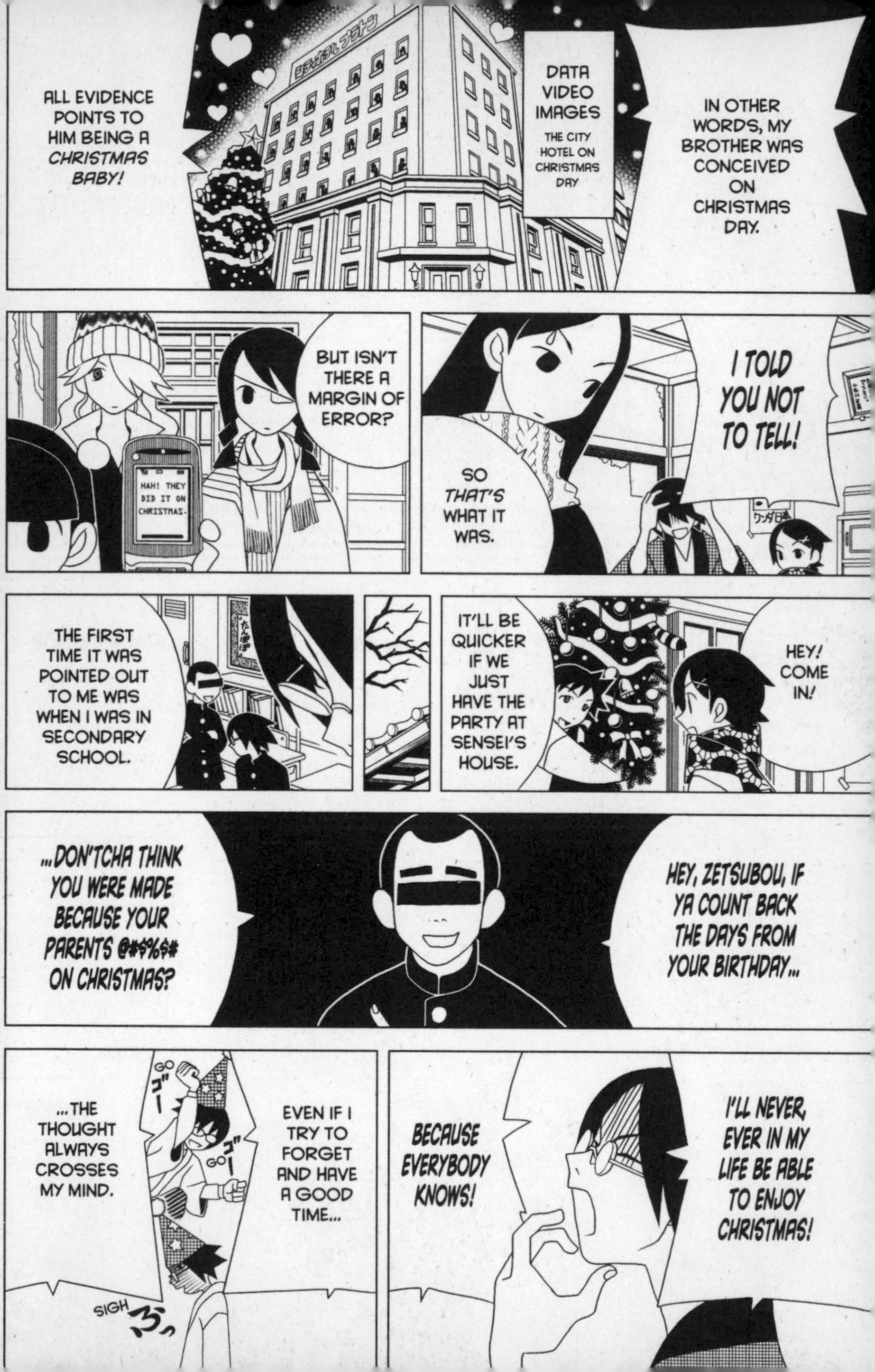
IN OTHER WORDS, MY BROTHER WAS CONCEIVED ON CHRISTMAS DAY.
DATA VIDEO IMAGES
THE CITY HOTEL ON CHRISTMAS DAY
ALL EVIDENCE POINTS TO HIM BEING A *CHRISTMAS BABY!*
I TOLD YOU NOT TO TELL!
SO *THAT'S* WHAT IT WAS.
BUT ISN'T THERE A MARGIN OF ERROR?
HAH! THEY DID IT ON CHRISTMAS.
HEY! COME IN!
IT'LL BE QUICKER IF WE JUST HAVE THE PARTY AT SENSEI'S HOUSE.
THE FIRST TIME IT WAS POINTED OUT TO ME WAS WHEN I WAS IN SECONDARY SCHOOL.
HEY, ZETSUBOU, IF YA COUNT BACK THE DAYS FROM YOUR BIRTHDAY...
...DON'TCHA THINK YOU WERE MADE BECAUSE YOUR PARENTS @#$%$# ON CHRISTMAS?
I'LL NEVER, EVER IN MY LIFE BE ABLE TO ENJOY CHRISTMAS!
BECAUSE EVERYBODY KNOWS!
EVEN IF I TRY TO FORGET AND HAVE A GOOD TIME...
GO
GO
...THE THOUGHT ALWAYS CROSSES MY MIND.
SIGH

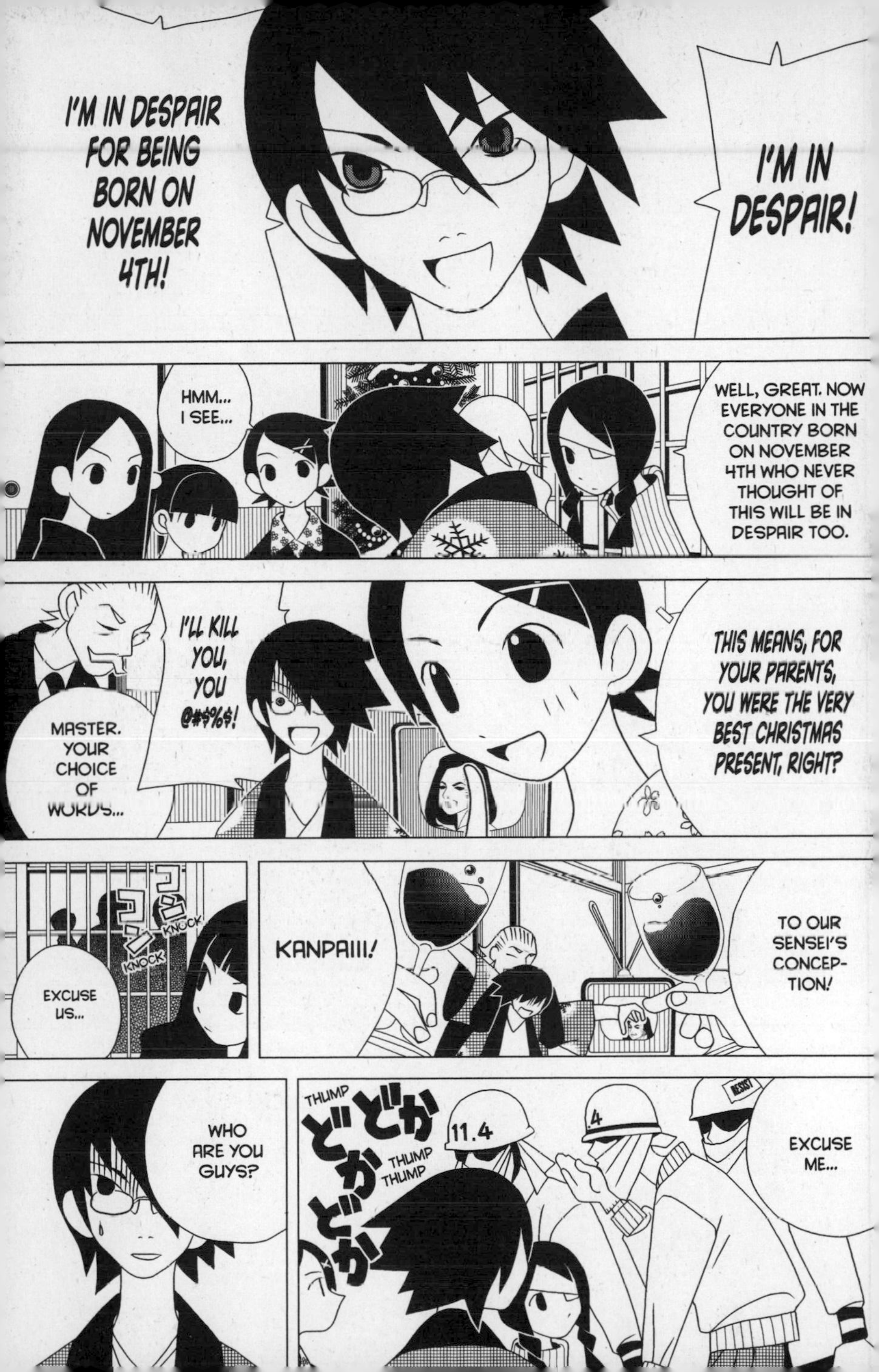
I'M IN DESPAIR!
I'M IN DESPAIR FOR BEING BORN ON NOVEMBER 4TH!
WELL, GREAT. NOW EVERYONE IN THE COUNTRY BORN ON NOVEMBER 4TH WHO NEVER THOUGHT OF THIS WILL BE IN DESPAIR TOO.
HMM... I SEE...
THIS MEANS, FOR YOUR PARENTS, YOU WERE THE VERY BEST CHRISTMAS PRESENT, RIGHT?
I'LL KILL YOU, YOU @#$%$!
MASTER. YOUR CHOICE OF WORDS...
TO OUR SENSEI'S CONCEPTION!
KANPAIII!
コン コン
KNOCK KNOCK
EXCUSE US...
EXCUSE ME...
RESIST
.4
11.4
どかどか どかどか
THUMP THUMP THUMP
WHO ARE YOU GUYS?

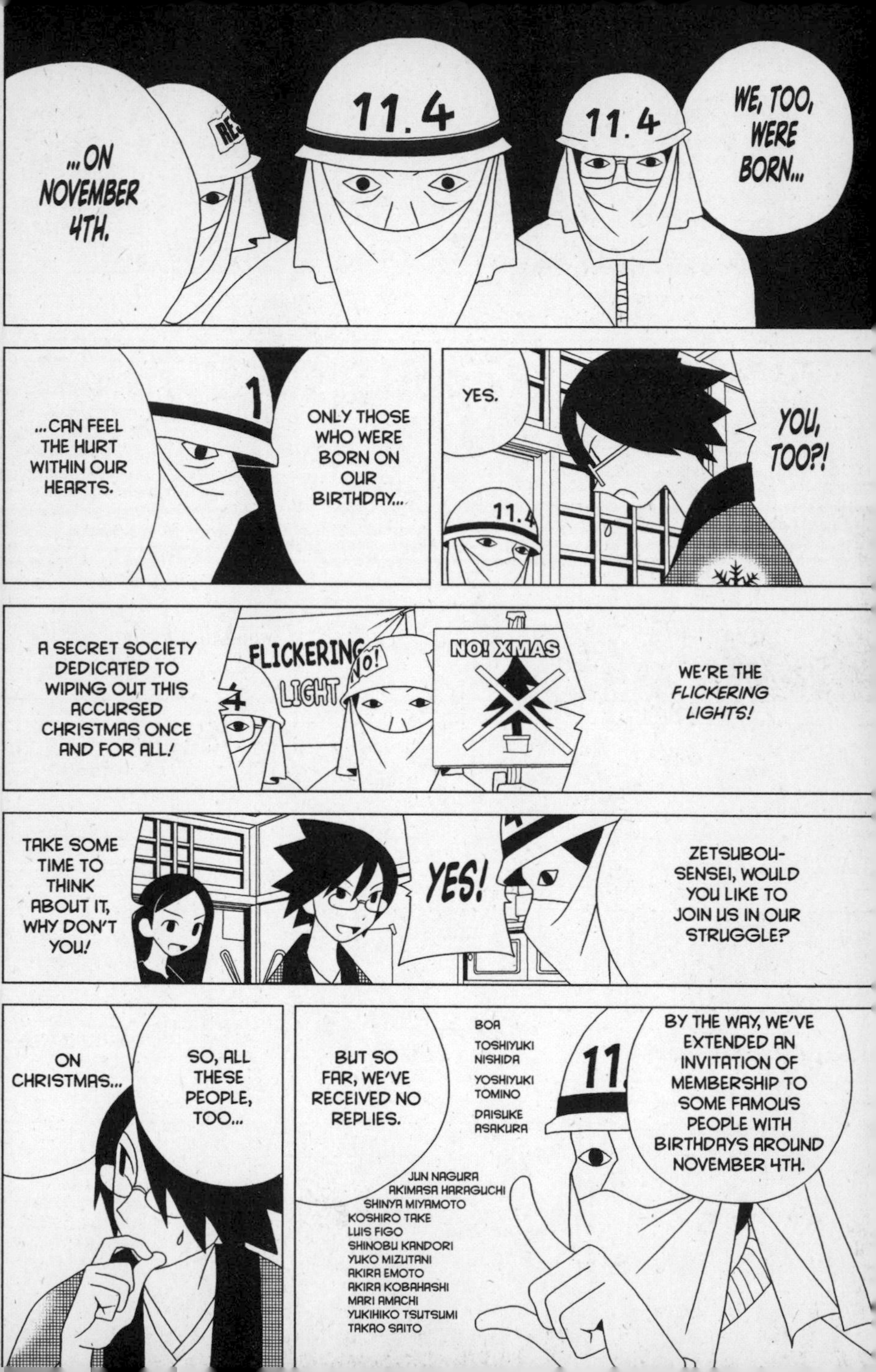
WE, TOO, WERE BORN...
11.4
11.4
RES
...ON NOVEMBER 4TH.
YOU, TOO?!
11.4
YES.
ONLY THOSE WHO WERE BORN ON OUR BIRTHDAY...
1
...CAN FEEL THE HURT WITHIN OUR HEARTS.
WE'RE THE FLICKERING LIGHTS!
NO! XMAS
NO!
FLICKERING LIGHT
A SECRET SOCIETY DEDICATED TO WIPING OUT THIS ACCURSED CHRISTMAS ONCE AND FOR ALL!
ZETSUBOU-SENSEI, WOULD YOU LIKE TO JOIN US IN OUR STRUGGLE?
YES!
TAKE SOME TIME TO THINK ABOUT IT, WHY DON'T YOU!
BY THE WAY, WE'VE EXTENDED AN INVITATION OF MEMBERSHIP TO SOME FAMOUS PEOPLE WITH BIRTHDAYS AROUND NOVEMBER 4TH.
BOA
TOSHIYUKI NISHIDA
YOSHIYUKI TOMINO
DAISUKE ASAKURA
JUN NAGURA
AKIMASA HARAGUCHI
SHINYA MIYAMOTO
KOSHIRO TAKE
LUIS FIGO
SHINOBU KANDORI
YUKO MIZUTANI
AKIRA EMOTO
AKIRA KOBAHASHI
MARI AMACHI
YUKIHIKO TSUTSUMI
TAKAO SAITO
BUT SO FAR, WE'VE RECEIVED NO REPLIES.
SO, ALL THESE PEOPLE, TOO...
ON CHRISTMAS...

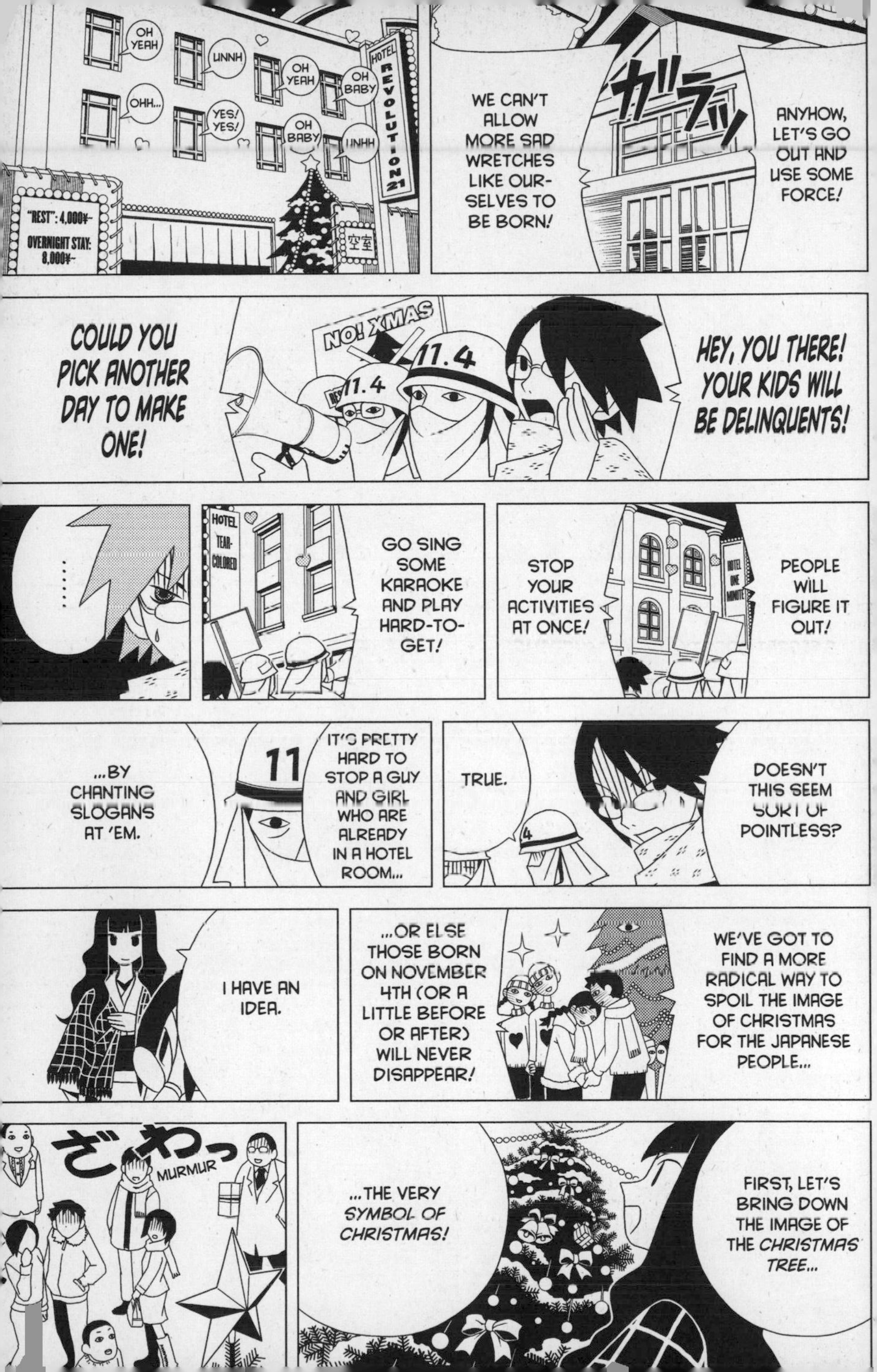
ANYHOW, LET'S GO OUT AND USE SOME FORCE!
ガラッ
WE CAN'T ALLOW MORE SAD WRETCHES LIKE OURSELVES TO BE BORN!
HOTEL REVOLUTION 21
OH YEAH
UNNH
OH YEAH
OH BABY
OHH...
YES! YES!
OH BABY
UNNH
"REST": 4,000¥~
OVERNIGHT STAY: 8,000¥~
空室
HEY, YOU THERE! YOUR KIDS WILL BE DELINQUENTS!
NO! XMAS
11.4
11.4
COULD YOU PICK ANOTHER DAY TO MAKE ONE!
PEOPLE WILL FIGURE IT OUT!
HOTEL ONE MINUTE
STOP YOUR ACTIVITIES AT ONCE!
GO SING SOME KARAOKE AND PLAY HARD-TO-GET!
HOTEL TEAR-COLORED
......
DOESN'T THIS SEEM SORT OF POINTLESS?
TRUE.
IT'S PRETTY HARD TO STOP A GUY AND GIRL WHO ARE ALREADY IN A HOTEL ROOM...
...BY CHANTING SLOGANS AT 'EM.
WE'VE GOT TO FIND A MORE RADICAL WAY TO SPOIL THE IMAGE OF CHRISTMAS FOR THE JAPANESE PEOPLE...
...OR ELSE THOSE BORN ON NOVEMBER 4TH (OR A LITTLE BEFORE OR AFTER) WILL NEVER DISAPPEAR!
I HAVE AN IDEA.
FIRST, LET'S BRING DOWN THE IMAGE OF THE CHRISTMAS TREE...
...THE VERY SYMBOL OF CHRISTMAS!
ざわっ
MURMUR

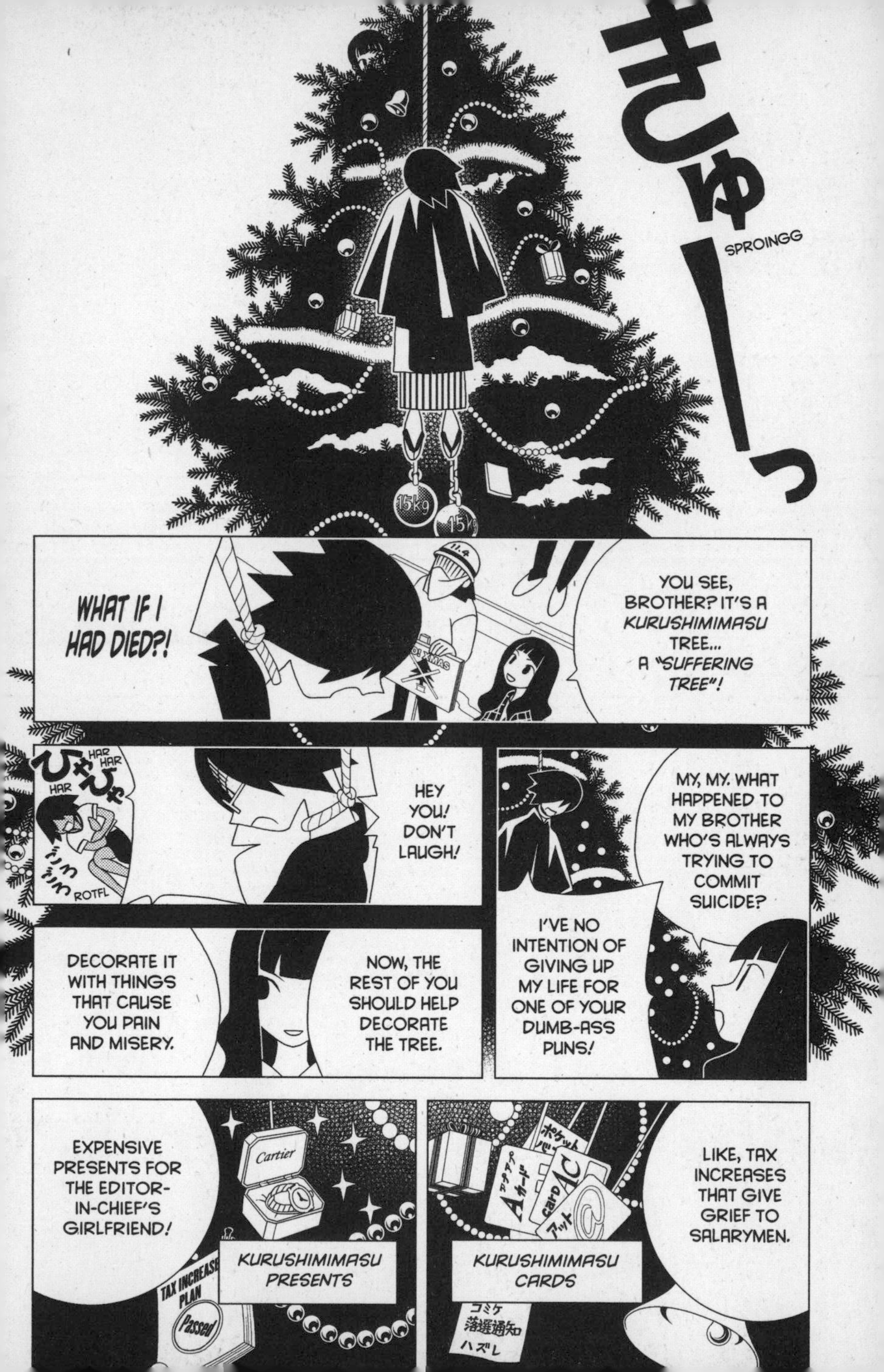
きゅーっ
SPROINGG
15kg
15kg
YOU SEE, BROTHER? IT'S A *KURUSHIMIMASU* TREE... A *"SUFFERING TREE"*!
WHAT IF I HAD DIED?!
MY, MY. WHAT HAPPENED TO MY BROTHER WHO'S ALWAYS TRYING TO COMMIT SUICIDE?
I'VE NO INTENTION OF GIVING UP MY LIFE FOR ONE OF YOUR DUMB-ASS PUNS!
HEY YOU! DON'T LAUGH!
ひゃひゃ
HAR HAR HAR
ROTFL
NOW, THE REST OF YOU SHOULD HELP DECORATE THE TREE.
DECORATE IT WITH THINGS THAT CAUSE YOU PAIN AND MISERY.
LIKE, TAX INCREASES THAT GIVE GRIEF TO SALARYMEN.
KURUSHIMIMASU CARDS
コミケ
落選通知
ハズレ
EXPENSIVE PRESENTS FOR THE EDITOR-IN-CHIEF'S GIRLFRIEND!
Cartier
KURUSHIMIMASU PRESENTS
TAX INCREASE PLAN
Passed

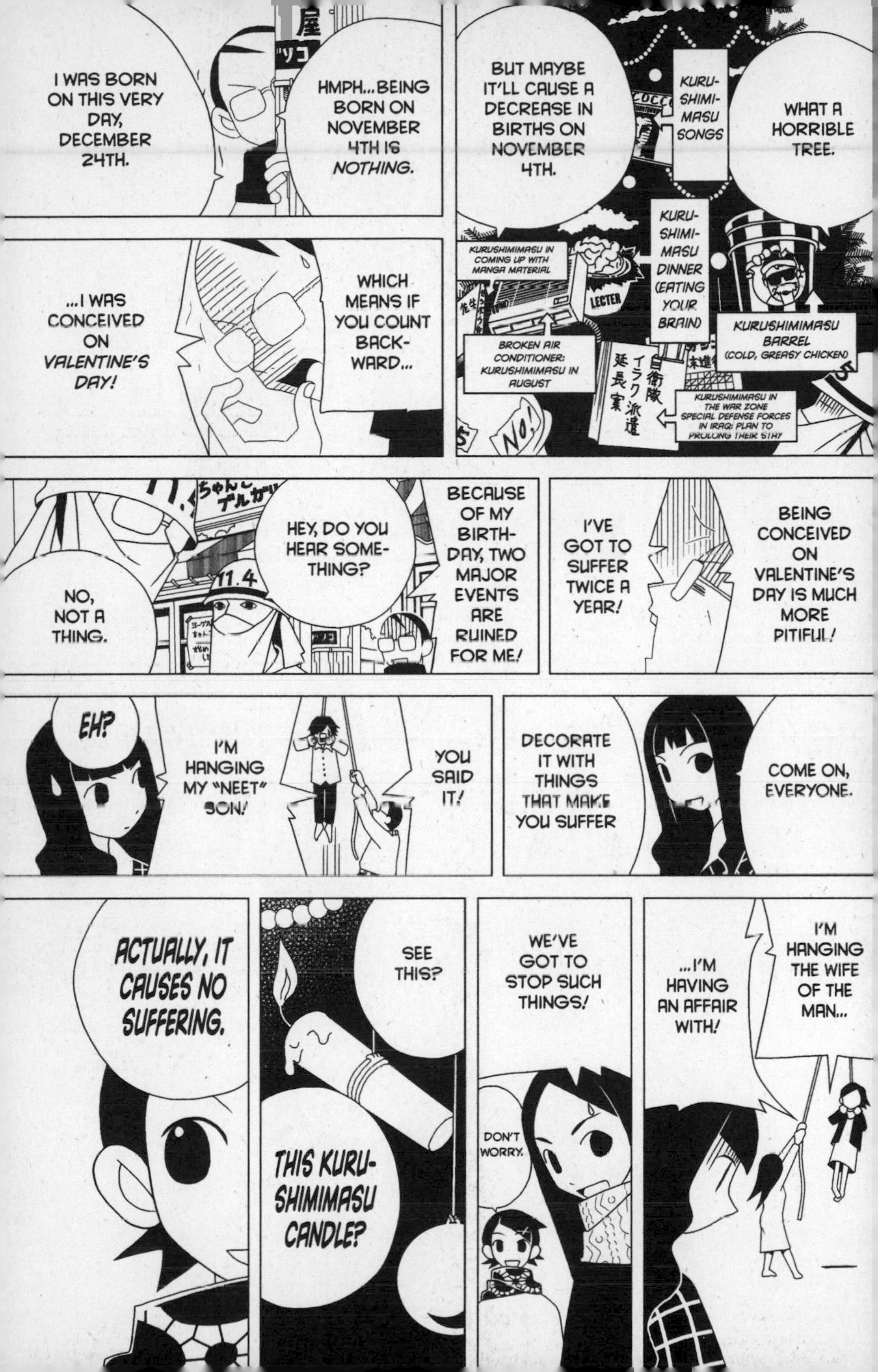
WHAT A HORRIBLE TREE.
KURU-SHIMI-MASU SONGS
BUT MAYBE IT'LL CAUSE A DECREASE IN BIRTHS ON NOVEMBER 4TH.
KURU-SHIMI-MASU DINNER (EATING YOUR BRAIN)
KURUSHIMIMASU IN COMING UP WITH MANGA MATERIAL
LECTER
KURUSHIMIMASU BARREL (COLD, GREASY CHICKEN)
BROKEN AIR CONDITIONER: KURUSHIMIMASU IN AUGUST
自衛隊 イラク派遣 延長案
KURUSHIMIMASU IN THE WAR ZONE SPECIAL DEFENSE FORCES IN IRAQ: PLAN TO PROLONG THEIR STAY
NO!
HMPH...BEING BORN ON NOVEMBER 4TH IS *NOTHING.*
I WAS BORN ON THIS VERY DAY, DECEMBER 24TH.
WHICH MEANS IF YOU COUNT BACKWARD...
...I WAS CONCEIVED ON VALENTINE'S DAY!
BEING CONCEIVED ON VALENTINE'S DAY IS MUCH MORE PITIFUL!
I'VE GOT TO SUFFER TWICE A YEAR!
BECAUSE OF MY BIRTHDAY, TWO MAJOR EVENTS ARE RUINED FOR ME!
HEY, DO YOU HEAR SOMETHING?
11.4
NO, NOT A THING.
COME ON, EVERYONE.
DECORATE IT WITH THINGS THAT MAKE YOU SUFFER
YOU SAID IT!
I'M HANGING MY "NEET" SON!
EH?
I'M HANGING THE WIFE OF THE MAN...
...I'M HAVING AN AFFAIR WITH!
WE'VE GOT TO STOP SUCH THINGS!
DON'T WORRY.
SEE THIS?
THIS KURUSHIMIMASU CANDLE?
ACTUALLY, IT CAUSES NO SUFFERING.

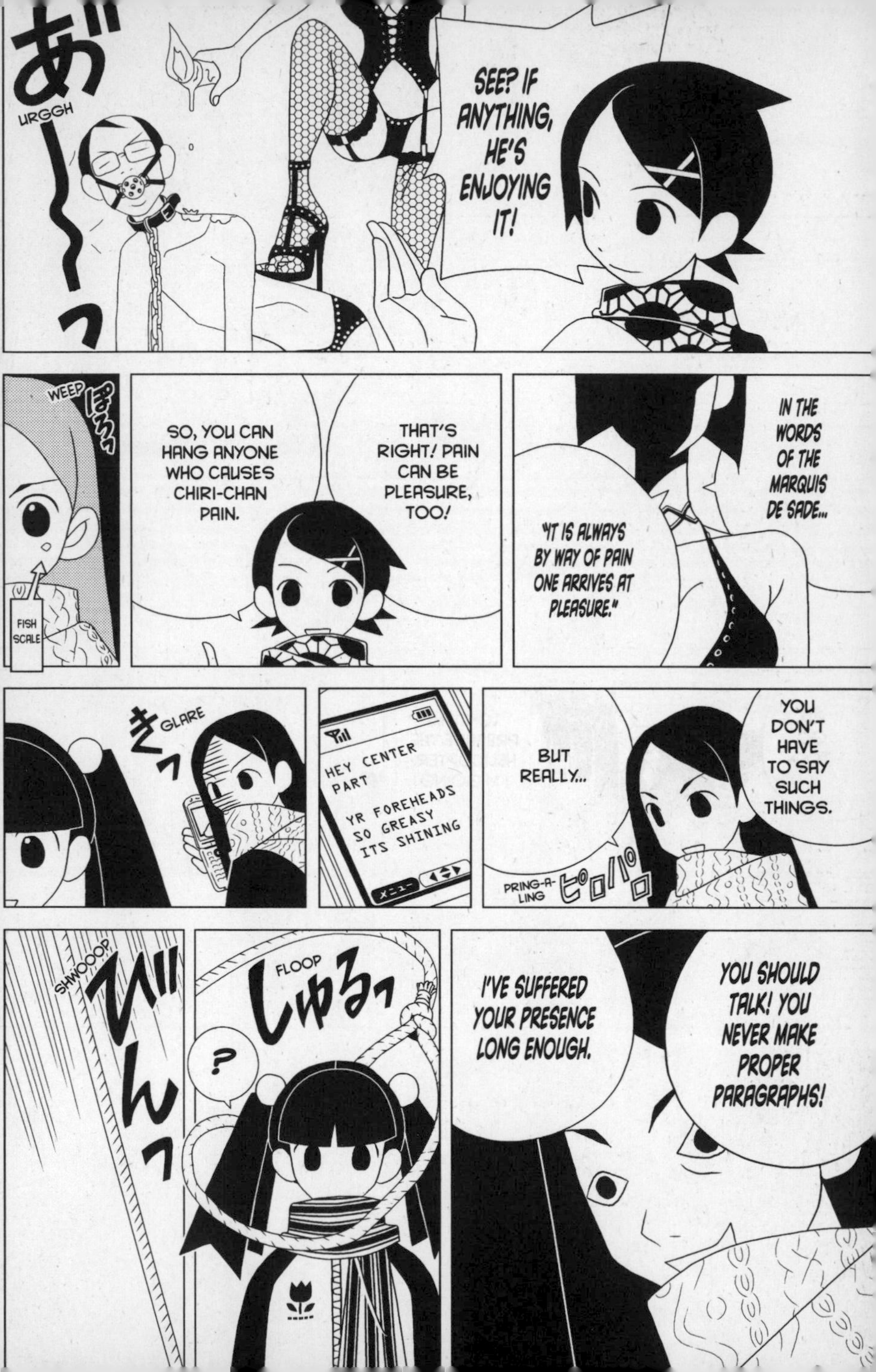
SEE? IF ANYTHING, HE'S ENJOYING IT!
あ゛ー〜っ
URGGH
IN THE WORDS OF THE MARQUIS DE SADE...
"IT IS ALWAYS BY WAY OF PAIN ONE ARRIVES AT PLEASURE."
THAT'S RIGHT! PAIN CAN BE PLEASURE, TOO!
SO, YOU CAN HANG ANYONE WHO CAUSES CHIRI-CHAN PAIN.
WEEP
ぽろっ
FISH SCALE
YOU DON'T HAVE TO SAY SUCH THINGS.
BUT REALLY...
PRING-A-LING
ピロパロ
HEY CENTER PART
YR FOREHEADS SO GREASY ITS SHINING
メニュー
きっ
GLARE
YOU SHOULD TALK! YOU NEVER MAKE PROPER PARAGRAPHS!
I'VE SUFFERED YOUR PRESENCE LONG ENOUGH.
FLOOP
しゅるっ
?
SHWOOOP
びんっ

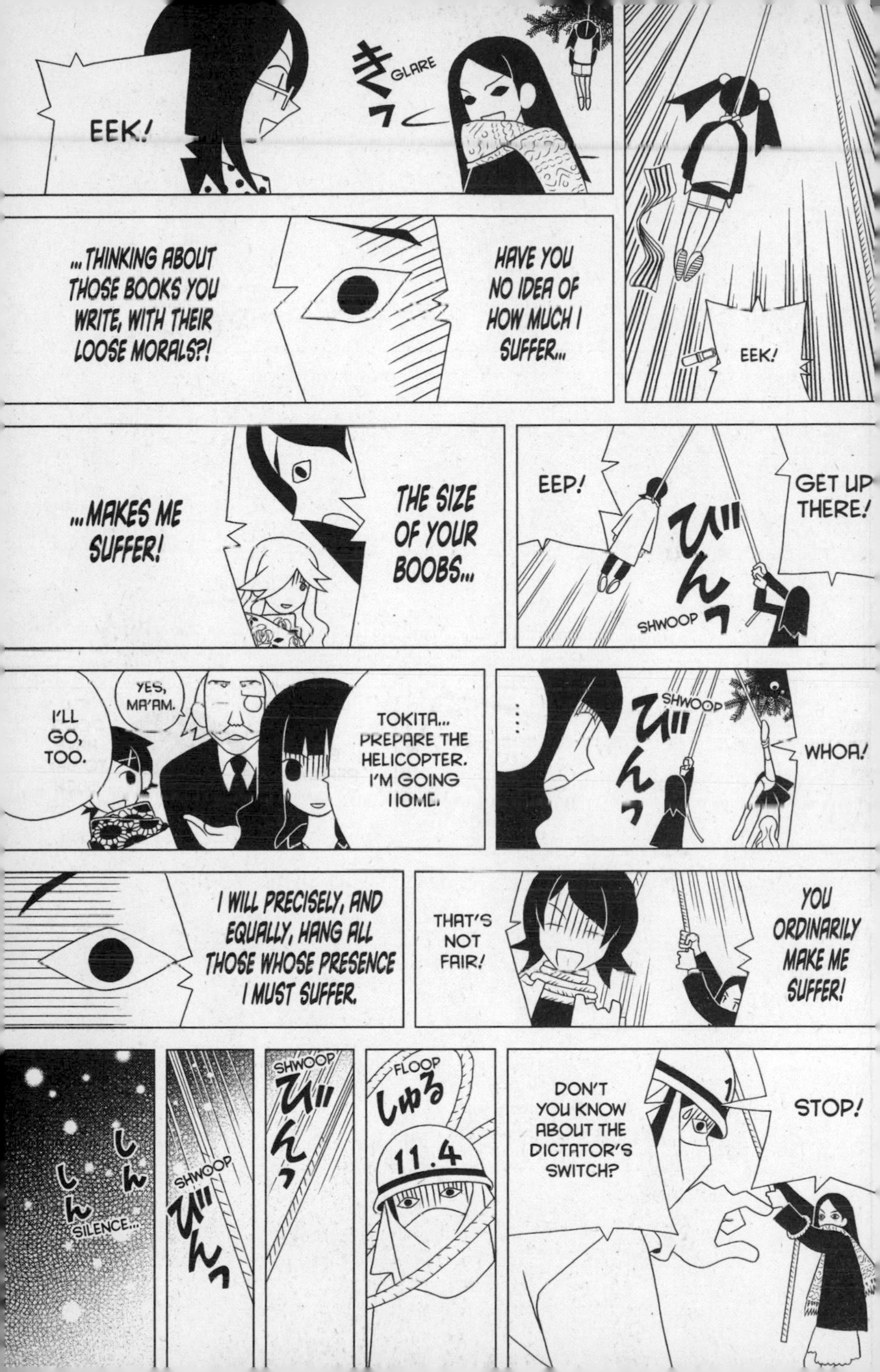
EEK!
きっ
GLARE
EEK!
HAVE YOU NO IDEA OF HOW MUCH I SUFFER...
...THINKING ABOUT THOSE BOOKS YOU WRITE, WITH THEIR LOOSE MORALS?!
GET UP THERE!
びんっ
SHWOOP
EEP!
THE SIZE OF YOUR BOOBS...
...MAKES ME SUFFER!
WHOA!
SHWOOP
びんっ
.....
TOKITA... PREPARE THE HELICOPTER. I'M GOING HOME.
YES, MA'AM.
I'LL GO, TOO.
YOU ORDINARILY MAKE ME SUFFER!
THAT'S NOT FAIR!
I WILL PRECISELY, AND EQUALLY, HANG ALL THOSE WHOSE PRESENCE I MUST SUFFER.
STOP!
DON'T YOU KNOW ABOUT THE DICTATOR'S SWITCH?
FLOOP
しゅる
SHWOOP
びんっ
11.4
SHWOOP
びんっ
しん
しん
SILENCE...

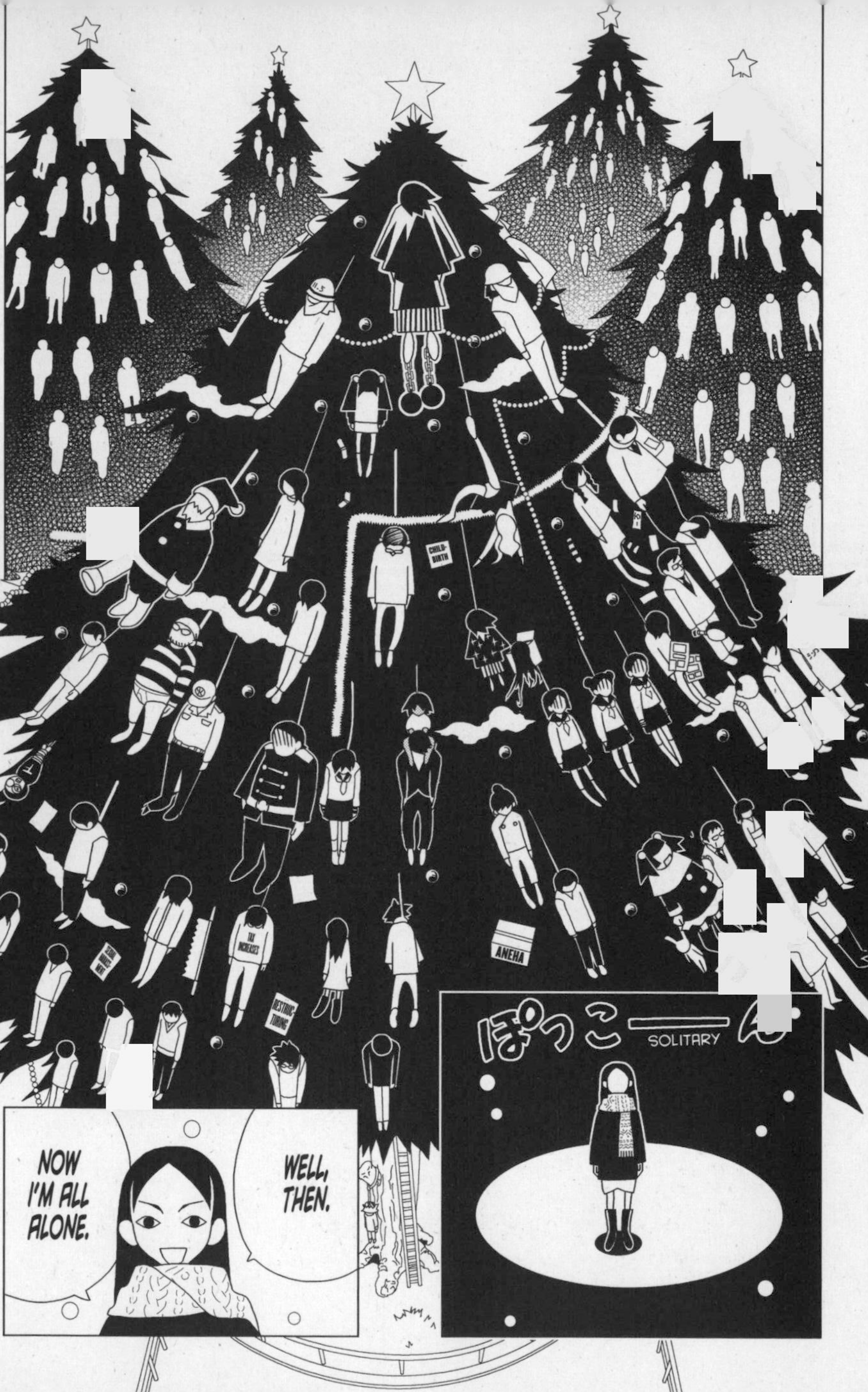
CHILD-BIRTH
ANEHA
TAX INCREASES
RESTRUC-TURING
SEXUAL HARASS-MENT
ぽっこーーん
SOLITARY
WELL, THEN.
NOW I'M ALL ALONE.

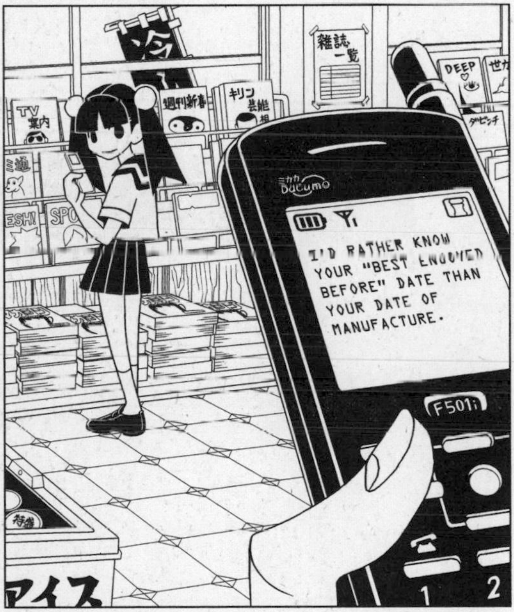
I'D RATHER KNOW YOUR "BEST ENDOWED BEFORE" DATE THAN YOUR DATE OF MANUFACTURE.
雑誌一覧
TV 案内
DEEP
F501i
アイス

DATE OF MANUFACTURE: MAY 12, 2007
DATE OF EXPIRY: MAY 12, 2014

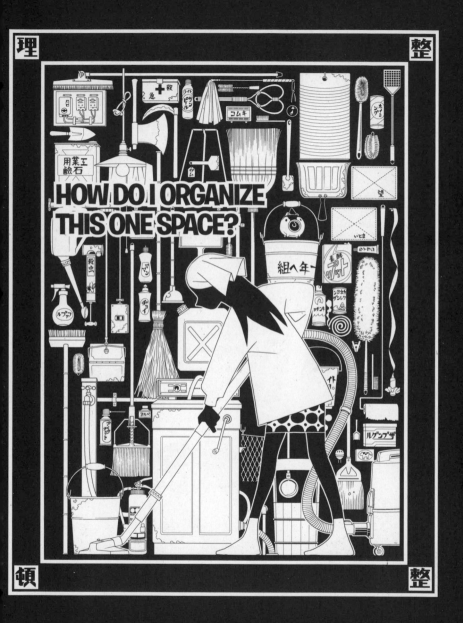

HOW DO I ORGANIZE
THIS ONE SPACE?

CHAPTER 33

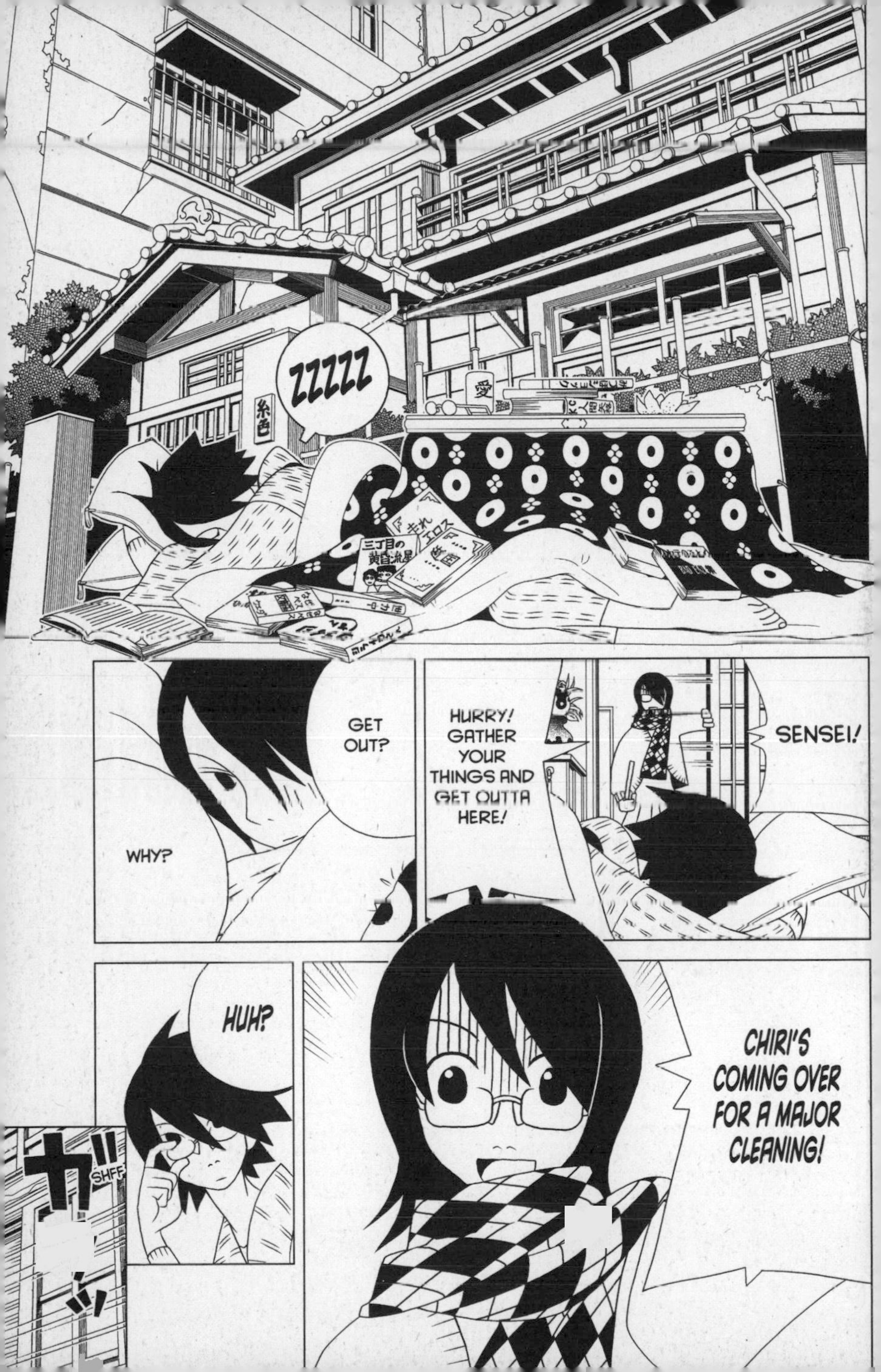
ZZZZZ
SENSEI!
HURRY! GATHER YOUR THINGS AND GET OUTTA HERE!
GET OUT?
WHY?
CHIRI'S COMING OVER FOR A MAJOR CLEANING!
HUH?
SHFF

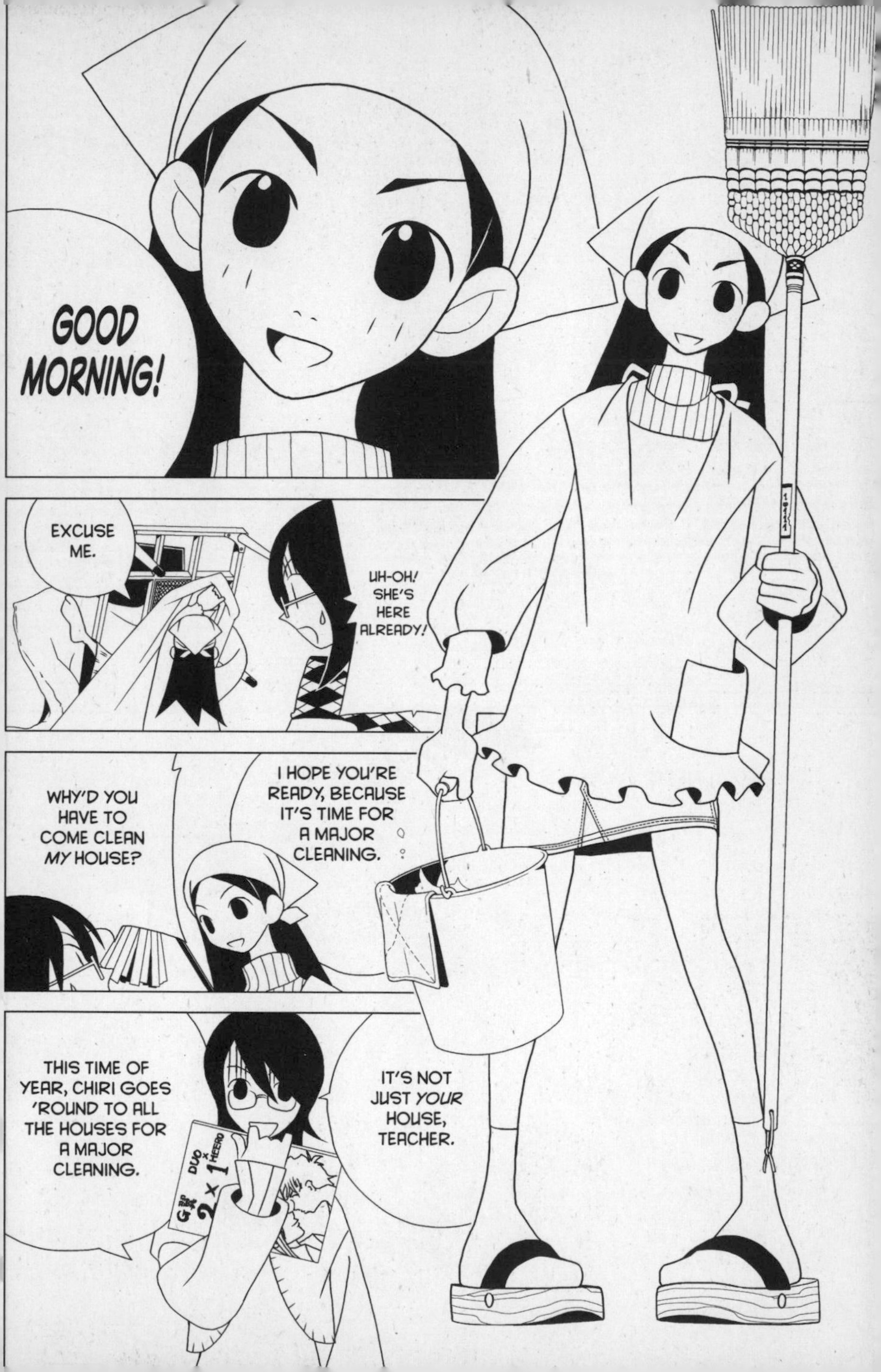
GOOD MORNING!
EXCUSE ME.
UH-OH! SHE'S HERE ALREADY!
I HOPE YOU'RE READY, BECAUSE IT'S TIME FOR A MAJOR CLEANING.
WHY'D YOU HAVE TO COME CLEAN *MY* HOUSE?
IT'S NOT JUST *YOUR* HOUSE, TEACHER.
THIS TIME OF YEAR, CHIRI GOES 'ROUND TO ALL THE HOUSES FOR A MAJOR CLEANING.

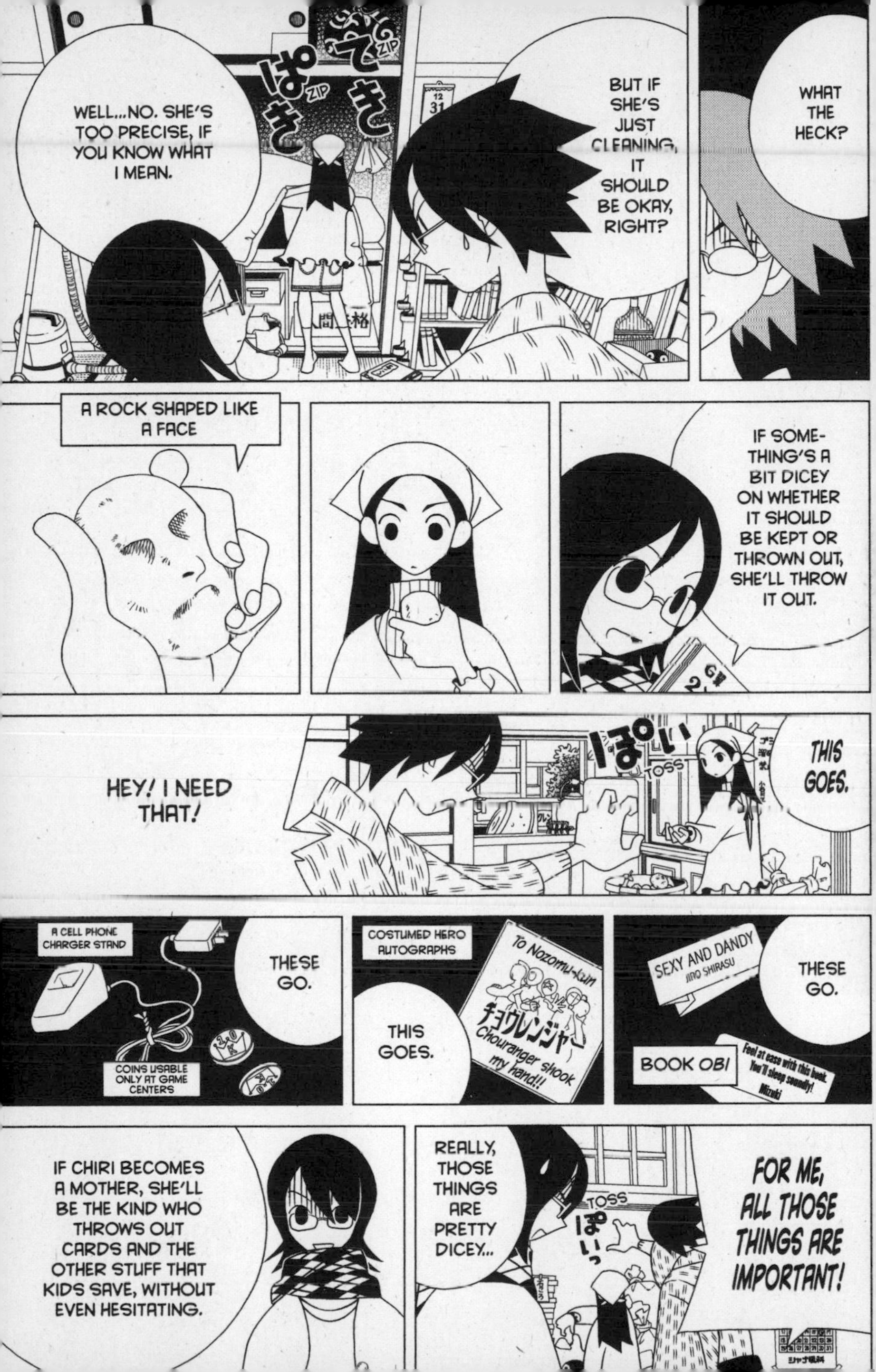
WHAT THE HECK?
BUT IF SHE'S JUST CLEANING, IT SHOULD BE OKAY, RIGHT?
ZIP
ZIP
WELL...NO. SHE'S TOO PRECISE, IF YOU KNOW WHAT I MEAN.
IF SOMETHING'S A BIT DICEY ON WHETHER IT SHOULD BE KEPT OR THROWN OUT, SHE'LL THROW IT OUT.
A ROCK SHAPED LIKE A FACE
THIS GOES.
TOSS
HEY! I NEED THAT!
THESE GO.
SEXY AND DANDY
JINO SHIRASU
BOOK OBI
Feel at ease with this book. You'll sleep soundly! Mizuki
COSTUMED HERO AUTOGRAPHS
To Nozomu-kun
チョウレンジャー
Chouranger shook my hand!!
THIS GOES.
A CELL PHONE CHARGER STAND
THESE GO.
COINS USABLE ONLY AT GAME CENTERS
FOR ME, ALL THOSE THINGS ARE IMPORTANT!
REALLY, THOSE THINGS ARE PRETTY DICEY...
TOSS
IF CHIRI BECOMES A MOTHER, SHE'LL BE THE KIND WHO THROWS OUT CARDS AND THE OTHER STUFF THAT KIDS SAVE, WITHOUT EVEN HESITATING.

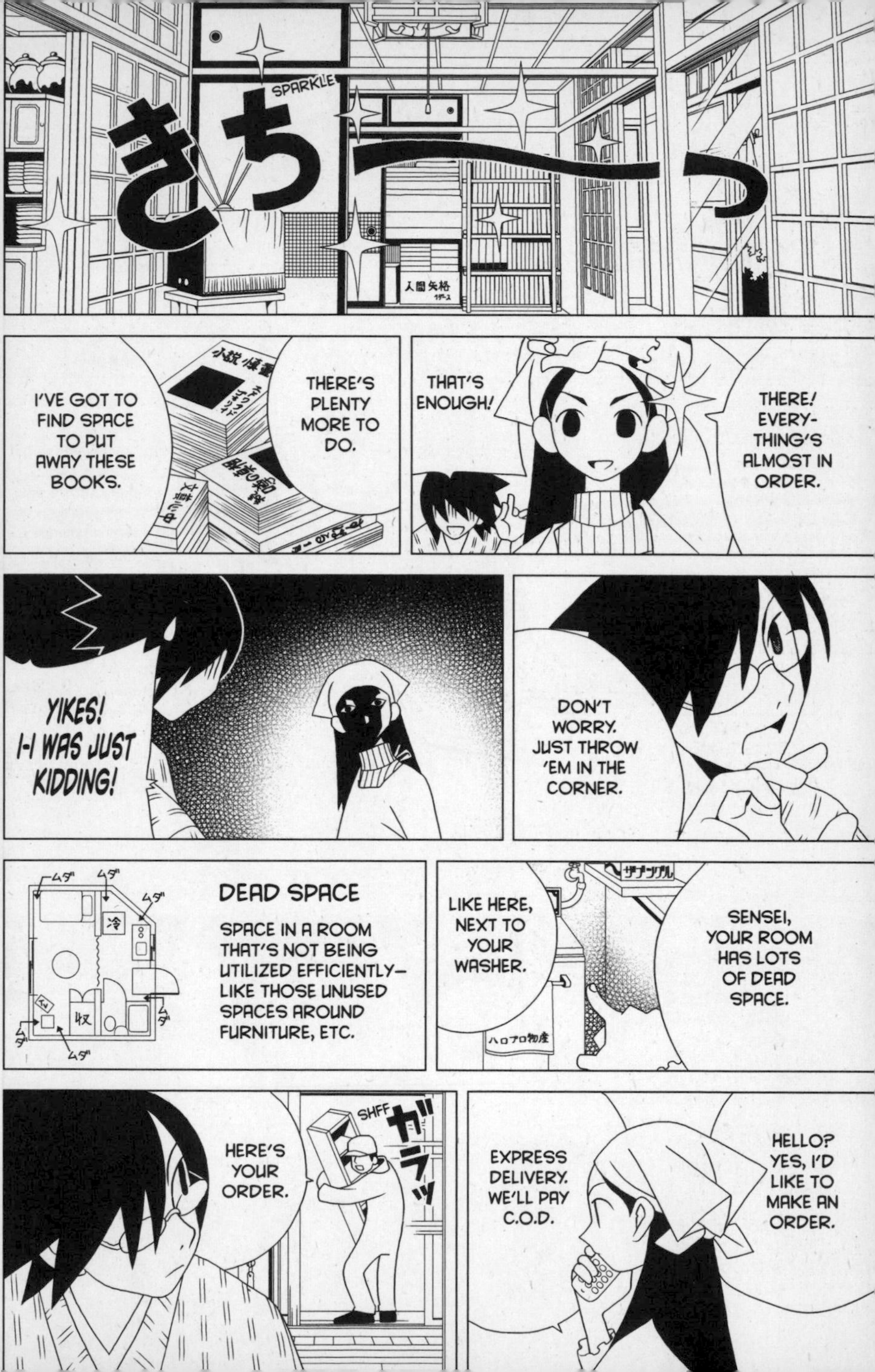
SPARKLE
きちーーっ
THERE! EVERY-THING'S ALMOST IN ORDER.
THAT'S ENOUGH!
THERE'S PLENTY MORE TO DO.
I'VE GOT TO FIND SPACE TO PUT AWAY THESE BOOKS.
DON'T WORRY. JUST THROW 'EM IN THE CORNER.
YIKES! I-I WAS JUST KIDDING!
SENSEI, YOUR ROOM HAS LOTS OF DEAD SPACE.
LIKE HERE, NEXT TO YOUR WASHER.
DEAD SPACE
SPACE IN A ROOM THAT'S NOT BEING UTILIZED EFFICIENTLY—LIKE THOSE UNUSED SPACES AROUND FURNITURE, ETC.
ムダ
HELLO? YES, I'D LIKE TO MAKE AN ORDER.
EXPRESS DELIVERY. WE'LL PAY C.O.D.
SHFF
ガラッ
HERE'S YOUR ORDER.

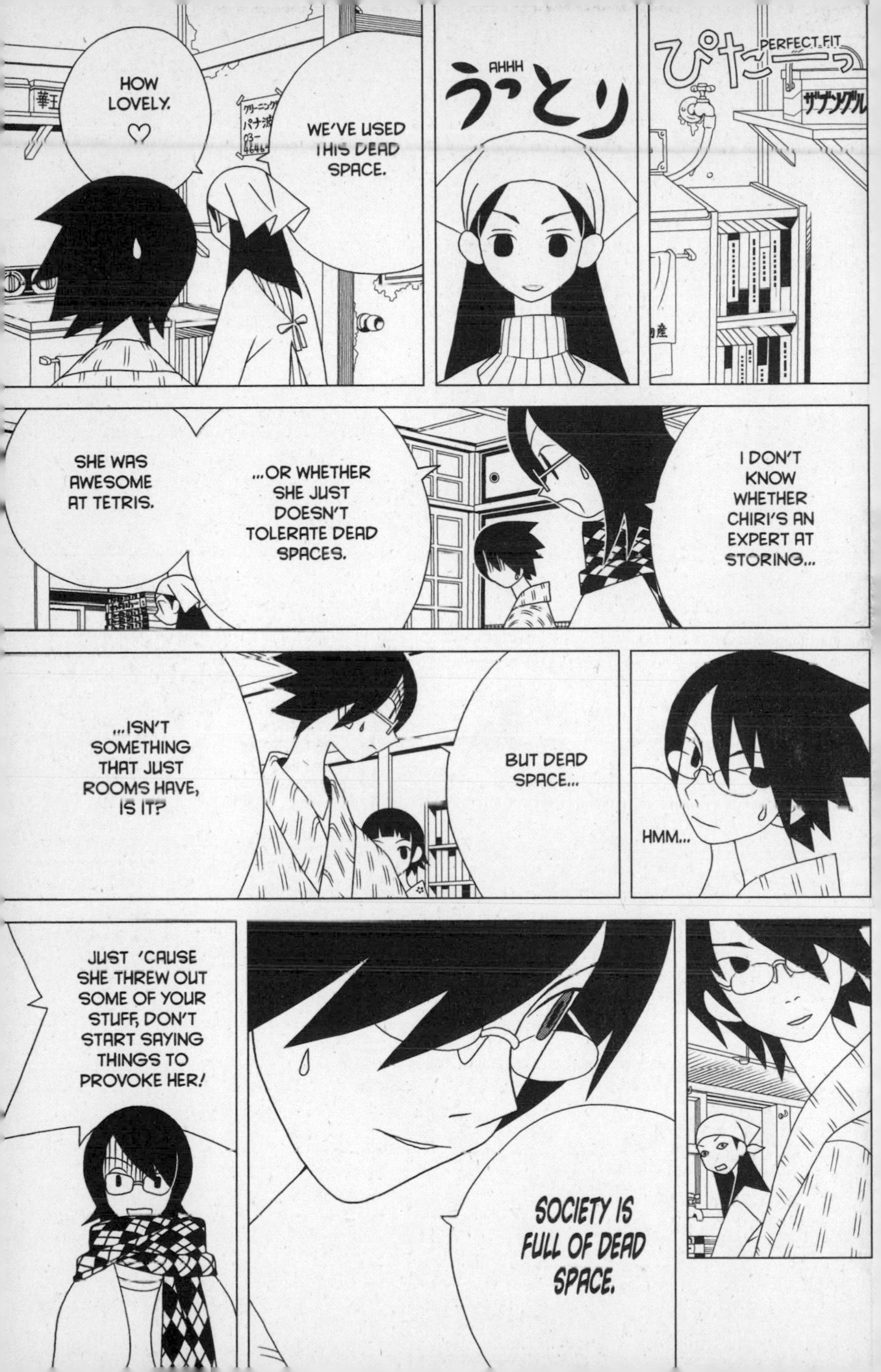
ぴたーっ
PERFECT FIT
ザブングル
うっとり
AHHH
WE'VE USED THIS DEAD SPACE.
HOW LOVELY. ♡
I DON'T KNOW WHETHER CHIRI'S AN EXPERT AT STORING...
...OR WHETHER SHE JUST DOESN'T TOLERATE DEAD SPACES.
SHE WAS AWESOME AT TETRIS.
HMM...
BUT DEAD SPACE...
...ISN'T SOMETHING THAT JUST ROOMS HAVE, IS IT?
SOCIETY IS FULL OF DEAD SPACE.
JUST 'CAUSE SHE THREW OUT SOME OF YOUR STUFF, DON'T START SAYING THINGS TO PROVOKE HER!

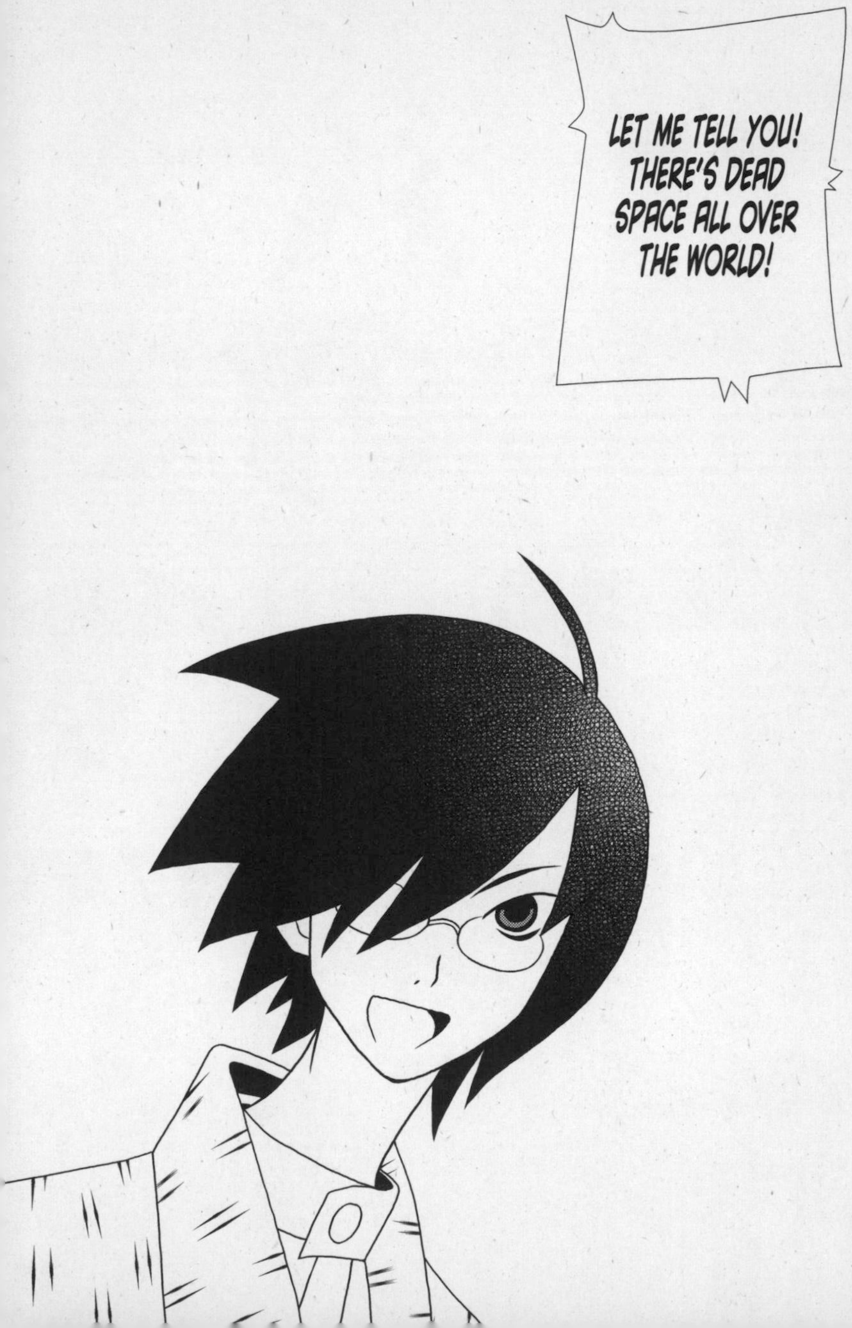
LET ME TELL YOU! THERE'S DEAD SPACE ALL OVER THE WORLD!

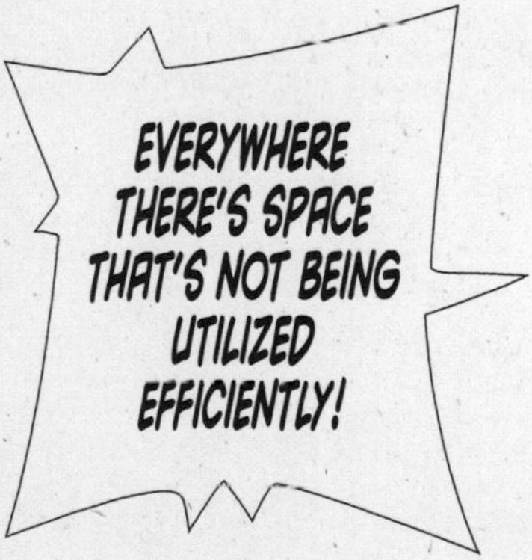
EVERYWHERE THERE'S SPACE THAT'S NOT BEING UTILIZED EFFICIENTLY!

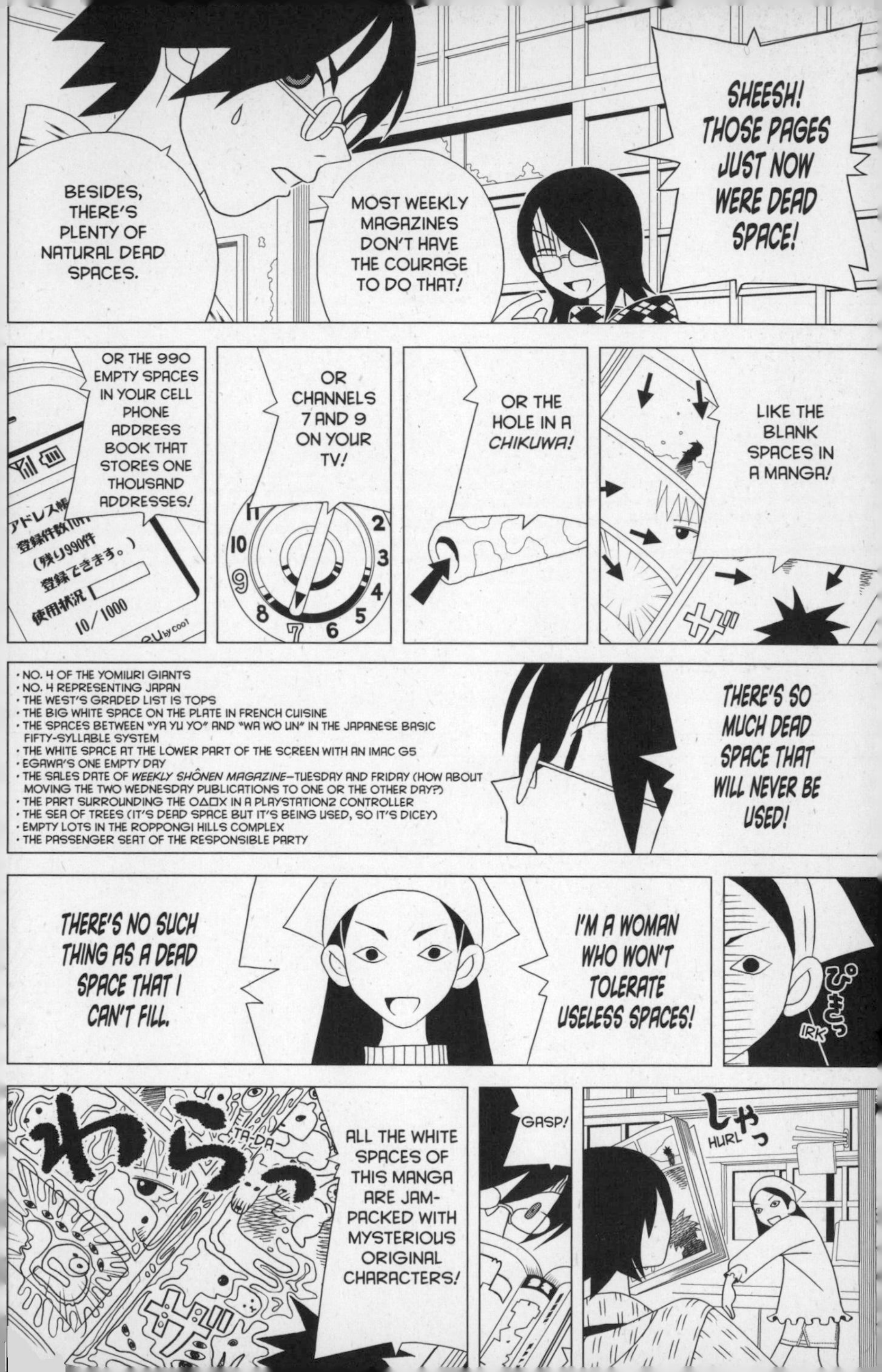
SHEESH! THOSE PAGES JUST NOW WERE DEAD SPACE!
MOST WEEKLY MAGAZINES DON'T HAVE THE COURAGE TO DO THAT!
BESIDES, THERE'S PLENTY OF NATURAL DEAD SPACES.
LIKE THE BLANK SPACES IN A MANGA!
ガ
OR THE HOLE IN A *CHIKUWA!*
OR CHANNELS 7 AND 9 ON YOUR TV!
11 2 10 3 9 4 8 5 7 6
OR THE 990 EMPTY SPACES IN YOUR CELL PHONE ADDRESS BOOK THAT STORES ONE THOUSAND ADDRESSES!
アドレス帳
(残り990件
登録できます。)
使用状況
10/1000
THERE'S SO MUCH DEAD SPACE THAT WILL NEVER BE USED!
• NO. 4 OF THE YOMIURI GIANTS
• NO. 4 REPRESENTING JAPAN
• THE WEST'S GRADED LIST IS TOPS
• THE BIG WHITE SPACE ON THE PLATE IN FRENCH CUISINE
• THE SPACES BETWEEN "YA YU YO" AND "WA WO UN" IN THE JAPANESE BASIC FIFTY-SYLLABLE SYSTEM
• THE WHITE SPACE AT THE LOWER PART OF THE SCREEN WITH AN IMAC G5
• EGAWA'S ONE EMPTY DAY
• THE SALES DATE OF *WEEKLY SHÔNEN MAGAZINE*—TUESDAY AND FRIDAY (HOW ABOUT MOVING THE TWO WEDNESDAY PUBLICATIONS TO ONE OR THE OTHER DAY?)
• THE PART SURROUNDING THE O△□X IN A PLAYSTATION2 CONTROLLER
• THE SEA OF TREES (IT'S DEAD SPACE BUT IT'S BEING USED, SO IT'S DICEY)
• EMPTY LOTS IN THE ROPPONGI HILLS COMPLEX
• THE PASSENGER SEAT OF THE RESPONSIBLE PARTY
ぴきっ
IRK
I'M A WOMAN WHO WON'T TOLERATE USELESS SPACES!
THERE'S NO SUCH THING AS A DEAD SPACE THAT I CAN'T FILL.
しゃっ
HURL
GASP!
ALL THE WHITE SPACES OF THIS MANGA ARE JAM-PACKED WITH MYSTERIOUS ORIGINAL CHARACTERS!
わらっ
TA-DA

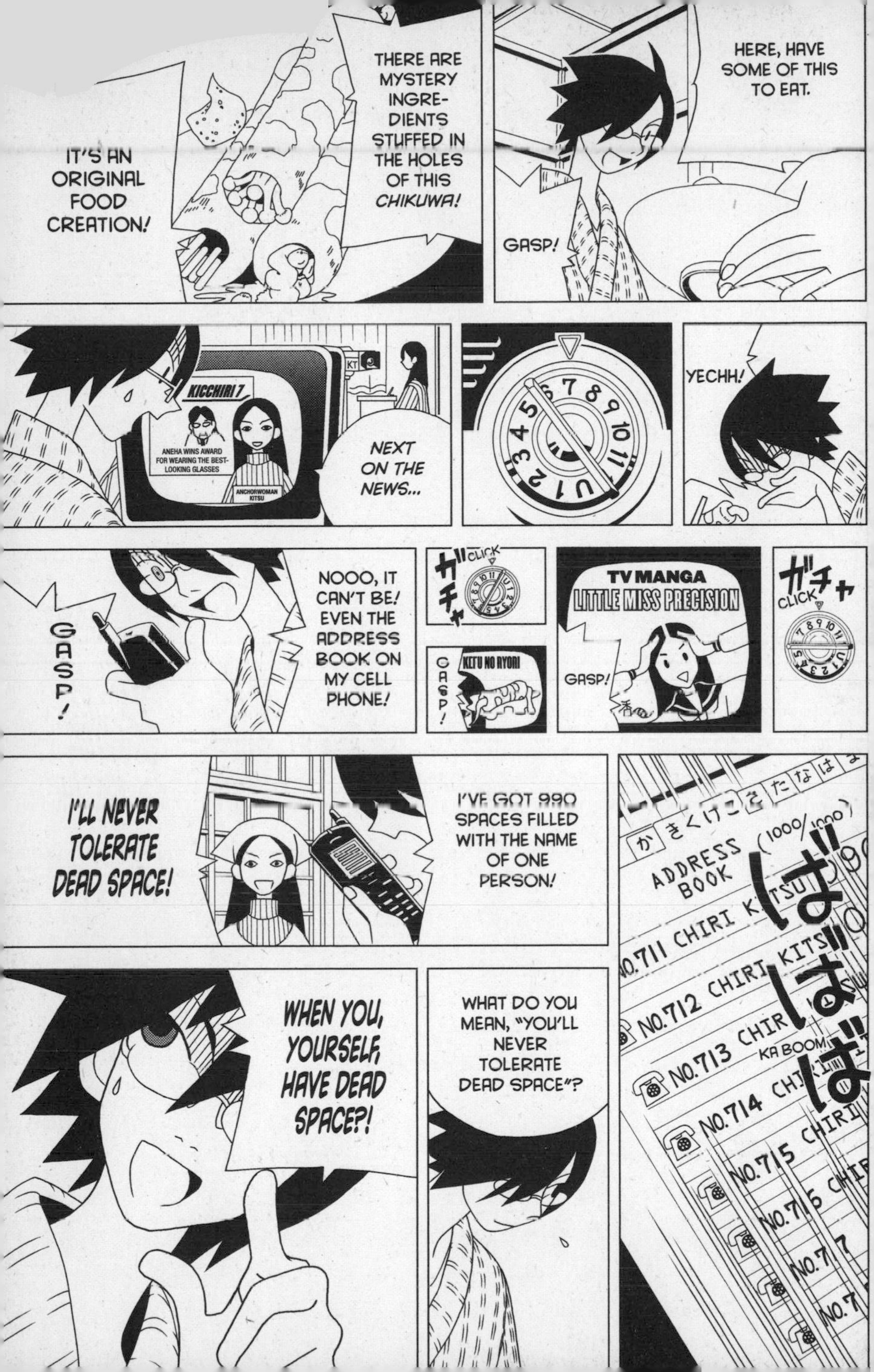
HERE, HAVE SOME OF THIS TO EAT.
GASP!
THERE ARE MYSTERY INGRE-DIENTS STUFFED IN THE HOLES OF THIS CHIKUWA!
IT'S AN ORIGINAL FOOD CREATION!
YECHH!
KT
KICCHIRI 7
ANEHA WINS AWARD FOR WEARING THE BEST-LOOKING GLASSES
ANCHORWOMAN KITSU
NEXT ON THE NEWS...
ガチャ
CLICK
TV MANGA
LITTLE MISS PRECISION
GASP!
ガチャ
CLICK
KETU NO RYORI
GASP!
NOOO, IT CAN'T BE! EVEN THE ADDRESS BOOK ON MY CELL PHONE!
GASP!
かきくけこさたなはま
ADDRESS BOOK (1000/1000)
NO.711 CHIRI KITSU
NO.712 CHIRI KITS
NO.713 CHIR
NO.714 CHIR
NO.715 CHIRI
NO.716 CHIR
ばばば
KA BOOM
I'VE GOT 990 SPACES FILLED WITH THE NAME OF ONE PERSON!
I'LL NEVER TOLERATE DEAD SPACE!
WHAT DO YOU MEAN, "YOU'LL NEVER TOLERATE DEAD SPACE"?
WHEN YOU, YOURSELF, HAVE DEAD SPACE?!

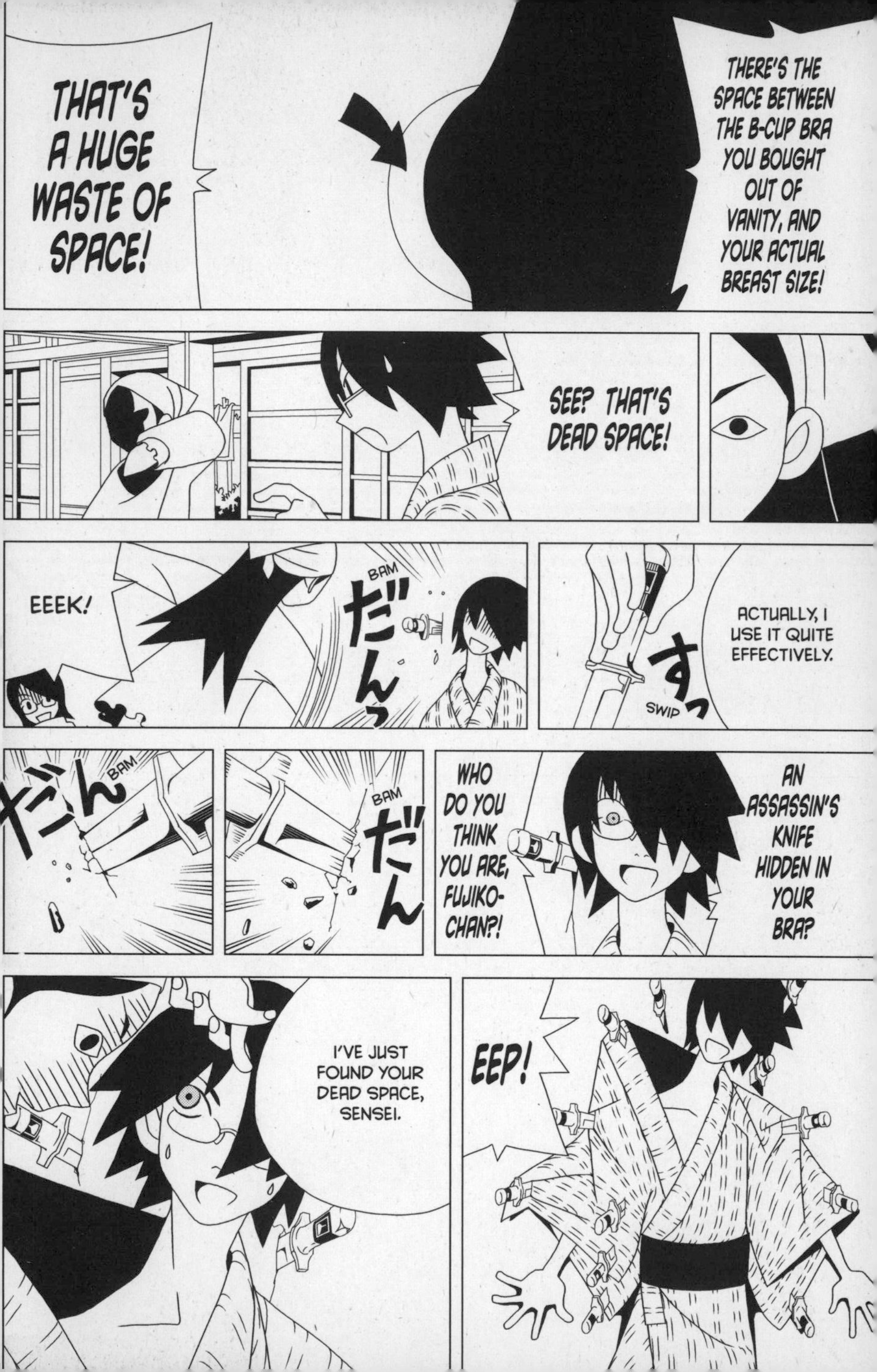
THERE'S THE SPACE BETWEEN THE B-CUP BRA YOU BOUGHT OUT OF VANITY, AND YOUR ACTUAL BREAST SIZE!
THAT'S A HUGE WASTE OF SPACE!
SEE? THAT'S DEAD SPACE!
ACTUALLY, I USE IT QUITE EFFECTIVELY.
すっ
SWIP
BAM
だんっ
EEEK!
AN ASSASSIN'S KNIFE HIDDEN IN YOUR BRA?
WHO DO YOU THINK YOU ARE, FUJIKO-CHAN?!
BAM
だん
BAM
だん
EEP!
I'VE JUST FOUND YOUR DEAD SPACE, SENSEI.

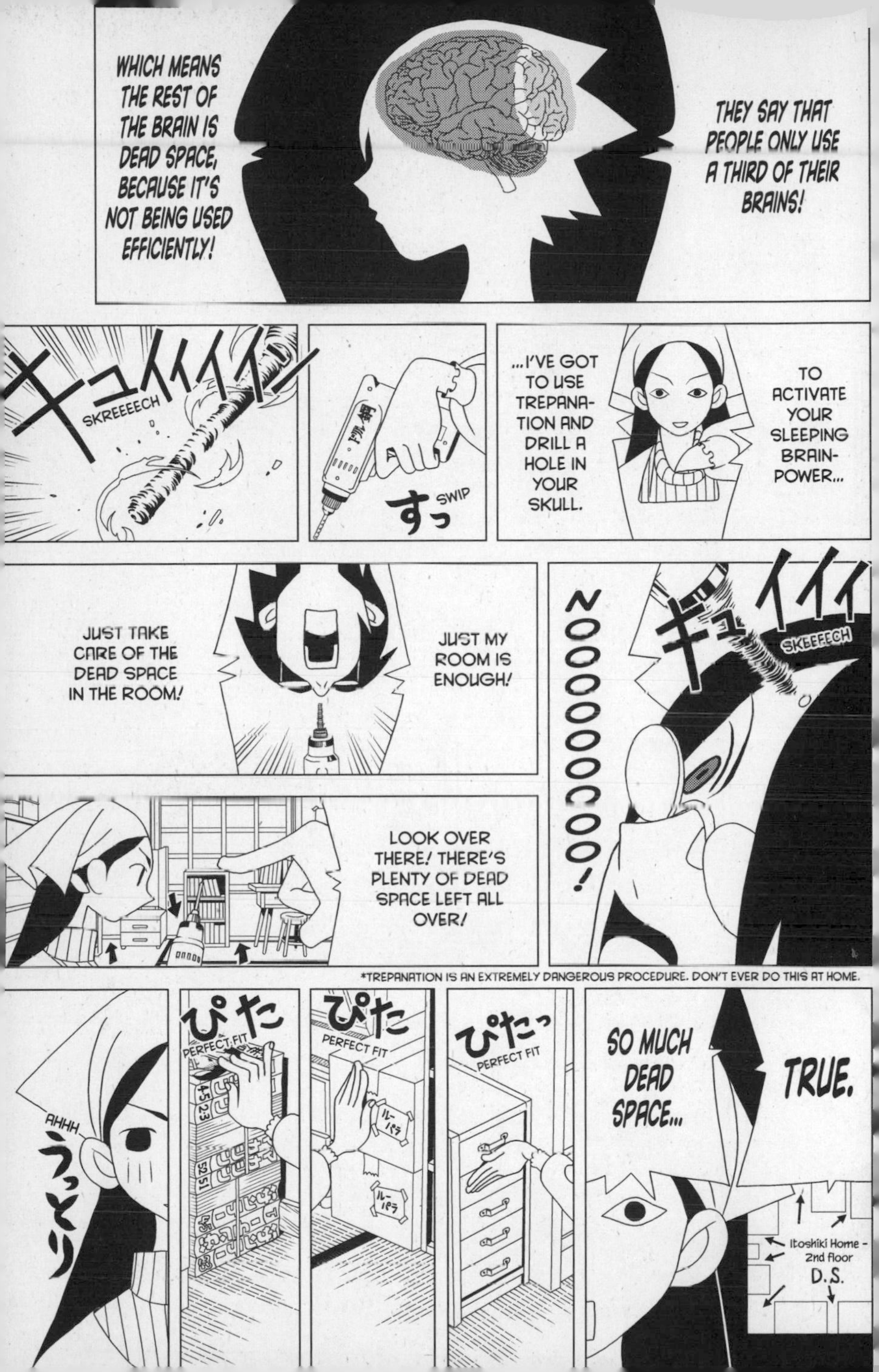
THEY SAY THAT PEOPLE ONLY USE A THIRD OF THEIR BRAINS!
WHICH MEANS THE REST OF THE BRAIN IS DEAD SPACE, BECAUSE IT'S NOT BEING USED EFFICIENTLY!
TO ACTIVATE YOUR SLEEPING BRAIN-POWER...
...I'VE GOT TO USE TREPANATION AND DRILL A HOLE IN YOUR SKULL.
すっ
SWIP
キュイイイン
SKREEEECH
キュイイイ
SKEEEECH
NOOOOOOOOO!
JUST MY ROOM IS ENOUGH!
JUST TAKE CARE OF THE DEAD SPACE IN THE ROOM!
LOOK OVER THERE! THERE'S PLENTY OF DEAD SPACE LEFT ALL OVER!
*TREPANATION IS AN EXTREMELY DANGEROUS PROCEDURE. DON'T EVER DO THIS AT HOME.
TRUE.
SO MUCH DEAD SPACE...
Itoshiki Home - 2nd floor
D.S.
ぴたっ
PERFECT FIT
ぴた
PERFECT FIT
ぴた
PERFECT FIT
うっとり
AHHH

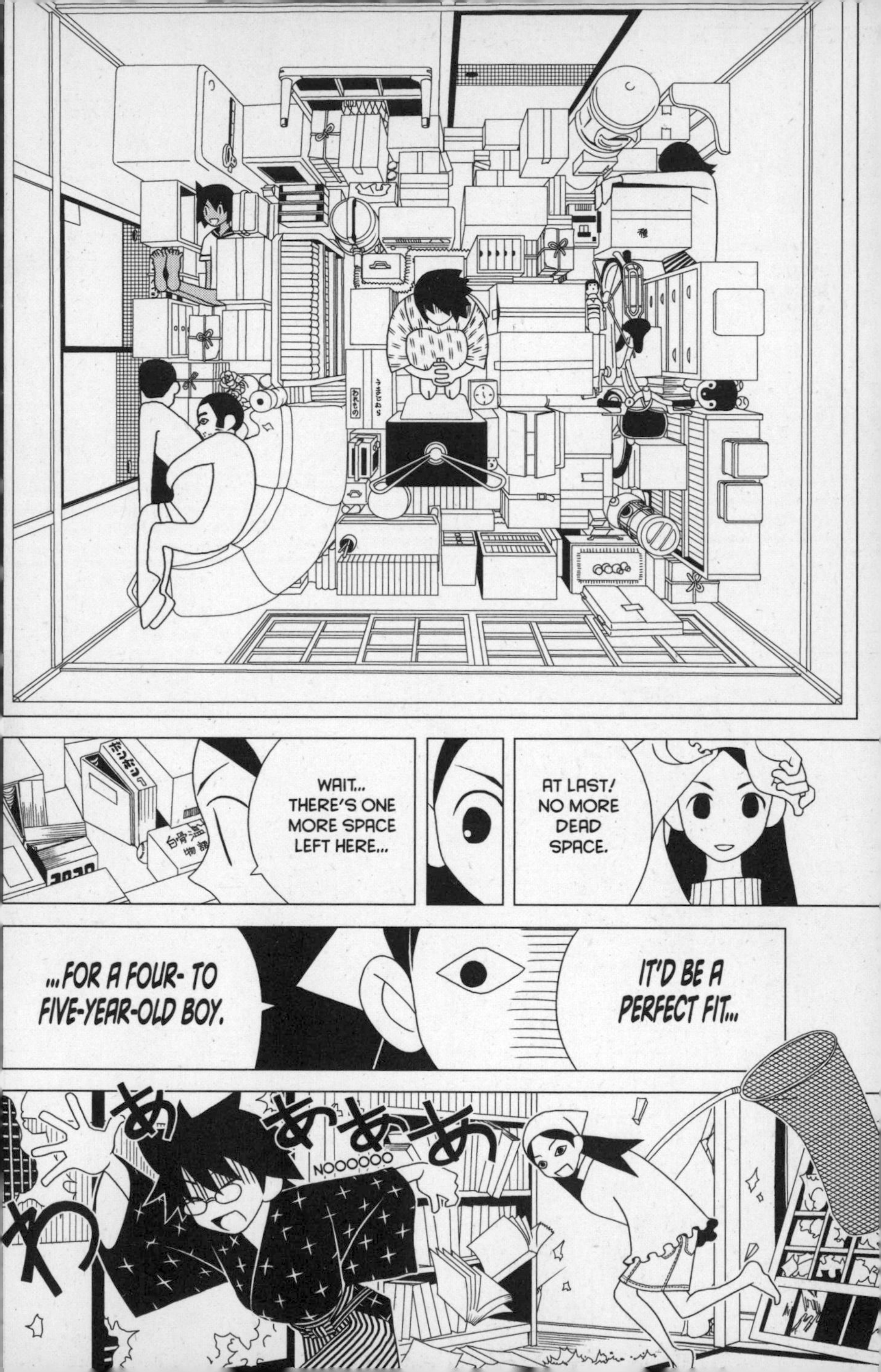
AT LAST! NO MORE DEAD SPACE.
WAIT... THERE'S ONE MORE SPACE LEFT HERE...
IT'D BE A PERFECT FIT...
...FOR A FOUR- TO FIVE-YEAR-OLD BOY.
わああああ
NOOOOOO

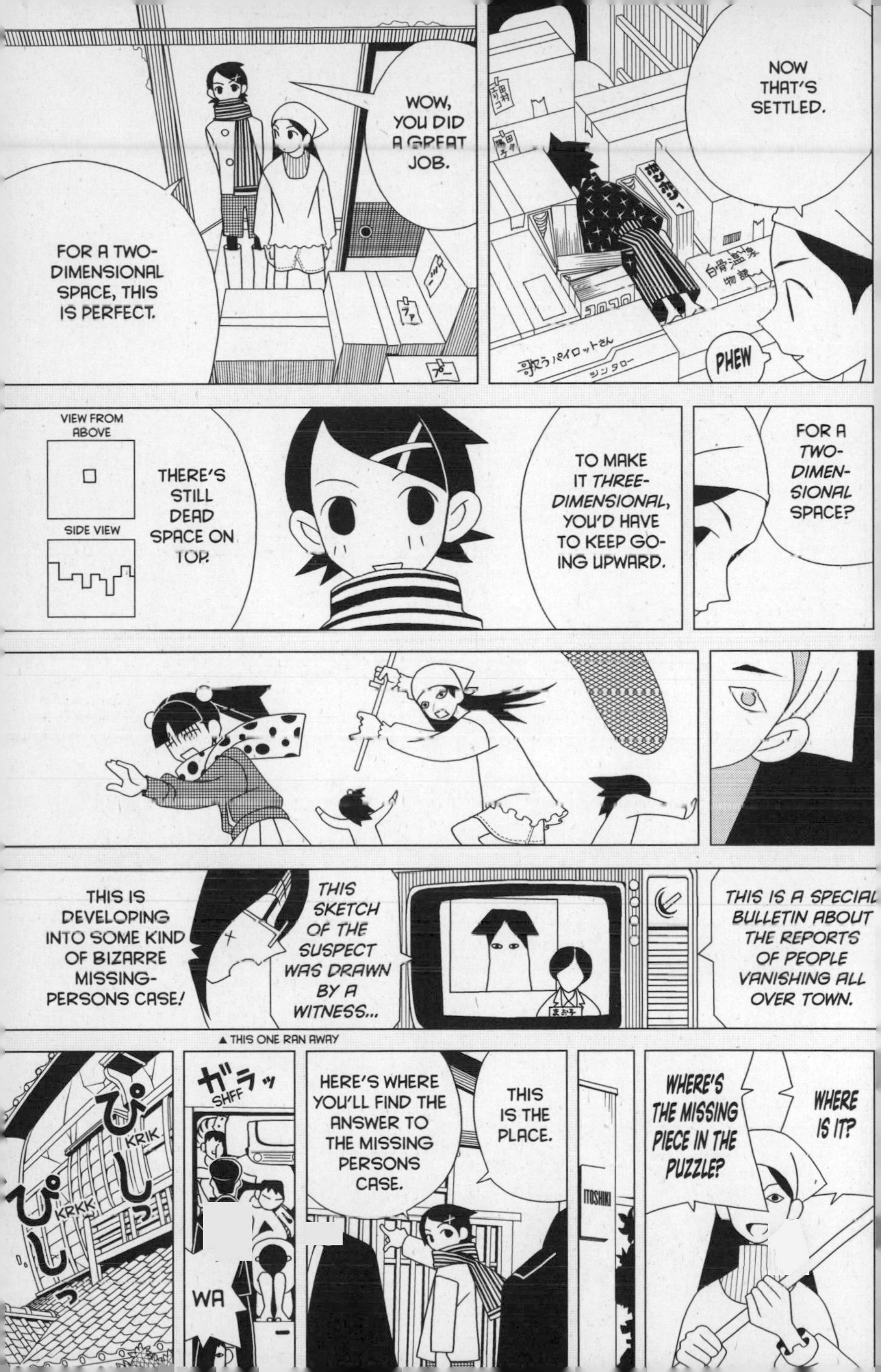
NOW THAT'S SETTLED.
PHEW
歌うパイロットさん
ジンタロー
WOW, YOU DID A GREAT JOB.
FOR A TWO-DIMENSIONAL SPACE, THIS IS PERFECT.
FOR A TWO-DIMENSIONAL SPACE?
TO MAKE IT THREE-DIMENSIONAL, YOU'D HAVE TO KEEP GOING UPWARD.
THERE'S STILL DEAD SPACE ON TOP.
VIEW FROM ABOVE
SIDE VIEW
THIS IS A SPECIAL BULLETIN ABOUT THE REPORTS OF PEOPLE VANISHING ALL OVER TOWN.
まお子
THIS SKETCH OF THE SUSPECT WAS DRAWN BY A WITNESS...
THIS IS DEVELOPING INTO SOME KIND OF BIZARRE MISSING-PERSONS CASE!
▲ THIS ONE RAN AWAY
WHERE IS IT?
WHERE'S THE MISSING PIECE IN THE PUZZLE?
ITOSHIKI
THIS IS THE PLACE.
HERE'S WHERE YOU'LL FIND THE ANSWER TO THE MISSING PERSONS CASE.
ガラッ
SHFF
WA
ぴしっ
KRIK
ぴしっ
KRKK

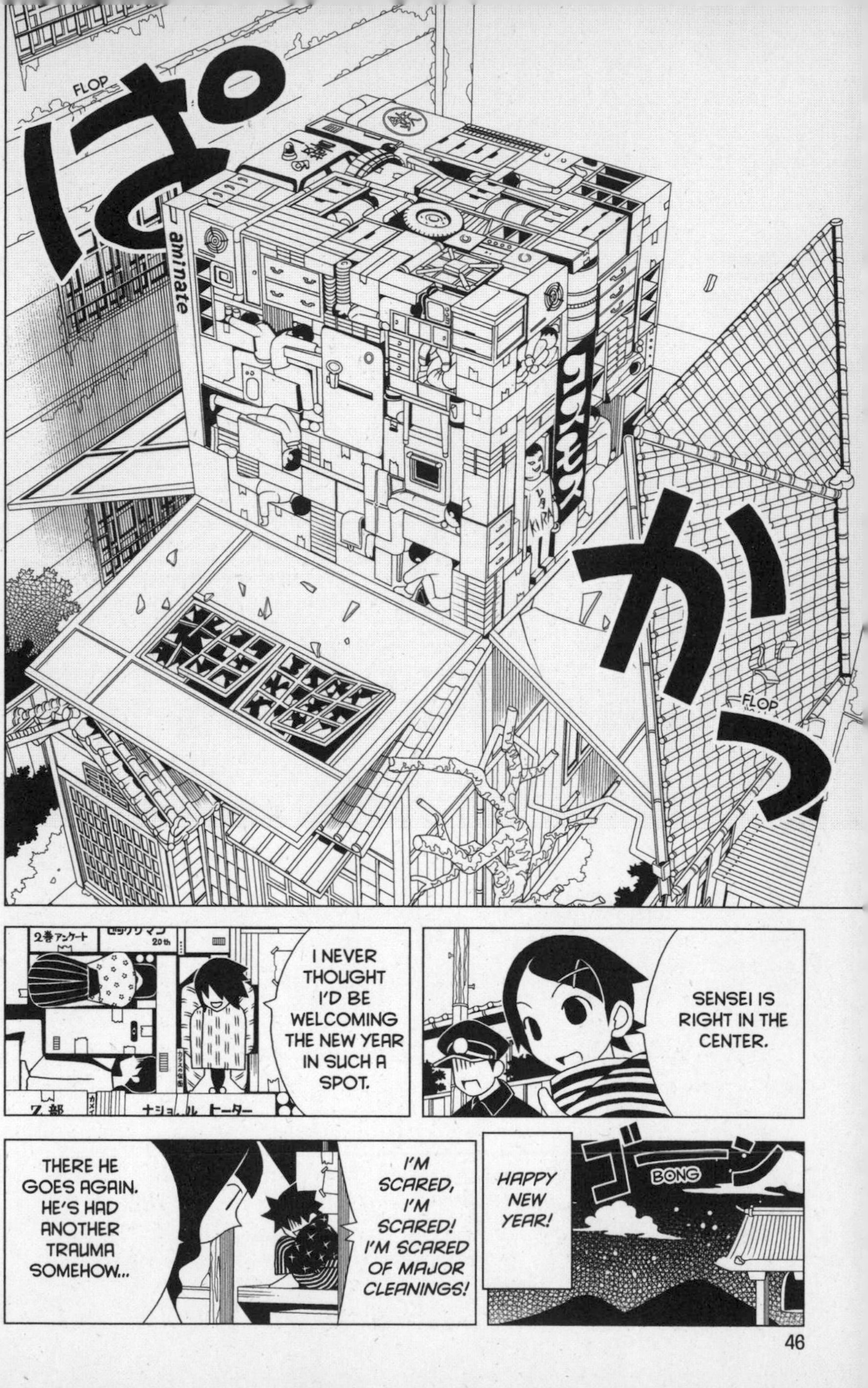
ぱ
FLOP
かっ
FLOP
aminate
SENSEI IS RIGHT IN THE CENTER.
I NEVER THOUGHT I'D BE WELCOMING THE NEW YEAR IN SUCH A SPOT.
ゴーン
BONG
HAPPY NEW YEAR!
I'M SCARED, I'M SCARED! I'M SCARED OF MAJOR CLEANINGS!
THERE HE GOES AGAIN. HE'S HAD ANOTHER TRAUMA SOMEHOW...

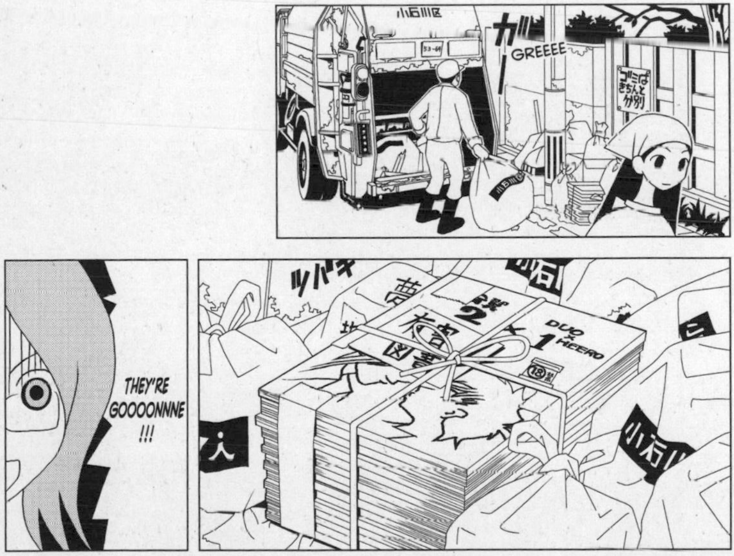
小石川区
ガー
GREEEE
ゴミは きちんと 分別
ツバキ
THEY'RE GOOOONNNE !!!

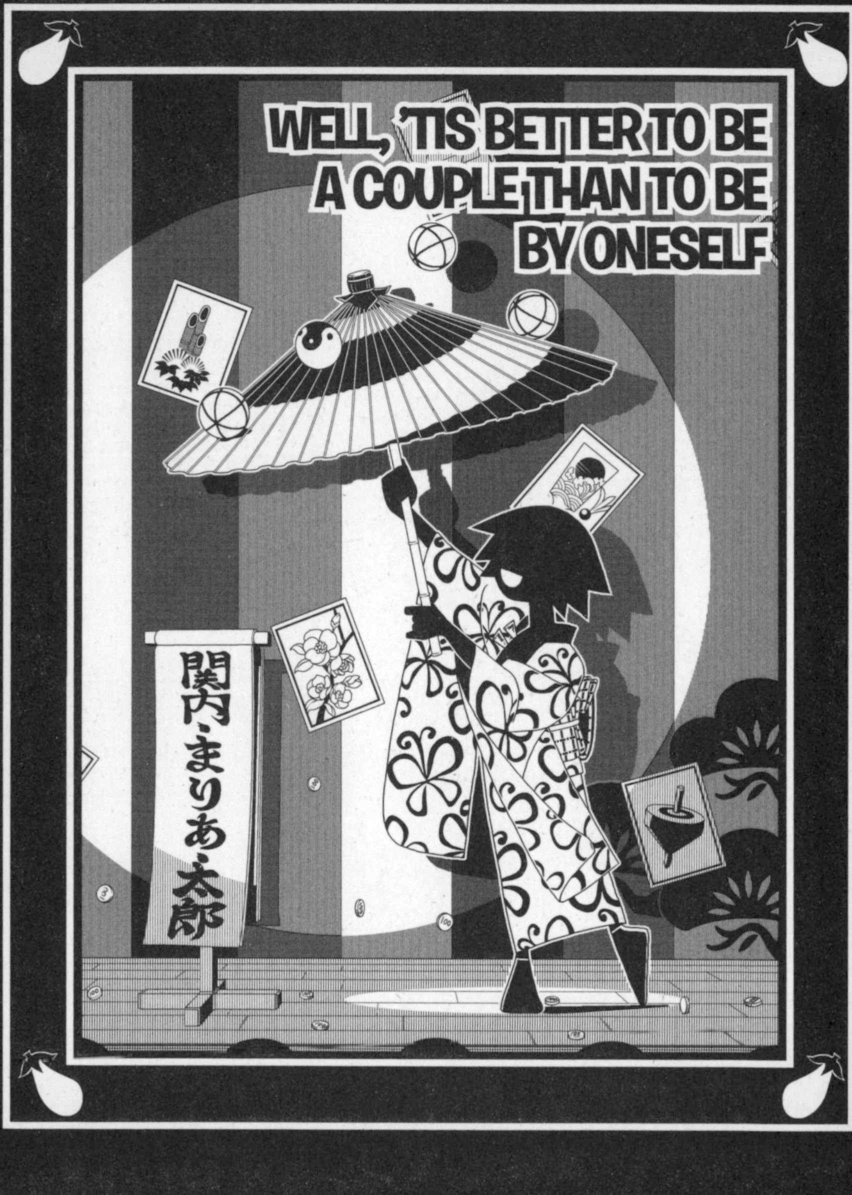
WELL, 'TIS BETTER TO BE A COUPLE THAN TO BE BY ONESELF
関内・まりあ・太郎

CHAPTER 34

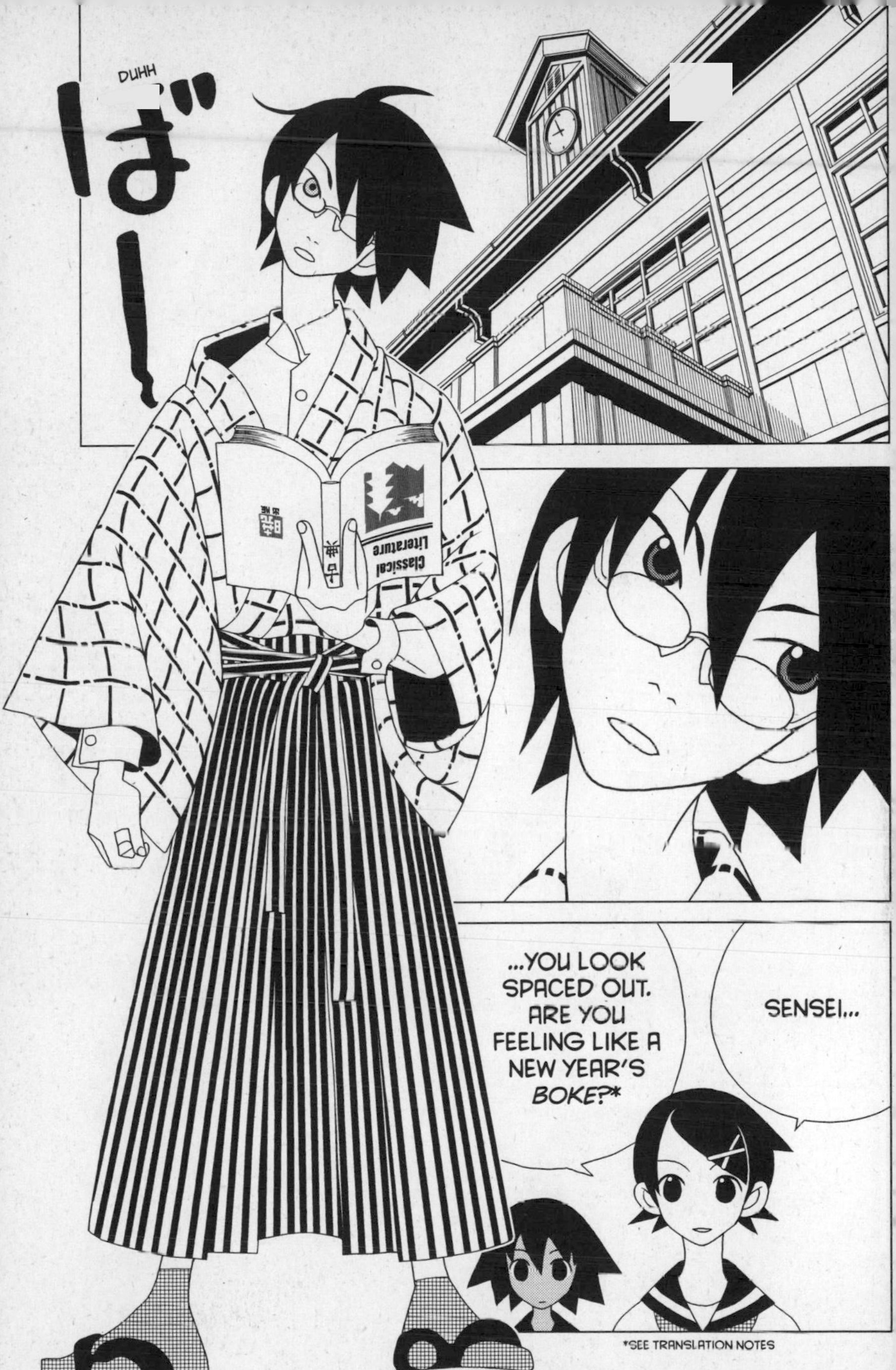
SENSEI...
...YOU LOOK SPACED OUT. ARE YOU FEELING LIKE A NEW YEAR'S *BOKE*?*
DUHH
ばー
Classical Literature

*SEE TRANSLATION NOTES

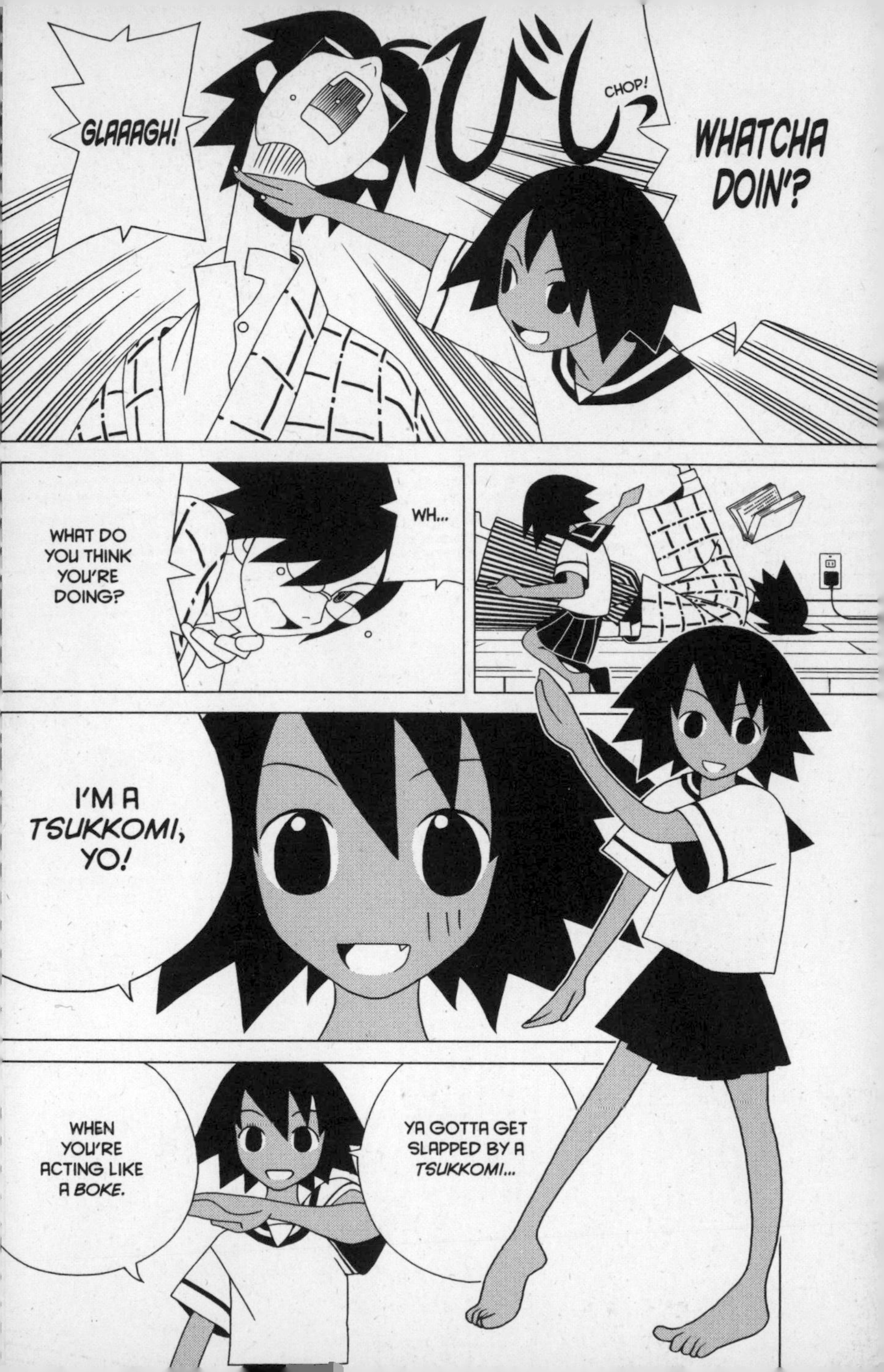
WHATCHA DOIN'?
びしっ
CHOP!
GLAAAGH!
WH...
WHAT DO YOU THINK YOU'RE DOING?
I'M A *TSUKKOMI*, YO!
YA GOTTA GET SLAPPED BY A *TSUKKOMI*...
WHEN YOU'RE ACTING LIKE A *BOKE*.

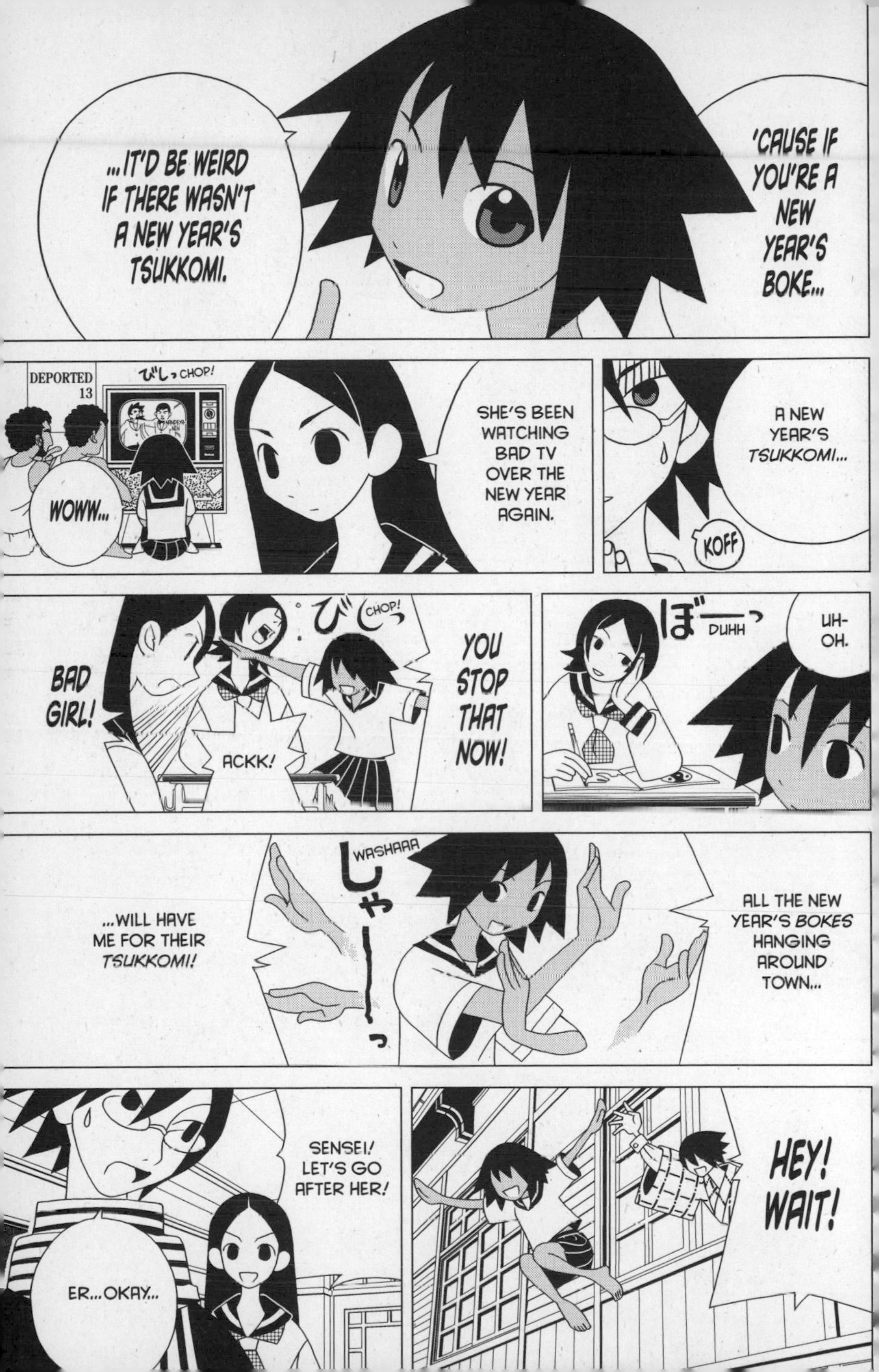
'CAUSE IF YOU'RE A NEW YEAR'S BOKE...
...IT'D BE WEIRD IF THERE WASN'T A NEW YEAR'S TSUKKOMI.
A NEW YEAR'S *TSUKKOMI*...
KOFF
SHE'S BEEN WATCHING BAD TV OVER THE NEW YEAR AGAIN.
DEPORTED 13
びしっ CHOP!
WOWW...
ぼーっ DUHH
UH-OH.
YOU STOP THAT NOW!
びしっ CHOP!
BAD GIRL!
ACKK!
ALL THE NEW YEAR'S *BOKES* HANGING AROUND TOWN...
しゃーっ WASHAAA
...WILL HAVE ME FOR THEIR *TSUKKOMI*!
HEY! WAIT!
SENSEI! LET'S GO AFTER HER!
ER...OKAY...

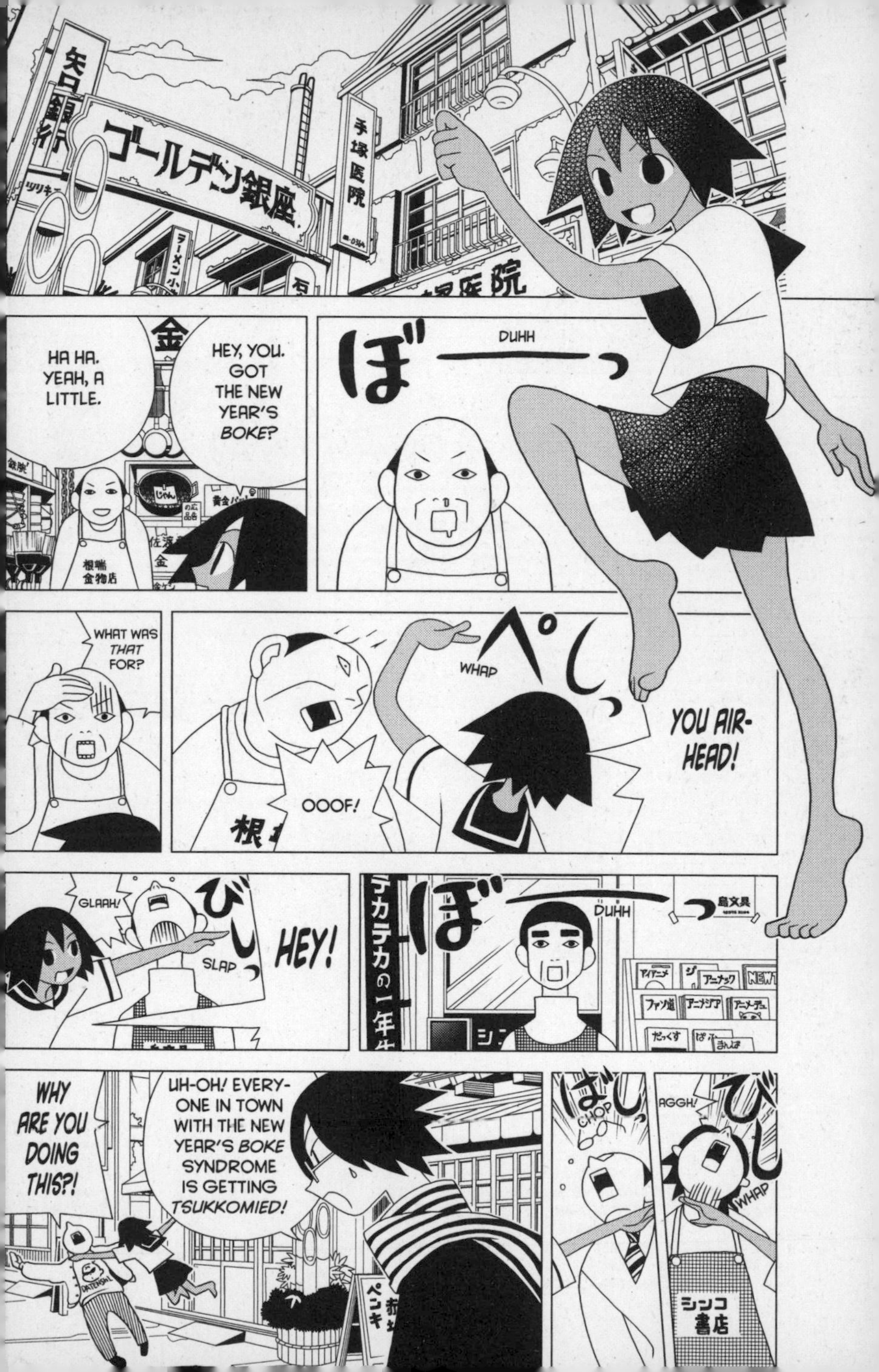

手塚医院
ゴールデン銀座
ぼーっ
DUHH
HEY, YOU. GOT THE NEW YEAR'S *BOKE*?
HA HA. YEAH, A LITTLE.
YOU AIR-HEAD!
ぺしっ
WHAP
OOOF!
WHAT WAS *THAT* FOR?
ぼーっ
DUHH
HEY!
びしっ
SLAP
GLAAH!
びしっ
AGGH!
WHAP
ばしっ
CHOP
UH-OH! EVERY-ONE IN TOWN WITH THE NEW YEAR'S *BOKE* SYNDROME IS GETTING *TSUKKOMIED!*
WHY ARE YOU DOING THIS?!

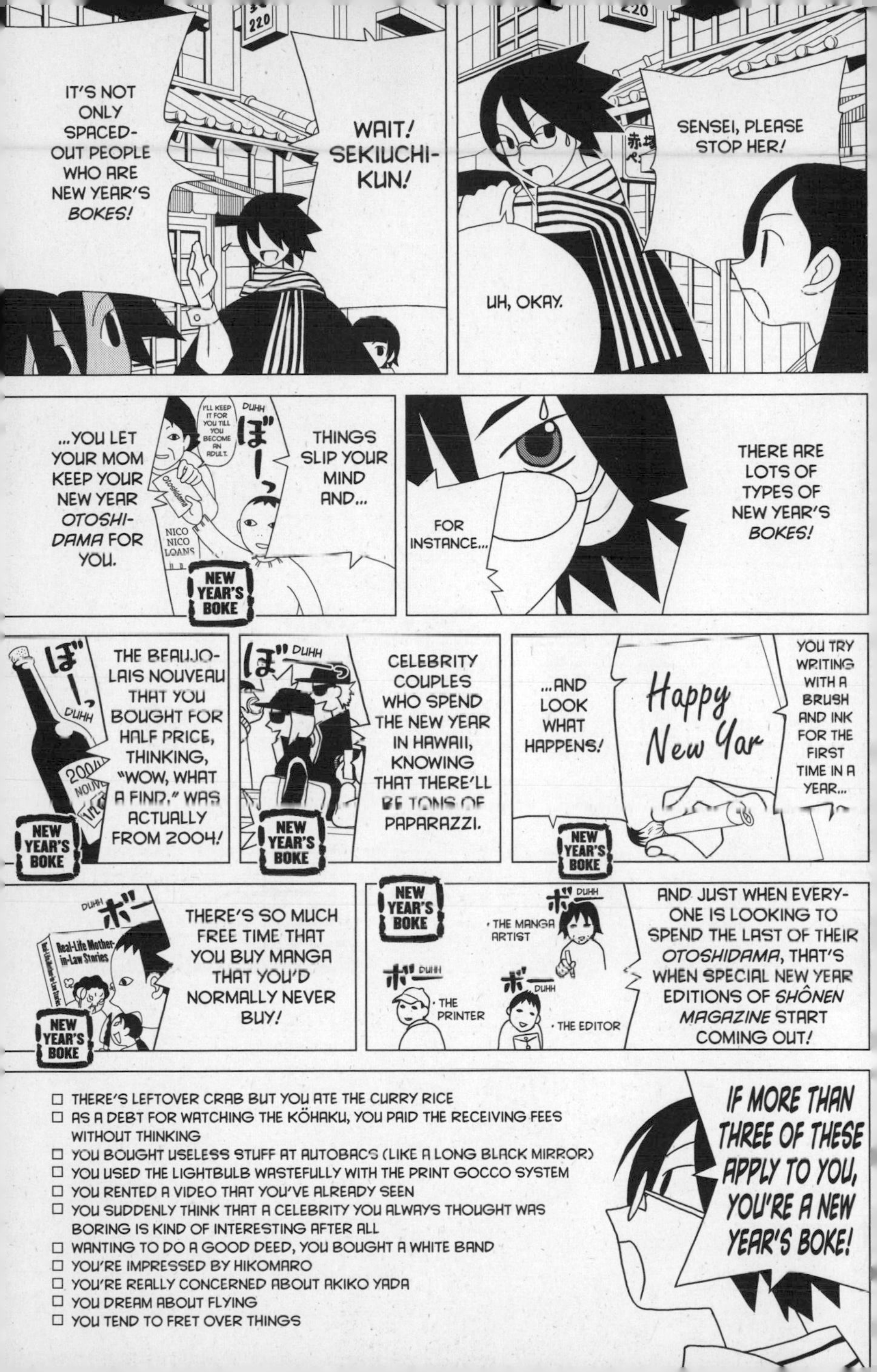

220
SENSEI, PLEASE STOP HER!
UH, OKAY.
WAIT! SEKIUCHI-KUN!
IT'S NOT ONLY SPACED-OUT PEOPLE WHO ARE NEW YEAR'S *BOKES*!
THERE ARE LOTS OF TYPES OF NEW YEAR'S *BOKES*!
FOR INSTANCE...
THINGS SLIP YOUR MIND AND...
DUHH
I'LL KEEP IT FOR YOU TILL YOU BECOME AN ADULT.
Otoshidama
NICO NICO LOANS
...YOU LET YOUR MOM KEEP YOUR NEW YEAR *OTOSHIDAMA* FOR YOU.
NEW YEAR'S BOKE
YOU TRY WRITING WITH A BRUSH AND INK FOR THE FIRST TIME IN A YEAR...
Happy New Yar
...AND LOOK WHAT HAPPENS!
NEW YEAR'S BOKE
CELEBRITY COUPLES WHO SPEND THE NEW YEAR IN HAWAII, KNOWING THAT THERE'LL BE TONS OF PAPARAZZI.
DUHH
NEW YEAR'S BOKE
THE BEAUJOLAIS NOUVEAU THAT YOU BOUGHT FOR HALF PRICE, THINKING, "WOW, WHAT A FIND," WAS ACTUALLY FROM 2004!
DUHH
NEW YEAR'S BOKE
AND JUST WHEN EVERYONE IS LOOKING TO SPEND THE LAST OF THEIR *OTOSHIDAMA*, THAT'S WHEN SPECIAL NEW YEAR EDITIONS OF *SHÔNEN MAGAZINE* START COMING OUT!
DUHH
· THE MANGA ARTIST
DUHH
· THE EDITOR
DUHH
· THE PRINTER
NEW YEAR'S BOKE
THERE'S SO MUCH FREE TIME THAT YOU BUY MANGA THAT YOU'D NORMALLY NEVER BUY!
DUHH
Real-Life Mother-in-Law Stories
NEW YEAR'S BOKE
IF MORE THAN THREE OF THESE APPLY TO YOU, YOU'RE A NEW YEAR'S BOKE!
☐ THERE'S LEFTOVER CRAB BUT YOU ATE THE CURRY RICE
☐ AS A DEBT FOR WATCHING THE KÔHAKU, YOU PAID THE RECEIVING FEES WITHOUT THINKING
☐ YOU BOUGHT USELESS STUFF AT AUTOBACS (LIKE A LONG BLACK MIRROR)
☐ YOU USED THE LIGHTBULB WASTEFULLY WITH THE PRINT GOCCO SYSTEM
☐ YOU RENTED A VIDEO THAT YOU'VE ALREADY SEEN
☐ YOU SUDDENLY THINK THAT A CELEBRITY YOU ALWAYS THOUGHT WAS BORING IS KIND OF INTERESTING AFTER ALL
☐ WANTING TO DO A GOOD DEED, YOU BOUGHT A WHITE BAND
☐ YOU'RE IMPRESSED BY HIKOMARO
☐ YOU'RE REALLY CONCERNED ABOUT AKIKO YADA
☐ YOU DREAM ABOUT FLYING
☐ YOU TEND TO FRET OVER THINGS

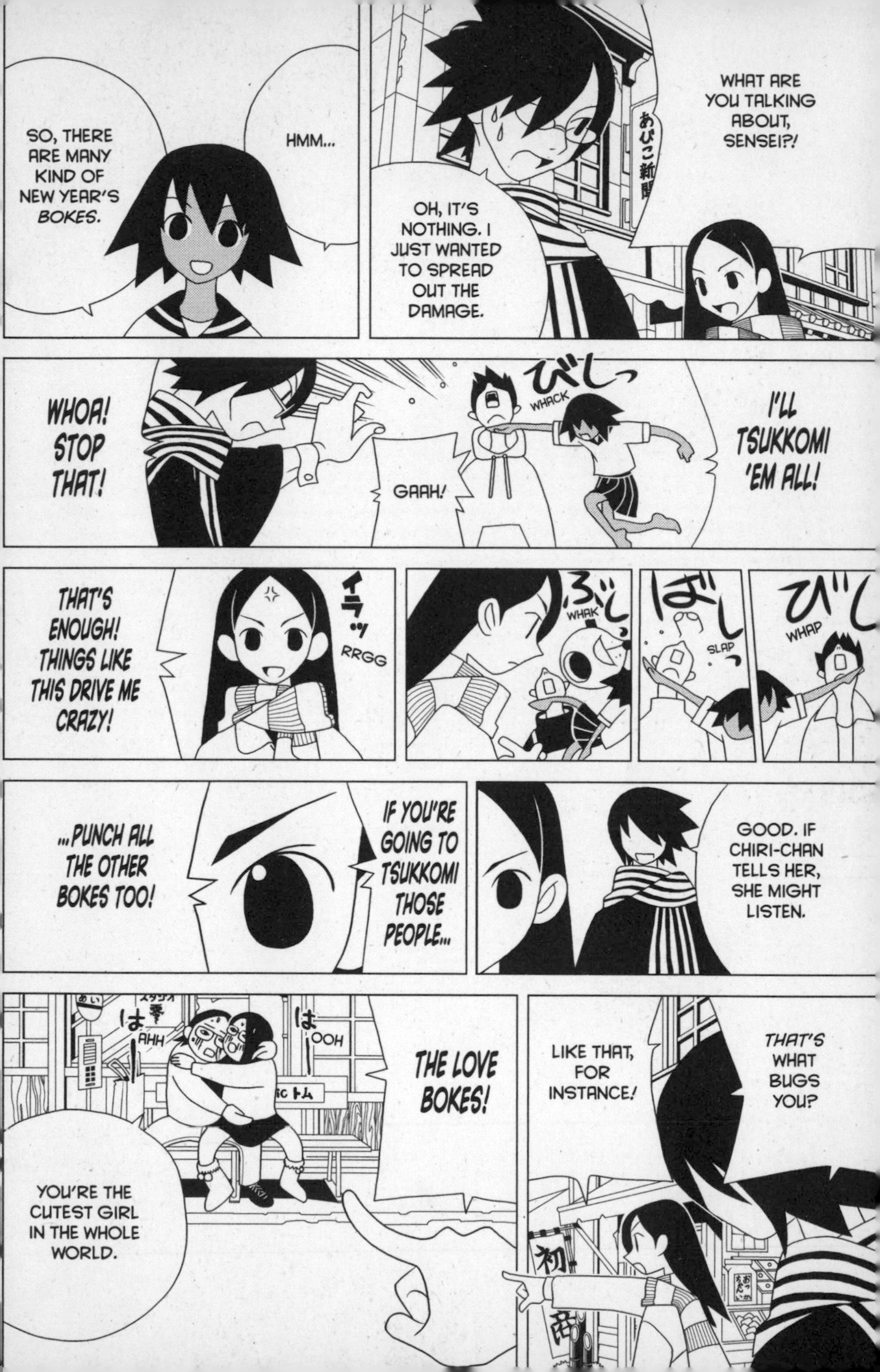
WHAT ARE YOU TALKING ABOUT, SENSEI?!
あびこ新聞
OH, IT'S NOTHING. I JUST WANTED TO SPREAD OUT THE DAMAGE.
HMM...
SO, THERE ARE MANY KIND OF NEW YEAR'S *BOKES*.
I'LL TSUKKOMI 'EM ALL!
びしっ
WHACK
GAAH!
WHOA! STOP THAT!
びし
WHAP
ばしっ
SLAP
ぶし
WHAK
イラッ
RRGG
THAT'S ENOUGH! THINGS LIKE THIS DRIVE ME CRAZY!
GOOD. IF CHIRI-CHAN TELLS HER, SHE MIGHT LISTEN.
IF YOU'RE GOING TO TSUKKOMI THOSE PEOPLE...
...PUNCH ALL THE OTHER BOKES TOO!
THAT'S WHAT BUGS YOU?
LIKE THAT, FOR INSTANCE!
THE LOVE BOKES!
はー
OOH
はー
AHH
YOU'RE THE CUTEST GIRL IN THE WHOLE WORLD.

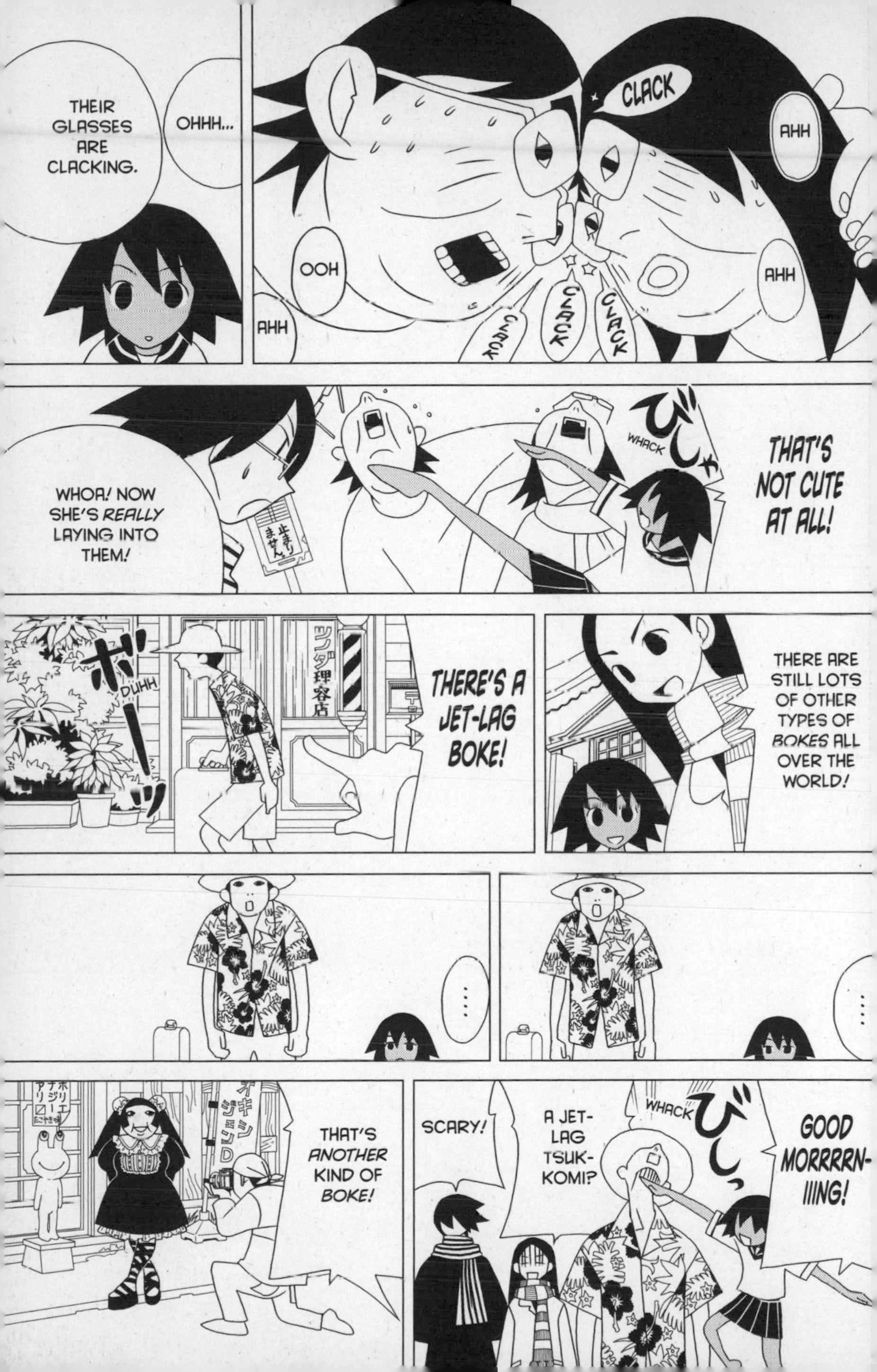
CLACK
AHH
AHH
CLACK
CLACK
CLACK
OOH
AHH
OHHH...
THEIR GLASSES ARE CLACKING.
THAT'S NOT CUTE AT ALL!
WHACK
止まりません
WHOA! NOW SHE'S *REALLY* LAYING INTO THEM!
THERE ARE STILL LOTS OF OTHER TYPES OF *BOKES* ALL OVER THE WORLD!
THERE'S A JET-LAG BOKE!
ツダ理容店
DUHH
....
....
GOOD MORRRRN-IIING!
WHACK
A JET-LAG TSUKKOMI?
SCARY!
THAT'S *ANOTHER* KIND OF *BOKE!*

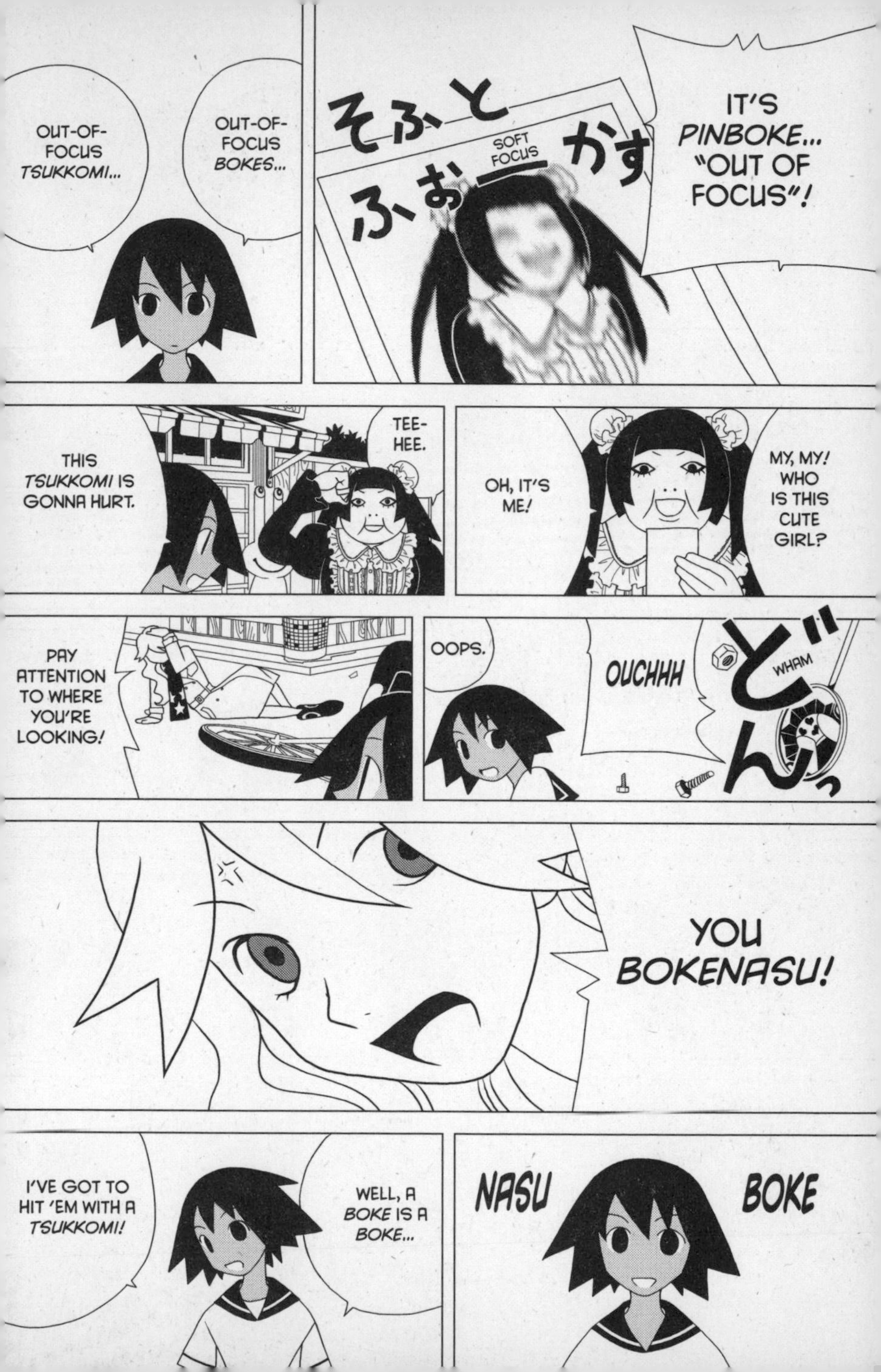
IT'S *PINBOKE*... "OUT OF FOCUS"!
そふと ふぉーかす
SOFT FOCUS
OUT-OF-FOCUS *BOKES*...
OUT-OF-FOCUS *TSUKKOMI*...
MY, MY! WHO IS THIS CUTE GIRL?
OH, IT'S ME!
TEE-HEE.
THIS *TSUKKOMI* IS GONNA HURT.
どん
WHAM
OUCHHH
OOPS.
PAY ATTENTION TO WHERE YOU'RE LOOKING!
YOU BOKENASU!
NASU
BOKE
WELL, A *BOKE* IS A BOKE...
I'VE GOT TO HIT 'EM WITH A *TSUKKOMI*!

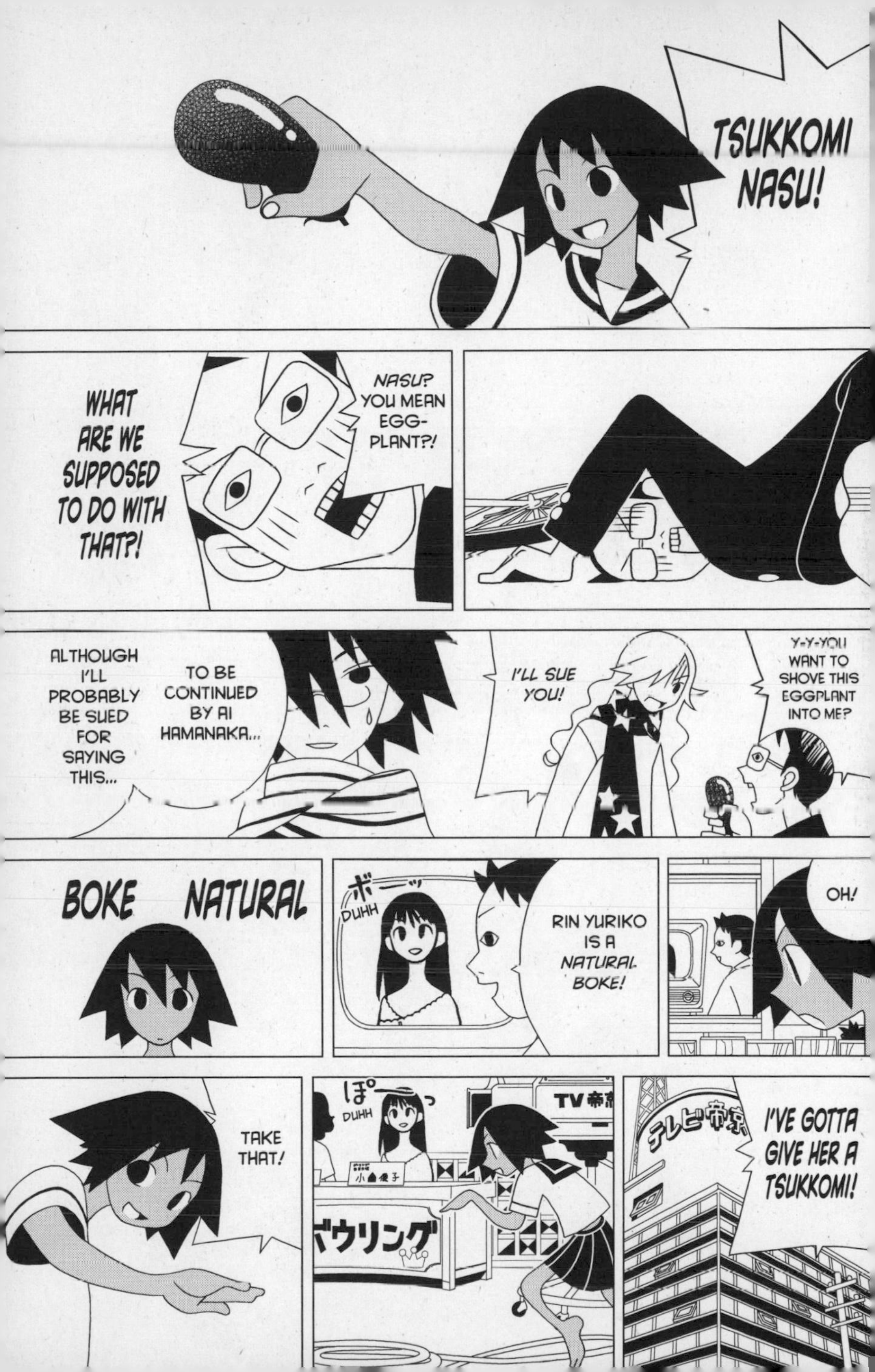
TSUKKOMI NASU!
NASU? YOU MEAN EGG-PLANT?!
WHAT ARE WE SUPPOSED TO DO WITH THAT?!
Y-Y-YOU WANT TO SHOVE THIS EGGPLANT INTO ME?
I'LL SUE YOU!
TO BE CONTINUED BY AI HAMANAKA...
ALTHOUGH I'LL PROBABLY BE SUED FOR SAYING THIS...
OH!
RIN YURIKO IS A NATURAL BOKE!
ボーッ
DUHH
BOKE NATURAL
テレビ帝京
I'VE GOTTA GIVE HER A TSUKKOMI!
ぽーっ
DUHH
ボウリング
TAKE THAT!

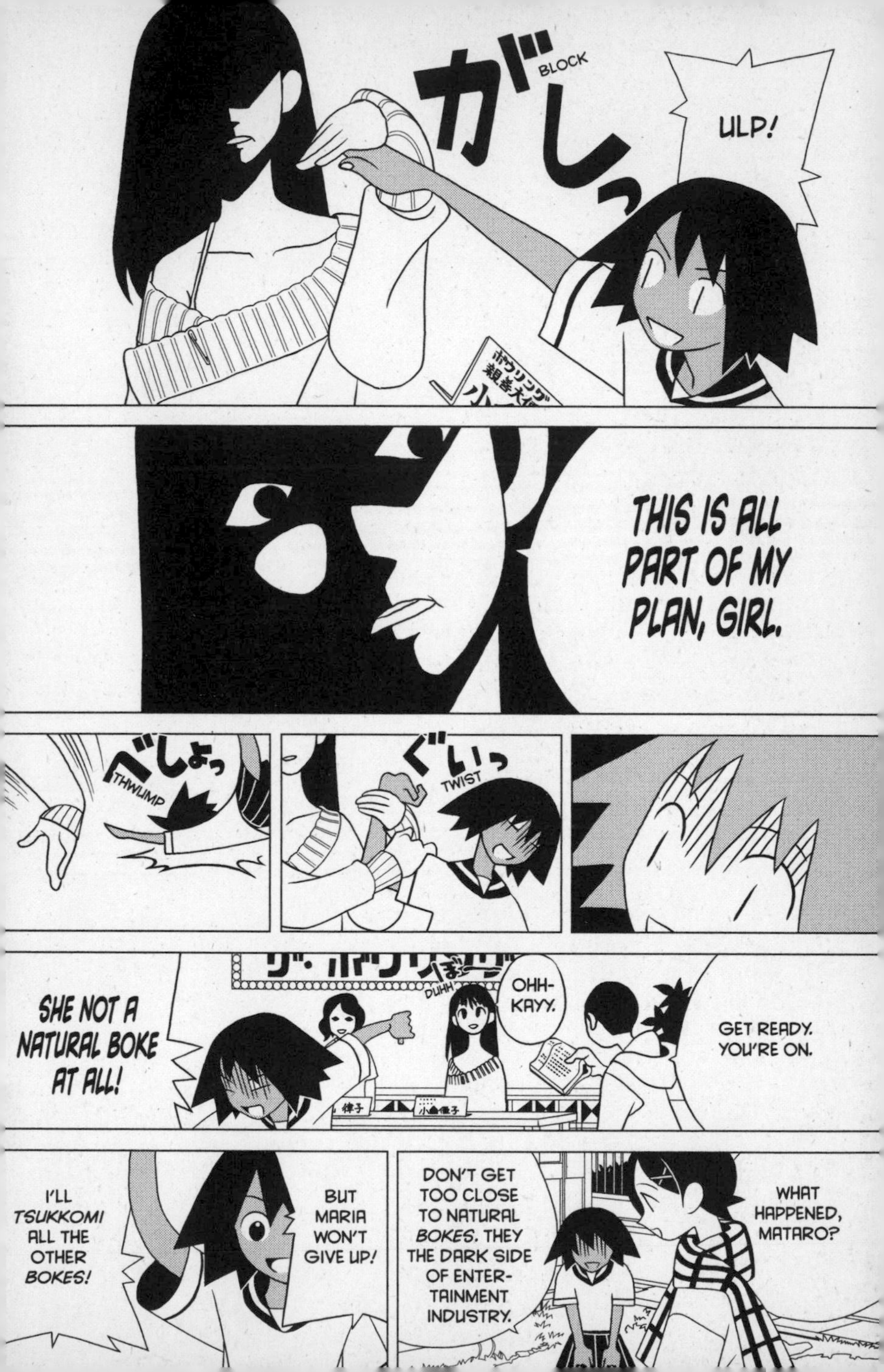

ULP!
がしっ
BLOCK
THIS IS ALL PART OF MY PLAN, GIRL.
ぐいっ
TWIST
べしょっ
THWUMP
GET READY. YOU'RE ON.
OHH-KAYY.
DUHH
SHE NOT A NATURAL BOKE AT ALL!
WHAT HAPPENED, MATARO?
DON'T GET TOO CLOSE TO NATURAL *BOKES*. THEY THE DARK SIDE OF ENTER-TAINMENT INDUSTRY.
BUT MARIA WON'T GIVE UP!
I'LL *TSUKKOMI* ALL THE OTHER *BOKES*!

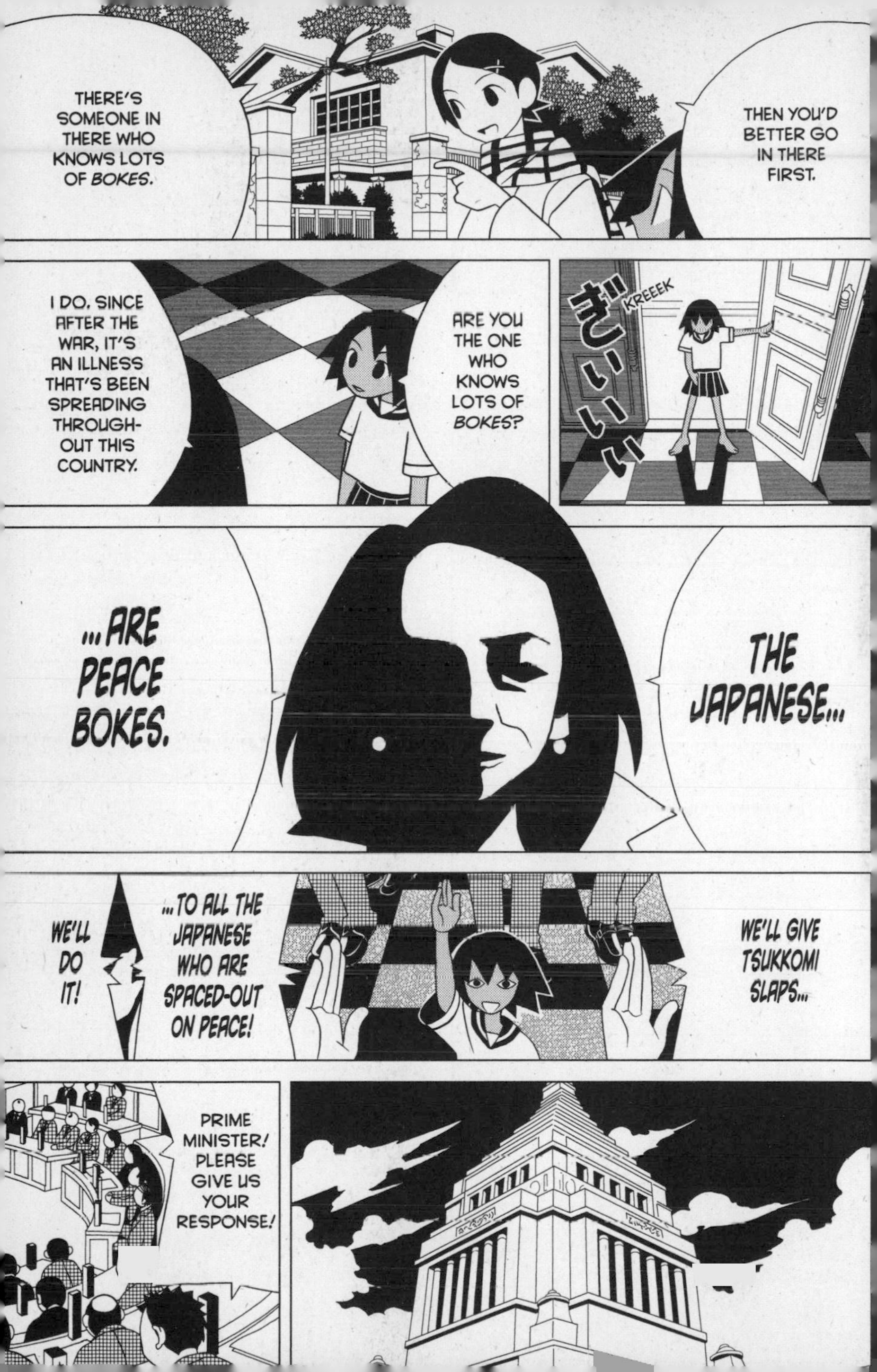
THERE'S SOMEONE IN THERE WHO KNOWS LOTS OF *BOKES*.
THEN YOU'D BETTER GO IN THERE FIRST.
ぎいいい
KREEEK
ARE YOU THE ONE WHO KNOWS LOTS OF *BOKES*?
I DO. SINCE AFTER THE WAR, IT'S AN ILLNESS THAT'S BEEN SPREADING THROUGH-OUT THIS COUNTRY.
THE JAPANESE...
...ARE PEACE BOKES.
WE'LL GIVE TSUKKOMI SLAPS...
...TO ALL THE JAPANESE WHO ARE SPACED-OUT ON PEACE!
WE'LL DO IT!
PRIME MINISTER! PLEASE GIVE US YOUR RESPONSE!

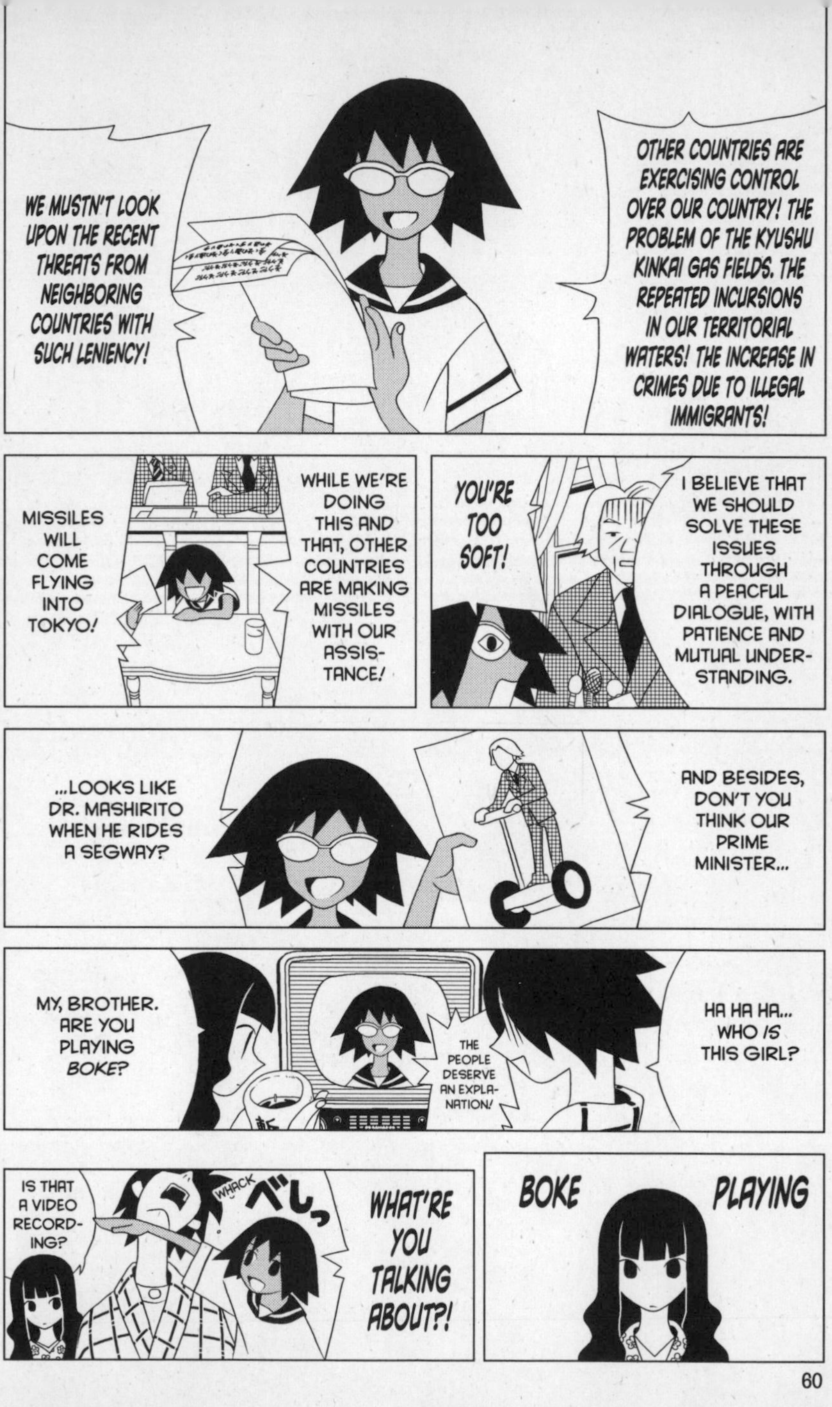
OTHER COUNTRIES ARE EXERCISING CONTROL OVER OUR COUNTRY! THE PROBLEM OF THE KYUSHU KINKAI GAS FIELDS. THE REPEATED INCURSIONS IN OUR TERRITORIAL WATERS! THE INCREASE IN CRIMES DUE TO ILLEGAL IMMIGRANTS!
WE MUSTN'T LOOK UPON THE RECENT THREATS FROM NEIGHBORING COUNTRIES WITH SUCH LENIENCY!
I BELIEVE THAT WE SHOULD SOLVE THESE ISSUES THROUGH A PEACFUL DIALOGUE, WITH PATIENCE AND MUTUAL UNDERSTANDING.
YOU'RE TOO SOFT!
WHILE WE'RE DOING THIS AND THAT, OTHER COUNTRIES ARE MAKING MISSILES WITH OUR ASSISTANCE!
MISSILES WILL COME FLYING INTO TOKYO!
AND BESIDES, DON'T YOU THINK OUR PRIME MINISTER...
...LOOKS LIKE DR. MASHIRITO WHEN HE RIDES A SEGWAY?
HA HA HA... WHO *IS* THIS GIRL?
THE PEOPLE DESERVE AN EXPLANATION!
MY, BROTHER. ARE YOU PLAYING *BOKE*?
BOKE PLAYING
WHAT'RE YOU TALKING ABOUT?!
べしっ WHACK
IS THAT A VIDEO RECORDING?

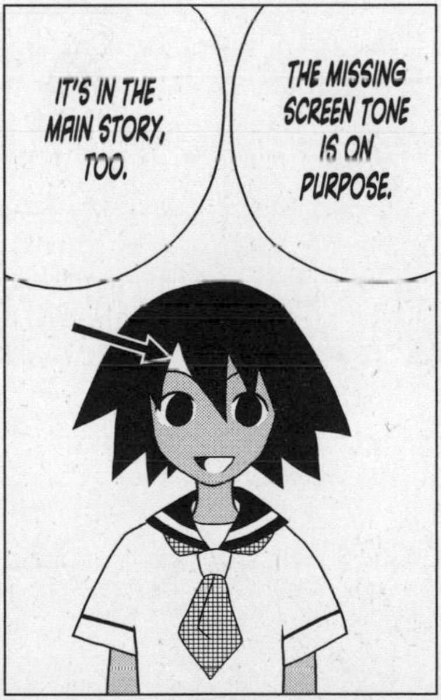
THE MISSING SCREEN TONE IS ON PURPOSE.
IT'S IN THE MAIN STORY, TOO.

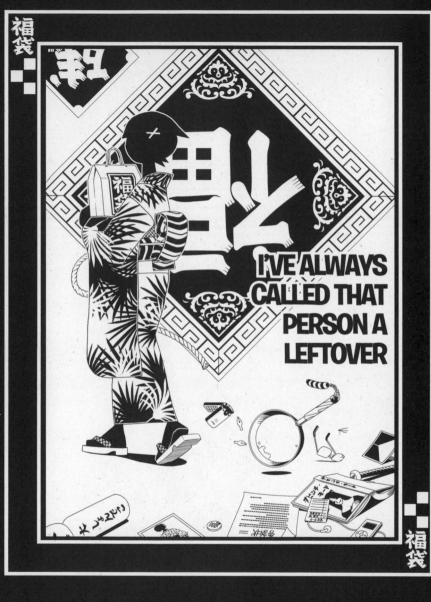

I'VE ALWAYS CALLED THAT PERSON A LEFTOVER

CHAPTER 35

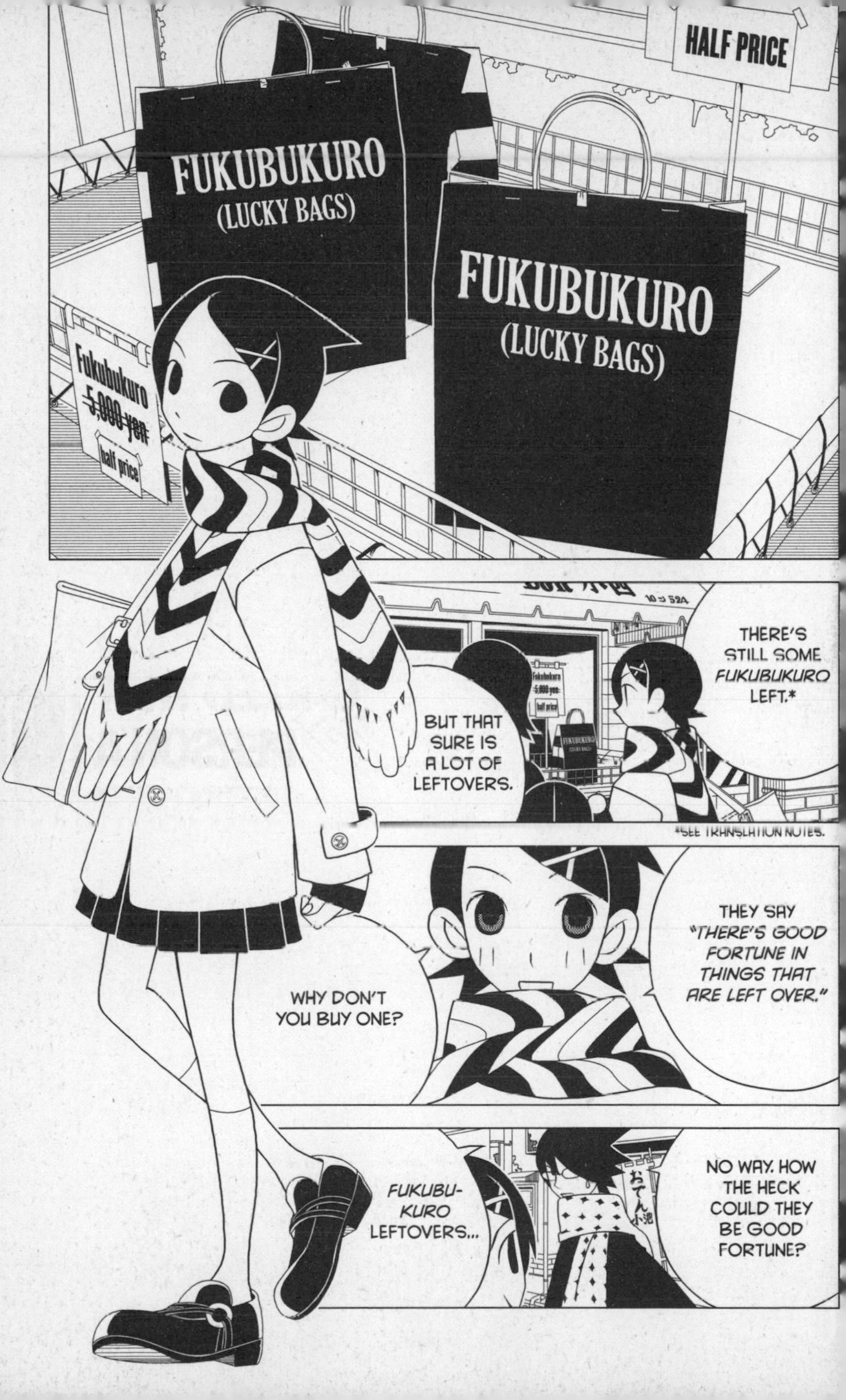
HALF PRICE
FUKUBUKURO (LUCKY BAGS)
FUKUBUKURO (LUCKY BAGS)
Fukubukuro 5,000 yen half price
THERE'S STILL SOME FUKUBUKURO LEFT.*
BUT THAT SURE IS A LOT OF LEFTOVERS.
*SEE TRANSLATION NOTES.
THEY SAY "THERE'S GOOD FORTUNE IN THINGS THAT ARE LEFT OVER."
WHY DON'T YOU BUY ONE?
NO WAY. HOW THE HECK COULD THEY BE GOOD FORTUNE?
おでん 小池
FUKUBUKURO LEFTOVERS...

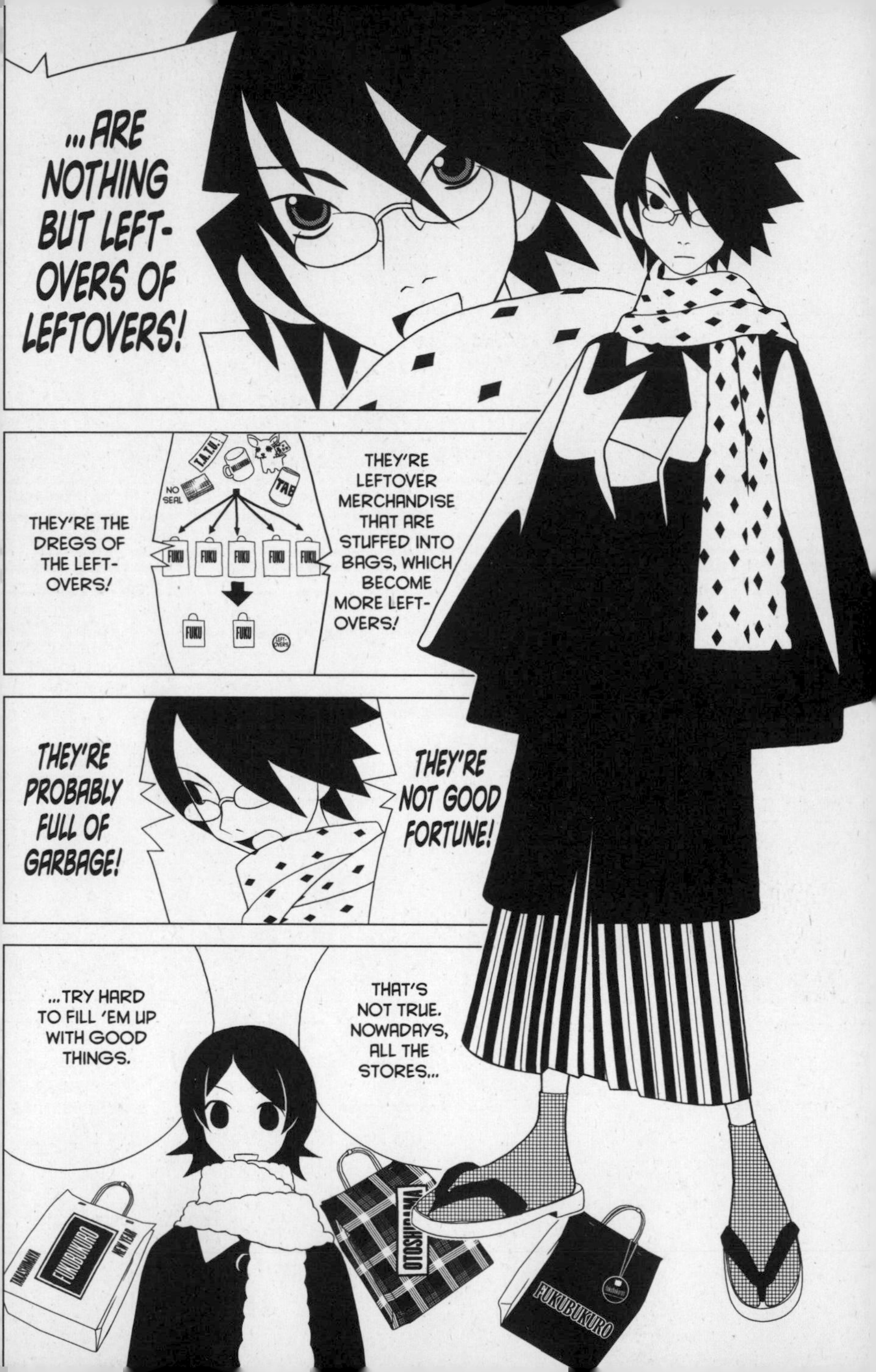
...ARE NOTHING BUT LEFT-OVERS OF LEFTOVERS!
THEY'RE LEFTOVER MERCHANDISE THAT ARE STUFFED INTO BAGS, WHICH BECOME MORE LEFT-OVERS!
T.A.T.U.
TAB
NO SEAL
FUKU
LEFT-OVERS
THEY'RE THE DREGS OF THE LEFT-OVERS!
THEY'RE NOT GOOD FORTUNE!
THEY'RE PROBABLY FULL OF GARBAGE!
THAT'S NOT TRUE. NOWADAYS, ALL THE STORES...
...TRY HARD TO FILL 'EM UP WITH GOOD THINGS.
FUKUBUKURO
NEW YEAR
FUKUBUKURO

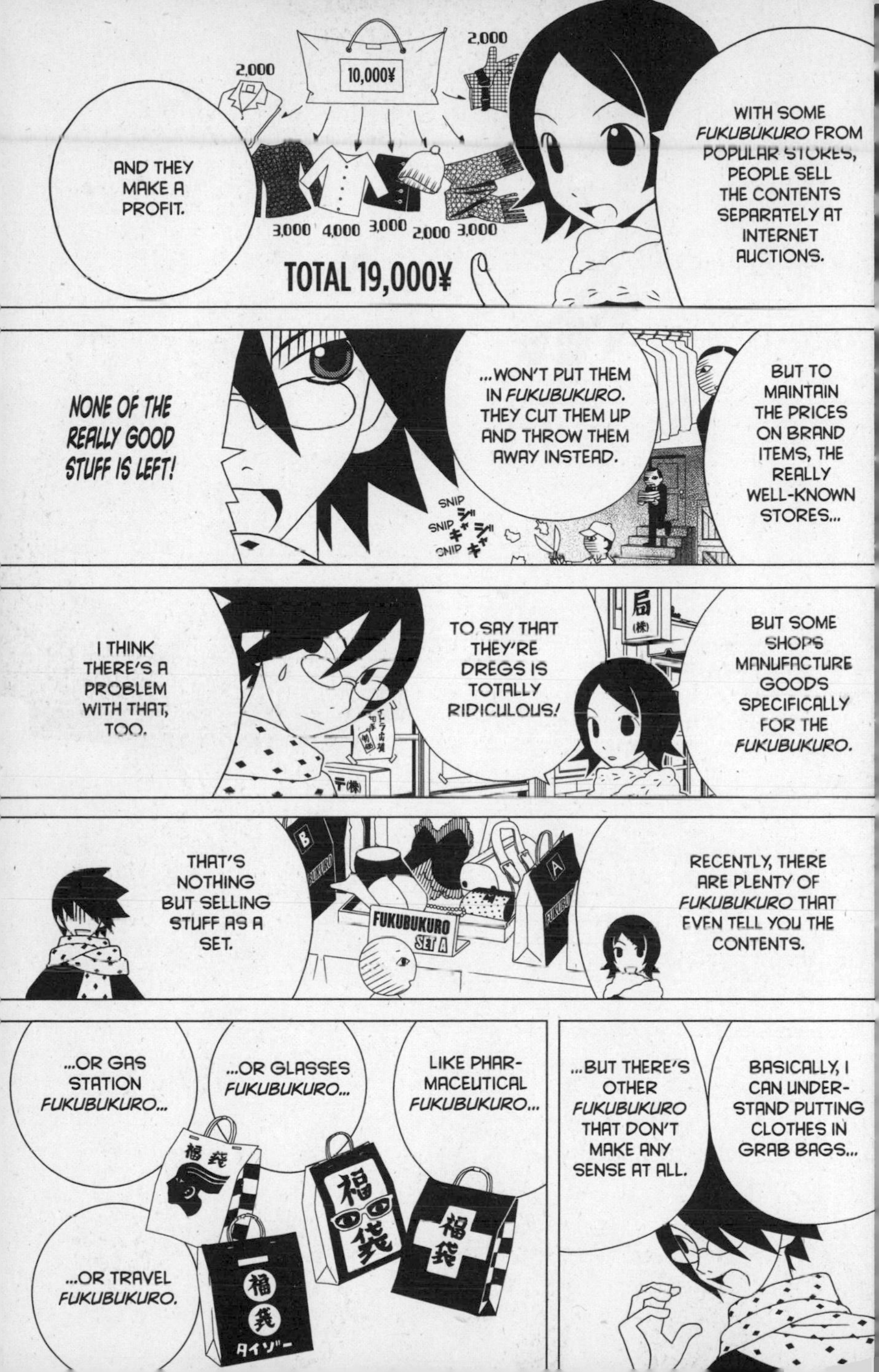
WITH SOME *FUKUBUKURO* FROM POPULAR STORES, PEOPLE SELL THE CONTENTS SEPARATELY AT INTERNET AUCTIONS.
2,000
10,000¥
2,000
3,000 4,000 3,000 2,000 3,000
TOTAL 19,000¥
AND THEY MAKE A PROFIT.
BUT TO MAINTAIN THE PRICES ON BRAND ITEMS, THE REALLY WELL-KNOWN STORES...
...WON'T PUT THEM IN *FUKUBUKURO*. THEY CUT THEM UP AND THROW THEM AWAY INSTEAD.
SNIP ジャキ SNIP ジャキ SNIP
NONE OF THE REALLY GOOD STUFF IS LEFT!
BUT SOME SHOPS MANUFACTURE GOODS SPECIFICALLY FOR THE *FUKUBUKURO*.
局 (株)
TO SAY THAT THEY'RE DREGS IS TOTALLY RIDICULOUS!
I THINK THERE'S A PROBLEM WITH THAT, TOO.
RECENTLY, THERE ARE PLENTY OF *FUKUBUKURO* THAT EVEN TELL YOU THE CONTENTS.
A
B
FUKUBUKURO SET A
THAT'S NOTHING BUT SELLING STUFF AS A SET.
BASICALLY, I CAN UNDERSTAND PUTTING CLOTHES IN GRAB BAGS...
...BUT THERE'S OTHER *FUKUBUKURO* THAT DON'T MAKE ANY SENSE AT ALL.
LIKE PHARMACEUTICAL *FUKUBUKURO*...
...OR GLASSES *FUKUBUKURO*...
...OR GAS STATION *FUKUBUKURO*...
...OR TRAVEL *FUKUBUKURO*.
福袋
福袋
福袋
一 福袋 タイゾー

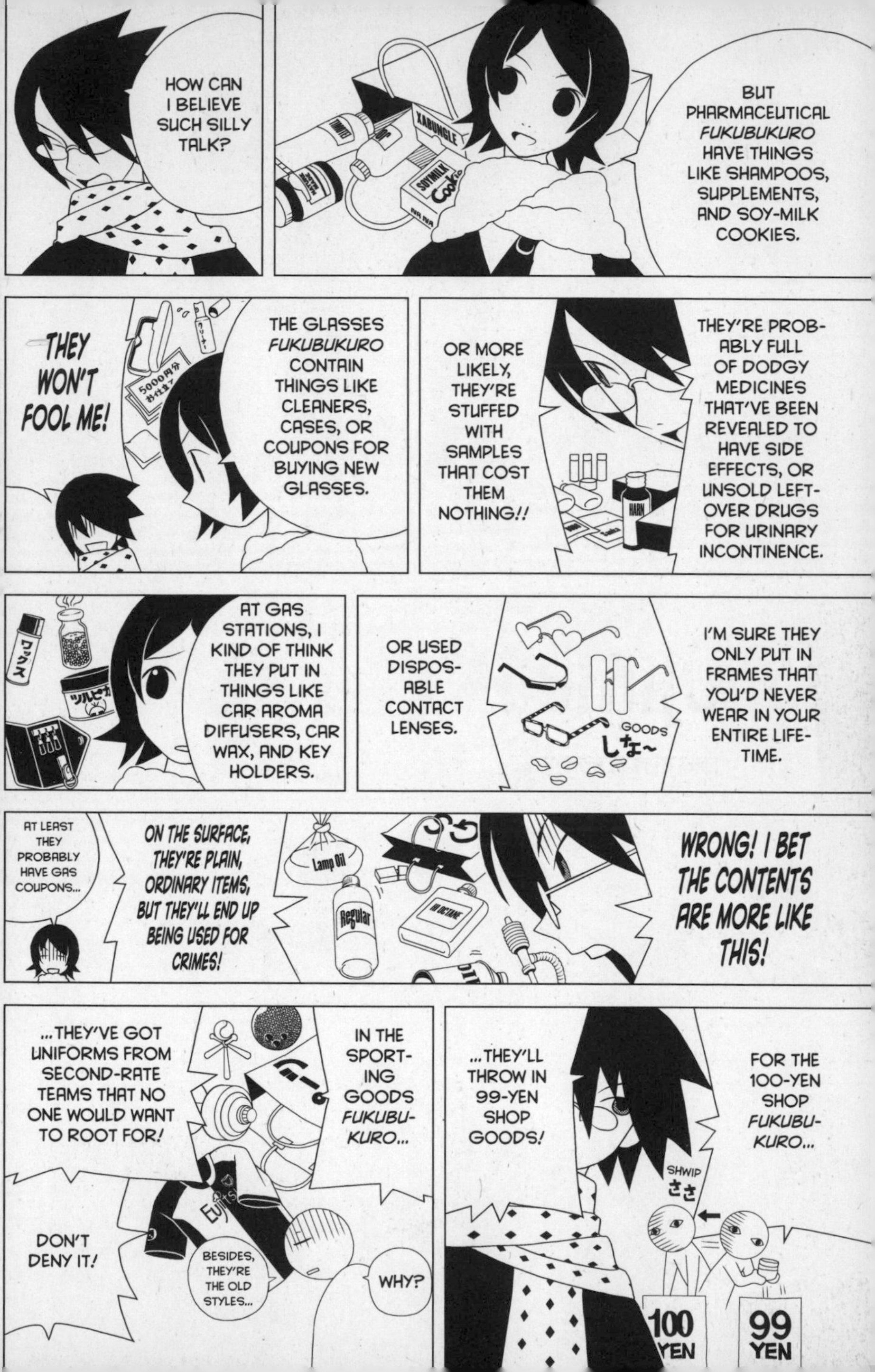
BUT PHARMACEUTICAL *FUKUBUKURO* HAVE THINGS LIKE SHAMPOOS, SUPPLEMENTS, AND SOY-MILK COOKIES.
XABUNGLE
SOYMILK Cookie
HOW CAN I BELIEVE SUCH SILLY TALK?
THEY'RE PROBABLY FULL OF DODGY MEDICINES THAT'VE BEEN REVEALED TO HAVE SIDE EFFECTS, OR UNSOLD LEFT-OVER DRUGS FOR URINARY INCONTINENCE.
HARN
OR MORE LIKELY, THEY'RE STUFFED WITH SAMPLES THAT COST THEM NOTHING!!
THE GLASSES *FUKUBUKURO* CONTAIN THINGS LIKE CLEANERS, CASES, OR COUPONS FOR BUYING NEW GLASSES.
クリーナー
5000円分お仕立て
THEY WON'T FOOL ME!
I'M SURE THEY ONLY PUT IN FRAMES THAT YOU'D NEVER WEAR IN YOUR ENTIRE LIFE-TIME.
GOODS
しな～
OR USED DISPOSABLE CONTACT LENSES.
AT GAS STATIONS, I KIND OF THINK THEY PUT IN THINGS LIKE CAR AROMA DIFFUSERS, CAR WAX, AND KEY HOLDERS.
ワックス
ツルピカ
WRONG! I BET THE CONTENTS ARE MORE LIKE THIS!
Lamp Oil
Regular
HI OCTANE
ON THE SURFACE, THEY'RE PLAIN, ORDINARY ITEMS, BUT THEY'LL END UP BEING USED FOR CRIMES!
AT LEAST THEY PROBABLY HAVE GAS COUPONS...
FOR THE 100-YEN SHOP *FUKUBUKURO*...
...THEY'LL THROW IN 99-YEN SHOP GOODS!
SHWIP
ささ
100 YEN
99 YEN
IN THE SPORTING GOODS *FUKUBUKURO*...
...THEY'VE GOT UNIFORMS FROM SECOND-RATE TEAMS THAT NO ONE WOULD WANT TO ROOT FOR!
WHY?
BESIDES, THEY'RE THE OLD STYLES...
DON'T DENY IT!

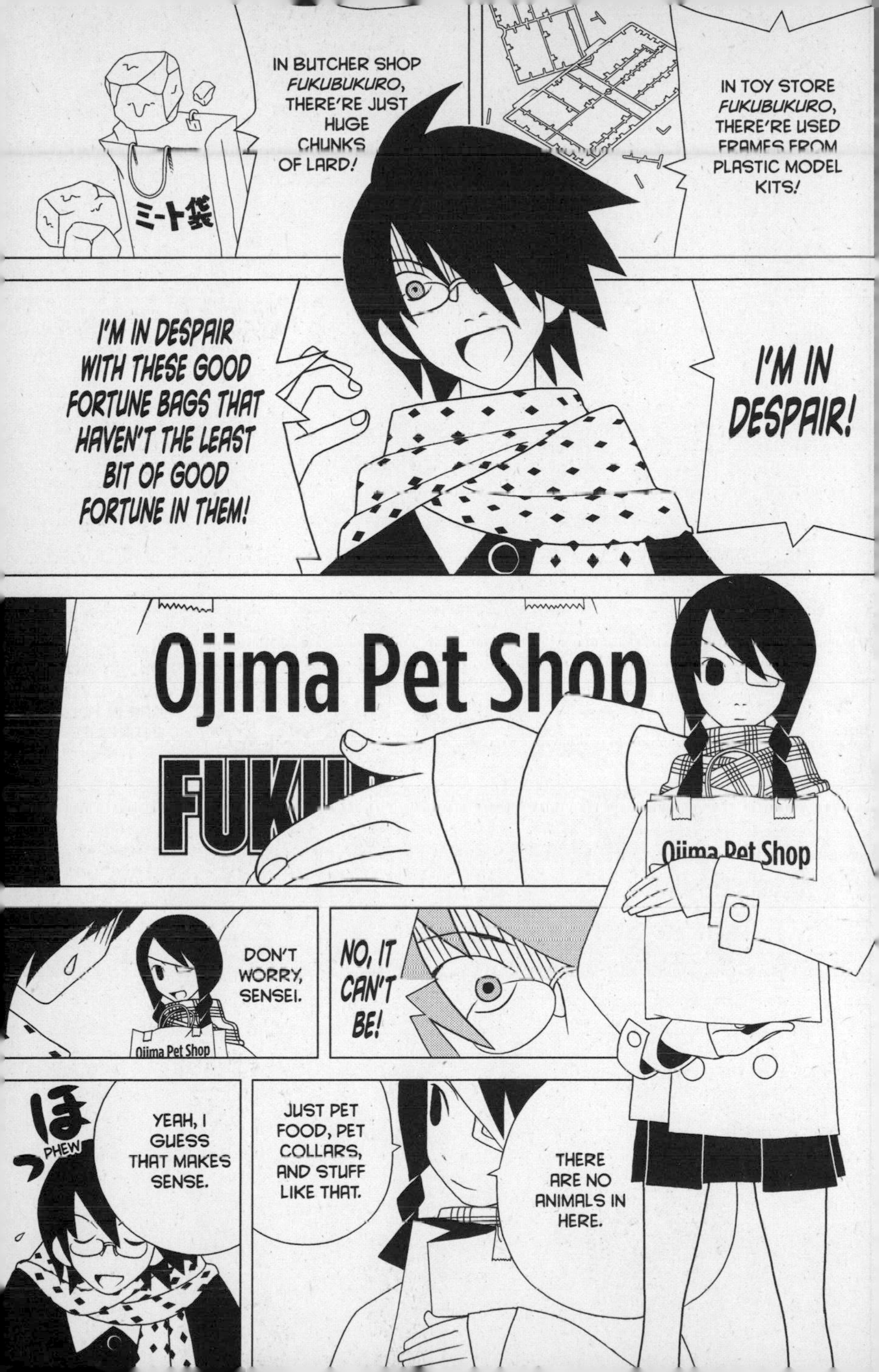
IN TOY STORE FUKUBUKURO, THERE'RE USED FRAMES FROM PLASTIC MODEL KITS!
IN BUTCHER SHOP FUKUBUKURO, THERE'RE JUST HUGE CHUNKS OF LARD!
ミート袋
I'M IN DESPAIR!
I'M IN DESPAIR WITH THESE GOOD FORTUNE BAGS THAT HAVEN'T THE LEAST BIT OF GOOD FORTUNE IN THEM!
Ojima Pet Shop
Ojima Pet Shop
FUKU
NO, IT CAN'T BE!
DON'T WORRY, SENSEI.
Ojima Pet Shop
THERE ARE NO ANIMALS IN HERE.
JUST PET FOOD, PET COLLARS, AND STUFF LIKE THAT.
YEAH, I GUESS THAT MAKES SENSE.
ほっ
PHEW

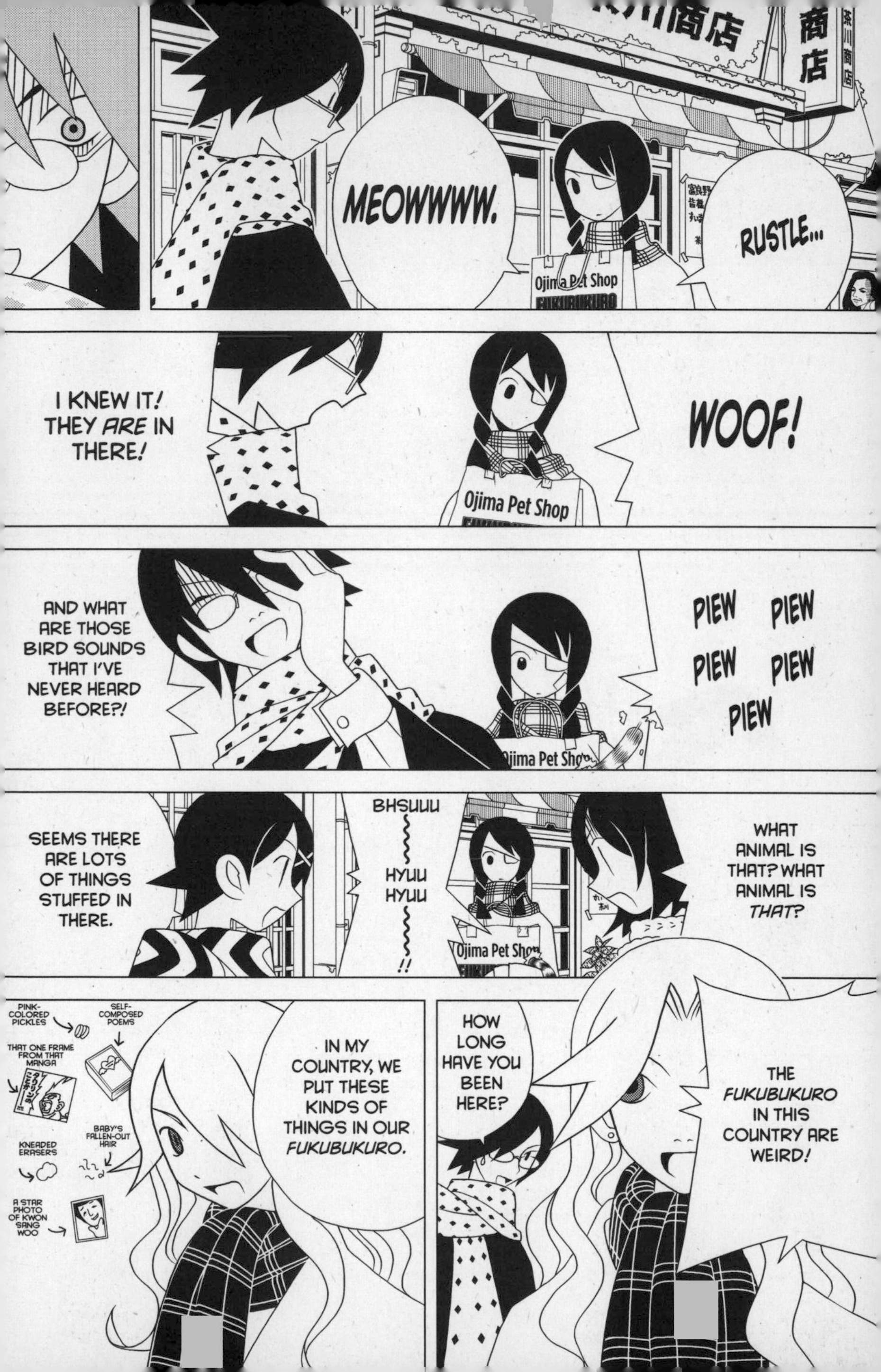
RUSTLE...
MEOWWWW.
Ojima Pet Shop
WOOF!
I KNEW IT! THEY *ARE* IN THERE!
Ojima Pet Shop
PIEW PIEW PIEW PIEW PIEW
AND WHAT ARE THOSE BIRD SOUNDS THAT I'VE NEVER HEARD BEFORE?!
WHAT ANIMAL IS THAT? WHAT ANIMAL IS *THAT*?
BHSUUU HYUU HYUU !!
SEEMS THERE ARE LOTS OF THINGS STUFFED IN THERE.
THE *FUKUBUKURO* IN THIS COUNTRY ARE WEIRD!
HOW LONG HAVE YOU BEEN HERE?
IN MY COUNTRY, WE PUT THESE KINDS OF THINGS IN OUR *FUKUBUKURO*.
PINK-COLORED PICKLES
SELF-COMPOSED POEMS
THAT ONE FRAME FROM THAT MANGA
BABY'S FALLEN-OUT HAIR
KNEADED ERASERS
A STAR PHOTO OF KWON SANG WOO

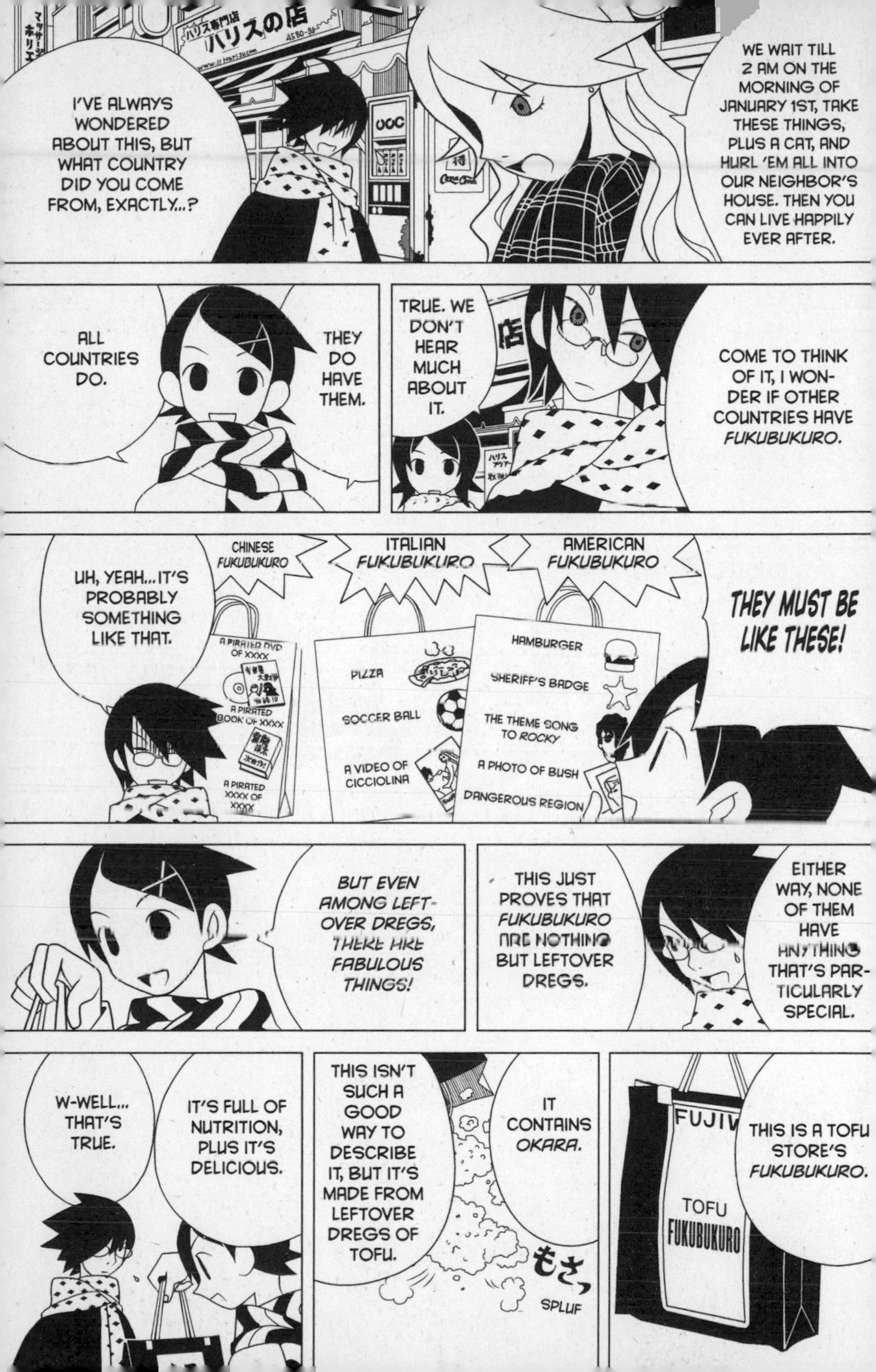

ハリス専門店
ハリスの店
WE WAIT TILL 2 AM ON THE MORNING OF JANUARY 1ST, TAKE THESE THINGS, PLUS A CAT, AND HURL 'EM ALL INTO OUR NEIGHBOR'S HOUSE. THEN YOU CAN LIVE HAPPILY EVER AFTER.
I'VE ALWAYS WONDERED ABOUT THIS, BUT WHAT COUNTRY DID YOU COME FROM, EXACTLY...?
COME TO THINK OF IT, I WONDER IF OTHER COUNTRIES HAVE *FUKUBUKURO.*
TRUE. WE DON'T HEAR MUCH ABOUT IT.
THEY DO HAVE THEM.
ALL COUNTRIES DO.
THEY MUST BE LIKE THESE!
AMERICAN *FUKUBUKURO*
HAMBURGER
SHERIFF'S BADGE
THE THEME SONG TO *ROCKY*
A PHOTO OF BUSH
DANGEROUS REGION
ITALIAN *FUKUBUKURO*
PIZZA
SOCCER BALL
A VIDEO OF CICCIOLINA
CHINESE *FUKUBUKURO*
A PIRATED DVD OF XXXX
A PIRATED BOOK OF XXXX
A PIRATED XXXX OF XXXX
UH, YEAH...IT'S PROBABLY SOMETHING LIKE THAT.
EITHER WAY, NONE OF THEM HAVE ANYTHING THAT'S PARTICULARLY SPECIAL.
THIS JUST PROVES THAT *FUKUBUKURO* ARE NOTHING BUT LEFTOVER DREGS.
BUT EVEN AMONG LEFTOVER DREGS, THERE ARE FABULOUS THINGS!
THIS IS A TOFU STORE'S *FUKUBUKURO.*
FUJIV
TOFU FUKUBUKURO
IT CONTAINS *OKARA.*
THIS ISN'T SUCH A GOOD WAY TO DESCRIBE IT, BUT IT'S MADE FROM LEFTOVER DREGS OF TOFU.
もさっ
SPLUF
IT'S FULL OF NUTRITION, PLUS IT'S DELICIOUS.
W-WELL... THAT'S TRUE.

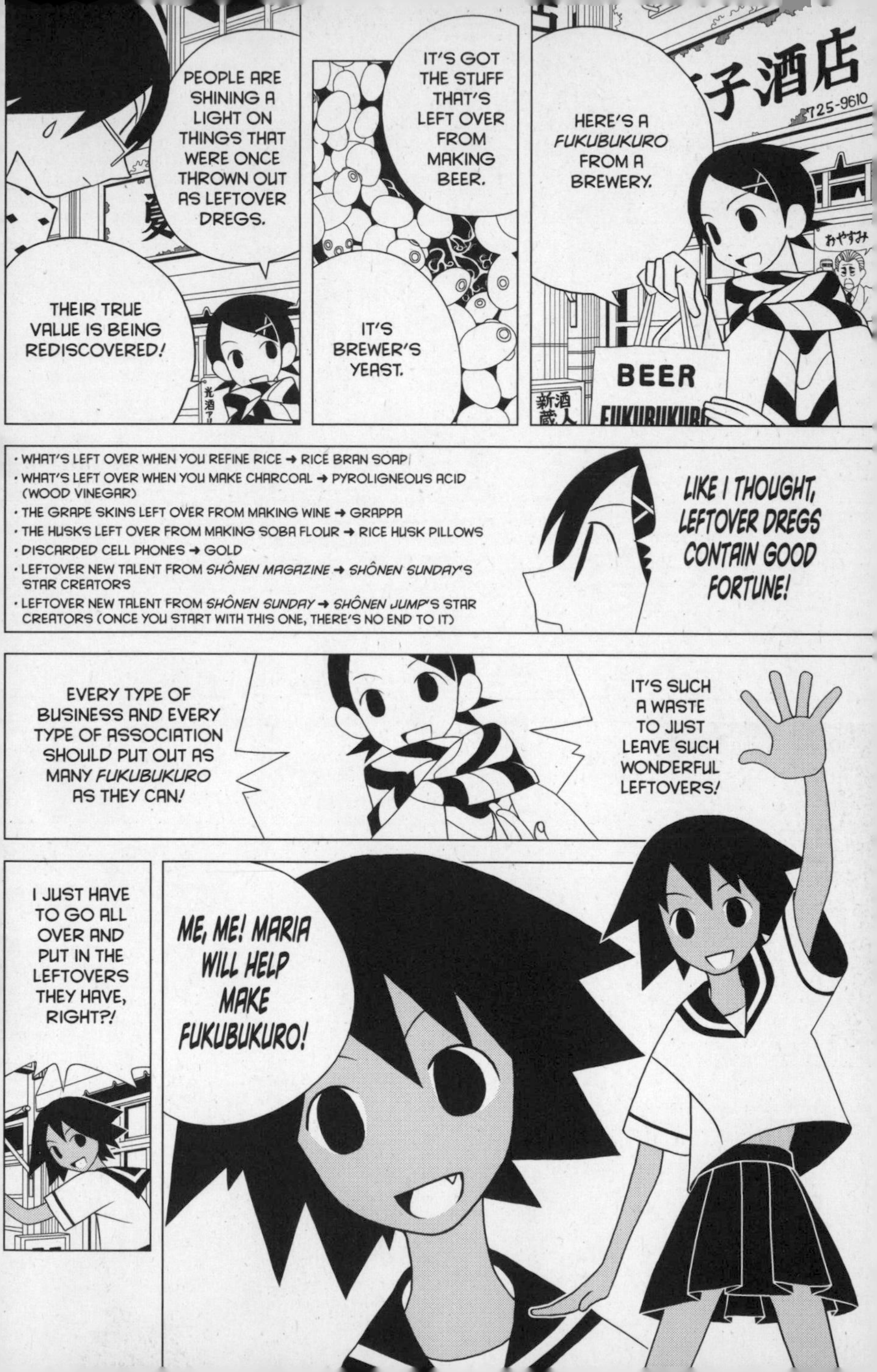

子酒店
725-9610
HERE'S A *FUKUBUKURO* FROM A BREWERY.
おやすみ
BEER
新酒
蔵人
IT'S GOT THE STUFF THAT'S LEFT OVER FROM MAKING BEER.
IT'S BREWER'S YEAST.
PEOPLE ARE SHINING A LIGHT ON THINGS THAT WERE ONCE THROWN OUT AS LEFTOVER DREGS.
THEIR TRUE VALUE IS BEING REDISCOVERED!
LIKE I THOUGHT, LEFTOVER DREGS CONTAIN GOOD FORTUNE!
• WHAT'S LEFT OVER WHEN YOU REFINE RICE → RICE BRAN SOAP
• WHAT'S LEFT OVER WHEN YOU MAKE CHARCOAL → PYROLIGNEOUS ACID (WOOD VINEGAR)
• THE GRAPE SKINS LEFT OVER FROM MAKING WINE → GRAPPA
• THE HUSKS LEFT OVER FROM MAKING SOBA FLOUR → RICE HUSK PILLOWS
• DISCARDED CELL PHONES → GOLD
• LEFTOVER NEW TALENT FROM *SHÔNEN MAGAZINE* → *SHÔNEN SUNDAY*'S STAR CREATORS
• LEFTOVER NEW TALENT FROM *SHÔNEN SUNDAY* → *SHÔNEN JUMP*'S STAR CREATORS (ONCE YOU START WITH THIS ONE, THERE'S NO END TO IT)
IT'S SUCH A WASTE TO JUST LEAVE SUCH WONDERFUL LEFTOVERS!
EVERY TYPE OF BUSINESS AND EVERY TYPE OF ASSOCIATION SHOULD PUT OUT AS MANY *FUKUBUKURO* AS THEY CAN!
ME, ME! MARIA WILL HELP MAKE FUKUBUKURO!
I JUST HAVE TO GO ALL OVER AND PUT IN THE LEFTOVERS THEY HAVE, RIGHT?!

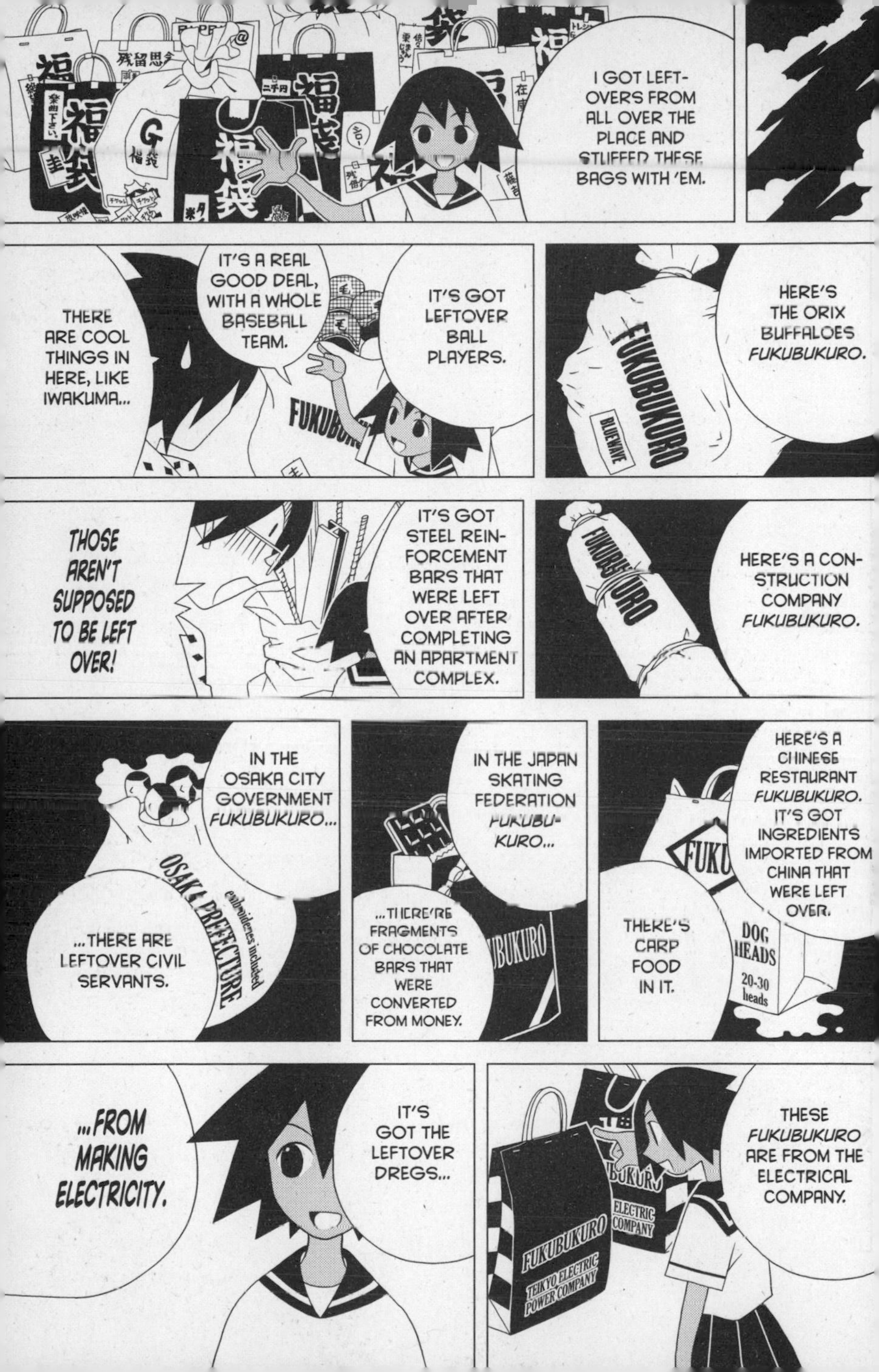
I GOT LEFT-OVERS FROM ALL OVER THE PLACE AND STUFFED THESE BAGS WITH 'EM.
HERE'S THE ORIX BUFFALOES *FUKUBUKURO*.
FUKUBUKURO
BLUEWAVE
IT'S GOT LEFTOVER BALL PLAYERS.
IT'S A REAL GOOD DEAL, WITH A WHOLE BASEBALL TEAM.
THERE ARE COOL THINGS IN HERE, LIKE IWAKUMA...
FUKUBU
HERE'S A CONSTRUCTION COMPANY *FUKUBUKURO*.
FUKUBUKURO
IT'S GOT STEEL REINFORCEMENT BARS THAT WERE LEFT OVER AFTER COMPLETING AN APARTMENT COMPLEX.
THOSE AREN'T SUPPOSED TO BE LEFT OVER!
HERE'S A CHINESE RESTAURANT *FUKUBUKURO*. IT'S GOT INGREDIENTS IMPORTED FROM CHINA THAT WERE LEFT OVER.
FUKU
THERE'S CARP FOOD IN IT.
DOG HEADS
20-30 heads
IN THE JAPAN SKATING FEDERATION *FUKUBU-KURO*...
...THERE'RE FRAGMENTS OF CHOCOLATE BARS THAT WERE CONVERTED FROM MONEY.
UBUKURO
IN THE OSAKA CITY GOVERNMENT *FUKUBUKURO*...
OSAKA PREFECTURE
embroideries included
...THERE ARE LEFTOVER CIVIL SERVANTS.
THESE *FUKUBUKURO* ARE FROM THE ELECTRICAL COMPANY.
FUKUBUKURO
TEIKYO ELECTRIC POWER COMPANY
ELECTRIC COMPANY
IT'S GOT THE LEFTOVER DREGS...
...FROM MAKING ELECTRICITY.

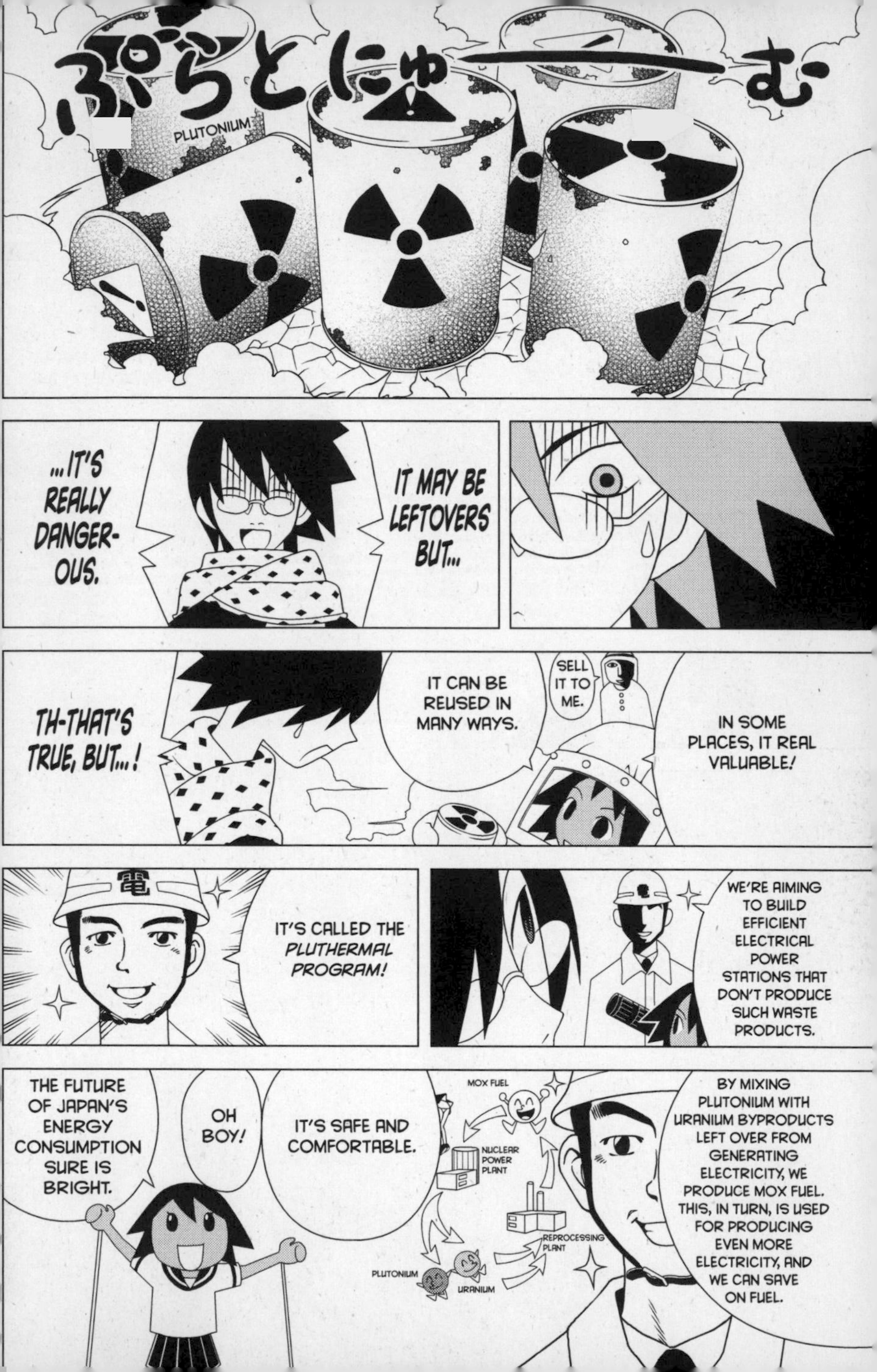
ぷらとにゅーーーむ
PLUTONIUM
IT MAY BE LEFTOVERS BUT...
...IT'S REALLY DANGER-OUS.
IN SOME PLACES, IT REAL VALUABLE!
SELL IT TO ME.
IT CAN BE REUSED IN MANY WAYS.
TH-THAT'S TRUE, BUT...!
WE'RE AIMING TO BUILD EFFICIENT ELECTRICAL POWER STATIONS THAT DON'T PRODUCE SUCH WASTE PRODUCTS.
IT'S CALLED THE *PLUTHERMAL PROGRAM!*
BY MIXING PLUTONIUM WITH URANIUM BYPRODUCTS LEFT OVER FROM GENERATING ELECTRICITY, WE PRODUCE MOX FUEL. THIS, IN TURN, IS USED FOR PRODUCING EVEN MORE ELECTRICITY, AND WE CAN SAVE ON FUEL.
MOX FUEL
NUCLEAR POWER PLANT
REPROCESSING PLANT
PLUTONIUM
URANIUM
IT'S SAFE AND COMFORTABLE.
OH BOY!
THE FUTURE OF JAPAN'S ENERGY CONSUMPTION SURE IS BRIGHT.

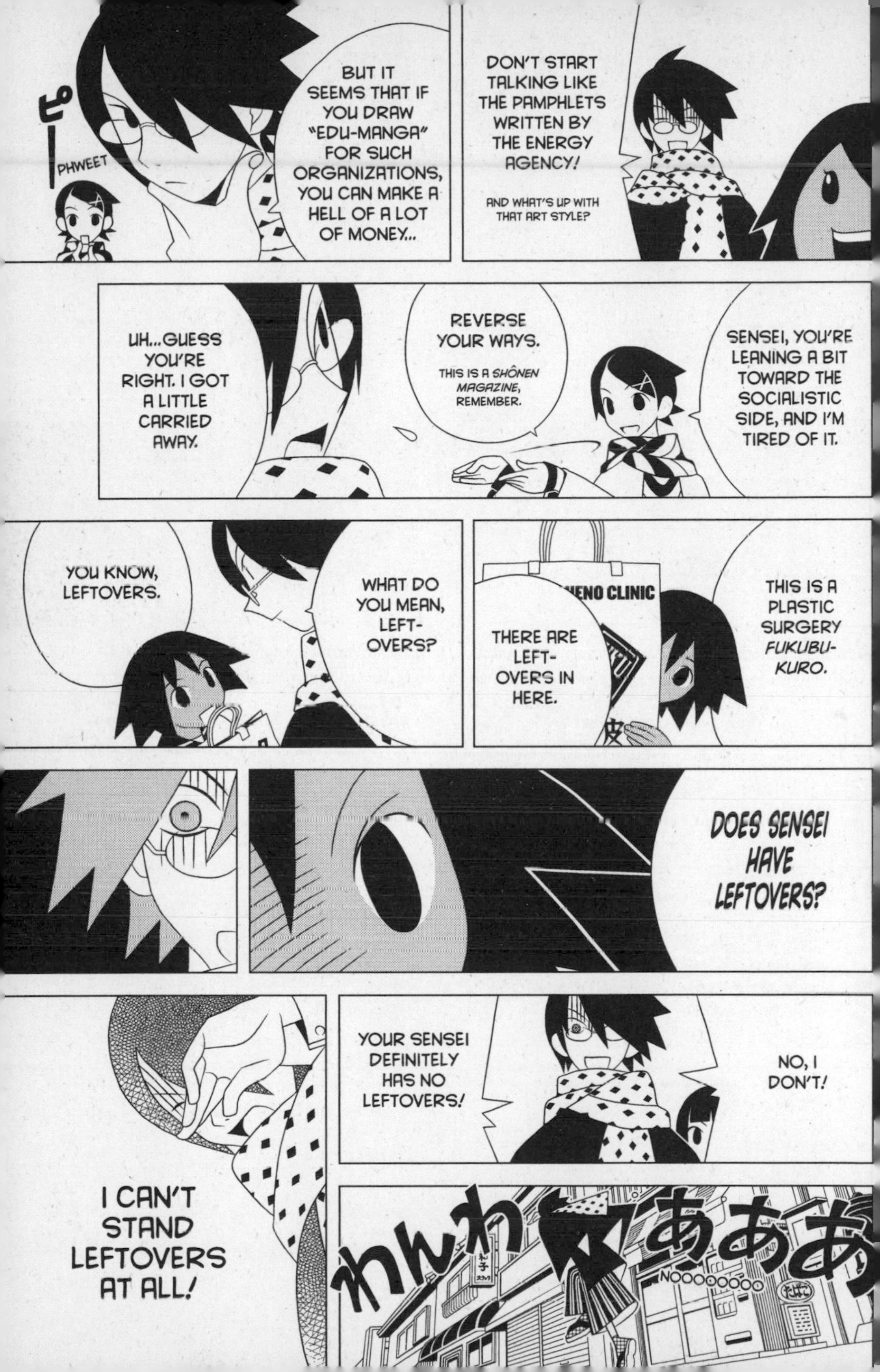
DON'T START TALKING LIKE THE PAMPHLETS WRITTEN BY THE ENERGY AGENCY!
AND WHAT'S UP WITH THAT ART STYLE?
BUT IT SEEMS THAT IF YOU DRAW "EDU-MANGA" FOR SUCH ORGANIZATIONS, YOU CAN MAKE A HELL OF A LOT OF MONEY...
ピー
PHWEET
SENSEI, YOU'RE LEANING A BIT TOWARD THE SOCIALISTIC SIDE, AND I'M TIRED OF IT.
REVERSE YOUR WAYS.
THIS IS A *SHÔNEN MAGAZINE*, REMEMBER.
UH...GUESS YOU'RE RIGHT. I GOT A LITTLE CARRIED AWAY.
THIS IS A PLASTIC SURGERY *FUKUBUKURO*.
THERE ARE LEFTOVERS IN HERE.
WHAT DO YOU MEAN, LEFTOVERS?
YOU KNOW, LEFTOVERS.
DOES SENSEI HAVE LEFTOVERS?
NO, I DON'T!
YOUR SENSEI DEFINITELY HAS NO LEFTOVERS!
わんわあああ
NOOOOOOOO
I CAN'T STAND LEFTOVERS AT ALL!

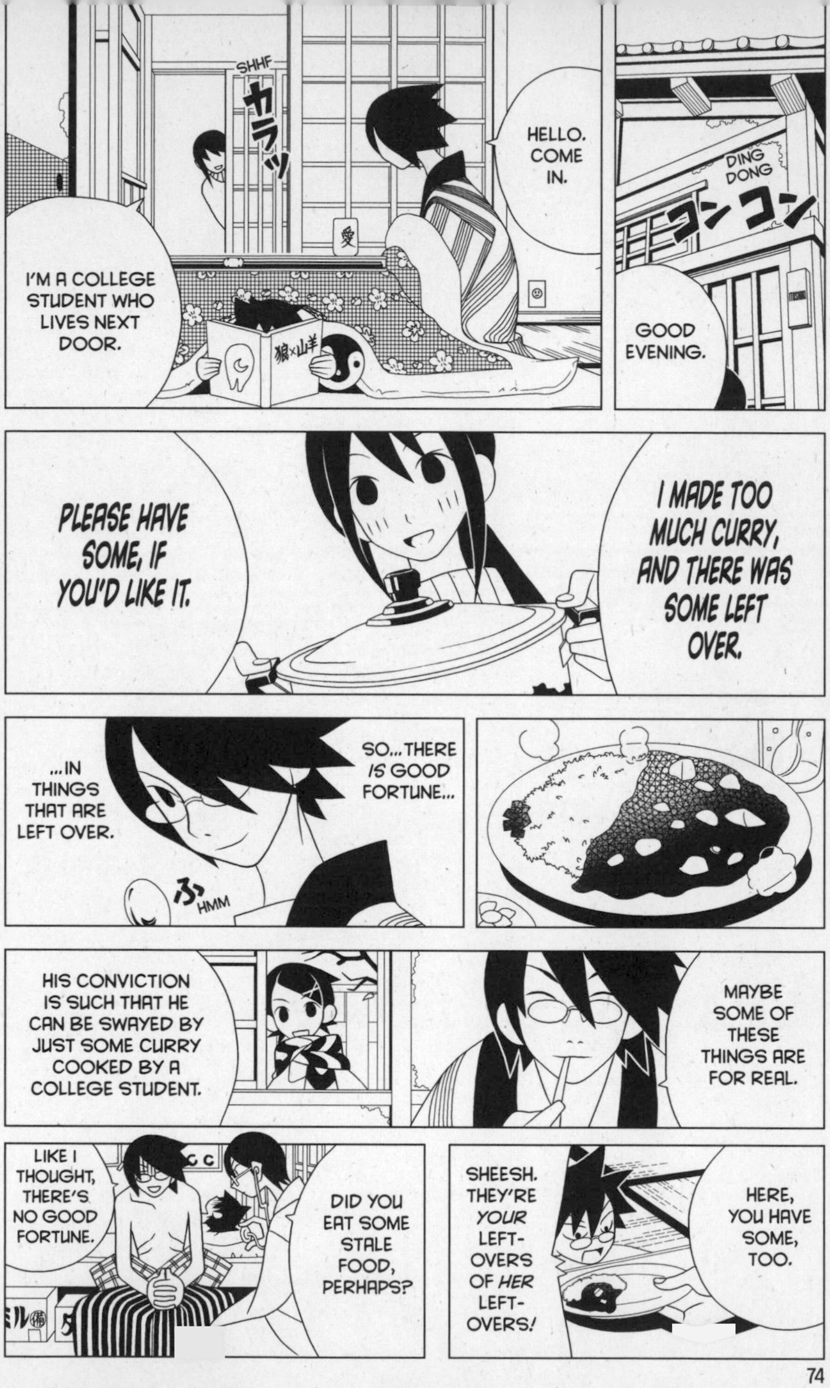
DING DONG
コンコン
GOOD EVENING.
HELLO. COME IN.
SHHF
カラッ
I'M A COLLEGE STUDENT WHO LIVES NEXT DOOR.
狼×山羊
I MADE TOO MUCH CURRY, AND THERE WAS SOME LEFT OVER.
PLEASE HAVE SOME, IF YOU'D LIKE IT.
SO... THERE *IS* GOOD FORTUNE...
...IN THINGS THAT ARE LEFT OVER.
ふ HMM
MAYBE SOME OF THESE THINGS ARE FOR REAL.
HIS CONVICTION IS SUCH THAT HE CAN BE SWAYED BY JUST SOME CURRY COOKED BY A COLLEGE STUDENT.
HERE, YOU HAVE SOME, TOO.
SHEESH. THEY'RE *YOUR* LEFT-OVERS OF *HER* LEFT-OVERS!
DID YOU EAT SOME STALE FOOD, PERHAPS?
LIKE I THOUGHT, THERE'S NO GOOD FORTUNE.

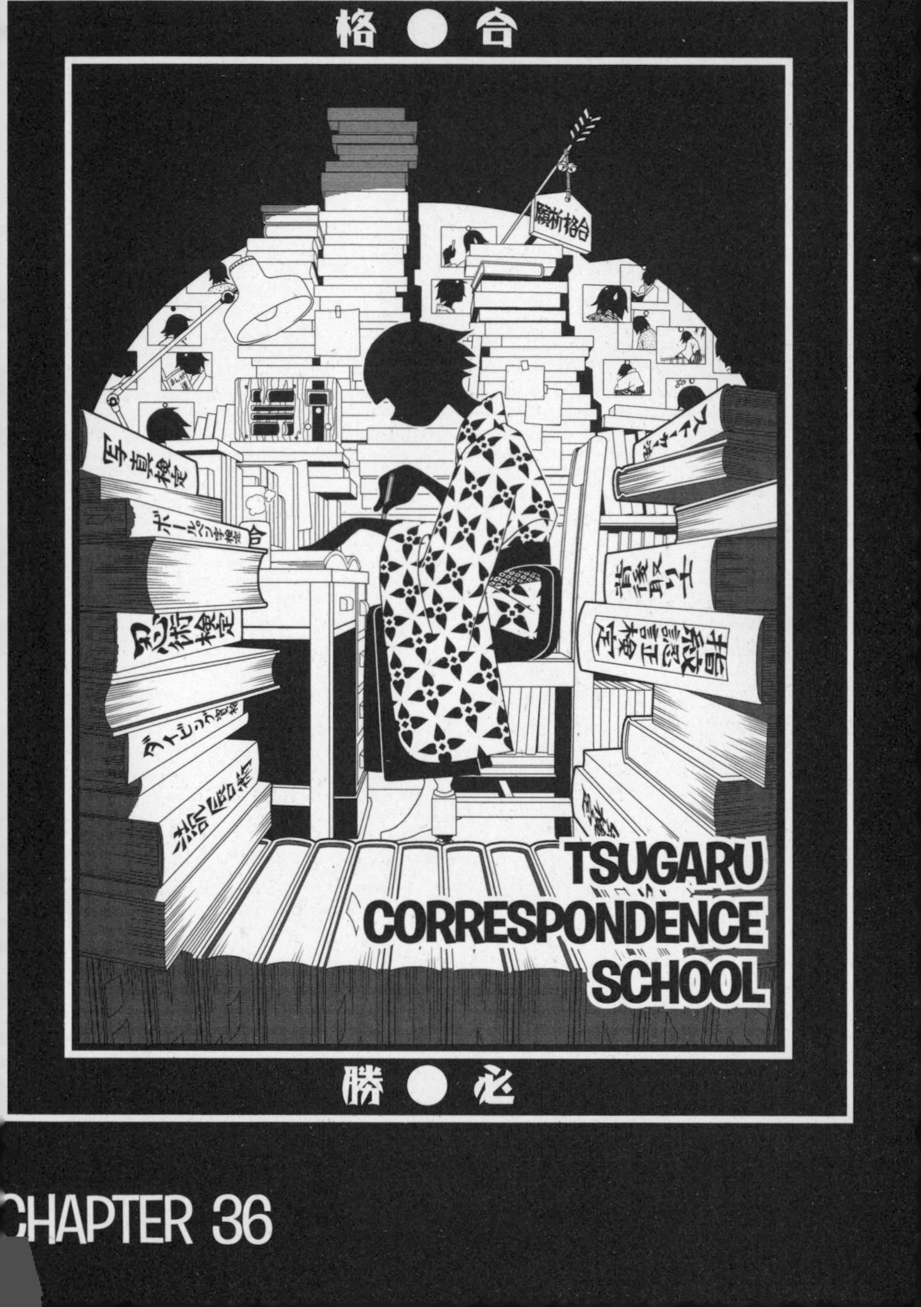
格●合
TSUGARU
CORRESPONDENCE
SCHOOL
勝●必

CHAPTER 36

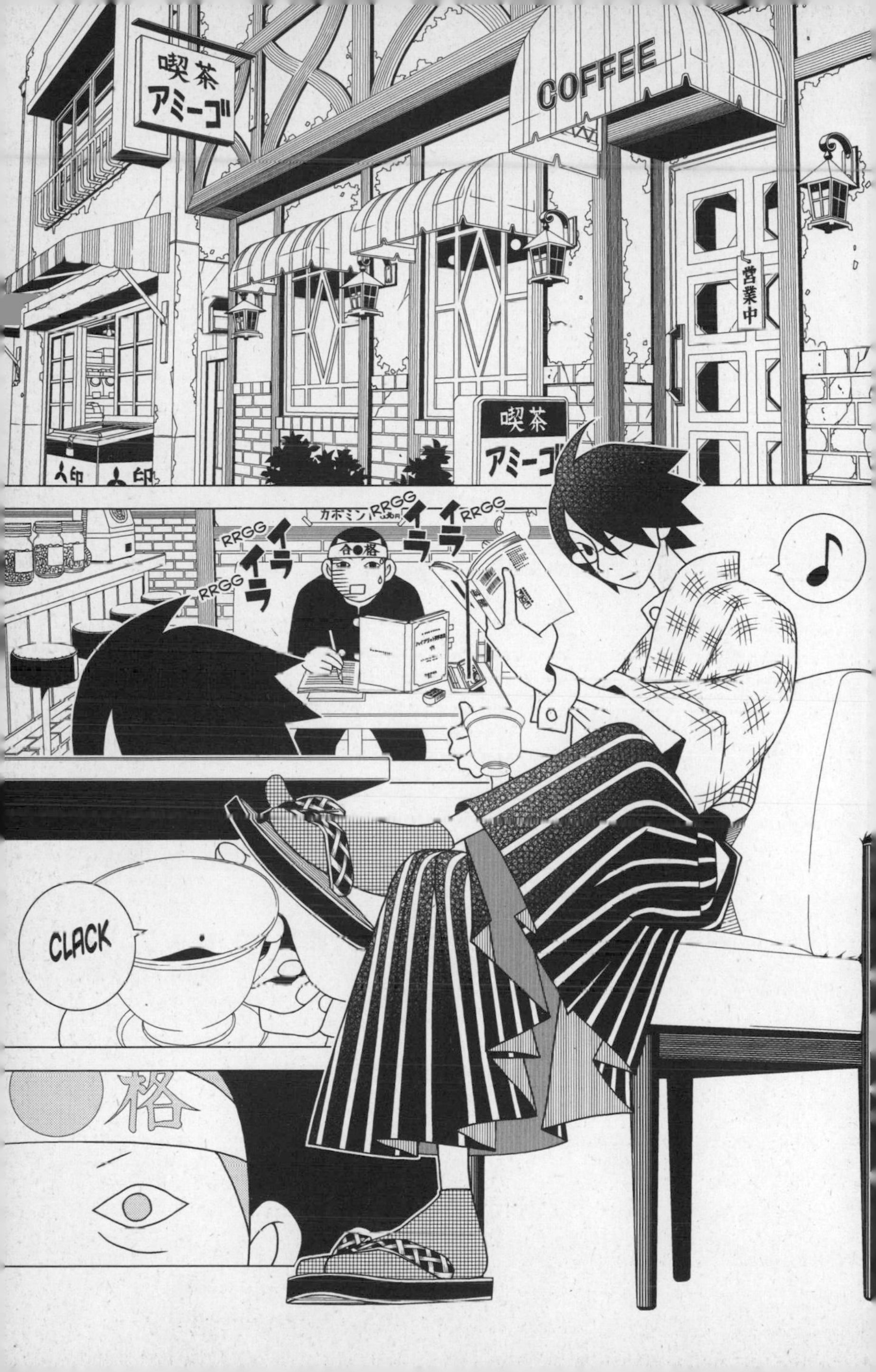
COFFEE
営業中
喫茶
アミーゴ
喫茶
アミーゴ
♪
RRGG
イラ
イラ
RRGG
イラ
イラ
RRGG
合格
CLACK
格

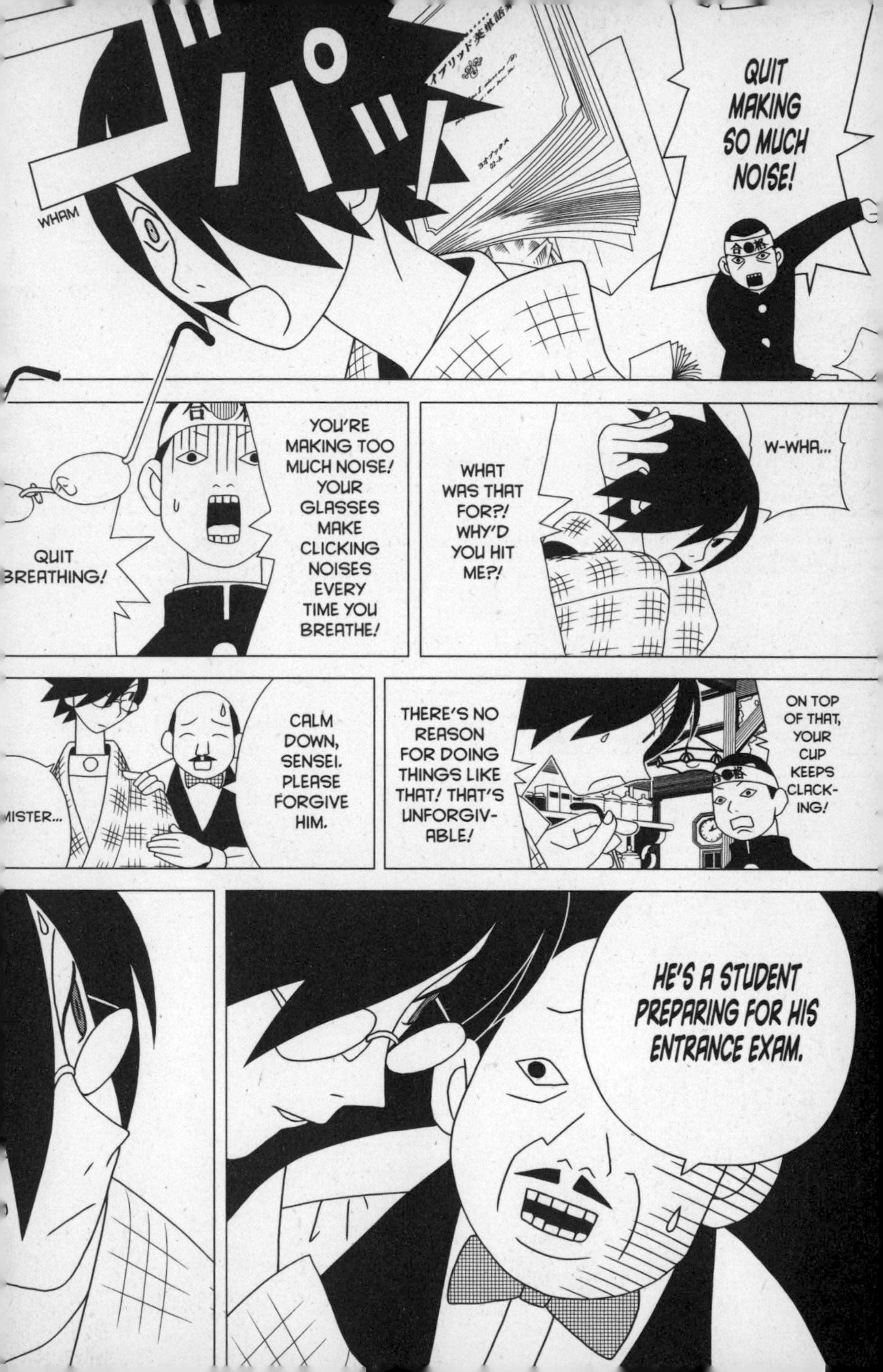
QUIT MAKING SO MUCH NOISE!
WHAM
W-WHA...
WHAT WAS THAT FOR?! WHY'D YOU HIT ME?!
YOU'RE MAKING TOO MUCH NOISE! YOUR GLASSES MAKE CLICKING NOISES EVERY TIME YOU BREATHE!
QUIT BREATHING!
ON TOP OF THAT, YOUR CUP KEEPS CLACKING!
THERE'S NO REASON FOR DOING THINGS LIKE THAT! THAT'S UNFORGIVABLE!
CALM DOWN, SENSEI. PLEASE FORGIVE HIM.
MISTER...
HE'S A STUDENT PREPARING FOR HIS ENTRANCE EXAM.

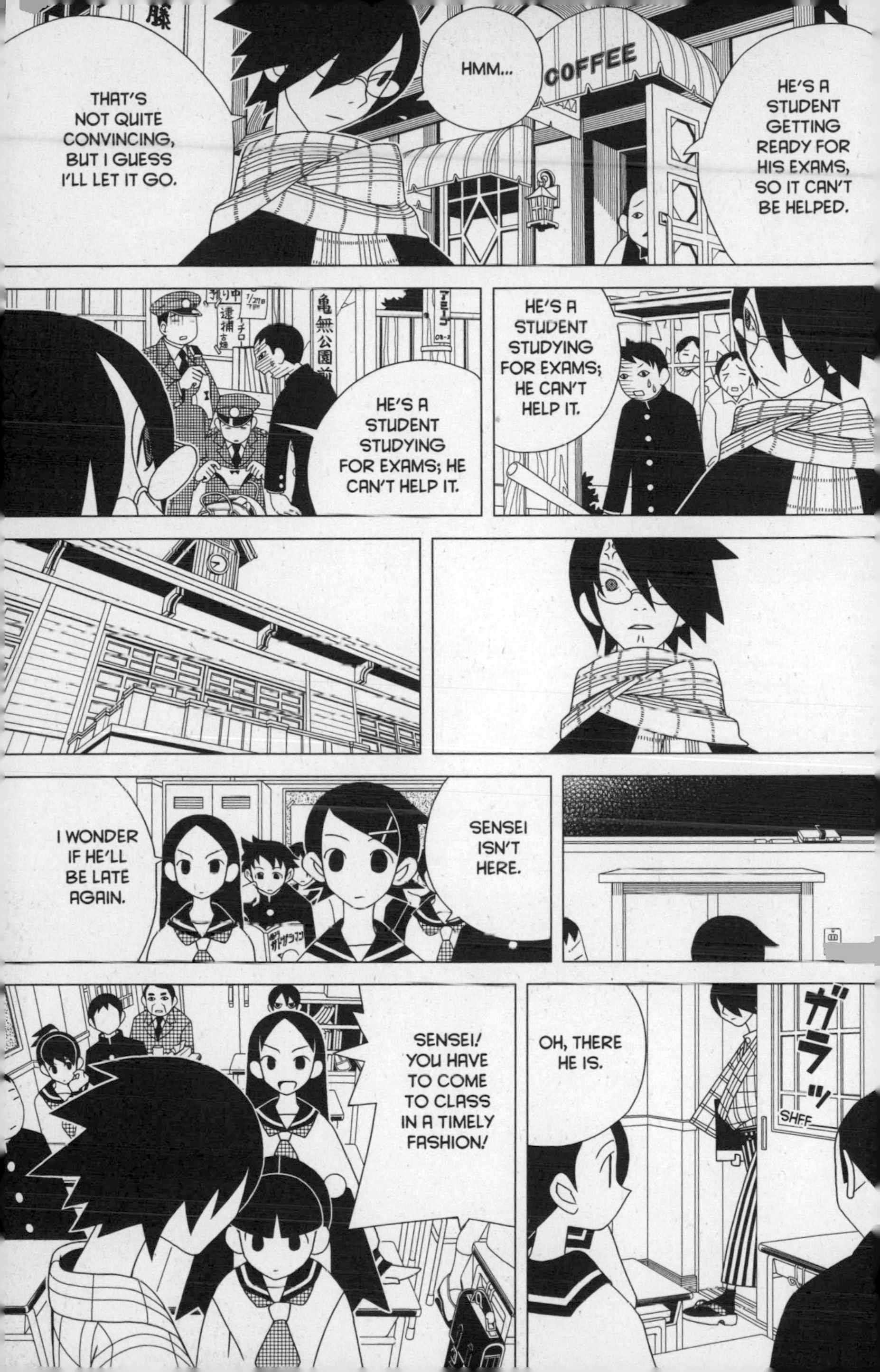
HE'S A STUDENT GETTING READY FOR HIS EXAMS, SO IT CAN'T BE HELPED.
COFFEE
HMM...
THAT'S NOT QUITE CONVINCING, BUT I GUESS I'LL LET IT GO.
HE'S A STUDENT STUDYING FOR EXAMS; HE CAN'T HELP IT.
亀無公園前
HE'S A STUDENT STUDYING FOR EXAMS; HE CAN'T HELP IT.
SENSEI ISN'T HERE.
I WONDER IF HE'LL BE LATE AGAIN.
ガラッ
SHFF
OH, THERE HE IS.
SENSEI! YOU HAVE TO COME TO CLASS IN A TIMELY FASHION!

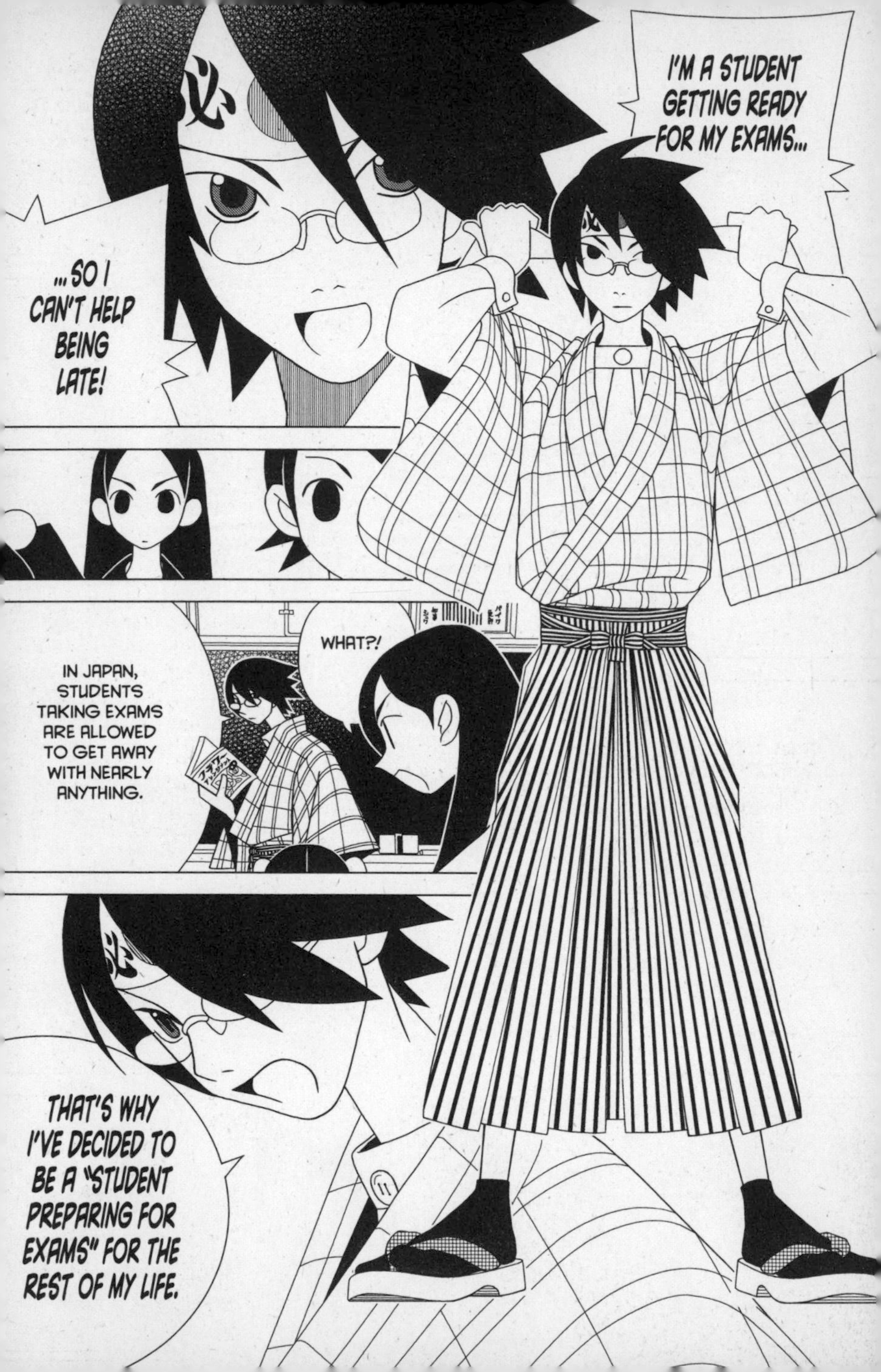
I'M A STUDENT GETTING READY FOR MY EXAMS...
...SO I CAN'T HELP BEING LATE!
WHAT?!
IN JAPAN, STUDENTS TAKING EXAMS ARE ALLOWED TO GET AWAY WITH NEARLY ANYTHING.
THAT'S WHY I'VE DECIDED TO BE A "STUDENT PREPARING FOR EXAMS" FOR THE REST OF MY LIFE.

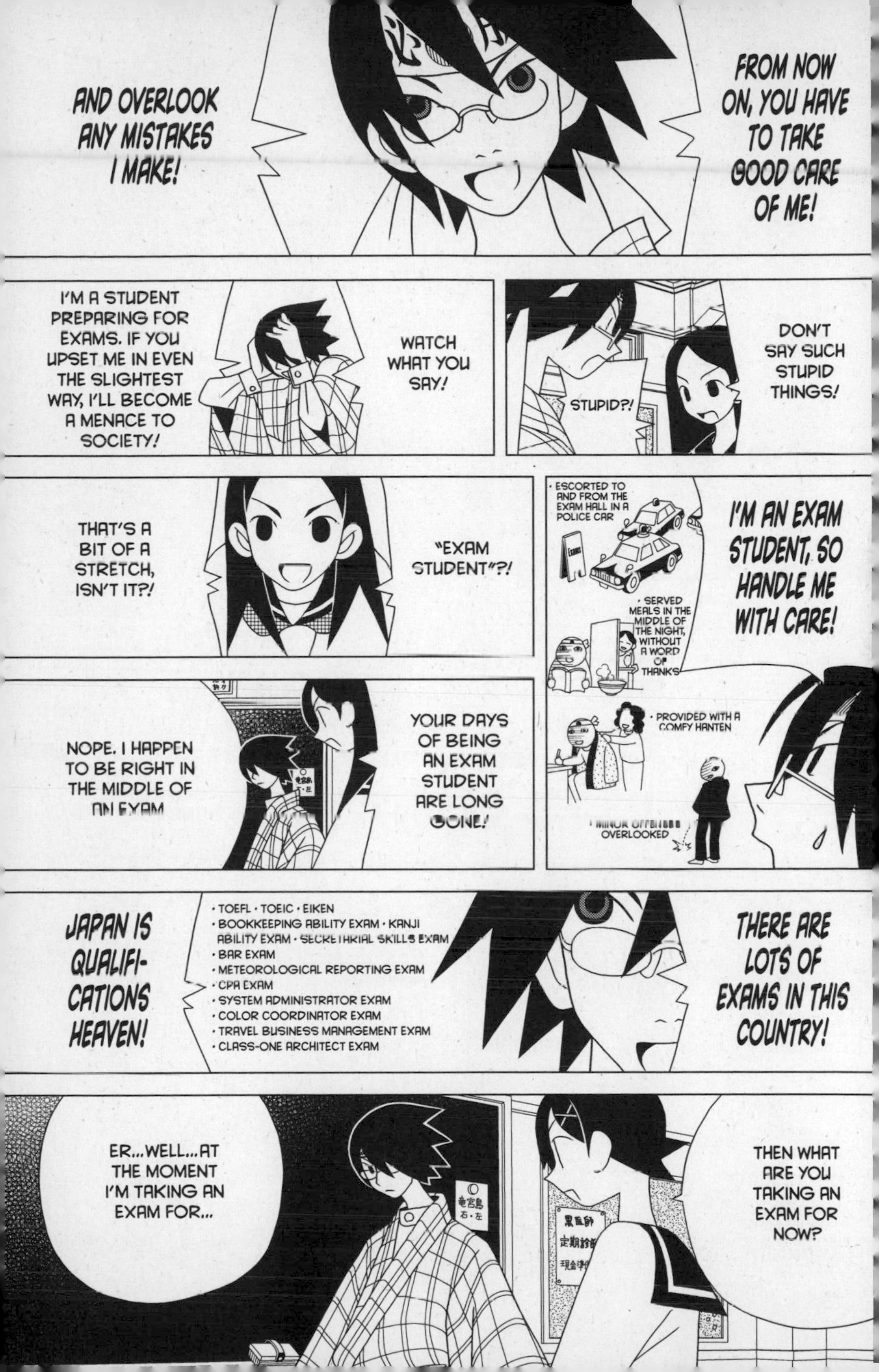
FROM NOW ON, YOU HAVE TO TAKE GOOD CARE OF ME!
AND OVERLOOK ANY MISTAKES I MAKE!
DON'T SAY SUCH STUPID THINGS!
STUPID?!
WATCH WHAT YOU SAY!
I'M A STUDENT PREPARING FOR EXAMS. IF YOU UPSET ME IN EVEN THE SLIGHTEST WAY, I'LL BECOME A MENACE TO SOCIETY!
I'M AN EXAM STUDENT, SO HANDLE ME WITH CARE!
• ESCORTED TO AND FROM THE EXAM HALL IN A POLICE CAR
EXAMS
• SERVED MEALS IN THE MIDDLE OF THE NIGHT, WITHOUT A WORD OF THANKS
• PROVIDED WITH A COMFY HANTEN
• MINOR OFFENSES OVERLOOKED
"EXAM STUDENT"?!
THAT'S A BIT OF A STRETCH, ISN'T IT?!
YOUR DAYS OF BEING AN EXAM STUDENT ARE LONG GONE!
NOPE. I HAPPEN TO BE RIGHT IN THE MIDDLE OF AN EXAM
THERE ARE LOTS OF EXAMS IN THIS COUNTRY!
• TOEFL • TOEIC • EIKEN
• BOOKKEEPING ABILITY EXAM • KANJI ABILITY EXAM • SECRETARIAL SKILLS EXAM
• BAR EXAM
• METEOROLOGICAL REPORTING EXAM
• CPA EXAM
• SYSTEM ADMINISTRATOR EXAM
• COLOR COORDINATOR EXAM
• TRAVEL BUSINESS MANAGEMENT EXAM
• CLASS-ONE ARCHITECT EXAM
JAPAN IS QUALIFI-CATIONS HEAVEN!
THEN WHAT ARE YOU TAKING AN EXAM FOR NOW?
ER...WELL...AT THE MOMENT I'M TAKING AN EXAM FOR...
竜宮島
石・左

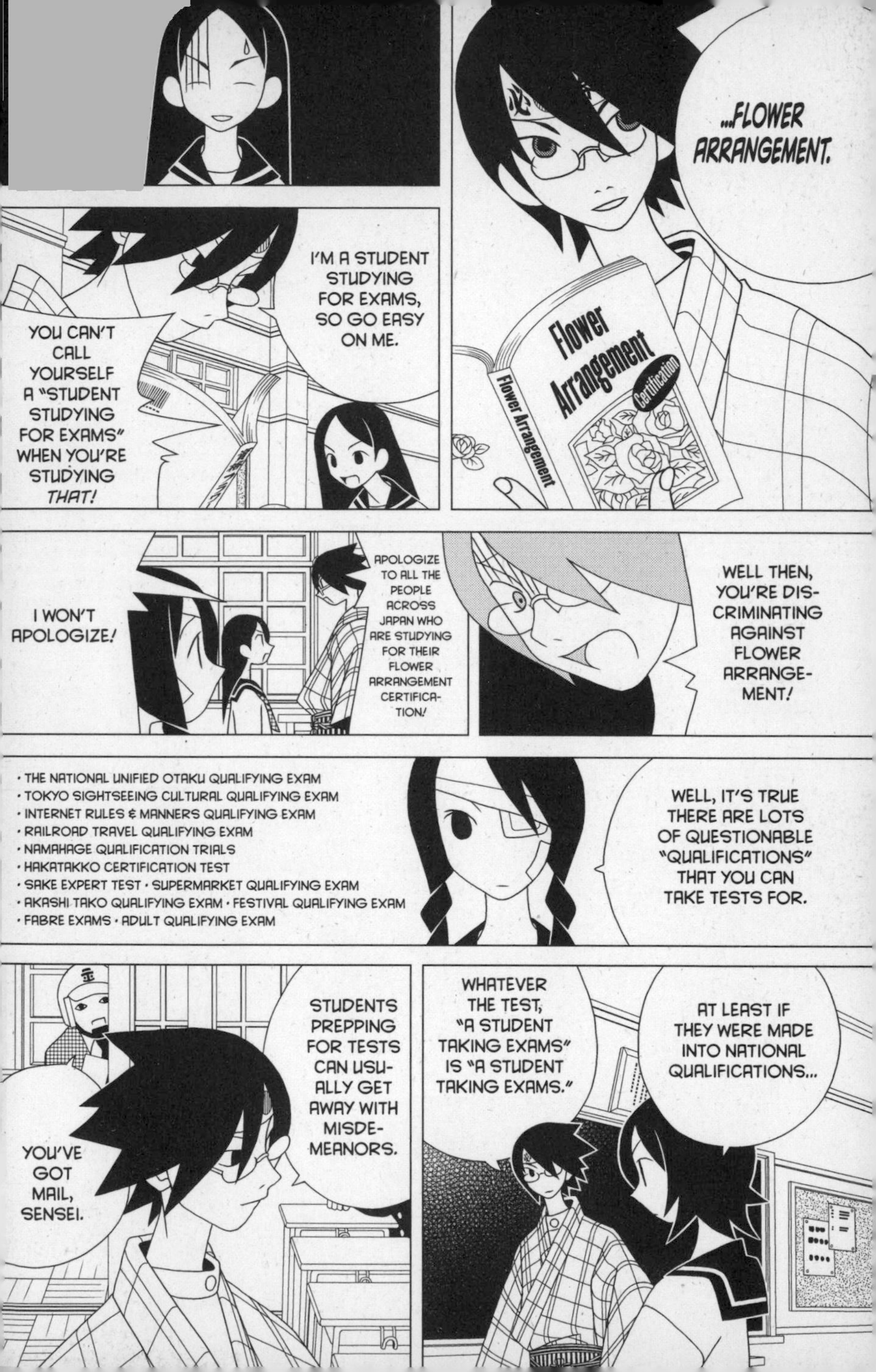
...FLOWER ARRANGEMENT.
Flower Arrangement
Certification
Flower Arrangement
I'M A STUDENT STUDYING FOR EXAMS, SO GO EASY ON ME.
YOU CAN'T CALL YOURSELF A "STUDENT STUDYING FOR EXAMS" WHEN YOU'RE STUDYING *THAT!*
WELL THEN, YOU'RE DISCRIMINATING AGAINST FLOWER ARRANGEMENT!
APOLOGIZE TO ALL THE PEOPLE ACROSS JAPAN WHO ARE STUDYING FOR THEIR FLOWER ARRANGEMENT CERTIFICATION!
I WON'T APOLOGIZE!
WELL, IT'S TRUE THERE ARE LOTS OF QUESTIONABLE "QUALIFICATIONS" THAT YOU CAN TAKE TESTS FOR.
• THE NATIONAL UNIFIED OTAKU QUALIFYING EXAM
• TOKYO SIGHTSEEING CULTURAL QUALIFYING EXAM
• INTERNET RULES & MANNERS QUALIFYING EXAM
• RAILROAD TRAVEL QUALIFYING EXAM
• NAMAHAGE QUALIFICATION TRIALS
• HAKATAKKO CERTIFICATION TEST
• SAKE EXPERT TEST • SUPERMARKET QUALIFYING EXAM
• AKASHI TAKO QUALIFYING EXAM • FESTIVAL QUALIFYING EXAM
• FABRE EXAMS • ADULT QUALIFYING EXAM
AT LEAST IF THEY WERE MADE INTO NATIONAL QUALIFICATIONS...
WHATEVER THE TEST, "A STUDENT TAKING EXAMS" IS "A STUDENT TAKING EXAMS."
STUDENTS PREPPING FOR TESTS CAN USUALLY GET AWAY WITH MISDEMEANORS.
YOU'VE GOT MAIL, SENSEI.

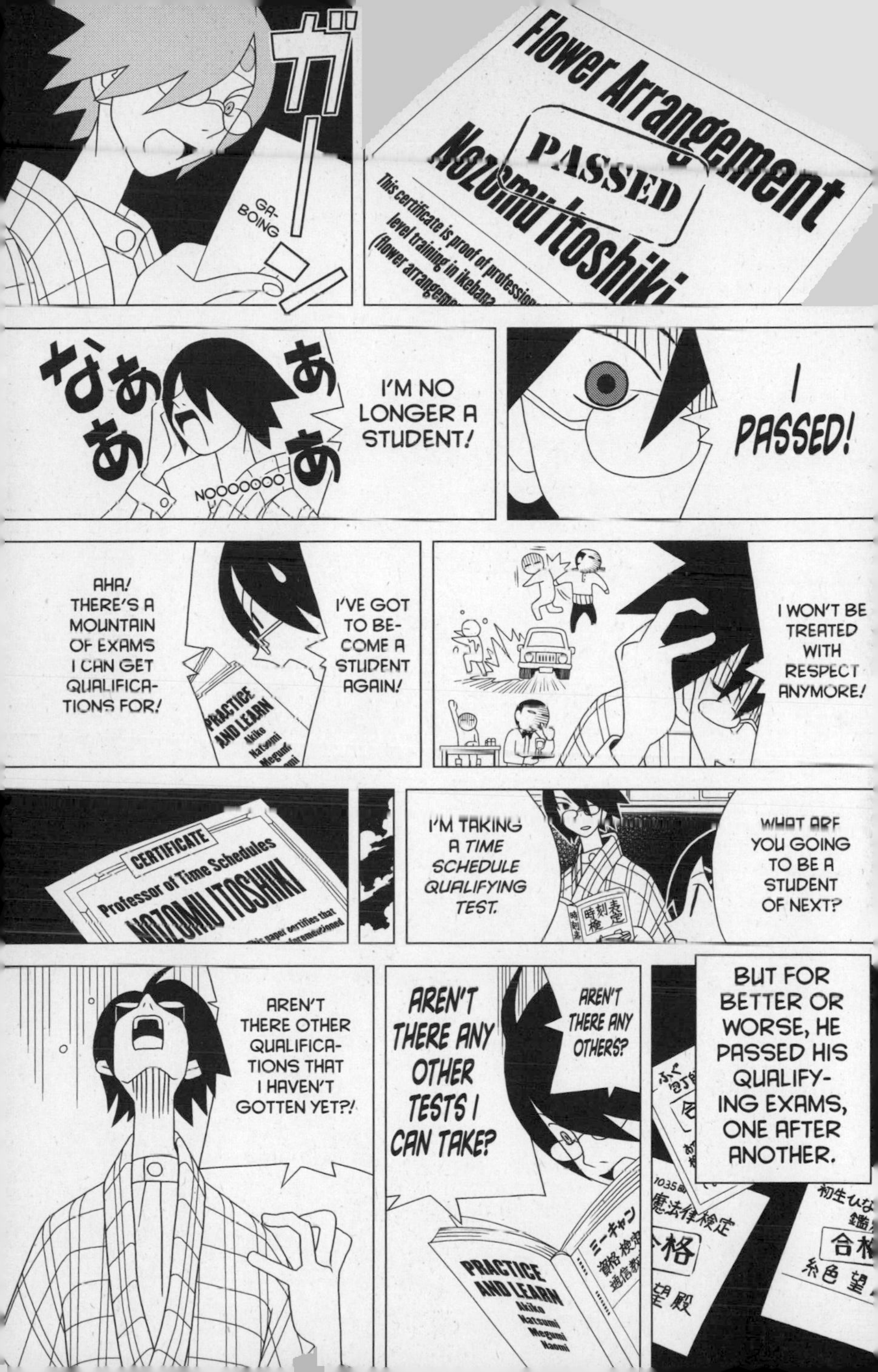
Flower Arrangement
PASSED
Nozomu Itoshiki
GA-BOING
I PASSED!
I'M NO LONGER A STUDENT!
なああ
ああ
NOOOOOOO
I WON'T BE TREATED WITH RESPECT ANYMORE!
I'VE GOT TO BE-COME A STUDENT AGAIN!
AHA! THERE'S A MOUNTAIN OF EXAMS I CAN GET QUALIFICA-TIONS FOR!
PRACTICE AND LEARN
WHAT ARE YOU GOING TO BE A STUDENT OF NEXT?
I'M TAKING A TIME SCHEDULE QUALIFYING TEST.
時刻表検定
CERTIFICATE
Professor of Time Schedules
NOZOMU ITOSHIKI
BUT FOR BETTER OR WORSE, HE PASSED HIS QUALIFY-ING EXAMS, ONE AFTER ANOTHER.
合格
合格
AREN'T THERE ANY OTHERS?
AREN'T THERE ANY OTHER TESTS I CAN TAKE?
PRACTICE AND LEARN
Akiko
Natsumi
Megumi
Naomi
AREN'T THERE OTHER QUALIFICA-TIONS THAT I HAVEN'T GOTTEN YET?!

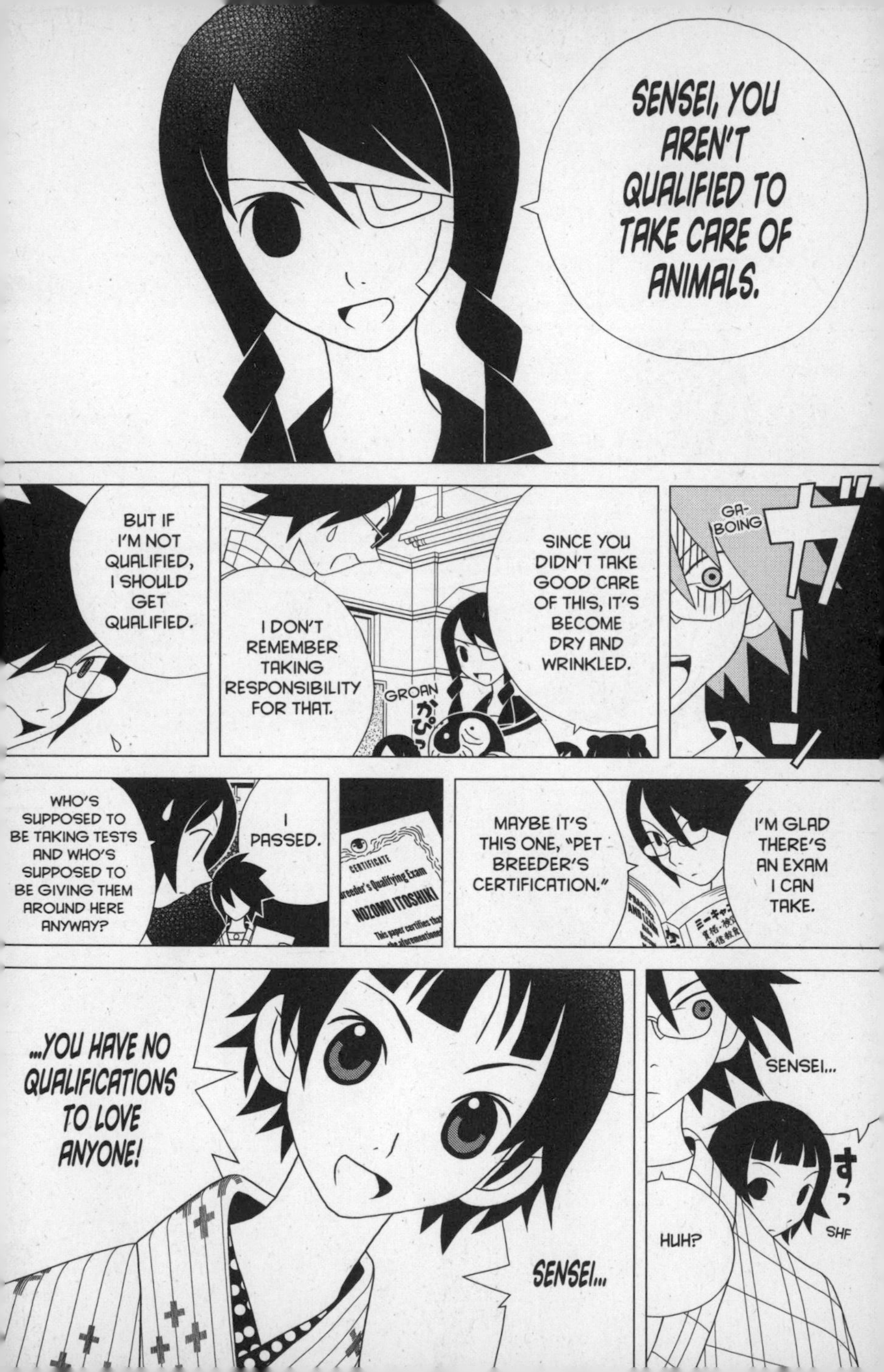
SENSEI, YOU AREN'T QUALIFIED TO TAKE CARE OF ANIMALS.
GA-BOING
SINCE YOU DIDN'T TAKE GOOD CARE OF THIS, IT'S BECOME DRY AND WRINKLED.
I DON'T REMEMBER TAKING RESPONSIBILITY FOR THAT.
GROAN
がぴっ
BUT IF I'M NOT QUALIFIED, I SHOULD GET QUALIFIED.
I'M GLAD THERE'S AN EXAM I CAN TAKE.
MAYBE IT'S THIS ONE, "PET BREEDER'S CERTIFICATION."
CERTIFICATE
NOZOMU ITOSHIKI
I PASSED.
WHO'S SUPPOSED TO BE TAKING TESTS AND WHO'S SUPPOSED TO BE GIVING THEM AROUND HERE ANYWAY?
SENSEI...
すっ
SHF
HUH?
SENSEI...
...YOU HAVE NO QUALIFICATIONS TO LOVE ANYONE!

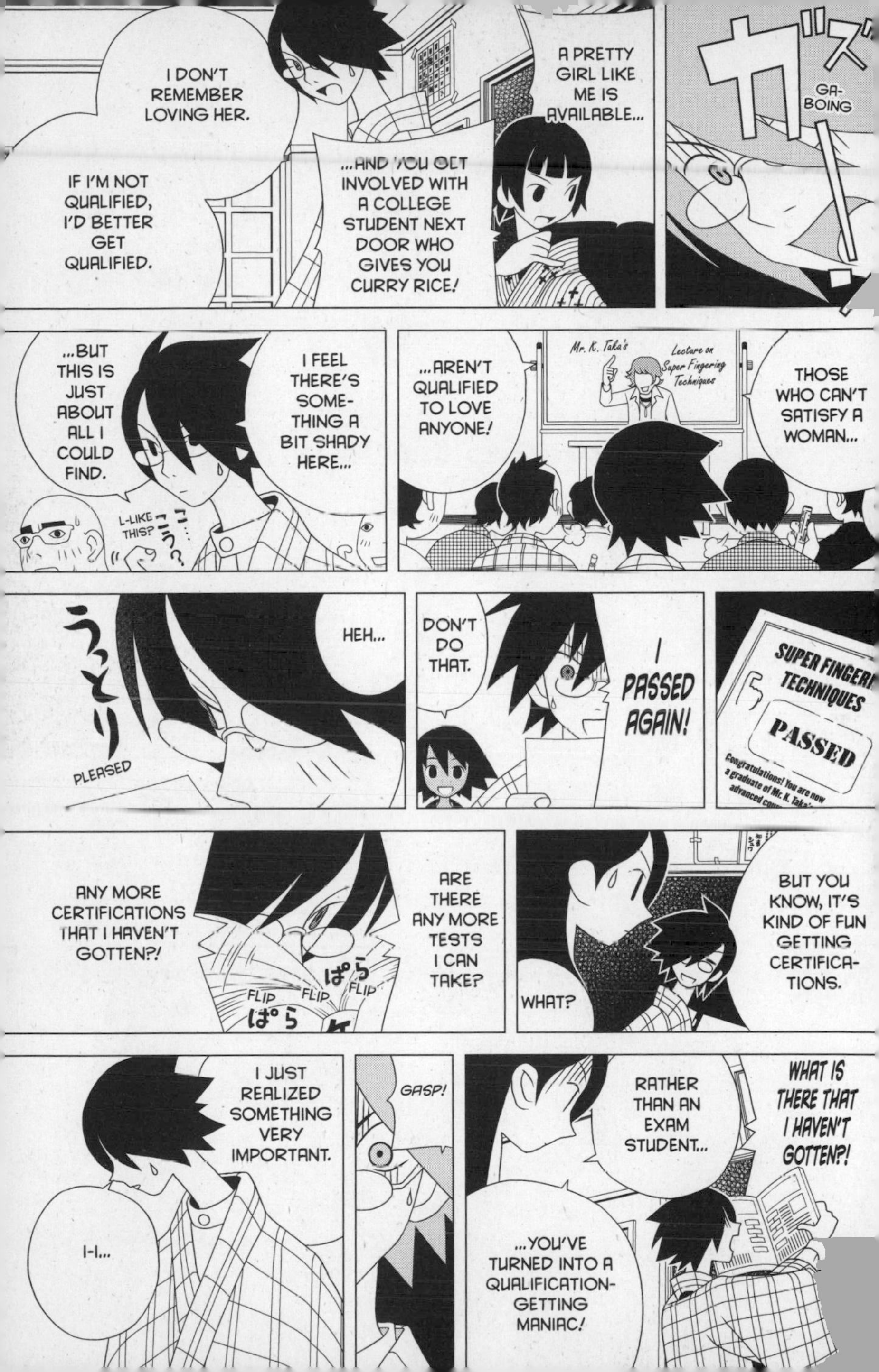
GA-BOING
A PRETTY GIRL LIKE ME IS AVAILABLE...
...AND YOU GET INVOLVED WITH A COLLEGE STUDENT NEXT DOOR WHO GIVES YOU CURRY RICE!
I DON'T REMEMBER LOVING HER.
IF I'M NOT QUALIFIED, I'D BETTER GET QUALIFIED.
Mr. K. Taka's
Lecture on Super Fingering Techniques
THOSE WHO CAN'T SATISFY A WOMAN...
...AREN'T QUALIFIED TO LOVE ANYONE!
I FEEL THERE'S SOME-THING A BIT SHADY HERE...
...BUT THIS IS JUST ABOUT ALL I COULD FIND.
L-LIKE THIS?
SUPER FINGERI
TECHNIQUES
PASSED
Congratulations! You are now a graduate of Mr. K. Taka's advanced cou
I PASSED AGAIN!
DON'T DO THAT.
HEH...
うっとり
PLEASED
BUT YOU KNOW, IT'S KIND OF FUN GETTING CERTIFICA-TIONS.
WHAT?
ARE THERE ANY MORE TESTS I CAN TAKE?
ANY MORE CERTIFICATIONS THAT I HAVEN'T GOTTEN?!
ぱら
FLIP
FLIP
FLIP
ぱら
WHAT IS THERE THAT I HAVEN'T GOTTEN?!
RATHER THAN AN EXAM STUDENT...
...YOU'VE TURNED INTO A QUALIFICATION-GETTING MANIAC!
GASP!
I JUST REALIZED SOMETHING VERY IMPORTANT.
I-I...

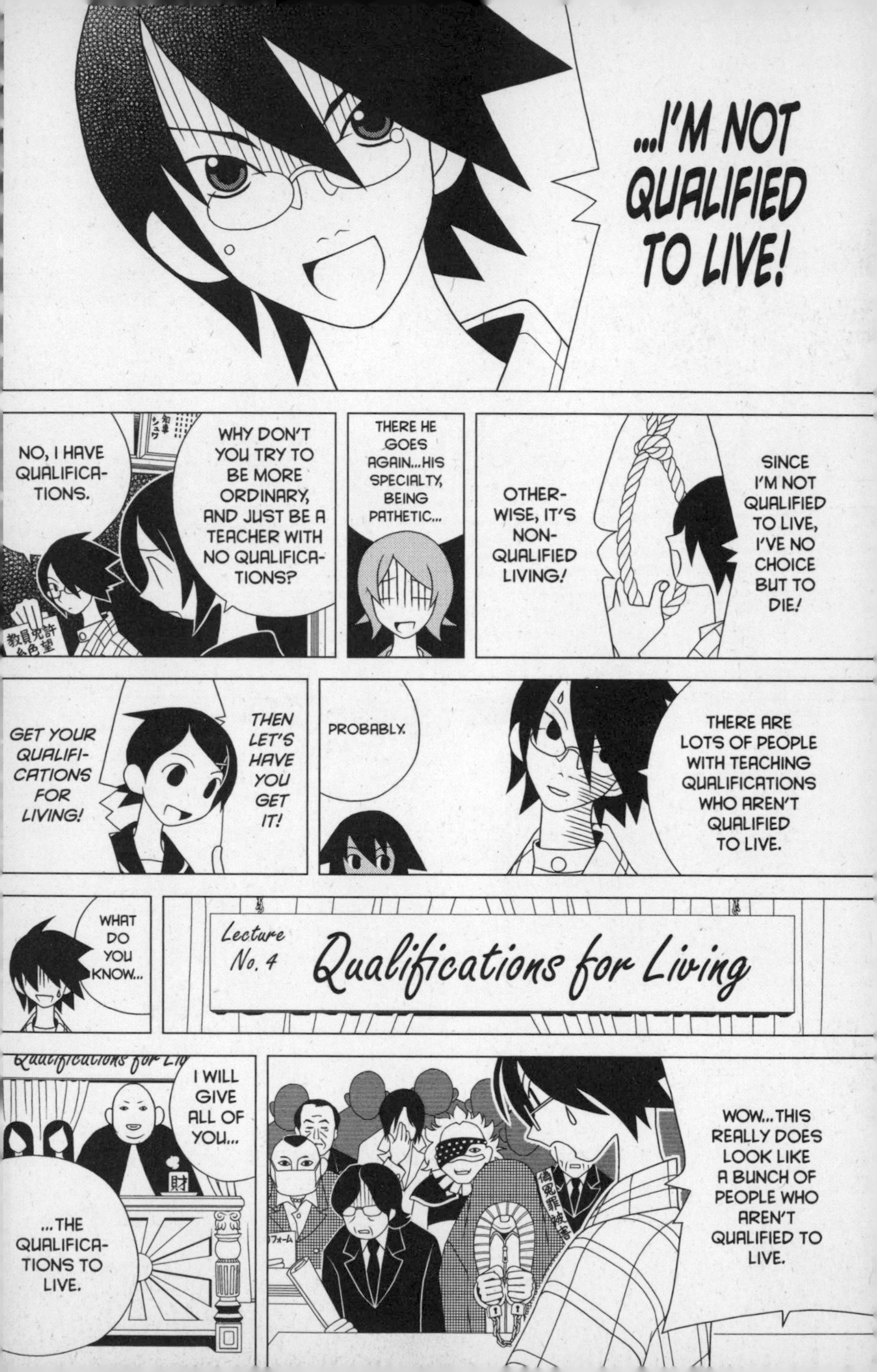
...I'M NOT QUALIFIED TO LIVE!
SINCE I'M NOT QUALIFIED TO LIVE, I'VE NO CHOICE BUT TO DIE!
OTHER-WISE, IT'S NON-QUALIFIED LIVING!
THERE HE GOES AGAIN...HIS SPECIALTY, BEING PATHETIC...
WHY DON'T YOU TRY TO BE MORE ORDINARY, AND JUST BE A TEACHER WITH NO QUALIFICA-TIONS?
NO, I HAVE QUALIFICA-TIONS.
THERE ARE LOTS OF PEOPLE WITH TEACHING QUALIFICATIONS WHO AREN'T QUALIFIED TO LIVE.
PROBABLY.
THEN LET'S HAVE YOU GET IT!
GET YOUR QUALIFI-CATIONS FOR LIVING!
Lecture No. 4 Qualifications for Living
WHAT DO YOU KNOW...
WOW...THIS REALLY DOES LOOK LIKE A BUNCH OF PEOPLE WHO AREN'T QUALIFIED TO LIVE.
I WILL GIVE ALL OF YOU...
...THE QUALIFICA-TIONS TO LIVE.

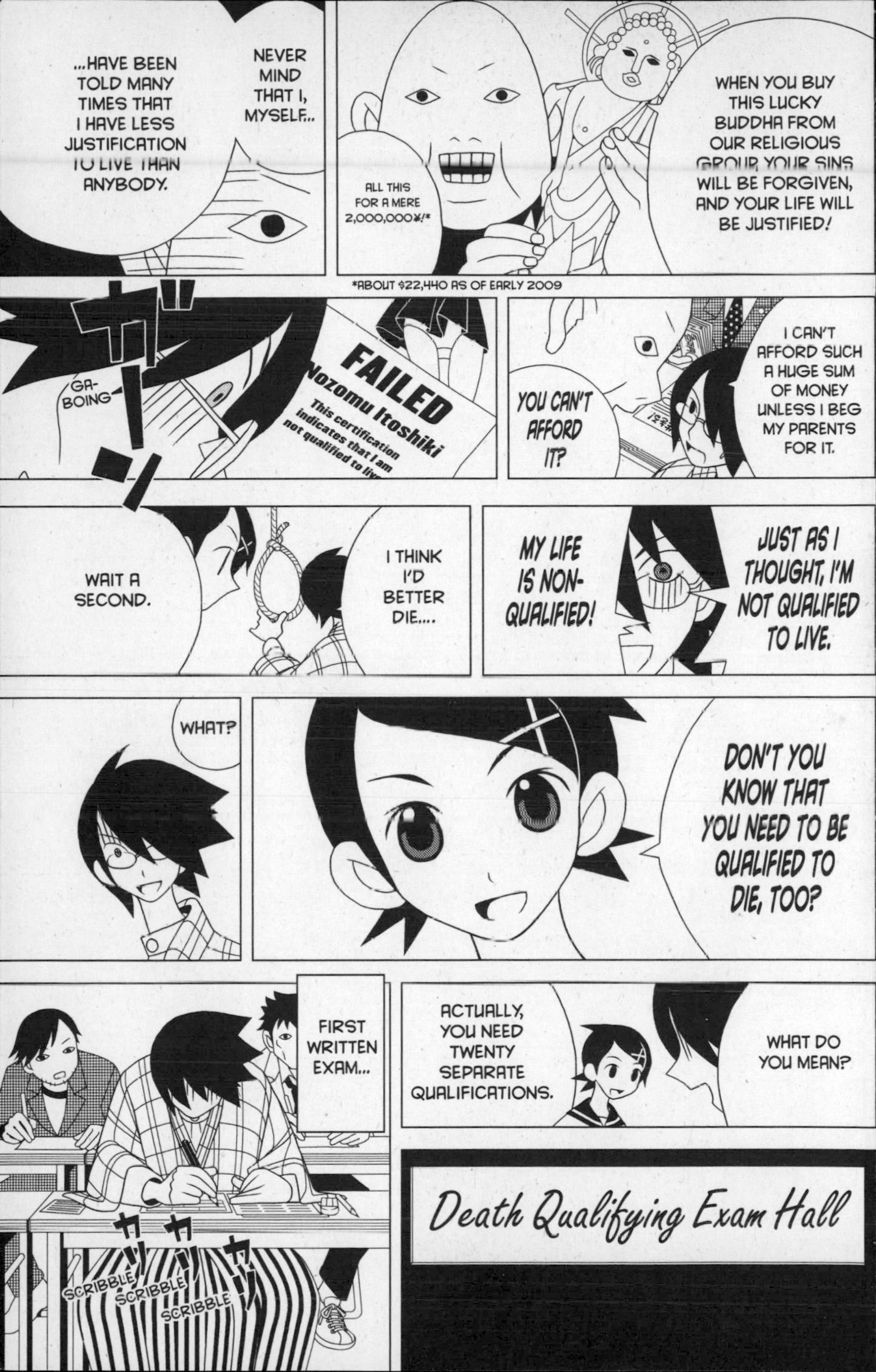
WHEN YOU BUY THIS LUCKY BUDDHA FROM OUR RELIGIOUS GROUP YOUR SINS WILL BE FORGIVEN, AND YOUR LIFE WILL BE JUSTIFIED!
ALL THIS FOR A MERE 2,000,000¥!*
NEVER MIND THAT I, MYSELF...
...HAVE BEEN TOLD MANY TIMES THAT I HAVE LESS JUSTIFICATION TO LIVE THAN ANYBODY.
*ABOUT $22,440 AS OF EARLY 2009
I CAN'T AFFORD SUCH A HUGE SUM OF MONEY UNLESS I BEG MY PARENTS FOR IT.
YOU CAN'T AFFORD IT?
FAILED
Nozomu Itoshiki
This certification indicates that I am not qualified to liv
GA-BOING
JUST AS I THOUGHT, I'M NOT QUALIFIED TO LIVE.
MY LIFE IS NON-QUALIFIED!
I THINK I'D BETTER DIE....
WAIT A SECOND.
DON'T YOU KNOW THAT YOU NEED TO BE QUALIFIED TO DIE, TOO?
WHAT?
WHAT DO YOU MEAN?
ACTUALLY, YOU NEED TWENTY SEPARATE QUALIFICATIONS.
Death Qualifying Exam Hall
FIRST WRITTEN EXAM...
SCRIBBLE
SCRIBBLE
SCRIBBLE

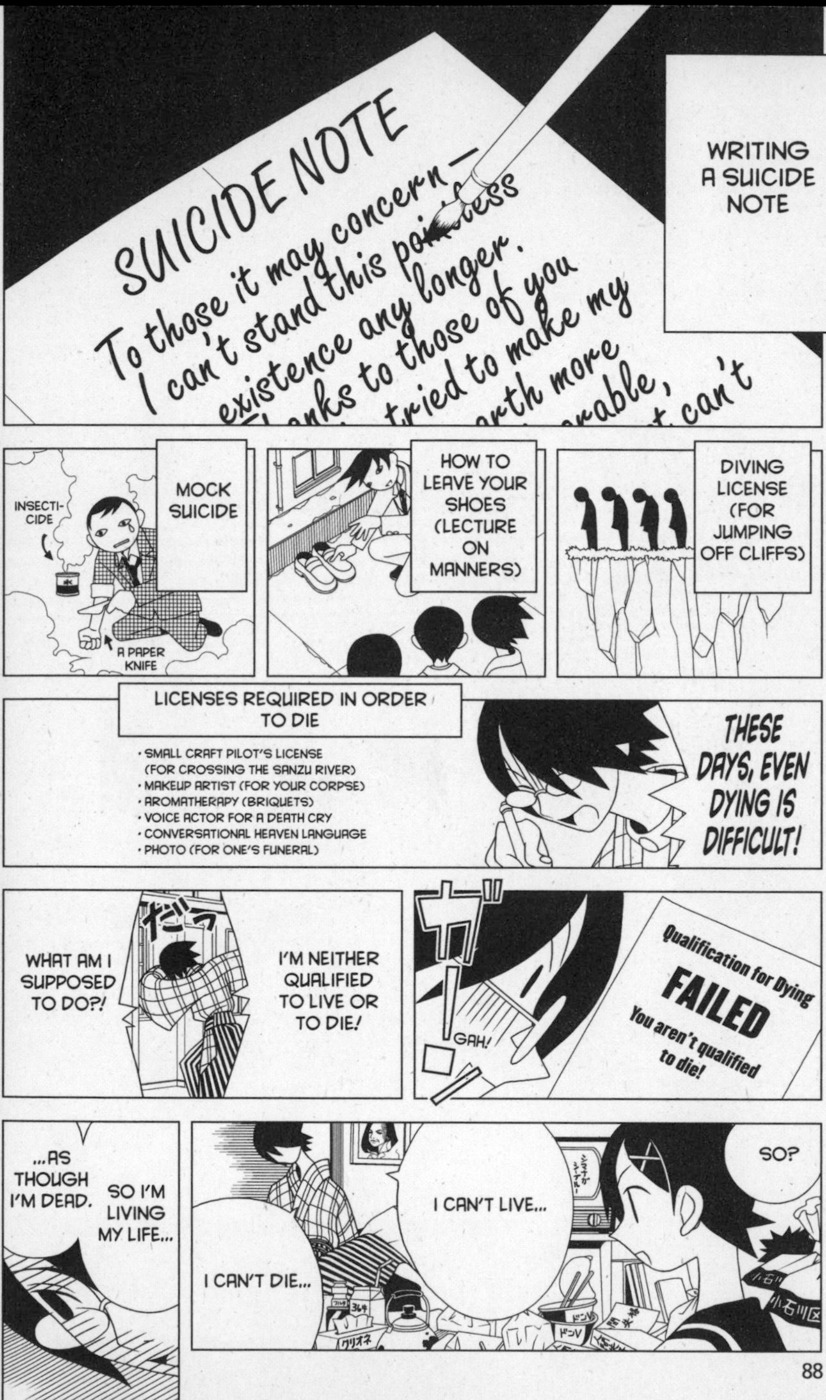
WRITING A SUICIDE NOTE
SUICIDE NOTE
To those it may concern—
I can't stand this po less
existence any longer.
nks to those of you
tried to make my
rth more
rable,
t can't
DIVING LICENSE (FOR JUMPING OFF CLIFFS)
HOW TO LEAVE YOUR SHOES (LECTURE ON MANNERS)
MOCK SUICIDE
INSECTICIDE
A PAPER KNIFE
LICENSES REQUIRED IN ORDER TO DIE
• SMALL CRAFT PILOT'S LICENSE (FOR CROSSING THE SANZU RIVER)
• MAKEUP ARTIST (FOR YOUR CORPSE)
• AROMATHERAPY (BRIQUETS)
• VOICE ACTOR FOR A DEATH CRY
• CONVERSATIONAL HEAVEN LANGUAGE
• PHOTO (FOR ONE'S FUNERAL)
THESE DAYS, EVEN DYING IS DIFFICULT!
Qualification for Dying
FAILED
You aren't qualified to die!
GAH!
I'M NEITHER QUALIFIED TO LIVE OR TO DIE!
WHAT AM I SUPPOSED TO DO?!
SO?
I CAN'T LIVE...
I CAN'T DIE...
SO I'M LIVING MY LIFE...
...AS THOUGH I'M DEAD.

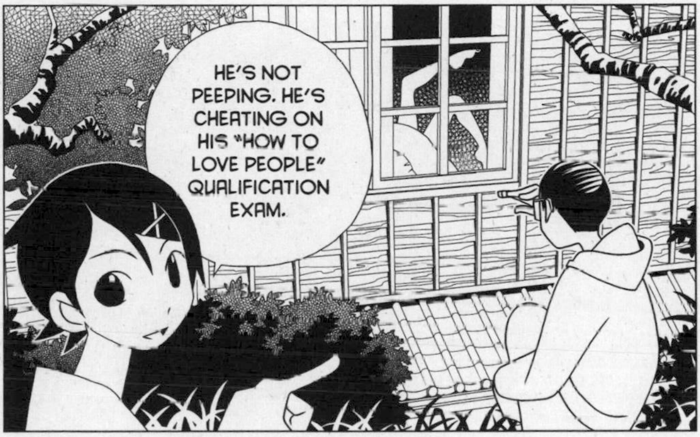
HE'S NOT PEEPING. HE'S CHEATING ON HIS "HOW TO LOVE PEOPLE" QUALIFICATION EXAM.

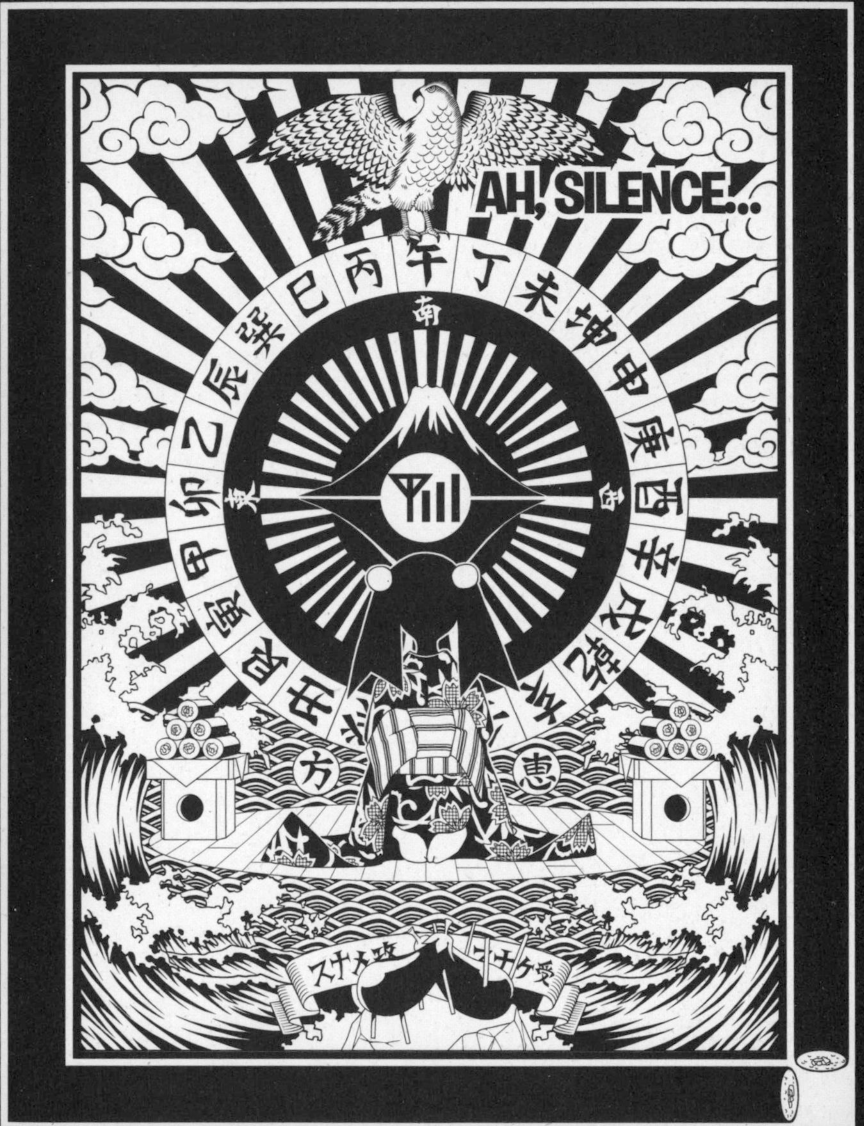
AH, SILENCE...
南
東
西
方
恵

CHAPTER 37

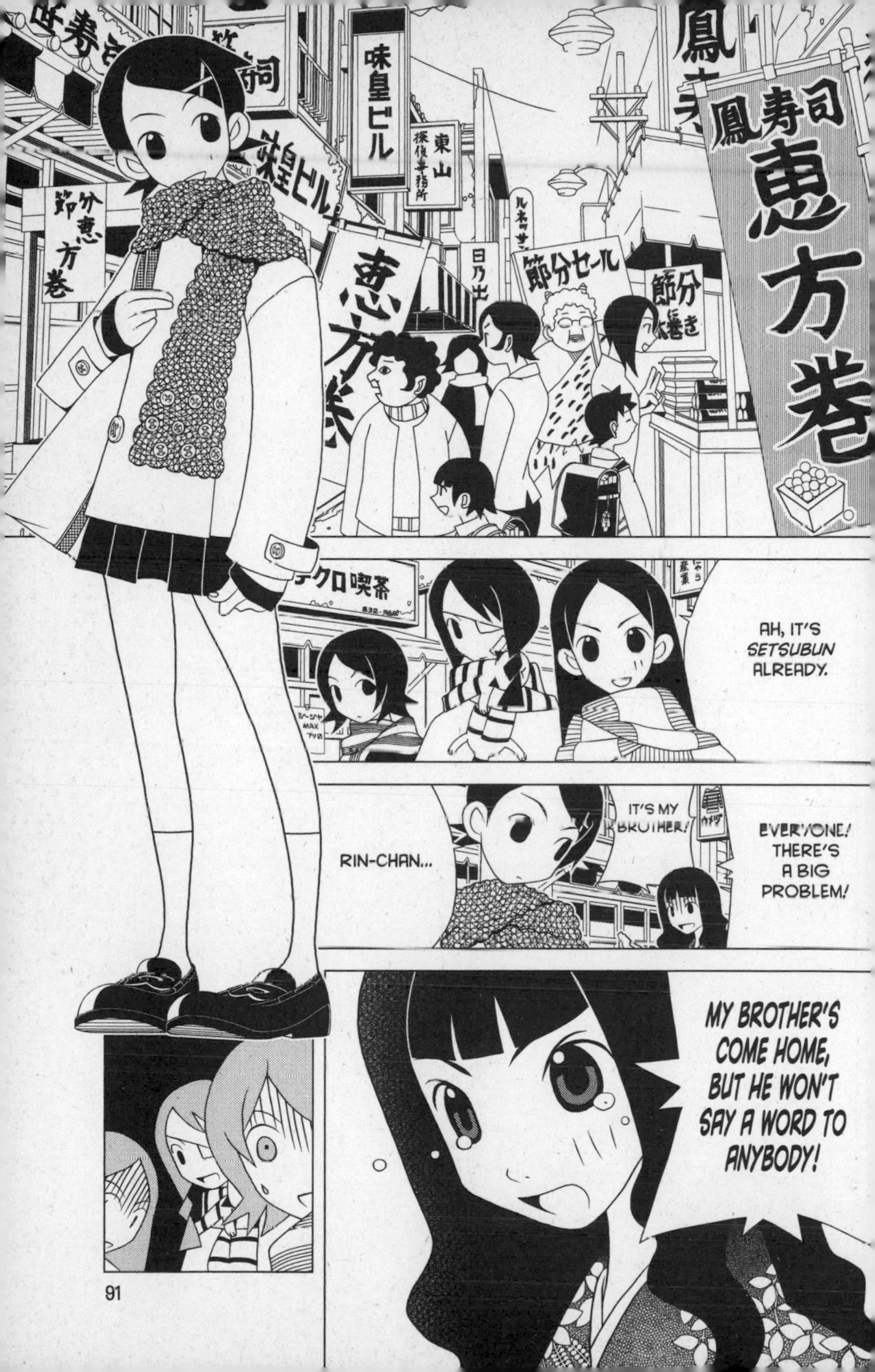
鳳寿司
恵方巻
節分セール
味皇ビル
東山
探偵事務所
日乃出
恵方巻
節分
恵方巻
AH, IT'S SETSUBUN ALREADY.
EVERYONE! THERE'S A BIG PROBLEM!
IT'S MY BROTHER!
RIN-CHAN...
MY BROTHER'S COME HOME, BUT HE WON'T SAY A WORD TO ANYBODY!

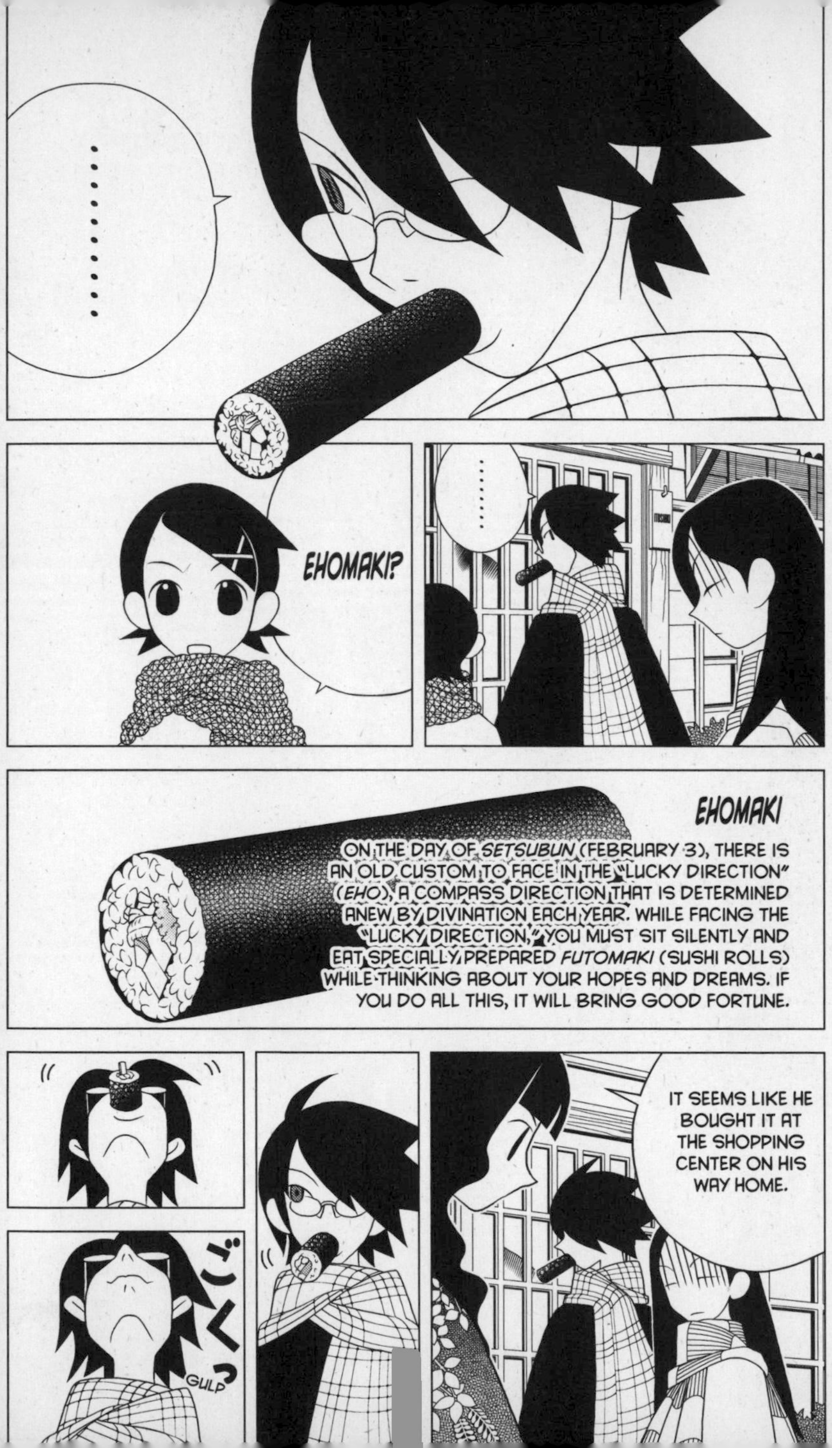
……
……
EHOMAKI?
EHOMAKI
ON THE DAY OF *SETSUBUN* (FEBRUARY 3), THERE IS AN OLD CUSTOM TO FACE IN THE "LUCKY DIRECTION" (*EHO*), A COMPASS DIRECTION THAT IS DETERMINED ANEW BY DIVINATION EACH YEAR. WHILE FACING THE "LUCKY DIRECTION," YOU MUST SIT SILENTLY AND EAT SPECIALLY PREPARED *FUTOMAKI* (SUSHI ROLLS) WHILE THINKING ABOUT YOUR HOPES AND DREAMS. IF YOU DO ALL THIS, IT WILL BRING GOOD FORTUNE.
IT SEEMS LIKE HE BOUGHT IT AT THE SHOPPING CENTER ON HIS WAY HOME.
GULP

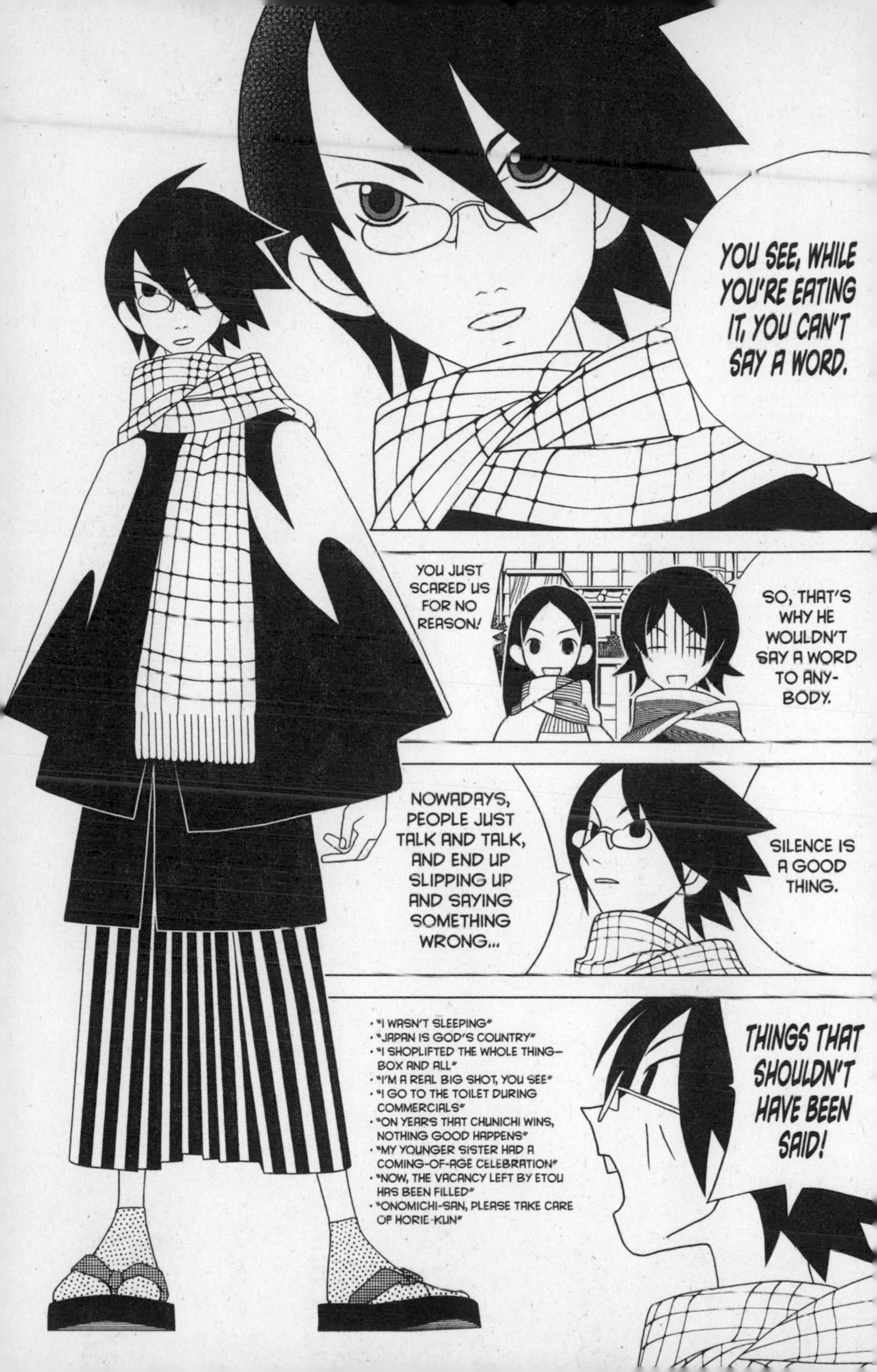
YOU SEE, WHILE YOU'RE EATING IT, YOU CAN'T SAY A WORD.
SO, THAT'S WHY HE WOULDN'T SAY A WORD TO ANY-BODY.
YOU JUST SCARED US FOR NO REASON!
SILENCE IS A GOOD THING.
NOWADAYS, PEOPLE JUST TALK AND TALK, AND END UP SLIPPING UP AND SAYING SOMETHING WRONG...
THINGS THAT SHOULDN'T HAVE BEEN SAID!
• "I WASN'T SLEEPING"
• "JAPAN IS GOD'S COUNTRY"
• "I SHOPLIFTED THE WHOLE THING—BOX AND ALL"
• "I'M A REAL BIG SHOT, YOU SEE"
• "I GO TO THE TOILET DURING COMMERCIALS"
• "ON YEARS THAT CHUNICHI WINS, NOTHING GOOD HAPPENS"
• "MY YOUNGER SISTER HAD A COMING-OF-AGE CELEBRATION"
• "NOW, THE VACANCY LEFT BY ETOU HAS BEEN FILLED"
• "ONOMICHI-SAN, PLEASE TAKE CARE OF HORIE-KUN"

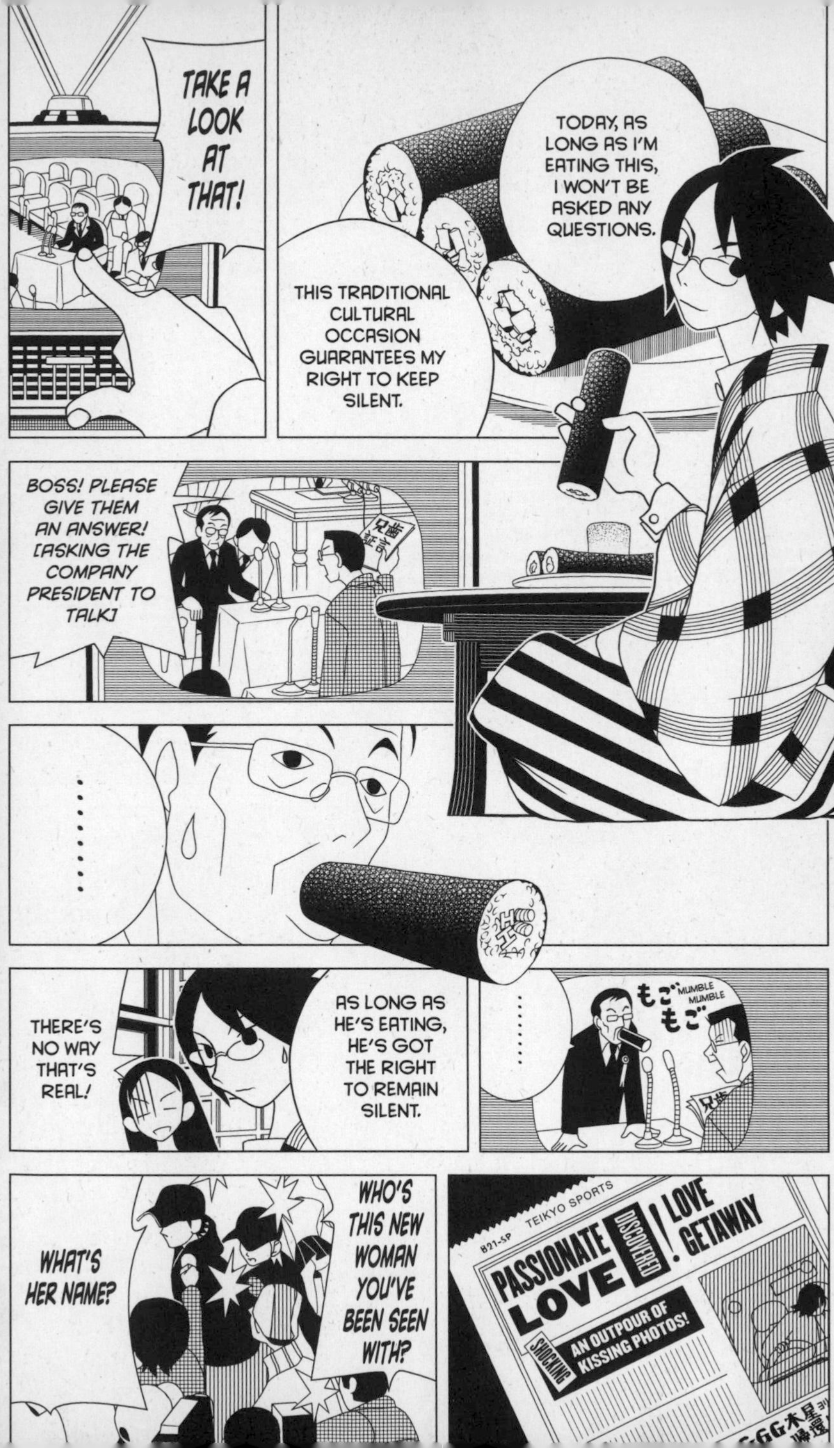
TODAY, AS LONG AS I'M EATING THIS, I WON'T BE ASKED ANY QUESTIONS.
THIS TRADITIONAL CULTURAL OCCASION GUARANTEES MY RIGHT TO KEEP SILENT.
TAKE A LOOK AT THAT!
BOSS! PLEASE GIVE THEM AN ANSWER! [ASKING THE COMPANY PRESIDENT TO TALK]
兄歯 証言
......
......
もご MUMBLE
もご MUMBLE
AS LONG AS HE'S EATING, HE'S GOT THE RIGHT TO REMAIN SILENT.
THERE'S NO WAY THAT'S REAL!
TEIKYO SPORTS
B21-SP
PASSIONATE LOVE
DISCOVERED
! LOVE GETAWAY
SHOCKING
AN OUTPOUR OF KISSING PHOTOS!
WHO'S THIS NEW WOMAN YOU'VE BEEN SEEN WITH?
WHAT'S HER NAME?

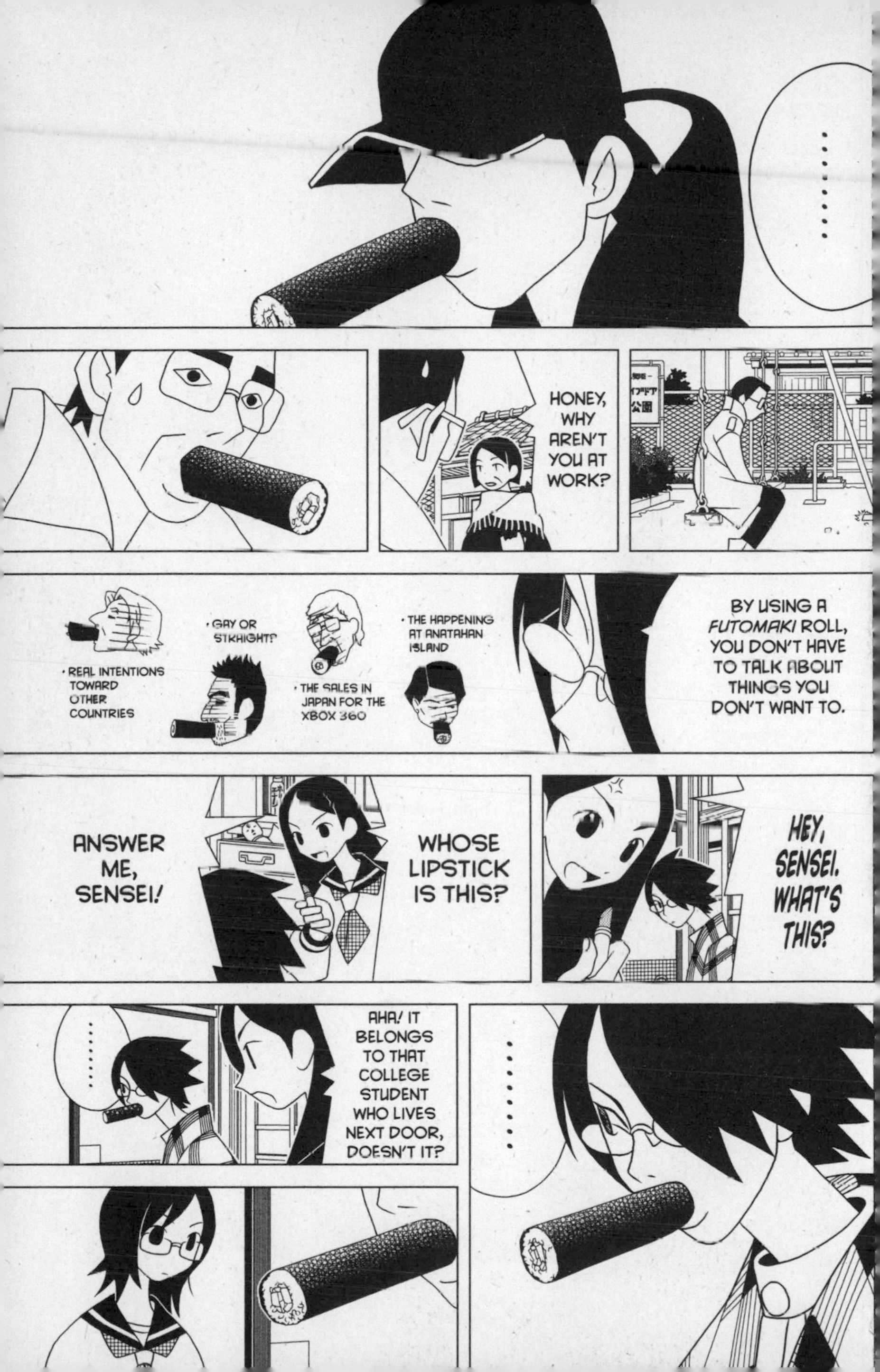
……
HONEY, WHY AREN'T YOU AT WORK?
BY USING A *FUTOMAKI* ROLL, YOU DON'T HAVE TO TALK ABOUT THINGS YOU DON'T WANT TO.
· THE HAPPENING AT ANATAHAN ISLAND
· THE SALES IN JAPAN FOR THE XBOX 360
· GAY OR STRAIGHT?
· REAL INTENTIONS TOWARD OTHER COUNTRIES
HEY, SENSEI. WHAT'S THIS?
WHOSE LIPSTICK IS THIS?
ANSWER ME, SENSEI!
……
AHA! IT BELONGS TO THAT COLLEGE STUDENT WHO LIVES NEXT DOOR, DOESN'T IT?
……

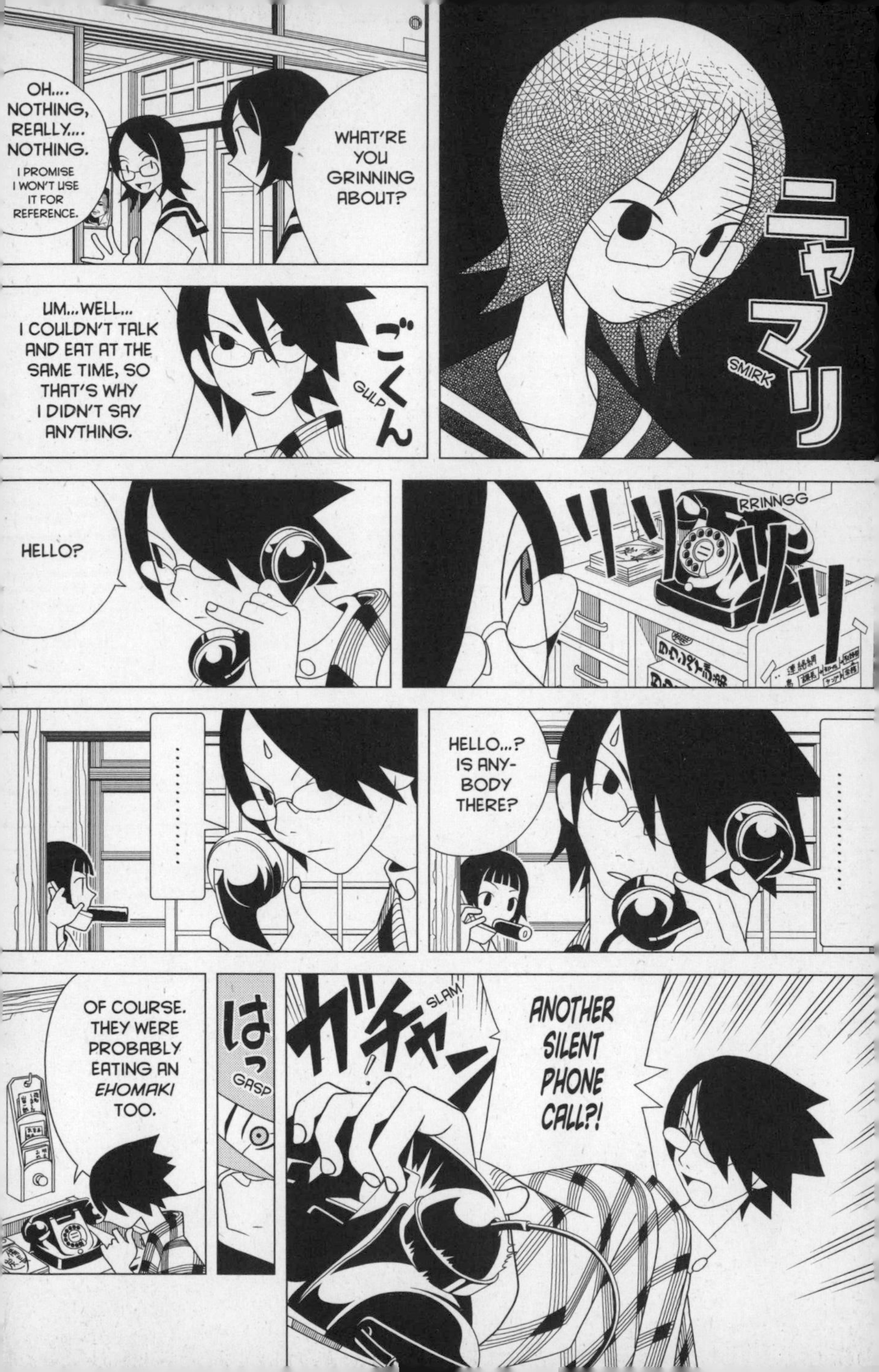
ニヤリ
SMIRK
WHAT'RE YOU GRINNING ABOUT?
OH.... NOTHING, REALLY.... NOTHING.
I PROMISE I WON'T USE IT FOR REFERENCE.
ごくん
GULP
UM...WELL... I COULDN'T TALK AND EAT AT THE SAME TIME, SO THAT'S WHY I DIDN'T SAY ANYTHING.
リリリリ
RRINNGG
HELLO?
......
HELLO...? IS ANYBODY THERE?
......
ANOTHER SILENT PHONE CALL?!
ガチャン
SLAM
はっ
GASP
OF COURSE. THEY WERE PROBABLY EATING AN *EHOMAKI* TOO.

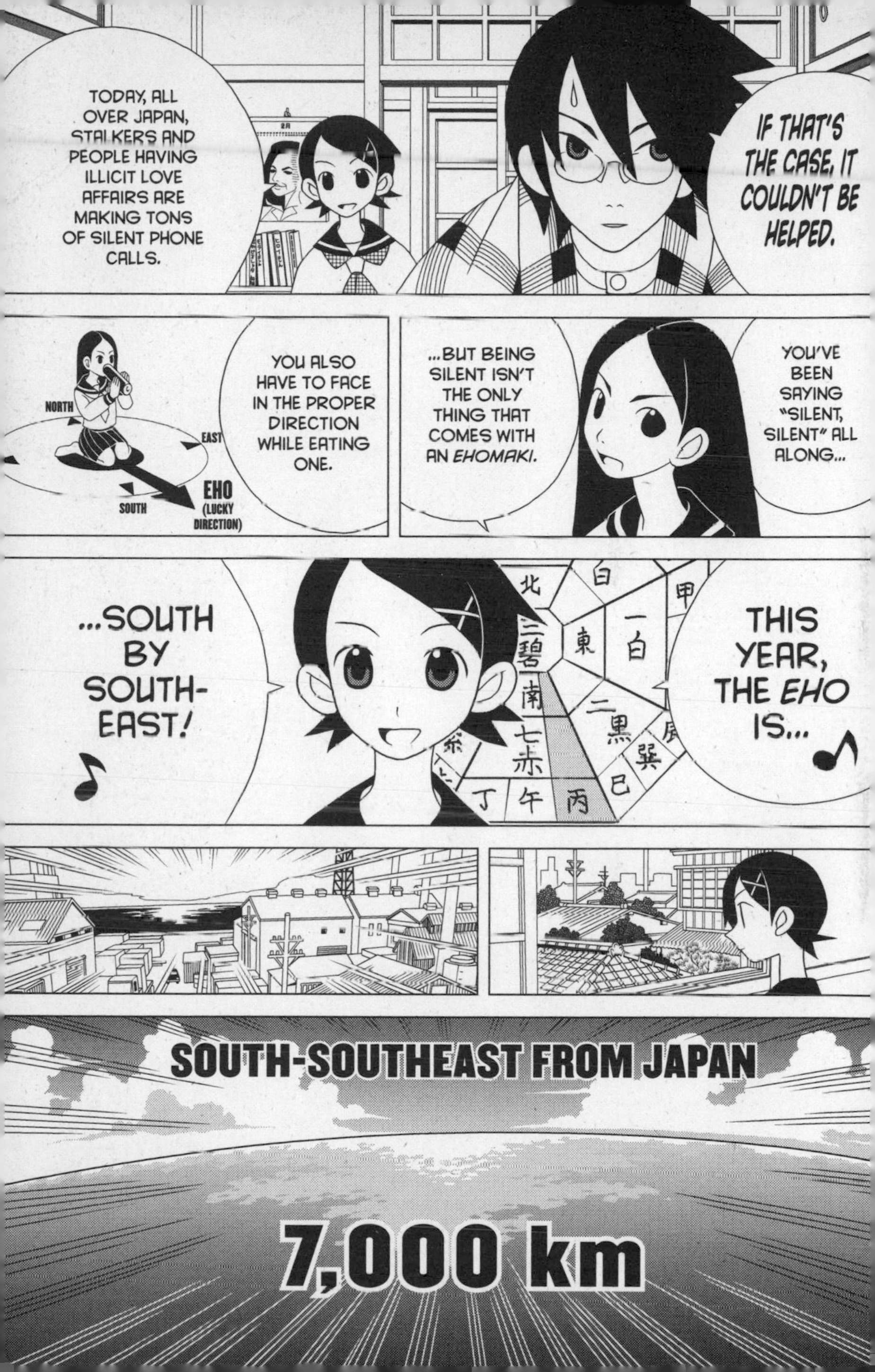
IF THAT'S THE CASE, IT COULDN'T BE HELPED.
TODAY, ALL OVER JAPAN, STALKERS AND PEOPLE HAVING ILLICIT LOVE AFFAIRS ARE MAKING TONS OF SILENT PHONE CALLS.
YOU'VE BEEN SAYING "SILENT, SILENT" ALL ALONG...
...BUT BEING SILENT ISN'T THE ONLY THING THAT COMES WITH AN *EHOMAKI*.
YOU ALSO HAVE TO FACE IN THE PROPER DIRECTION WHILE EATING ONE.
NORTH
EAST
EHO (LUCKY DIRECTION)
SOUTH
THIS YEAR, THE *EHO* IS...
...SOUTH BY SOUTH-EAST!
SOUTH-SOUTHEAST FROM JAPAN
7,000 km

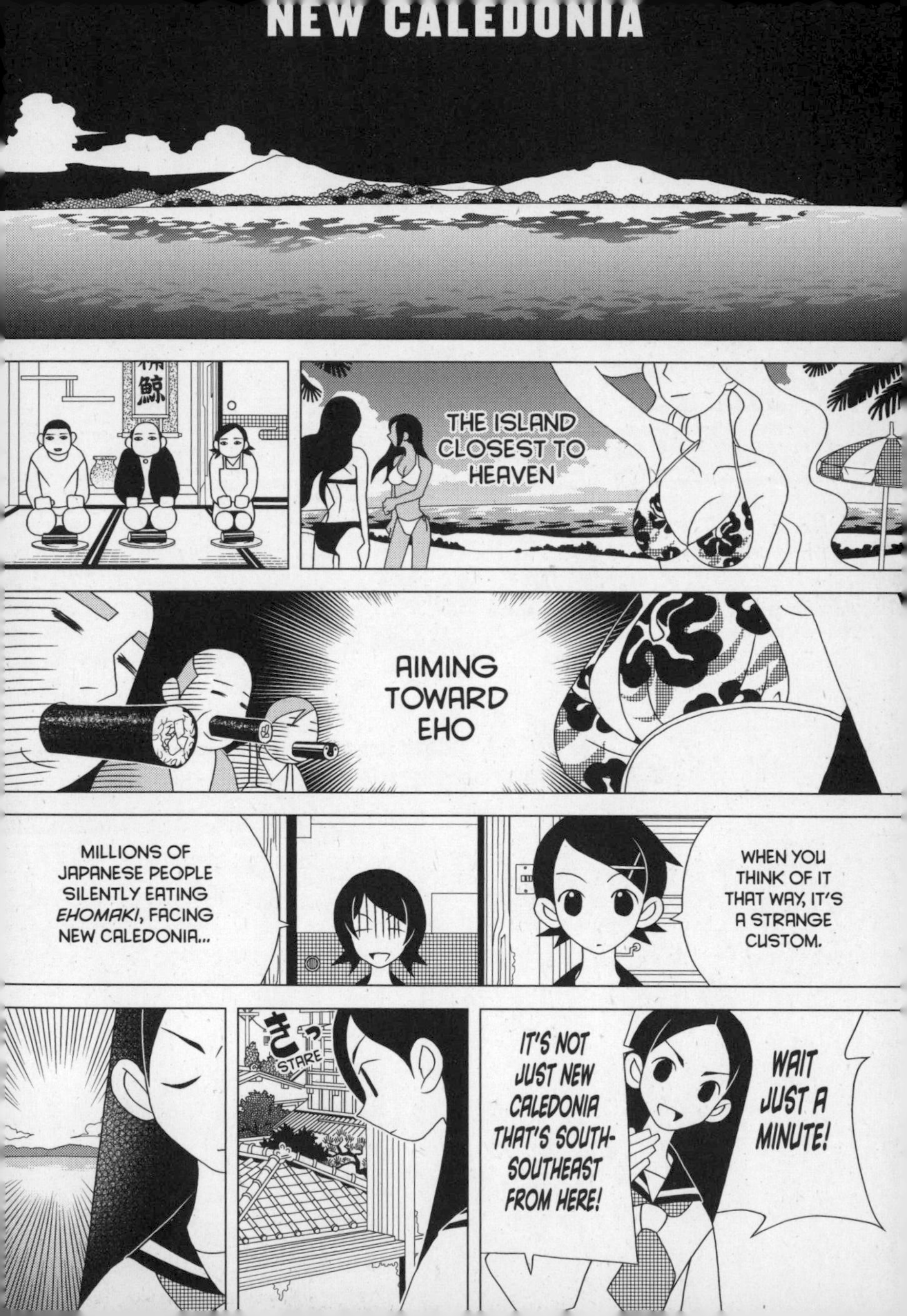
NEW CALEDONIA
THE ISLAND CLOSEST TO HEAVEN
AIMING TOWARD EHO
WHEN YOU THINK OF IT THAT WAY, IT'S A STRANGE CUSTOM.
MILLIONS OF JAPANESE PEOPLE SILENTLY EATING *EHOMAKI*, FACING NEW CALEDONIA...
WAIT JUST A MINUTE!
IT'S NOT JUST NEW CALEDONIA THAT'S SOUTH-SOUTHEAST FROM HERE!
きっ STARE

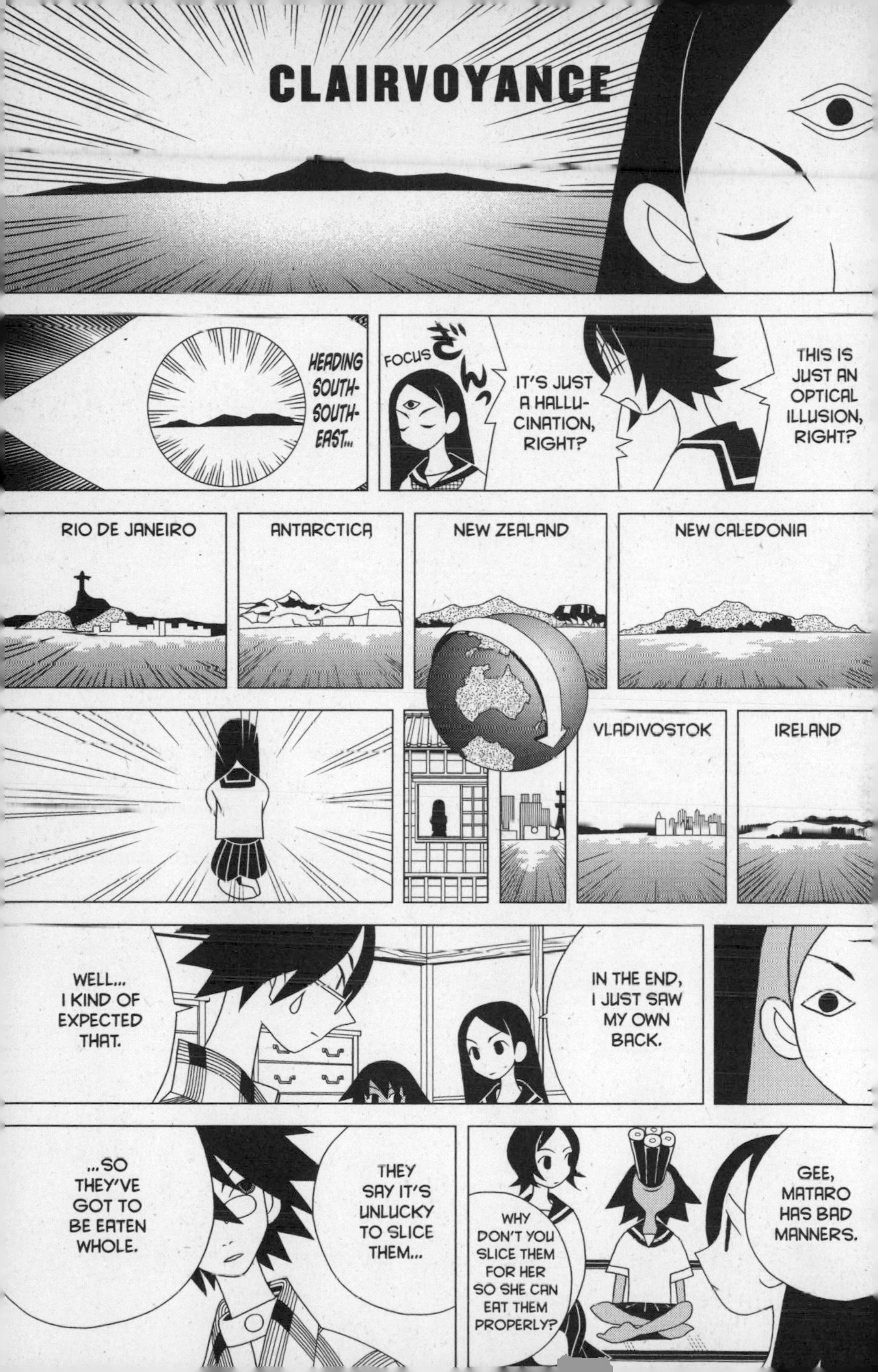
CLAIRVOYANCE
THIS IS JUST AN OPTICAL ILLUSION, RIGHT?
IT'S JUST A HALLUCINATION, RIGHT?
FOCUS ぎんっ
HEADING SOUTH-SOUTH-EAST...
NEW CALEDONIA
NEW ZEALAND
ANTARCTICA
RIO DE JANEIRO
IRELAND
VLADIVOSTOK
IN THE END, I JUST SAW MY OWN BACK.
WELL... I KIND OF EXPECTED THAT.
GEE, MATARO HAS BAD MANNERS.
WHY DON'T YOU SLICE THEM FOR HER SO SHE CAN EAT THEM PROPERLY?
THEY SAY IT'S UNLUCKY TO SLICE THEM...
...SO THEY'VE GOT TO BE EATEN WHOLE.

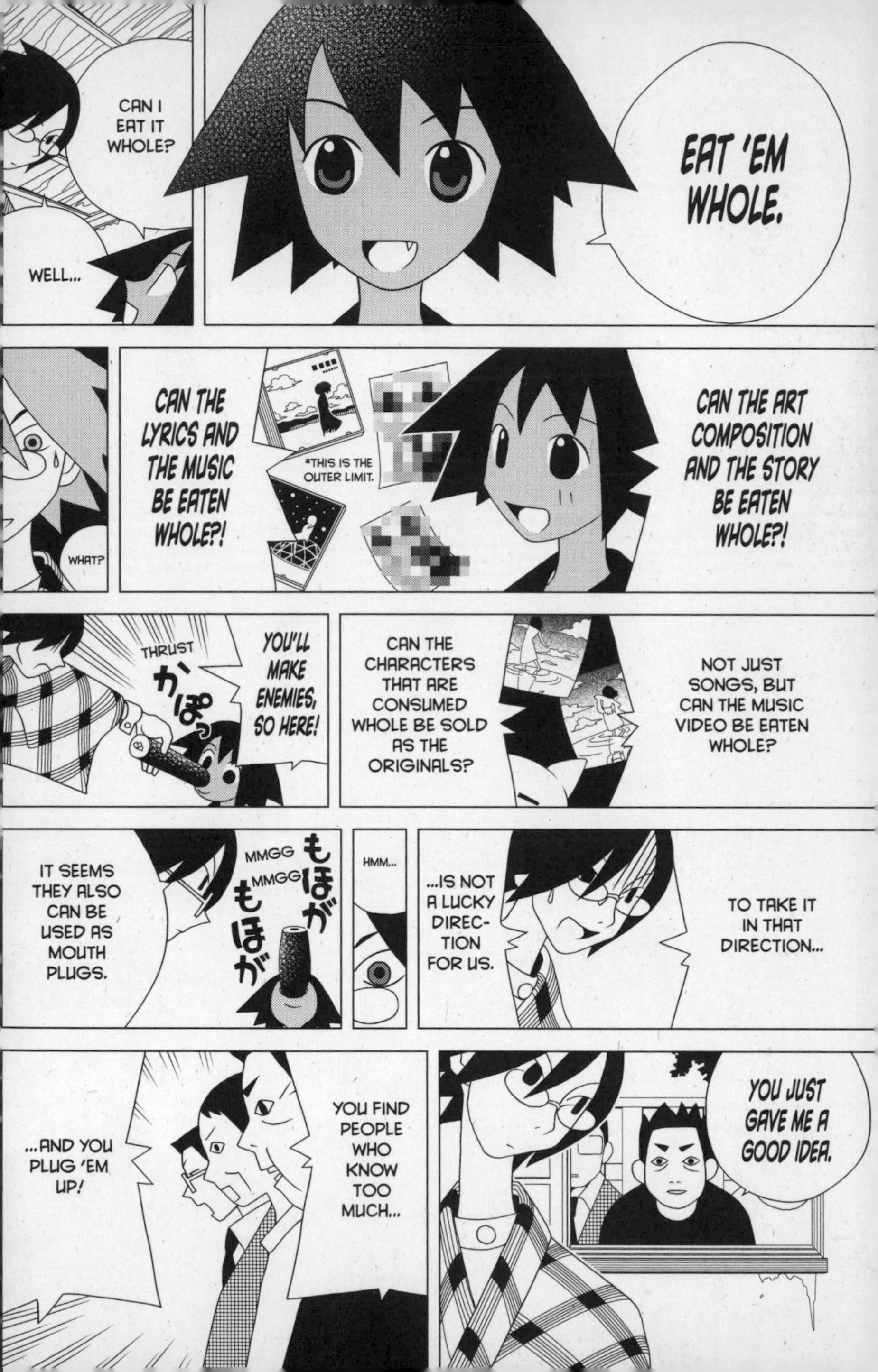
EAT 'EM WHOLE.
CAN I EAT IT WHOLE?
WELL...
CAN THE ART COMPOSITION AND THE STORY BE EATEN WHOLE?!
*THIS IS THE OUTER LIMIT.
CAN THE LYRICS AND THE MUSIC BE EATEN WHOLE?!
WHAT?
NOT JUST SONGS, BUT CAN THE MUSIC VIDEO BE EATEN WHOLE?
CAN THE CHARACTERS THAT ARE CONSUMED WHOLE BE SOLD AS THE ORIGINALS?
YOU'LL MAKE ENEMIES, SO HERE!
THRUST
かぽっ
TO TAKE IT IN THAT DIRECTION...
...IS NOT A LUCKY DIRECTION FOR US.
HMM...
MMGG
もほが
MMGG
もほが
IT SEEMS THEY ALSO CAN BE USED AS MOUTH PLUGS.
YOU JUST GAVE ME A GOOD IDEA.
YOU FIND PEOPLE WHO KNOW TOO MUCH...
...AND YOU PLUG 'EM UP!

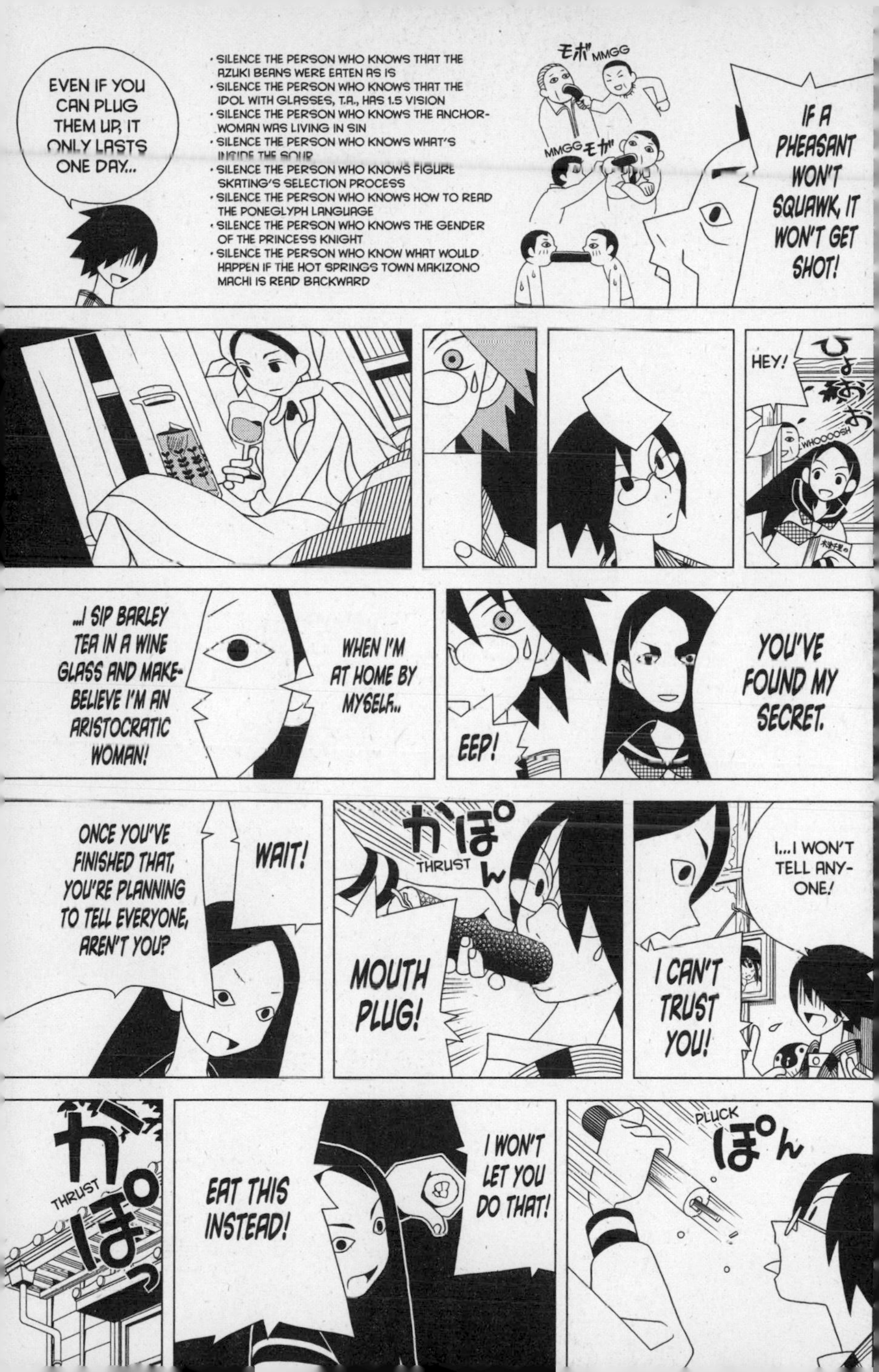
IF A PHEASANT WON'T SQUAWK, IT WON'T GET SHOT!
モゴ MMGG
MMGG モガ
• SILENCE THE PERSON WHO KNOWS THAT THE AZUKI BEANS WERE EATEN AS IS
• SILENCE THE PERSON WHO KNOWS THAT THE IDOL WITH GLASSES, T.A., HAS 1.5 VISION
• SILENCE THE PERSON WHO KNOWS THE ANCHORWOMAN WAS LIVING IN SIN
• SILENCE THE PERSON WHO KNOWS WHAT'S INSIDE THE SOUP
• SILENCE THE PERSON WHO KNOWS FIGURE SKATING'S SELECTION PROCESS
• SILENCE THE PERSON WHO KNOWS HOW TO READ THE PONEGLYPH LANGUAGE
• SILENCE THE PERSON WHO KNOWS THE GENDER OF THE PRINCESS KNIGHT
• SILENCE THE PERSON WHO KNOW WHAT WOULD HAPPEN IF THE HOT SPRINGS TOWN MAKIZONO MACHI IS READ BACKWARD
EVEN IF YOU CAN PLUG THEM UP, IT ONLY LASTS ONE DAY...
HEY!
ひょおぉ
WHOOOOSH
YOU'VE FOUND MY SECRET.
EEP!
WHEN I'M AT HOME BY MYSELF...
...I SIP BARLEY TEA IN A WINE GLASS AND MAKE-BELIEVE I'M AN ARISTOCRATIC WOMAN!
I...I WON'T TELL ANYONE!
I CAN'T TRUST YOU!
かぽん
THRUST
MOUTH PLUG!
WAIT!
ONCE YOU'VE FINISHED THAT, YOU'RE PLANNING TO TELL EVERYONE, AREN'T YOU?
ぽん
PLUCK
I WON'T LET YOU DO THAT!
EAT THIS INSTEAD!
かぽっ
THRUST

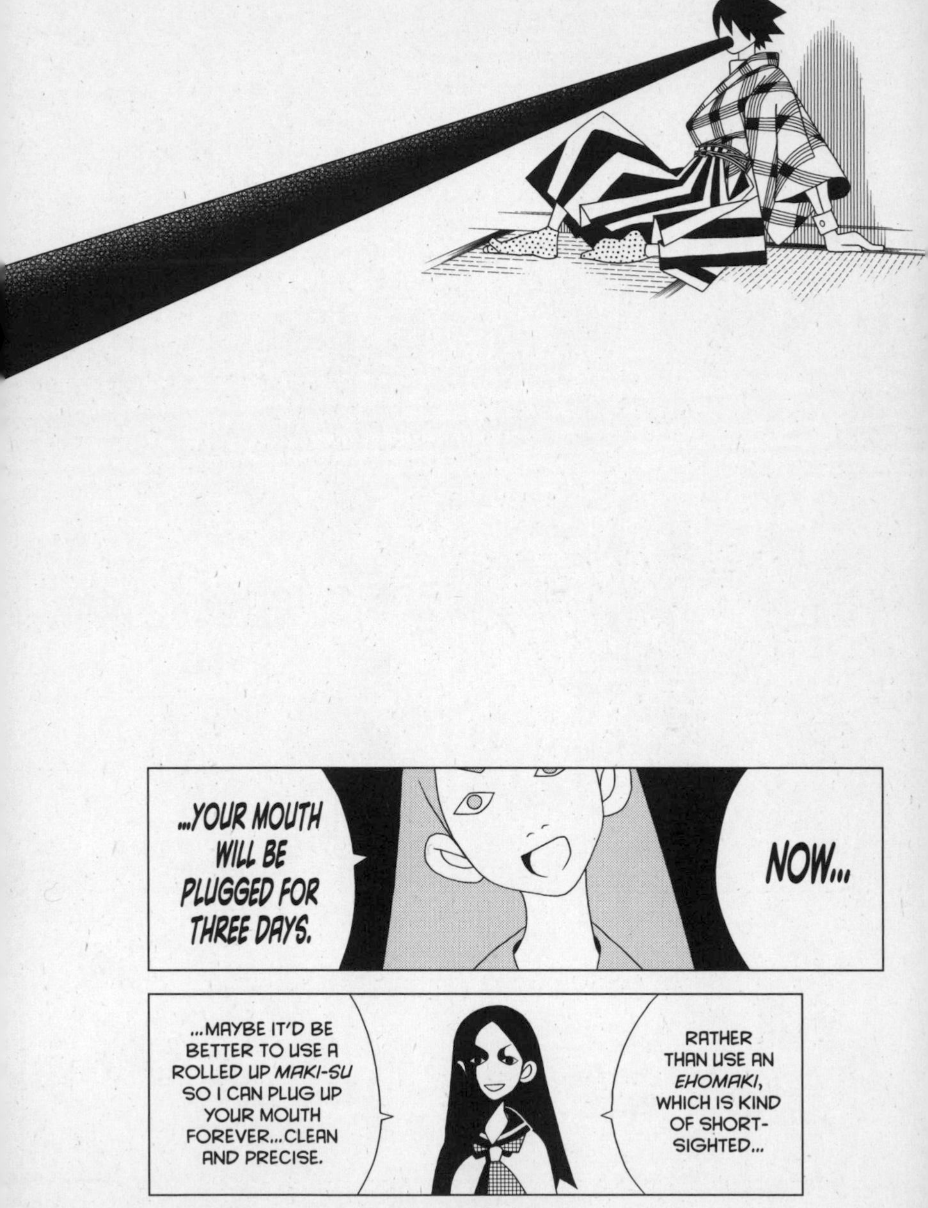
NOW...
...YOUR MOUTH WILL BE PLUGGED FOR THREE DAYS.
RATHER THAN USE AN *EHOMAKI*, WHICH IS KIND OF SHORT-SIGHTED...
...MAYBE IT'D BE BETTER TO USE A ROLLED UP *MAKI-SU* SO I CAN PLUG UP YOUR MOUTH FOREVER...CLEAN AND PRECISE.

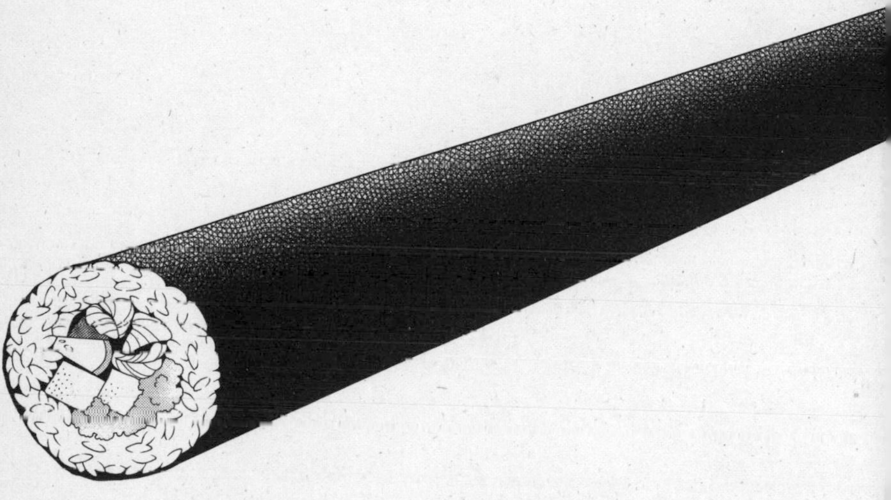

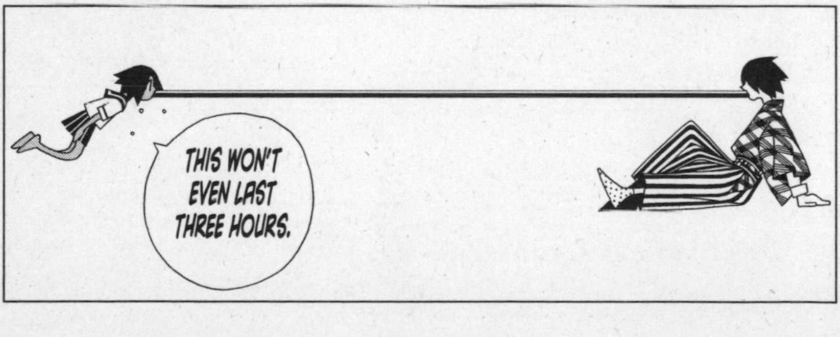
THIS WON'T EVEN LAST THREE HOURS.

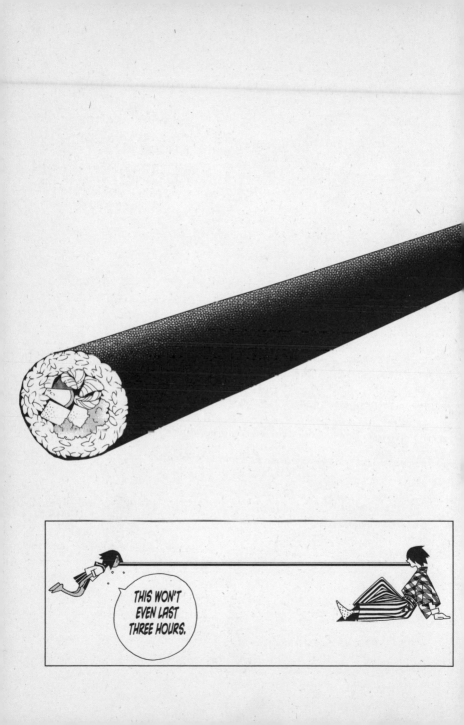

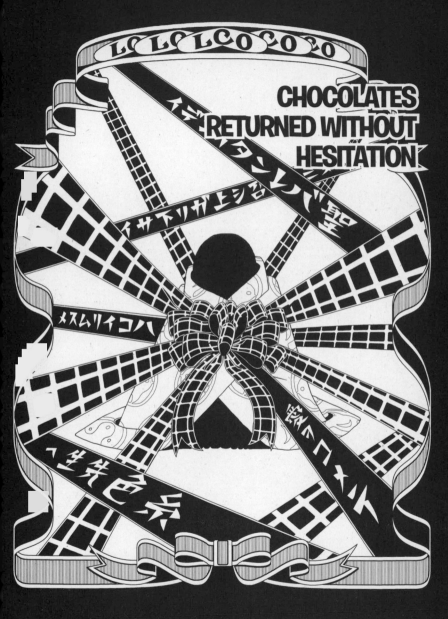

CHOCOLATES
RETURNED WITHOUT
HESITATION

CHAPTER 38

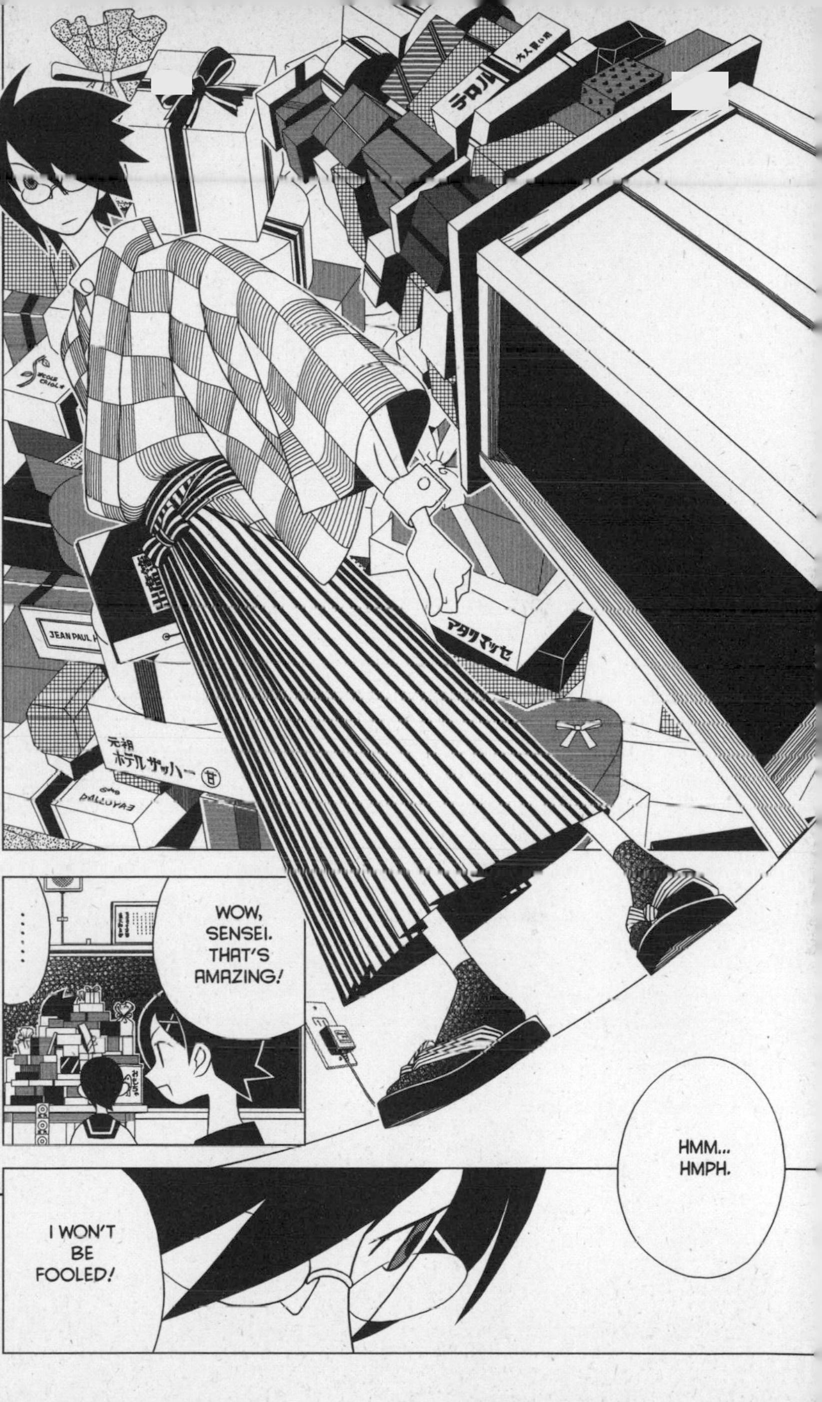
HMM... HMPH.
WOW, SENSEI. THAT'S AMAZING!
......
I WON'T BE FOOLED!

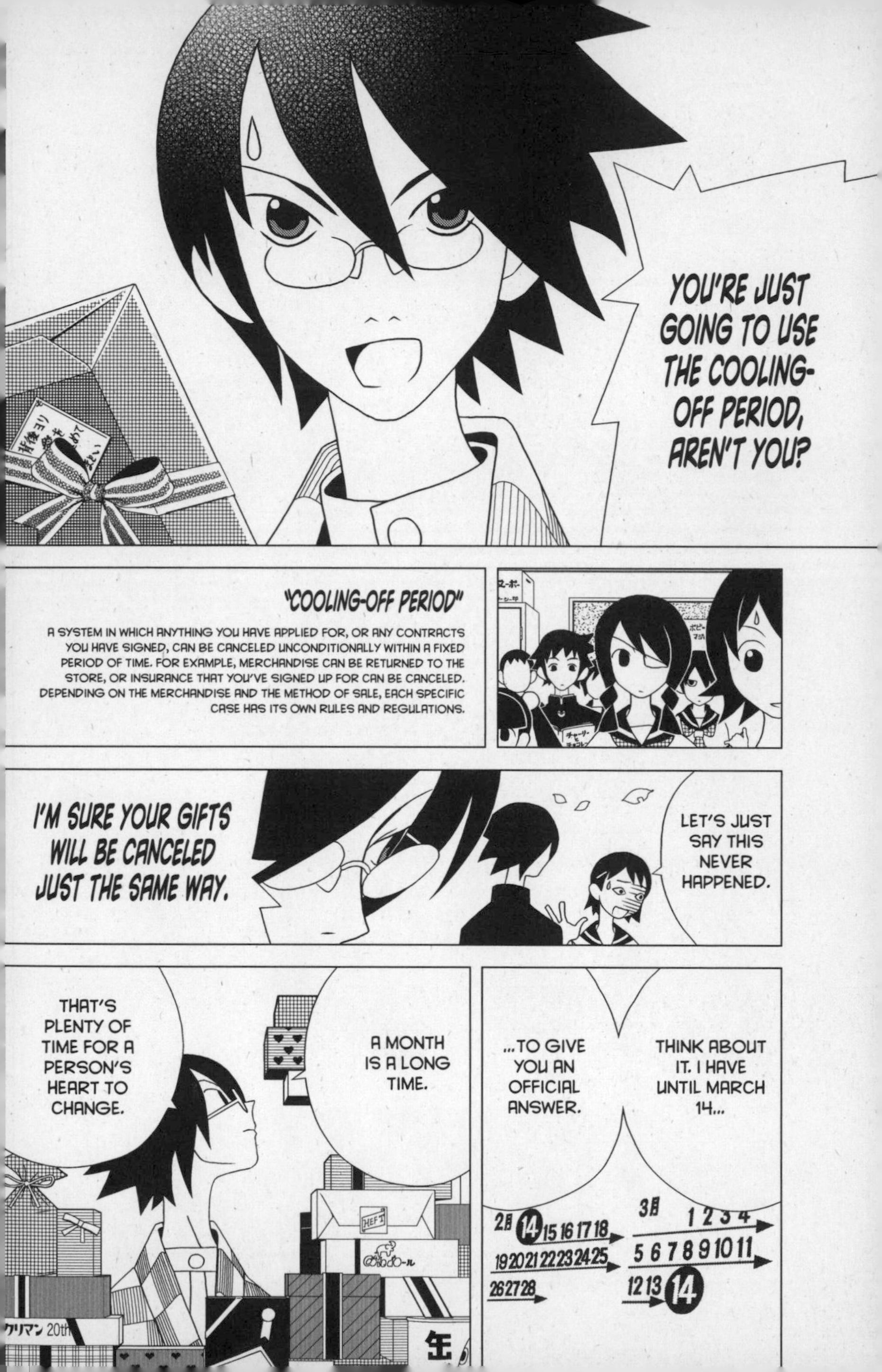
YOU'RE JUST GOING TO USE THE COOLING-OFF PERIOD, AREN'T YOU?
"COOLING-OFF PERIOD"
A SYSTEM IN WHICH ANYTHING YOU HAVE APPLIED FOR, OR ANY CONTRACTS YOU HAVE SIGNED, CAN BE CANCELED UNCONDITIONALLY WITHIN A FIXED PERIOD OF TIME. FOR EXAMPLE, MERCHANDISE CAN BE RETURNED TO THE STORE, OR INSURANCE THAT YOU'VE SIGNED UP FOR CAN BE CANCELED. DEPENDING ON THE MERCHANDISE AND THE METHOD OF SALE, EACH SPECIFIC CASE HAS ITS OWN RULES AND REGULATIONS.
LET'S JUST SAY THIS NEVER HAPPENED.
I'M SURE YOUR GIFTS WILL BE CANCELED JUST THE SAME WAY.
THINK ABOUT IT. I HAVE UNTIL MARCH 14...
...TO GIVE YOU AN OFFICIAL ANSWER.
A MONTH IS A LONG TIME.
THAT'S PLENTY OF TIME FOR A PERSON'S HEART TO CHANGE.

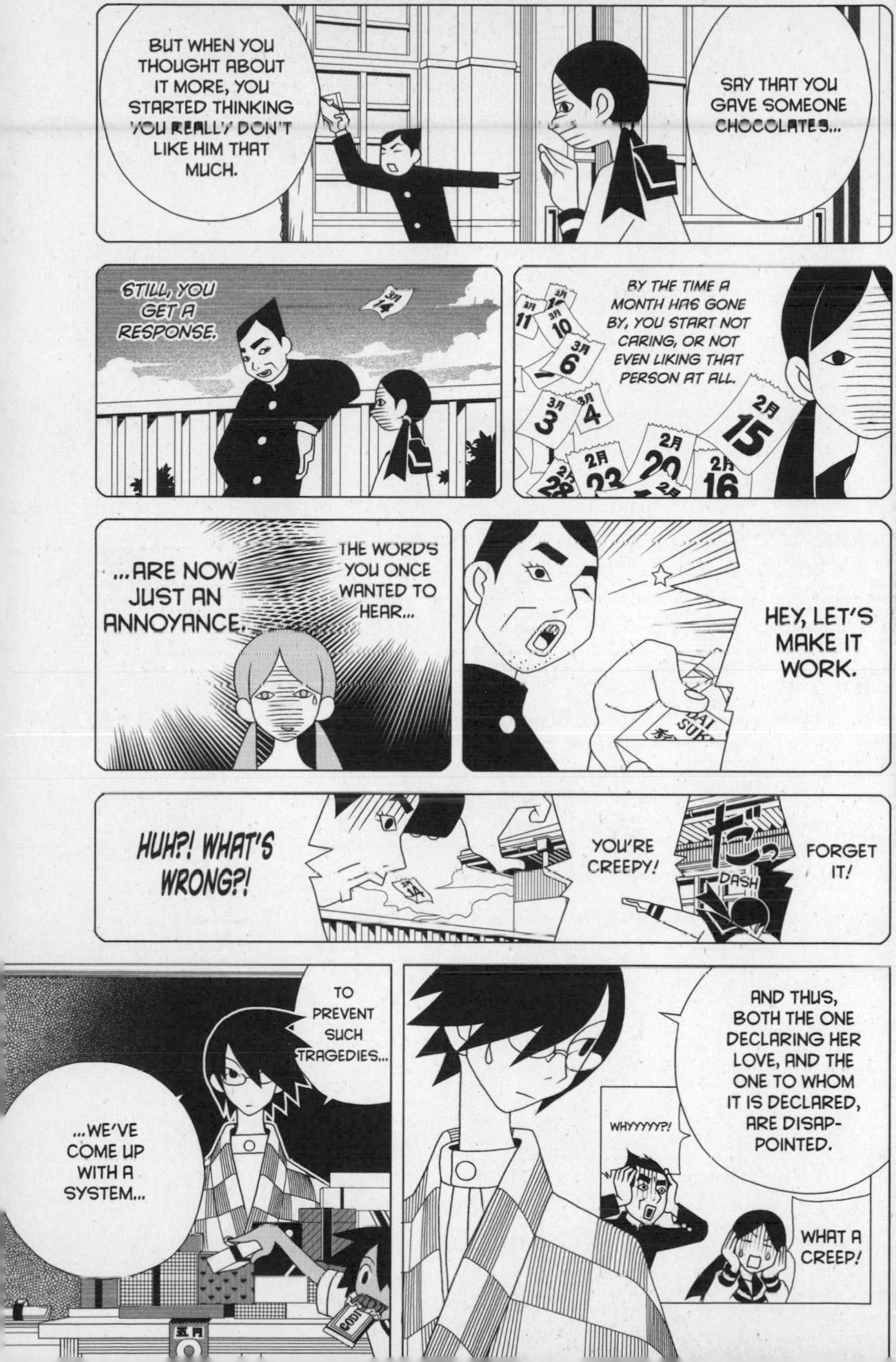
SAY THAT YOU GAVE SOMEONE CHOCOLATES...
BUT WHEN YOU THOUGHT ABOUT IT MORE, YOU STARTED THINKING YOU REALLY DON'T LIKE HIM THAT MUCH.
BY THE TIME A MONTH HAS GONE BY, YOU START NOT CARING, OR NOT EVEN LIKING THAT PERSON AT ALL.
STILL, YOU GET A RESPONSE.
HEY, LET'S MAKE IT WORK.
THE WORDS YOU ONCE WANTED TO HEAR...
...ARE NOW JUST AN ANNOYANCE.
FORGET IT!
だっ
DASH
YOU'RE CREEPY!
HUH?! WHAT'S WRONG?!
AND THUS, BOTH THE ONE DECLARING HER LOVE, AND THE ONE TO WHOM IT IS DECLARED, ARE DISAPPOINTED.
WHAT A CREEP!
WHYYYYY?!
TO PREVENT SUCH TRAGEDIES...
...WE'VE COME UP WITH A SYSTEM...

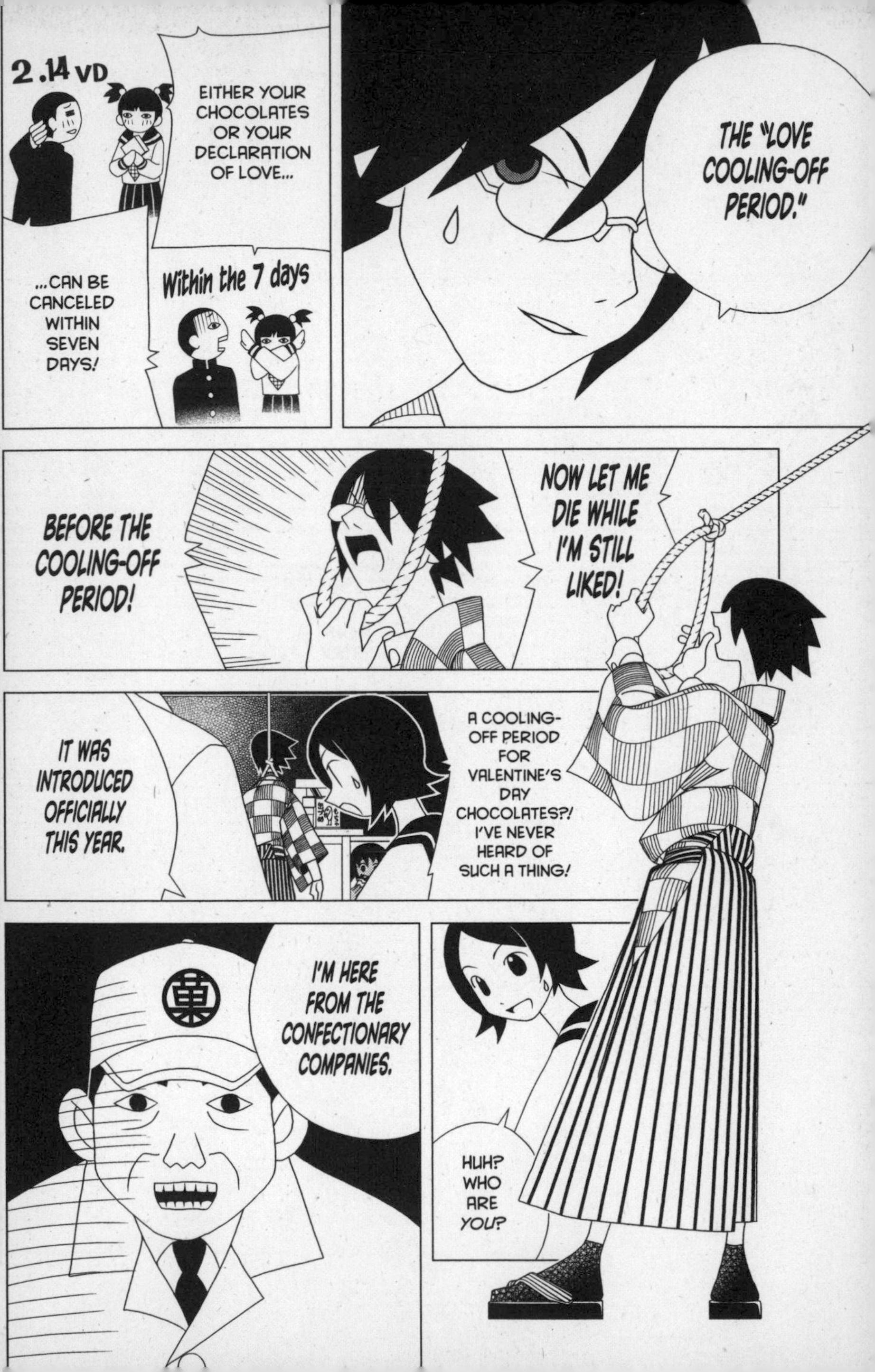
THE "LOVE COOLING-OFF PERIOD."
2.14 VD
EITHER YOUR CHOCOLATES OR YOUR DECLARATION OF LOVE...
Within the 7 days
...CAN BE CANCELED WITHIN SEVEN DAYS!
NOW LET ME DIE WHILE I'M STILL LIKED!
BEFORE THE COOLING-OFF PERIOD!
A COOLING-OFF PERIOD FOR VALENTINE'S DAY CHOCOLATES?! I'VE NEVER HEARD OF SUCH A THING!
IT WAS INTRODUCED OFFICIALLY THIS YEAR.
HUH? WHO ARE YOU?
I'M HERE FROM THE CONFECTIONARY COMPANIES.

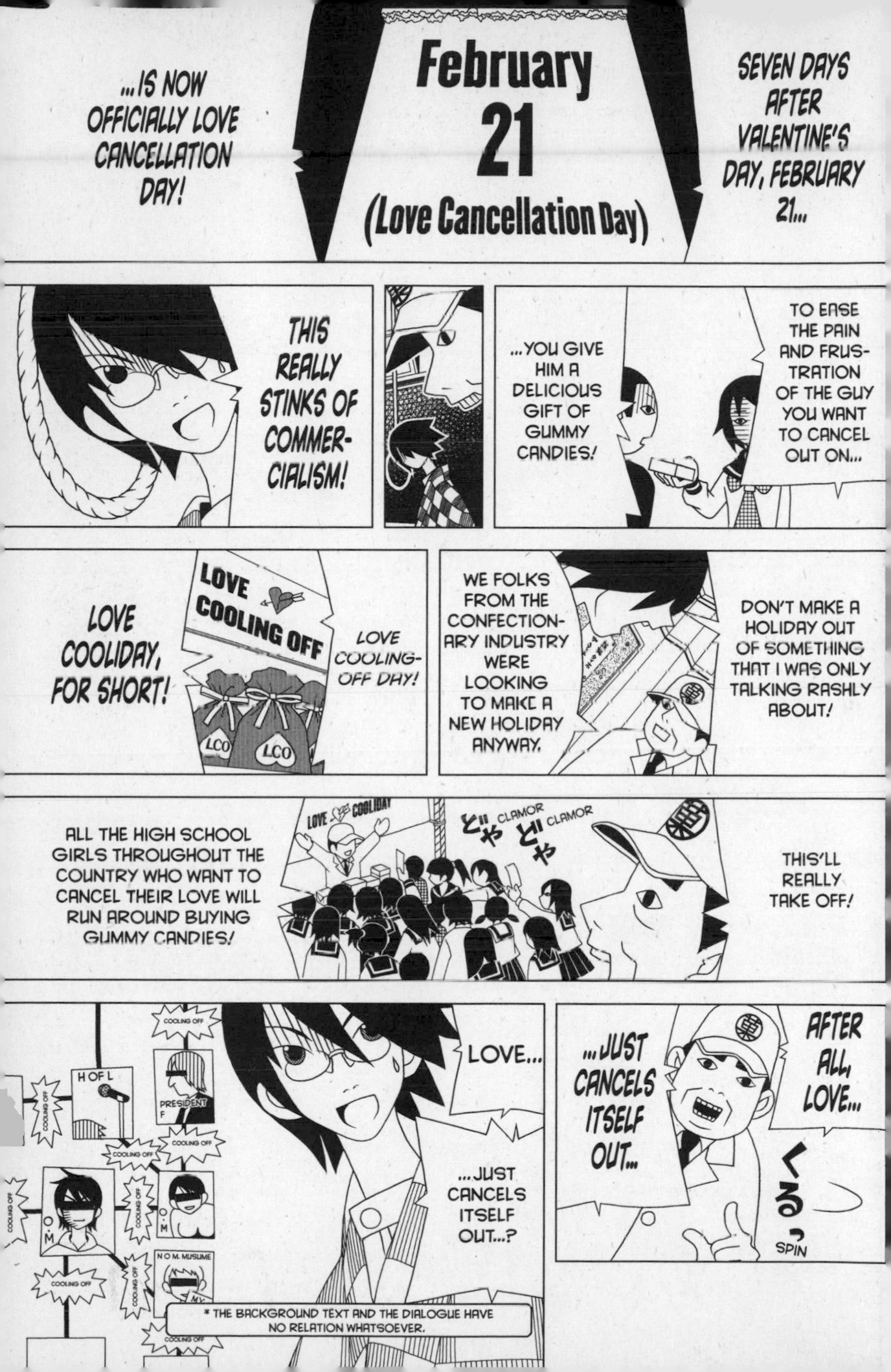
SEVEN DAYS AFTER VALENTINE'S DAY, FEBRUARY 21...
February 21 (Love Cancellation Day)
...IS NOW OFFICIALLY LOVE CANCELLATION DAY!
TO EASE THE PAIN AND FRUS-TRATION OF THE GUY YOU WANT TO CANCEL OUT ON...
...YOU GIVE HIM A DELICIOUS GIFT OF GUMMY CANDIES!
THIS REALLY STINKS OF COMMER-CIALISM!
DON'T MAKE A HOLIDAY OUT OF SOMETHING THAT I WAS ONLY TALKING RASHLY ABOUT!
WE FOLKS FROM THE CONFECTION-ARY INDUSTRY WERE LOOKING TO MAKE A NEW HOLIDAY ANYWAY.
LOVE COOLING-OFF DAY!
LOVE COOLING OFF
LCO
LCO
LOVE COOLIDAY, FOR SHORT!
THIS'LL REALLY TAKE OFF!
どや CLAMOR
どや CLAMOR
LOVE COOLIDAY
ALL THE HIGH SCHOOL GIRLS THROUGHOUT THE COUNTRY WHO WANT TO CANCEL THEIR LOVE WILL RUN AROUND BUYING GUMMY CANDIES!
AFTER ALL, LOVE...
...JUST CANCELS ITSELF OUT...
くる SPIN
LOVE...
...JUST CANCELS ITSELF OUT...?
COOLING OFF
H OF L
PRESIDENT F
O·M
N O M. MUSUME
MY
* THE BACKGROUND TEXT AND THE DIALOGUE HAVE NO RELATION WHATSOEVER.

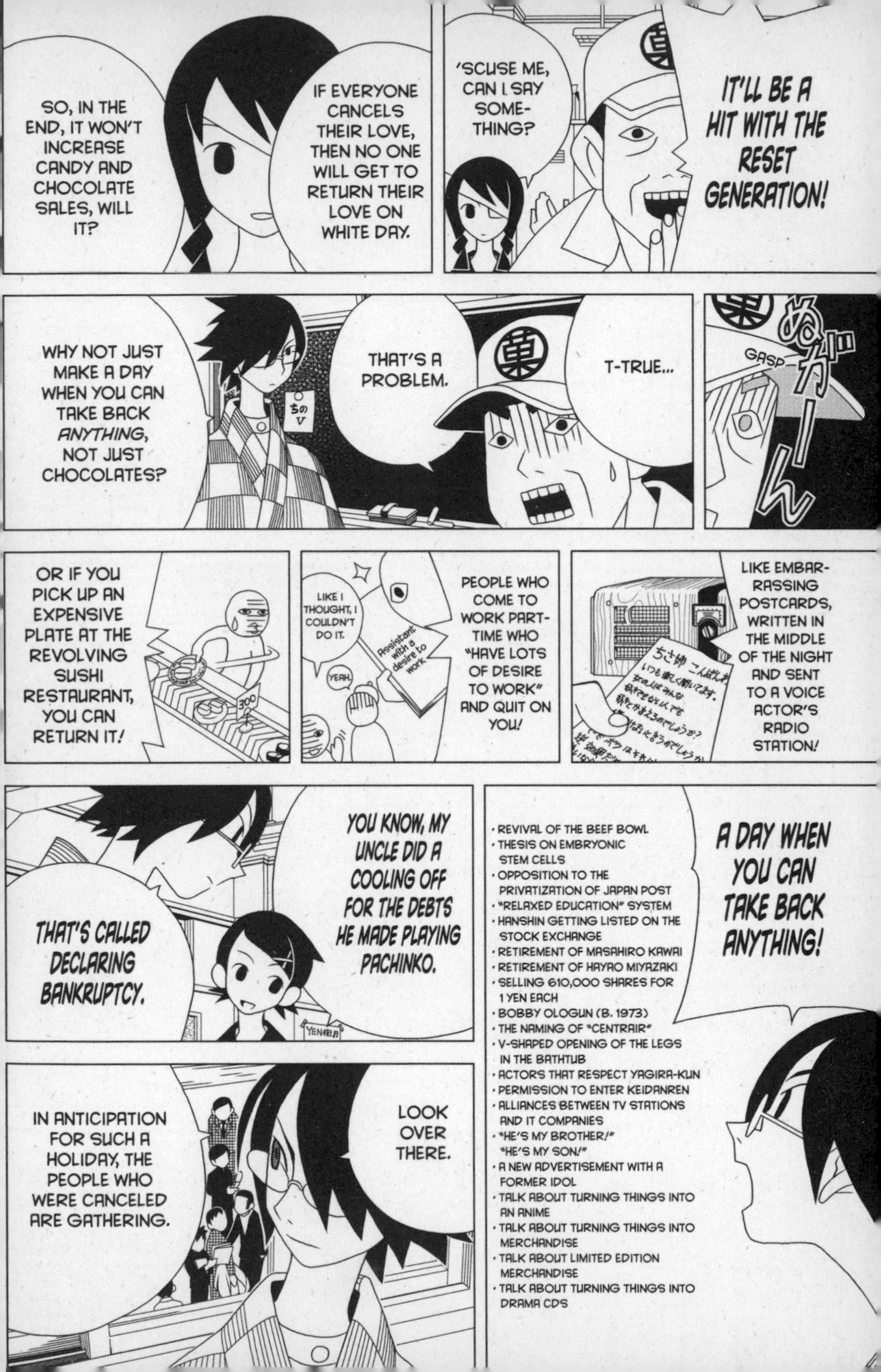
IT'LL BE A HIT WITH THE RESET GENERATION!
'SCUSE ME, CAN I SAY SOME-THING?
IF EVERYONE CANCELS THEIR LOVE, THEN NO ONE WILL GET TO RETURN THEIR LOVE ON WHITE DAY.
SO, IN THE END, IT WON'T INCREASE CANDY AND CHOCOLATE SALES, WILL IT?
ぬがーん
GASP
T-TRUE...
THAT'S A PROBLEM.
ちのV
WHY NOT JUST MAKE A DAY WHEN YOU CAN TAKE BACK *ANYTHING*, NOT JUST CHOCOLATES?
LIKE EMBARRASSING POSTCARDS, WRITTEN IN THE MIDDLE OF THE NIGHT AND SENT TO A VOICE ACTOR'S RADIO STATION!
PEOPLE WHO COME TO WORK PART-TIME WHO "HAVE LOTS OF DESIRE TO WORK" AND QUIT ON YOU!
LIKE I THOUGHT, I COULDN'T DO IT.
Assistant with a desire to work
YEAH.
OR IF YOU PICK UP AN EXPENSIVE PLATE AT THE REVOLVING SUSHI RESTAURANT, YOU CAN RETURN IT!
300
A DAY WHEN YOU CAN TAKE BACK ANYTHING!
• REVIVAL OF THE BEEF BOWL
• THESIS ON EMBRYONIC STEM CELLS
• OPPOSITION TO THE PRIVATIZATION OF JAPAN POST
• "RELAXED EDUCATION" SYSTEM
• HANSHIN GETTING LISTED ON THE STOCK EXCHANGE
• RETIREMENT OF MASAHIRO KAWAI
• RETIREMENT OF HAYAO MIYAZAKI
• SELLING 610,000 SHARES FOR 1 YEN EACH
• BOBBY OLOGUN (B. 1973)
• THE NAMING OF "CENTRAIR"
• V-SHAPED OPENING OF THE LEGS IN THE BATHTUB
• ACTORS THAT RESPECT YAGIRA-KUN
• PERMISSION TO ENTER KEIDANREN
• ALLIANCES BETWEEN TV STATIONS AND IT COMPANIES
• "HE'S MY BROTHER!" "HE'S MY SON!"
• A NEW ADVERTISEMENT WITH A FORMER IDOL
• TALK ABOUT TURNING THINGS INTO AN ANIME
• TALK ABOUT TURNING THINGS INTO MERCHANDISE
• TALK ABOUT LIMITED EDITION MERCHANDISE
• TALK ABOUT TURNING THINGS INTO DRAMA CDS
YOU KNOW, MY UNCLE DID A COOLING OFF FOR THE DEBTS HE MADE PLAYING PACHINKO.
THAT'S CALLED DECLARING BANKRUPTCY.
LOOK OVER THERE.
IN ANTICIPATION FOR SUCH A HOLIDAY, THE PEOPLE WHO WERE CANCELED ARE GATHERING.

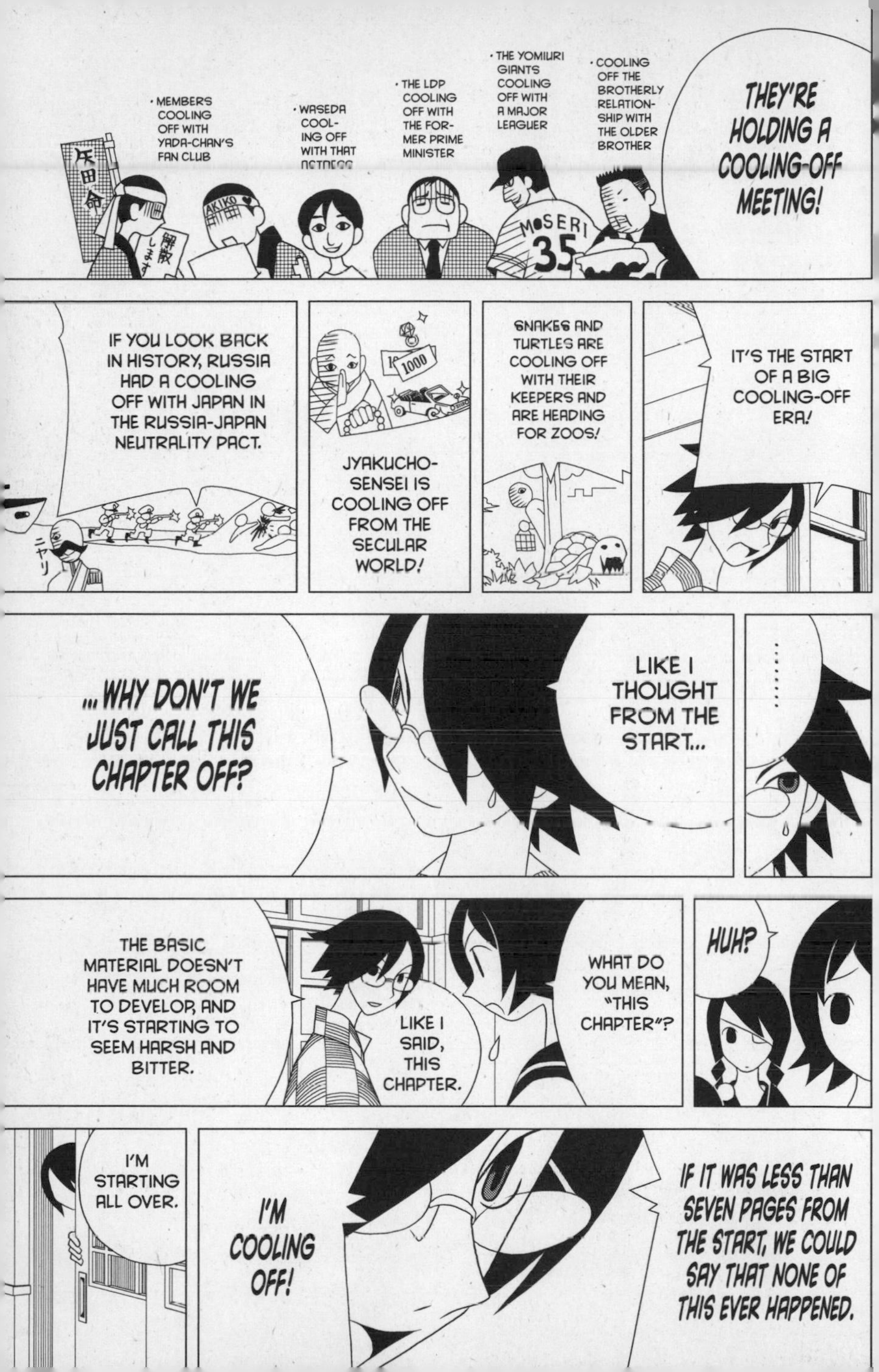

THEY'RE HOLDING A COOLING-OFF MEETING!
· COOLING OFF THE BROTHERLY RELATION-SHIP WITH THE OLDER BROTHER
· THE YOMIURI GIANTS COOLING OFF WITH A MAJOR LEAGUER
MOSERI 35
· THE LDP COOLING OFF WITH THE FOR-MER PRIME MINISTER
· WASEDA COOL-ING OFF WITH THAT
AKIKO
解散します
· MEMBERS COOLING OFF WITH YADA-CHAN'S FAN CLUB
矢田命
IT'S THE START OF A BIG COOLING-OFF ERA!
SNAKES AND TURTLES ARE COOLING OFF WITH THEIR KEEPERS AND ARE HEADING FOR ZOOS!
1000
JYAKUCHO-SENSEI IS COOLING OFF FROM THE SECULAR WORLD!
IF YOU LOOK BACK IN HISTORY, RUSSIA HAD A COOLING OFF WITH JAPAN IN THE RUSSIA-JAPAN NEUTRALITY PACT.
ニヤリ
……
LIKE I THOUGHT FROM THE START...
...WHY DON'T WE JUST CALL THIS CHAPTER OFF?
HUH?
WHAT DO YOU MEAN, "THIS CHAPTER"?
LIKE I SAID, THIS CHAPTER.
THE BASIC MATERIAL DOESN'T HAVE MUCH ROOM TO DEVELOP, AND IT'S STARTING TO SEEM HARSH AND BITTER.
IF IT WAS LESS THAN SEVEN PAGES FROM THE START, WE COULD SAY THAT NONE OF THIS EVER HAPPENED.
I'M COOLING OFF!
I'M STARTING ALL OVER.

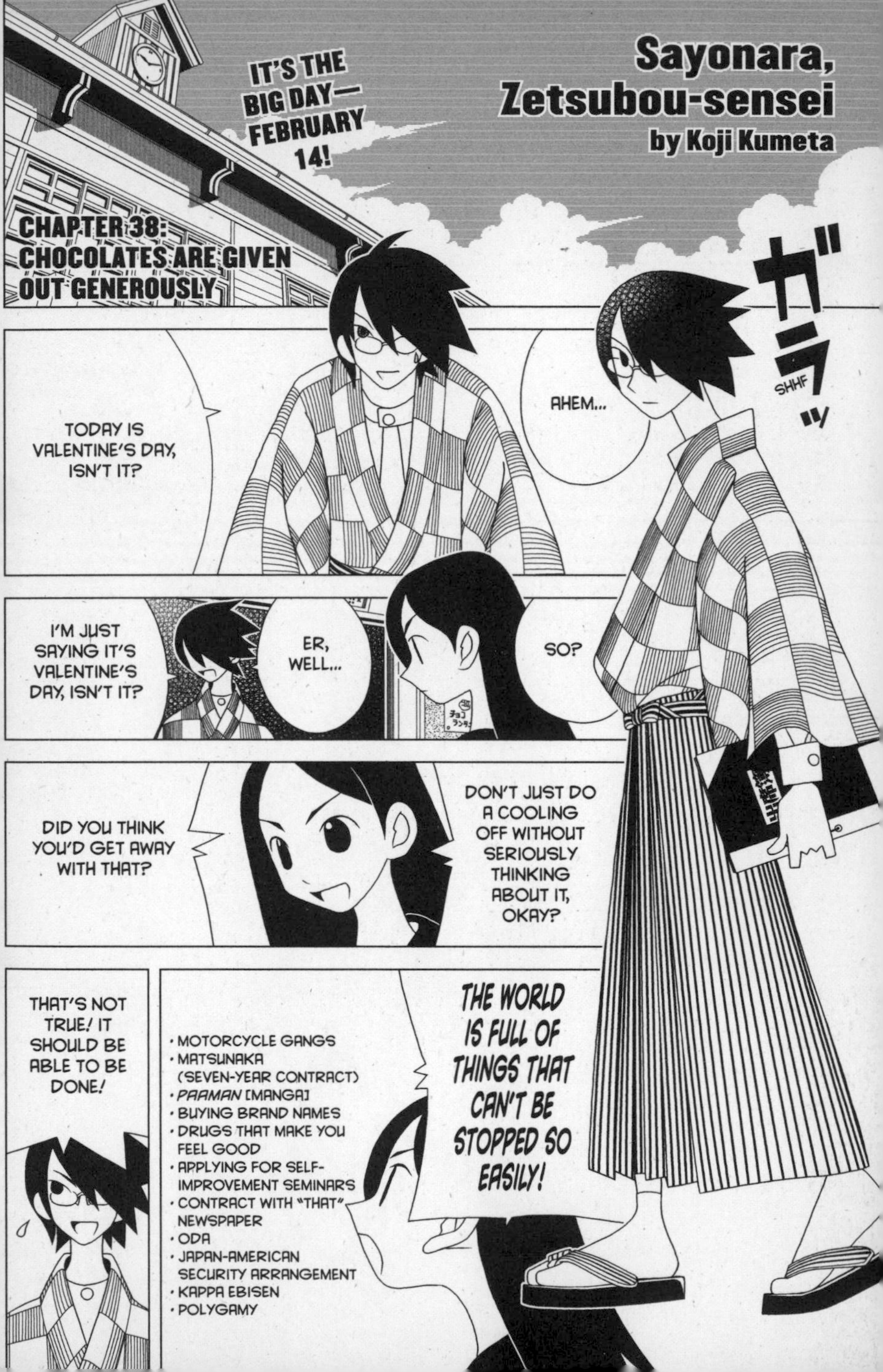
Sayonara, Zetsubou-sensei
by Koji Kumeta
IT'S THE BIG DAY— FEBRUARY 14!
CHAPTER 38: CHOCOLATES ARE GIVEN OUT GENEROUSLY
ガラッ
SHHF
AHEM...
TODAY IS VALENTINE'S DAY, ISN'T IT?
SO?
ER, WELL...
I'M JUST SAYING IT'S VALENTINE'S DAY, ISN'T IT?
DON'T JUST DO A COOLING OFF WITHOUT SERIOUSLY THINKING ABOUT IT, OKAY?
DID YOU THINK YOU'D GET AWAY WITH THAT?
THE WORLD IS FULL OF THINGS THAT CAN'T BE STOPPED SO EASILY!
• MOTORCYCLE GANGS
• MATSUNAKA (SEVEN-YEAR CONTRACT)
• *PAAMAN* [MANGA]
• BUYING BRAND NAMES
• DRUGS THAT MAKE YOU FEEL GOOD
• APPLYING FOR SELF-IMPROVEMENT SEMINARS
• CONTRACT WITH "THAT" NEWSPAPER
• ODA
• JAPAN-AMERICAN SECURITY ARRANGEMENT
• KAPPA EBISEN
• POLYGAMY
THAT'S NOT TRUE! IT SHOULD BE ABLE TO BE DONE!

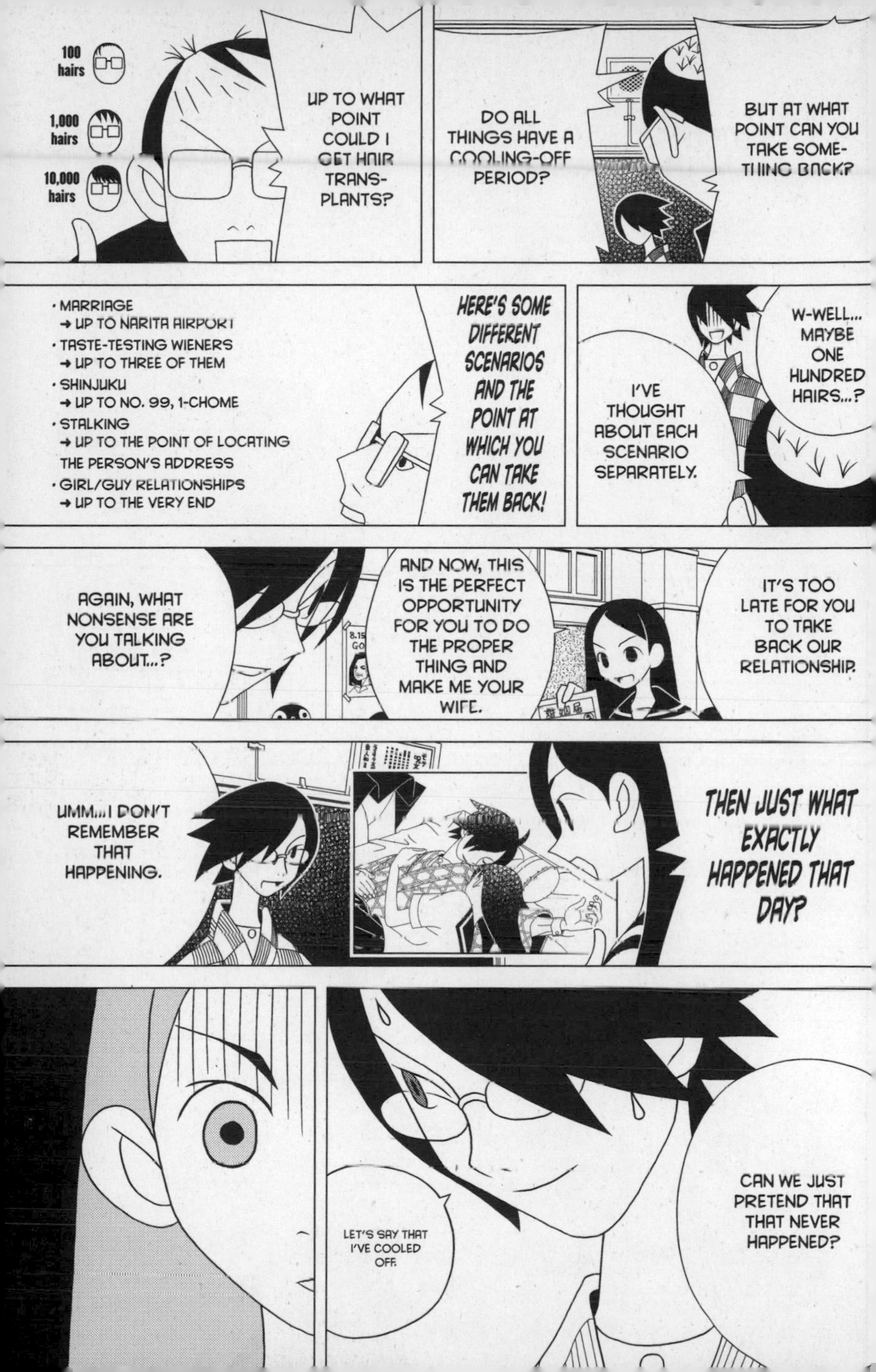
BUT AT WHAT POINT CAN YOU TAKE SOME-THING BACK?
DO ALL THINGS HAVE A COOLING-OFF PERIOD?
UP TO WHAT POINT COULD I GET HAIR TRANS-PLANTS?
100 hairs
1,000 hairs
10,000 hairs
W-WELL... MAYBE ONE HUNDRED HAIRS...?
I'VE THOUGHT ABOUT EACH SCENARIO SEPARATELY.
HERE'S SOME DIFFERENT SCENARIOS AND THE POINT AT WHICH YOU CAN TAKE THEM BACK!
• MARRIAGE → UP TO NARITA AIRPORT
• TASTE-TESTING WIENERS → UP TO THREE OF THEM
• SHINJUKU → UP TO NO. 99, 1-CHOME
• STALKING → UP TO THE POINT OF LOCATING THE PERSON'S ADDRESS
• GIRL/GUY RELATIONSHIPS → UP TO THE VERY END
IT'S TOO LATE FOR YOU TO TAKE BACK OUR RELATIONSHIP.
AND NOW, THIS IS THE PERFECT OPPORTUNITY FOR YOU TO DO THE PROPER THING AND MAKE ME YOUR WIFE.
AGAIN, WHAT NONSENSE ARE YOU TALKING ABOUT...?
THEN JUST WHAT EXACTLY HAPPENED THAT DAY?
UMM... I DON'T REMEMBER THAT HAPPENING.
CAN WE JUST PRETEND THAT THAT NEVER HAPPENED?
LET'S SAY THAT I'VE COOLED OFF.

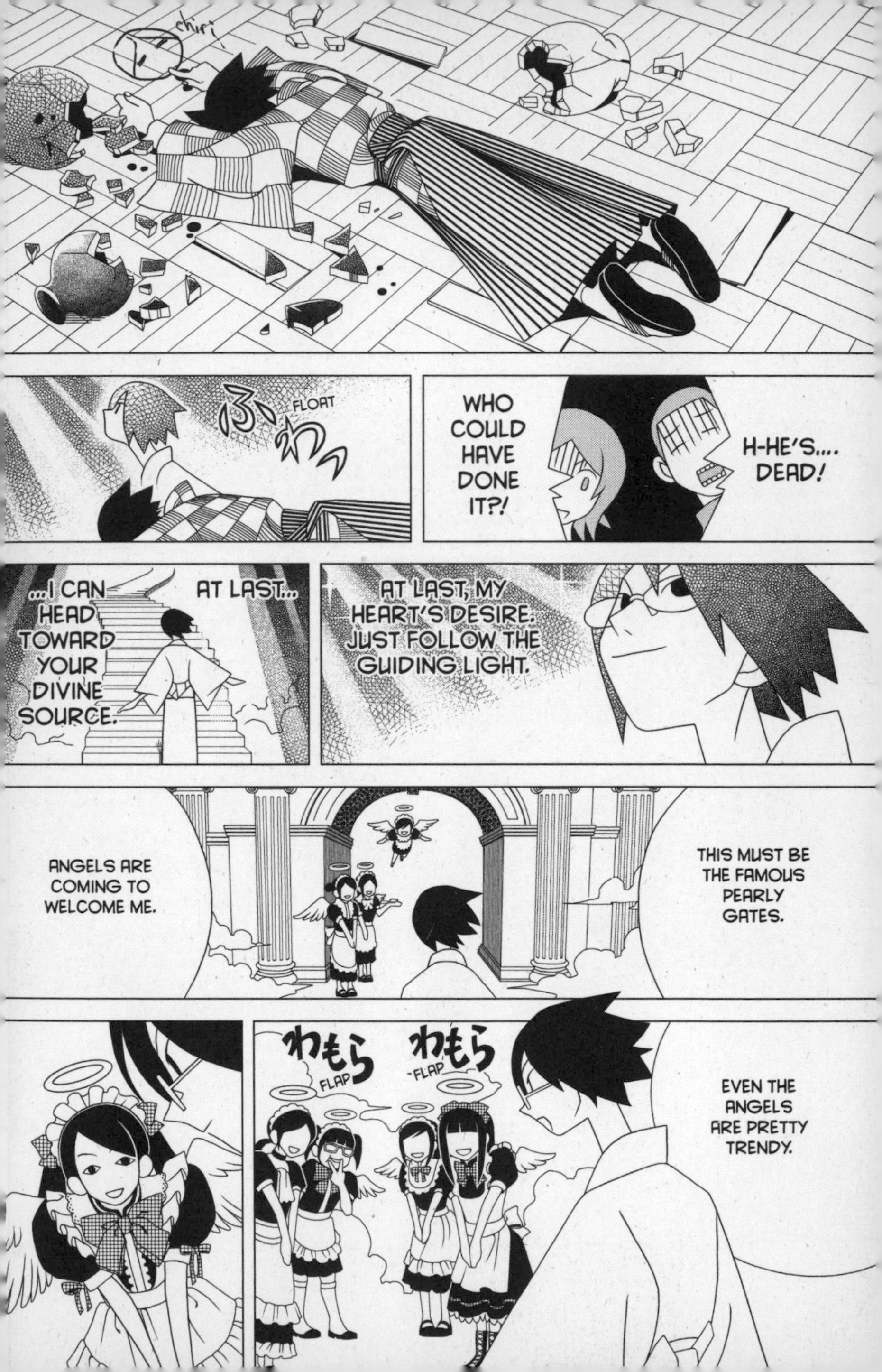
chiri
H-HE'S.... DEAD!
WHO COULD HAVE DONE IT?!
ふわ
FLOAT
AT LAST, MY HEART'S DESIRE. JUST FOLLOW THE GUIDING LIGHT.
AT LAST...
...I CAN HEAD TOWARD YOUR DIVINE SOURCE.
THIS MUST BE THE FAMOUS PEARLY GATES.
ANGELS ARE COMING TO WELCOME ME.
EVEN THE ANGELS ARE PRETTY TRENDY.
わもら
FLAP
わもら
FLAP

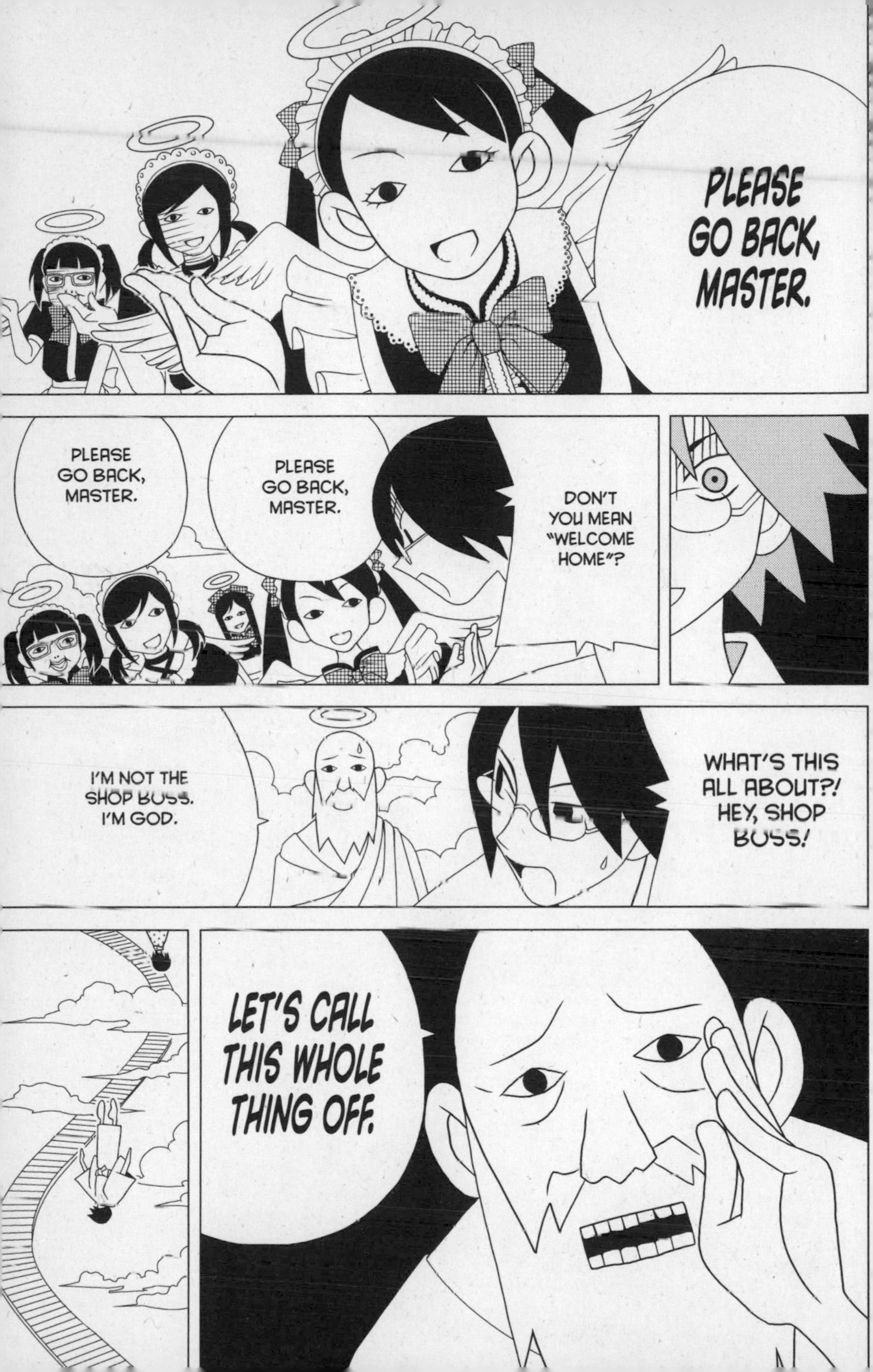
PLEASE GO BACK, MASTER.
DON'T YOU MEAN "WELCOME HOME"?
PLEASE GO BACK, MASTER.
PLEASE GO BACK, MASTER.
WHAT'S THIS ALL ABOUT?! HEY, SHOP BOSS!
I'M NOT THE SHOP BOSS. I'M GOD.
LET'S CALL THIS WHOLE THING OFF.

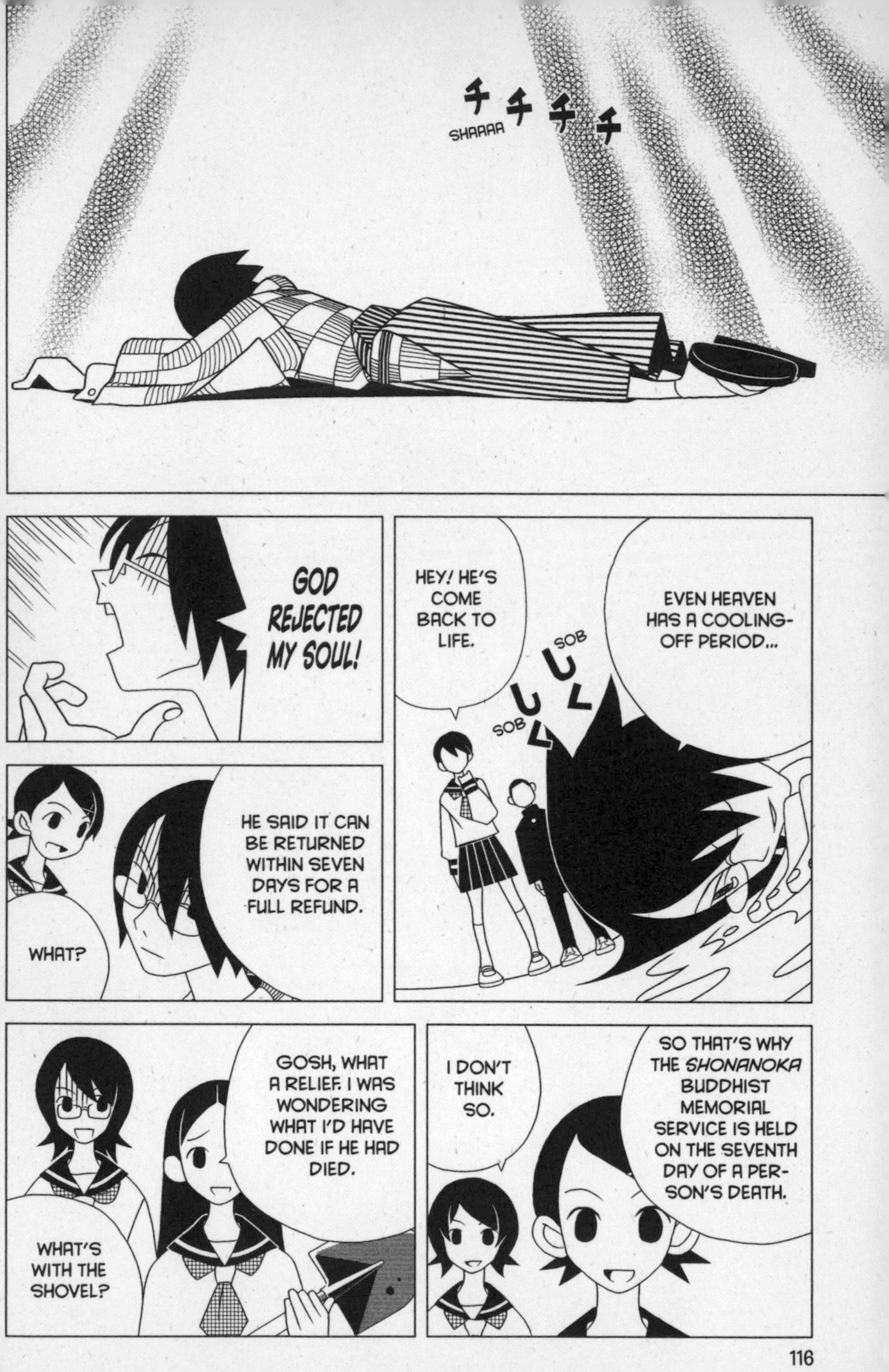
チチチチ
SHAAAA
EVEN HEAVEN HAS A COOLING-OFF PERIOD...
HEY! HE'S COME BACK TO LIFE.
SOB
SOB
GOD REJECTED MY SOUL!
HE SAID IT CAN BE RETURNED WITHIN SEVEN DAYS FOR A FULL REFUND.
WHAT?
SO THAT'S WHY THE *SHONANOKA* BUDDHIST MEMORIAL SERVICE IS HELD ON THE SEVENTH DAY OF A PERSON'S DEATH.
I DON'T THINK SO.
GOSH, WHAT A RELIEF. I WAS WONDERING WHAT I'D HAVE DONE IF HE HAD DIED.
WHAT'S WITH THE SHOVEL?

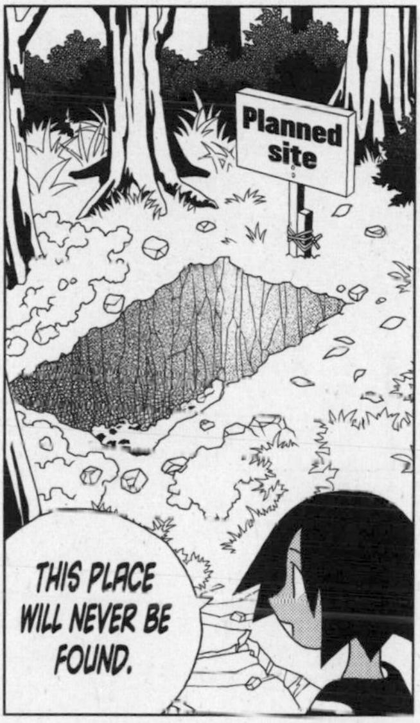
Planned site
THIS PLACE WILL NEVER BE FOUND.

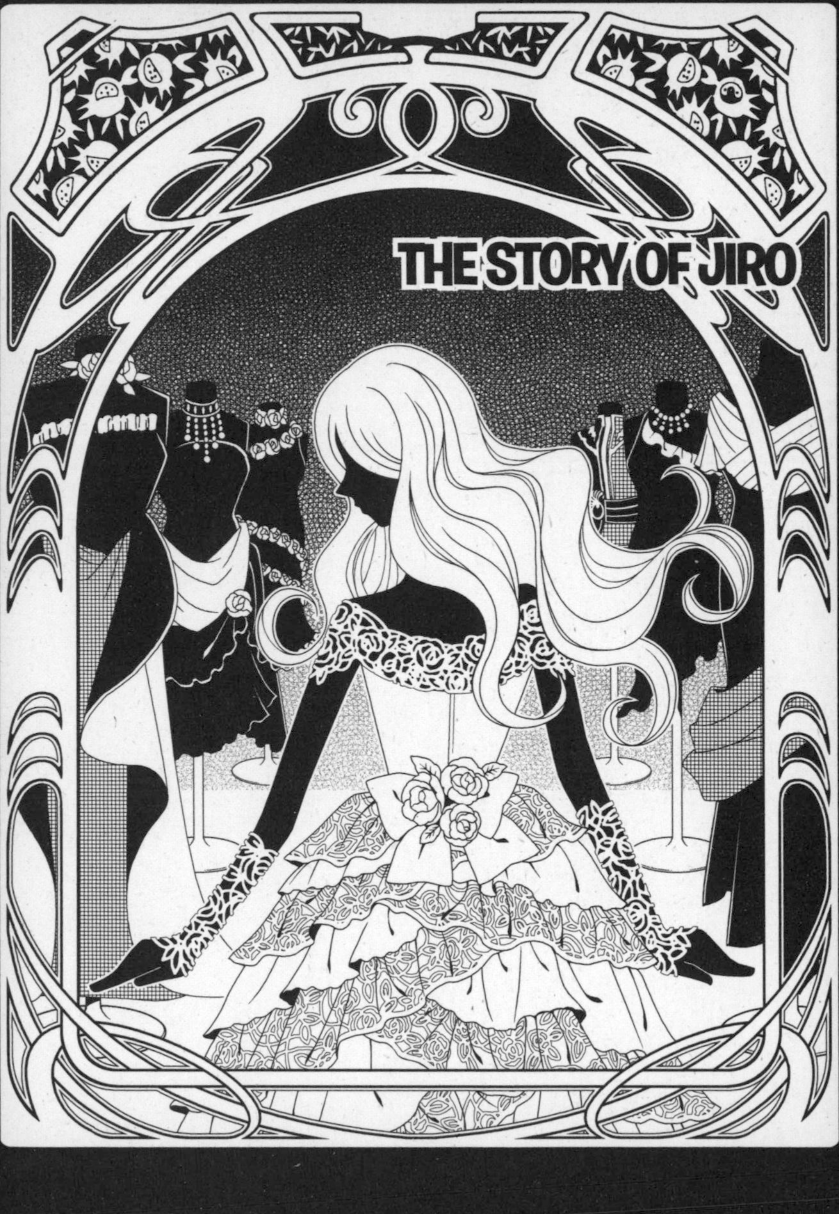
THE STORY OF JIRO

CHAPTER 39

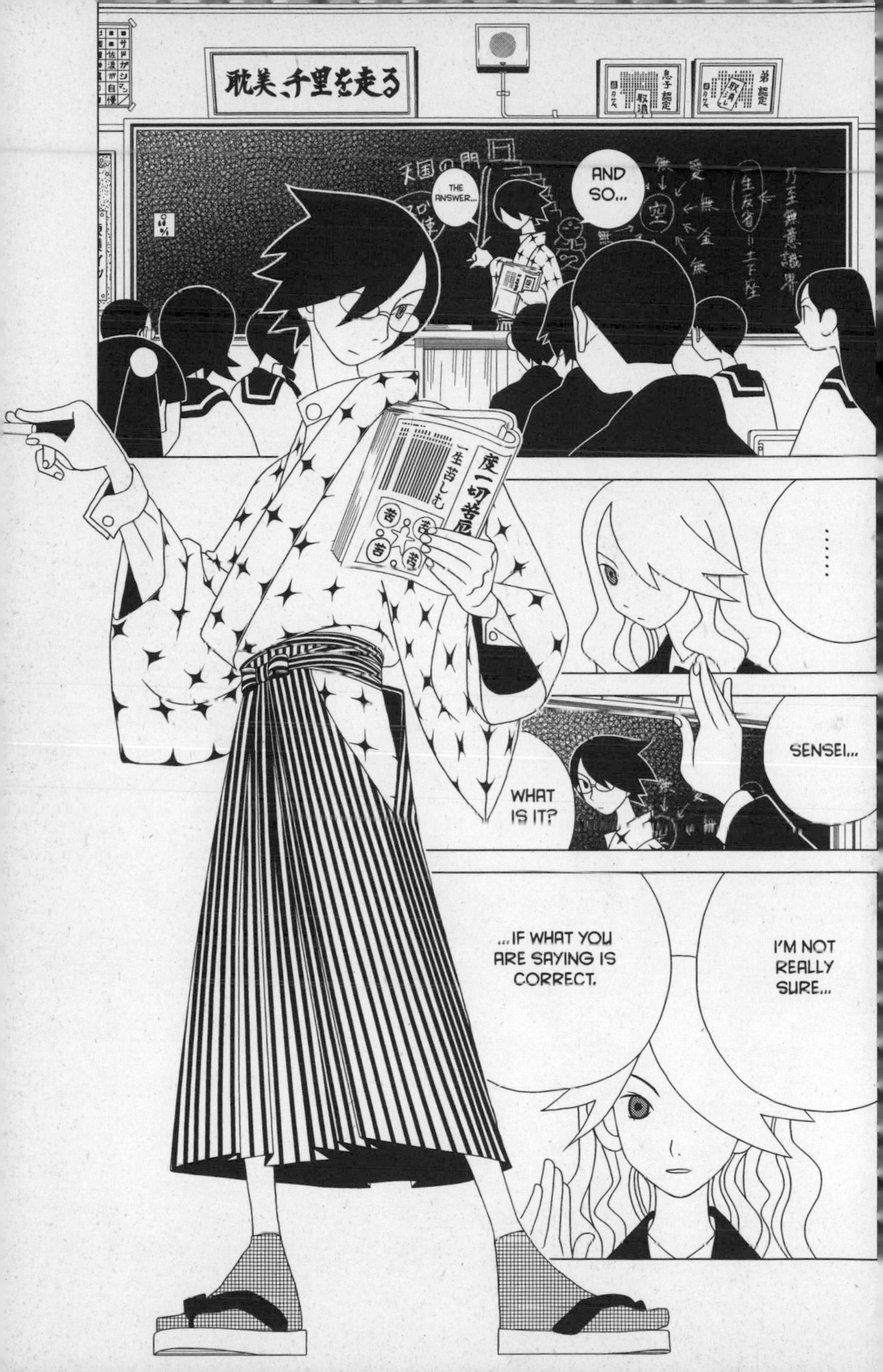

耽美、千里を走る
AND SO...
THE ANSWER...
......
SENSEI...
WHAT IS IT?
I'M NOT REALLY SURE...
...IF WHAT YOU ARE SAYING IS CORRECT.

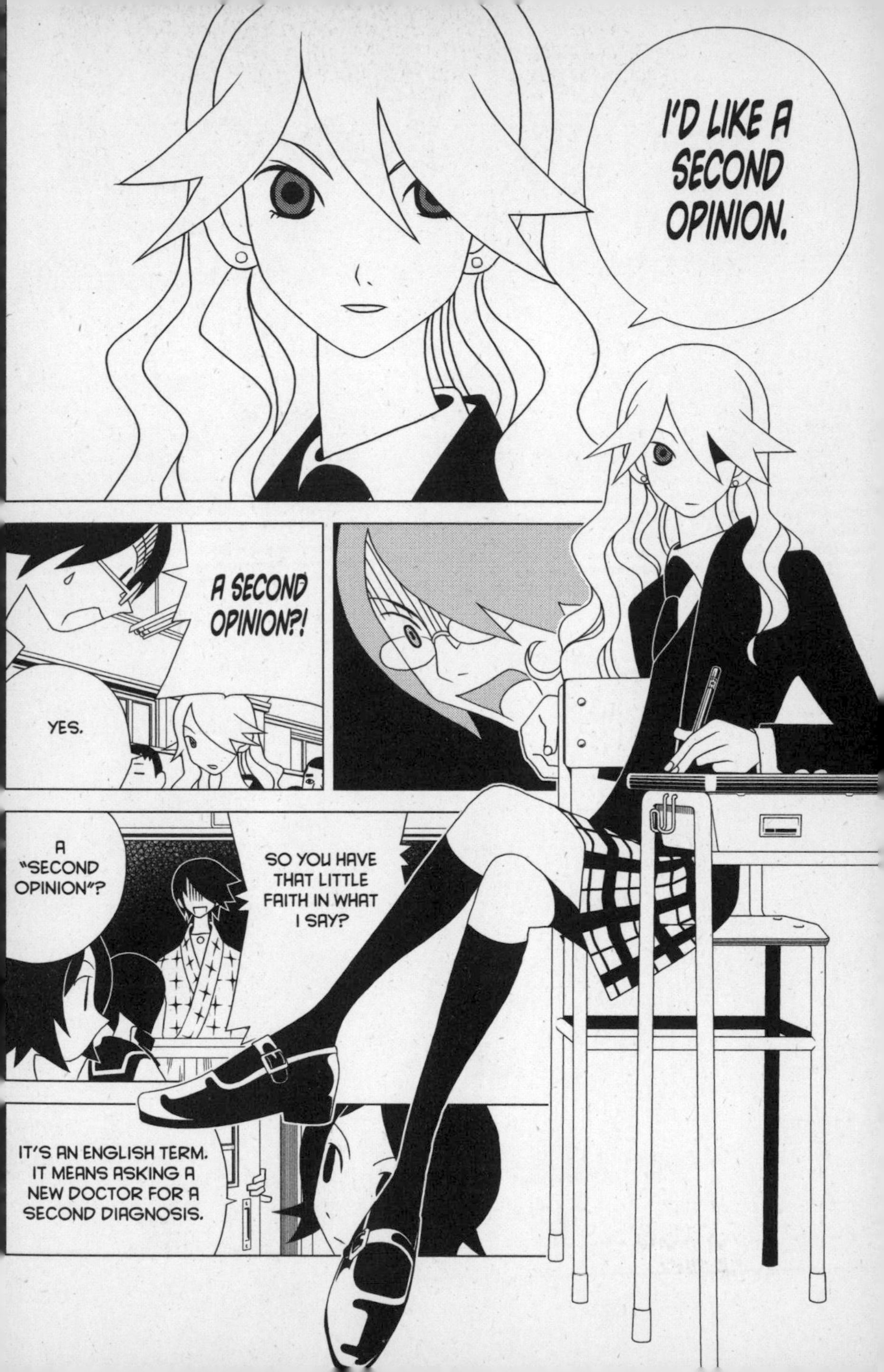
I'D LIKE A SECOND OPINION.
A SECOND OPINION?!
YES.
SO YOU HAVE THAT LITTLE FAITH IN WHAT I SAY?
A "SECOND OPINION"?
IT'S AN ENGLISH TERM. IT MEANS ASKING A NEW DOCTOR FOR A SECOND DIAGNOSIS.

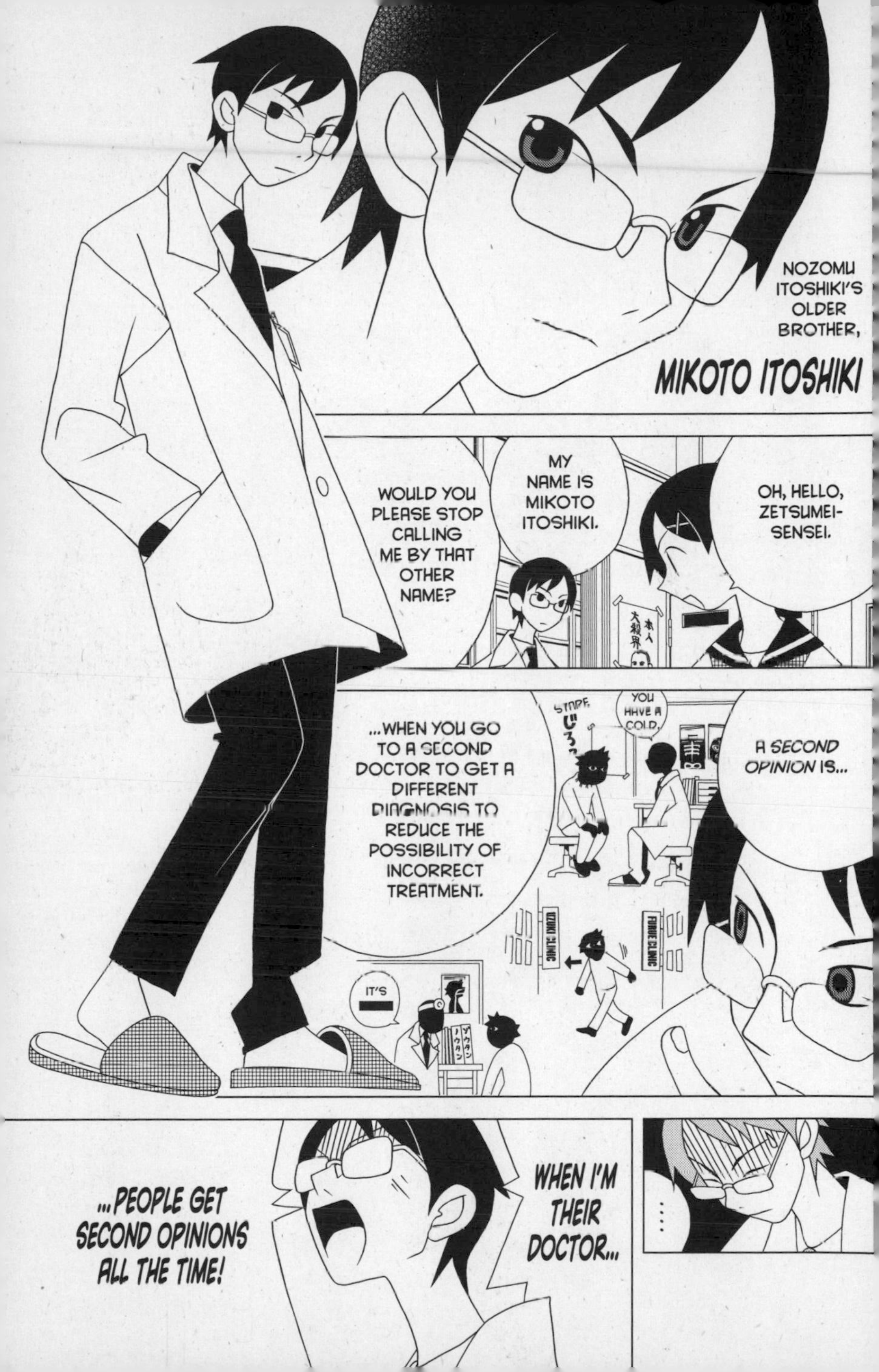
NOZOMU ITOSHIKI'S OLDER BROTHER,
MIKOTO ITOSHIKI
OH, HELLO, ZETSUMEI-SENSEI.
MY NAME IS MIKOTO ITOSHIKI.
WOULD YOU PLEASE STOP CALLING ME BY THAT OTHER NAME?
A SECOND OPINION IS...
YOU HAVE A COLD.
STARE
...WHEN YOU GO TO A SECOND DOCTOR TO GET A DIFFERENT DIAGNOSIS TO REDUCE THE POSSIBILITY OF INCORRECT TREATMENT.
IT'S [redacted]
....
WHEN I'M THEIR DOCTOR...
...PEOPLE GET SECOND OPINIONS ALL THE TIME!

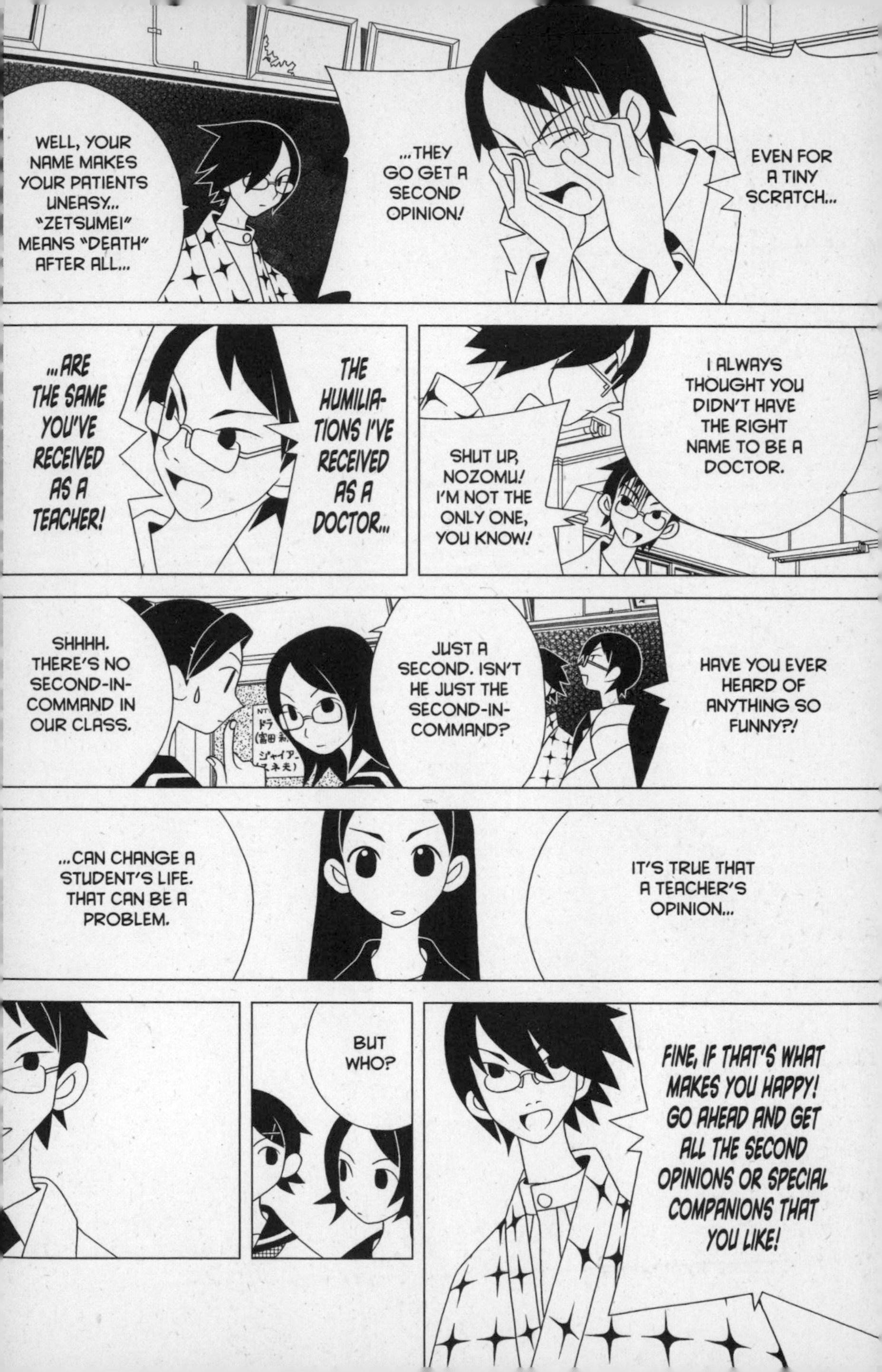
EVEN FOR A TINY SCRATCH...
...THEY GO GET A SECOND OPINION!
WELL, YOUR NAME MAKES YOUR PATIENTS UNEASY... "ZETSUMEI" MEANS "DEATH" AFTER ALL...
I ALWAYS THOUGHT YOU DIDN'T HAVE THE RIGHT NAME TO BE A DOCTOR.
SHUT UP, NOZOMU! I'M NOT THE ONLY ONE, YOU KNOW!
THE HUMILIA-TIONS I'VE RECEIVED AS A DOCTOR...
...ARE THE SAME YOU'VE RECEIVED AS A TEACHER!
HAVE YOU EVER HEARD OF ANYTHING SO FUNNY?!
JUST A SECOND. ISN'T HE JUST THE SECOND-IN-COMMAND?
SHHHH. THERE'S NO SECOND-IN-COMMAND IN OUR CLASS.
IT'S TRUE THAT A TEACHER'S OPINION...
...CAN CHANGE A STUDENT'S LIFE. THAT CAN BE A PROBLEM.
FINE, IF THAT'S WHAT MAKES YOU HAPPY! GO AHEAD AND GET ALL THE SECOND OPINIONS OR SPECIAL COMPANIONS THAT YOU LIKE!
BUT WHO?

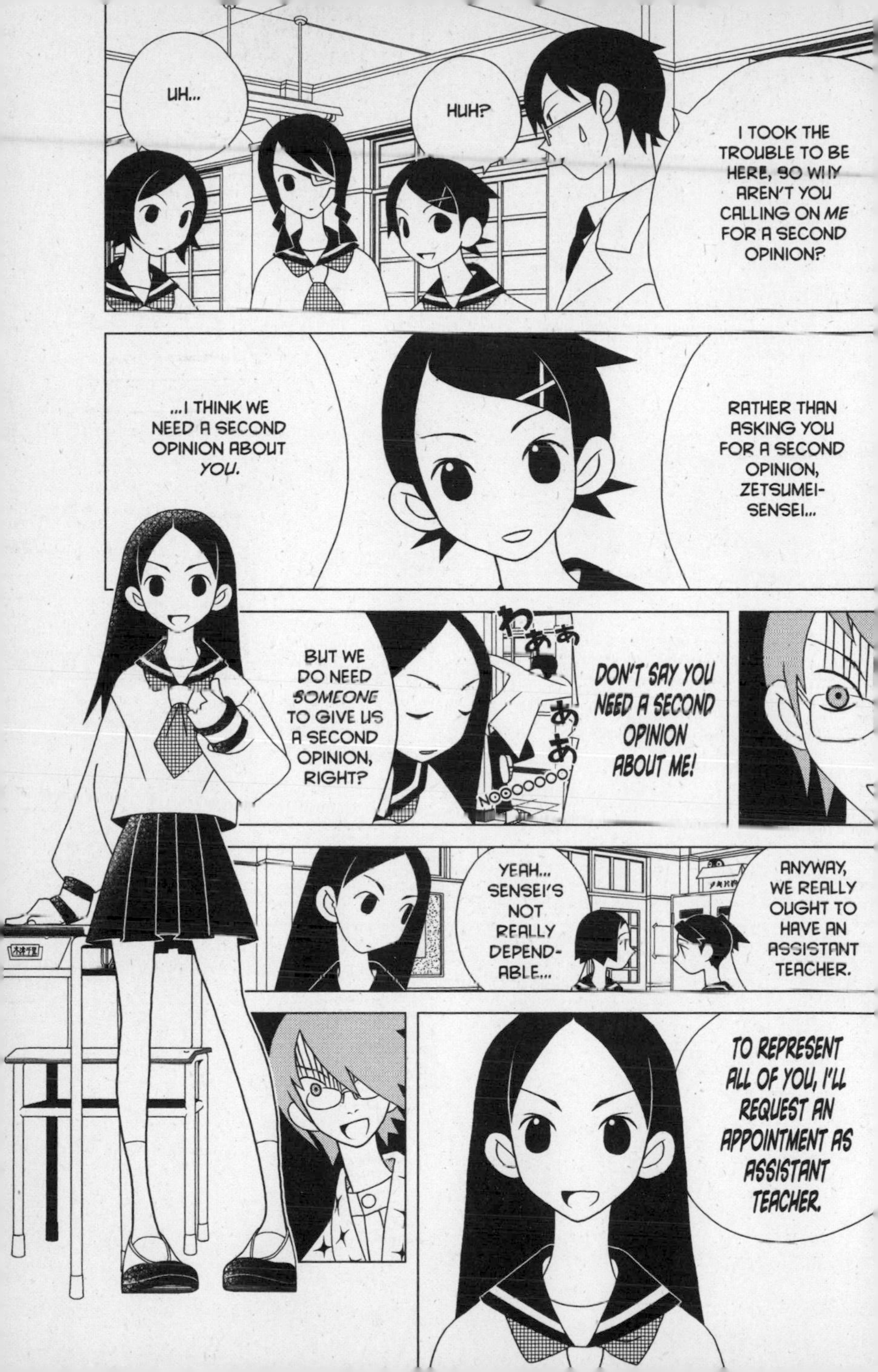
I TOOK THE TROUBLE TO BE HERE, SO WHY AREN'T YOU CALLING ON *ME* FOR A SECOND OPINION?
HUH?
UH...
RATHER THAN ASKING YOU FOR A SECOND OPINION, ZETSUMEI-SENSEI...
...I THINK WE NEED A SECOND OPINION ABOUT *YOU*.
DON'T SAY YOU NEED A SECOND OPINION ABOUT ME!
わああああ
NOOOOOOO
BUT WE DO NEED *SOMEONE* TO GIVE US A SECOND OPINION, RIGHT?
ANYWAY, WE REALLY OUGHT TO HAVE AN ASSISTANT TEACHER.
YEAH... SENSEI'S NOT REALLY DEPENDABLE...
TO REPRESENT ALL OF YOU, I'LL REQUEST AN APPOINTMENT AS ASSISTANT TEACHER.

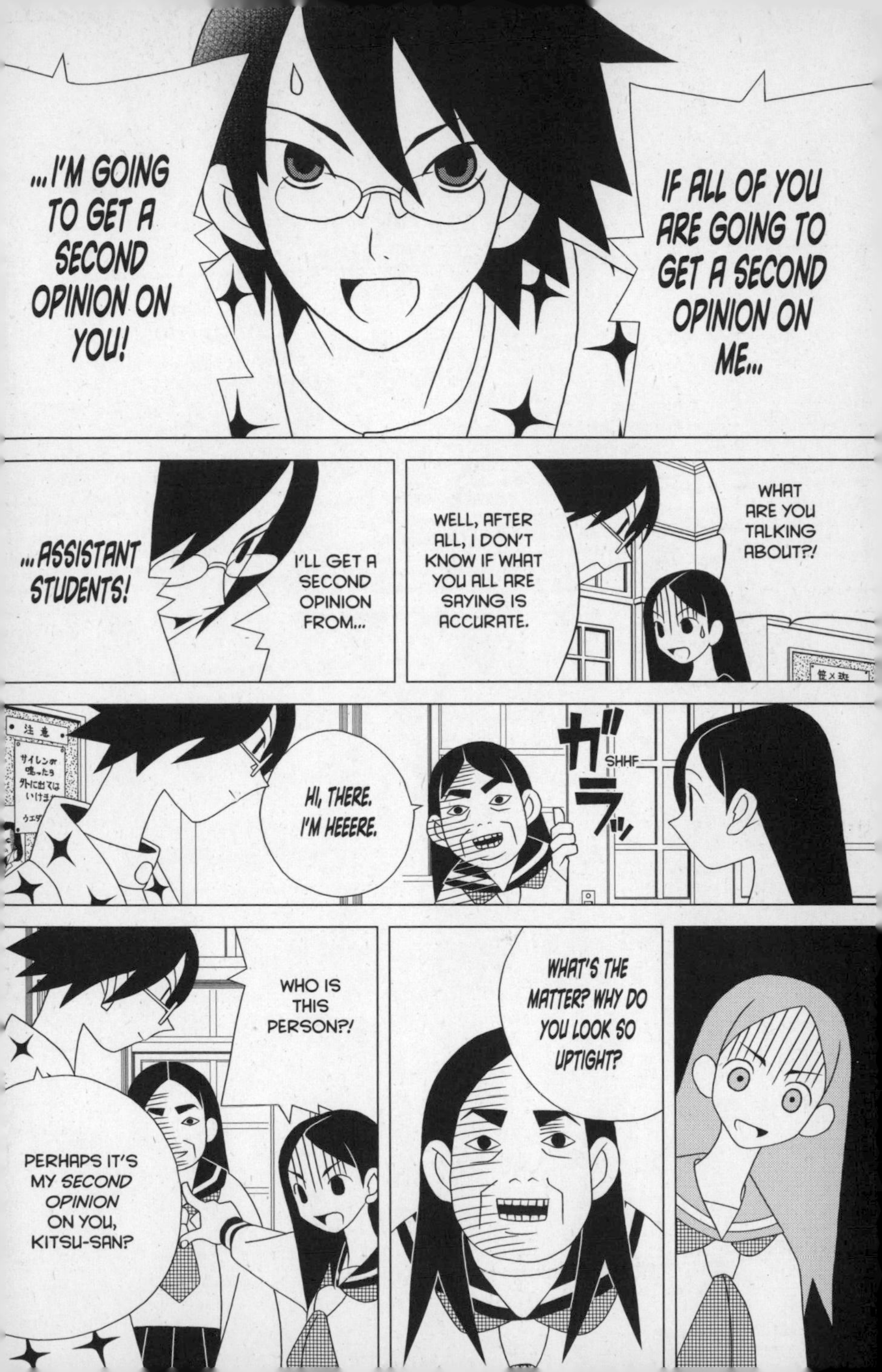
IF ALL OF YOU ARE GOING TO GET A SECOND OPINION ON ME...
...I'M GOING TO GET A SECOND OPINION ON YOU!
WHAT ARE YOU TALKING ABOUT?!
WELL, AFTER ALL, I DON'T KNOW IF WHAT YOU ALL ARE SAYING IS ACCURATE.
I'LL GET A SECOND OPINION FROM...
...ASSISTANT STUDENTS!
ガラッ
SHHF
HI, THERE. I'M HEEERE.
注意
WHAT'S THE MATTER? WHY DO YOU LOOK SO UPTIGHT?
WHO IS THIS PERSON?!
PERHAPS IT'S MY *SECOND OPINION* ON YOU, KITSU-SAN?

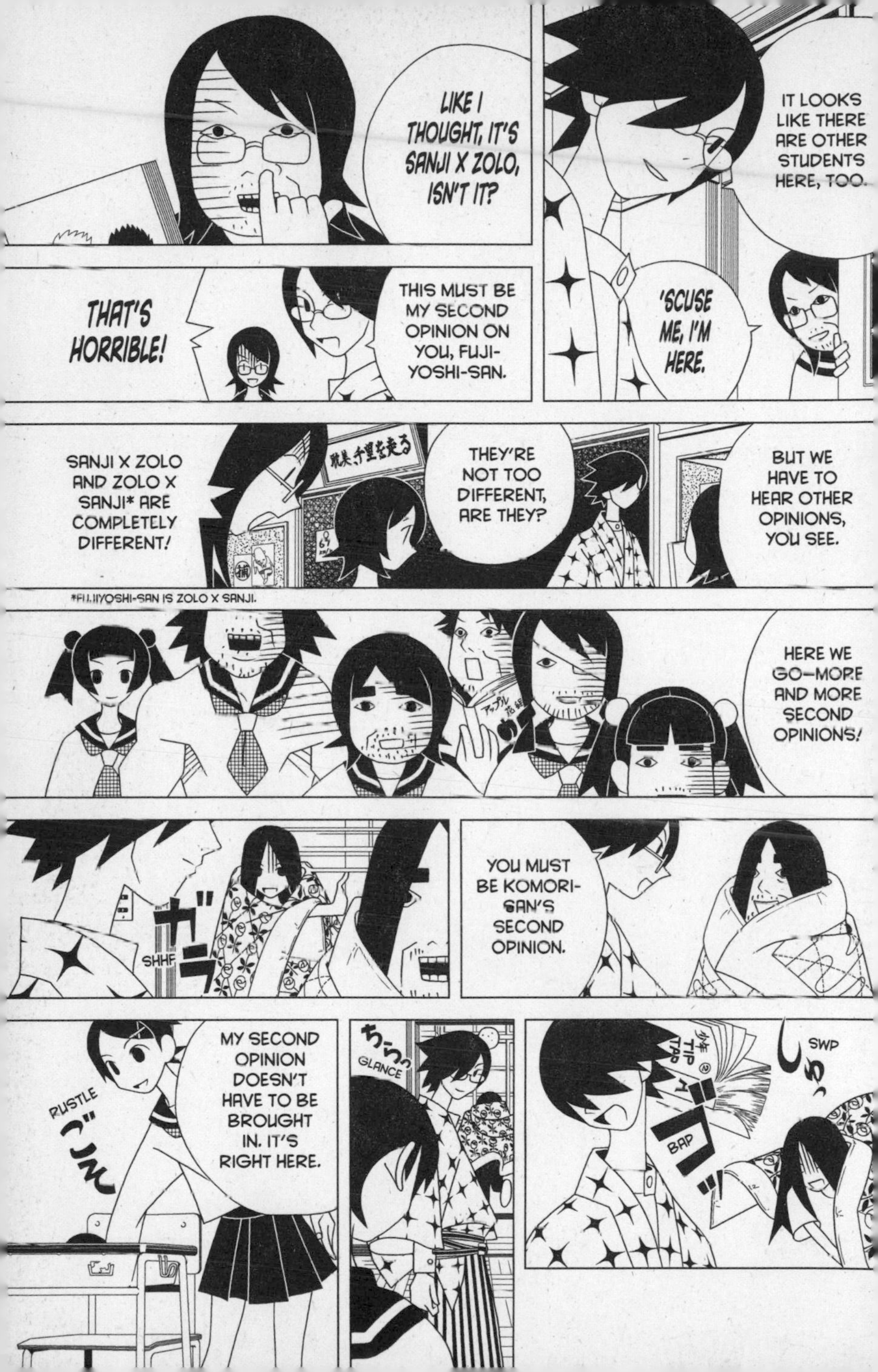
IT LOOKS LIKE THERE ARE OTHER STUDENTS HERE, TOO.
LIKE I THOUGHT, IT'S SANJI X ZOLO, ISN'T IT?
'SCUSE ME, I'M HERE.
THIS MUST BE MY SECOND OPINION ON YOU, FUJI-YOSHI-SAN.
THAT'S HORRIBLE!
BUT WE HAVE TO HEAR OTHER OPINIONS, YOU SEE.
THEY'RE NOT TOO DIFFERENT, ARE THEY?
SANJI X ZOLO AND ZOLO X SANJI* ARE COMPLETELY DIFFERENT!
*FUJIYOSHI-SAN IS ZOLO X SANJI.
HERE WE GO—MORE AND MORE SECOND OPINIONS!
YOU MUST BE KOMORI-SAN'S SECOND OPINION.
SHHF
SWP
TIP TAP
BAP
GLANCE
MY SECOND OPINION DOESN'T HAVE TO BE BROUGHT IN. IT'S RIGHT HERE.
RUSTLE

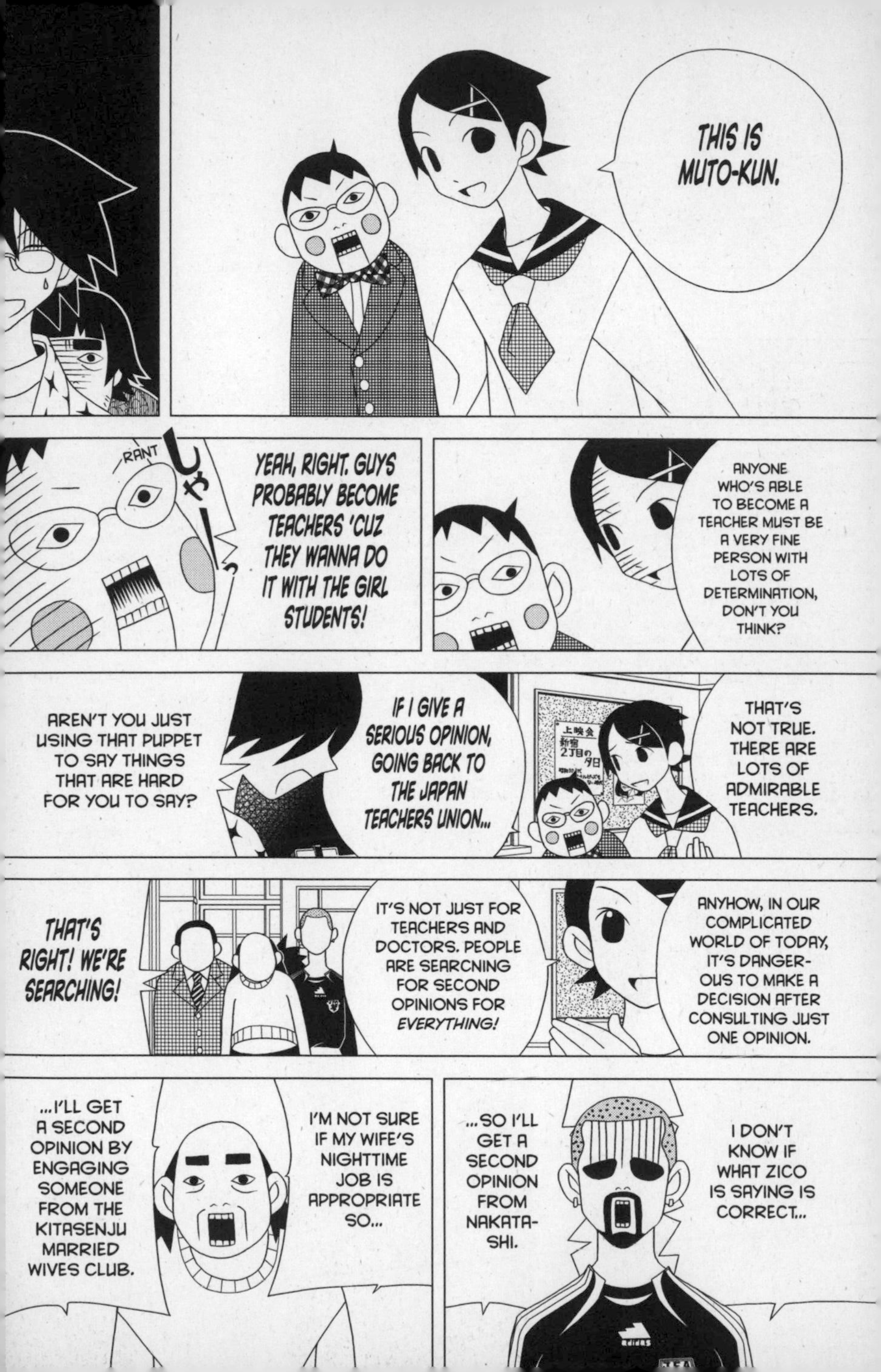
THIS IS MUTO-KUN.
ANYONE WHO'S ABLE TO BECOME A TEACHER MUST BE A VERY FINE PERSON WITH LOTS OF DETERMINATION, DON'T YOU THINK?
YEAH, RIGHT. GUYS PROBABLY BECOME TEACHERS 'CUZ THEY WANNA DO IT WITH THE GIRL STUDENTS!
RANT
THAT'S NOT TRUE. THERE ARE LOTS OF ADMIRABLE TEACHERS.
上映会
新宿
2丁目の夕日
IF I GIVE A SERIOUS OPINION, GOING BACK TO THE JAPAN TEACHERS UNION...
AREN'T YOU JUST USING THAT PUPPET TO SAY THINGS THAT ARE HARD FOR YOU TO SAY?
ANYHOW, IN OUR COMPLICATED WORLD OF TODAY, IT'S DANGER-OUS TO MAKE A DECISION AFTER CONSULTING JUST ONE OPINION.
IT'S NOT JUST FOR TEACHERS AND DOCTORS. PEOPLE ARE SEARCNING FOR SECOND OPINIONS FOR *EVERYTHING!*
THAT'S RIGHT! WE'RE SEARCHING!
I DON'T KNOW IF WHAT ZICO IS SAYING IS CORRECT...
...SO I'LL GET A SECOND OPINION FROM NAKATA-SHI.
I'M NOT SURE IF MY WIFE'S NIGHTTIME JOB IS APPROPRIATE SO...
...I'LL GET A SECOND OPINION BY ENGAGING SOMEONE FROM THE KITASENJU MARRIED WIVES CLUB.

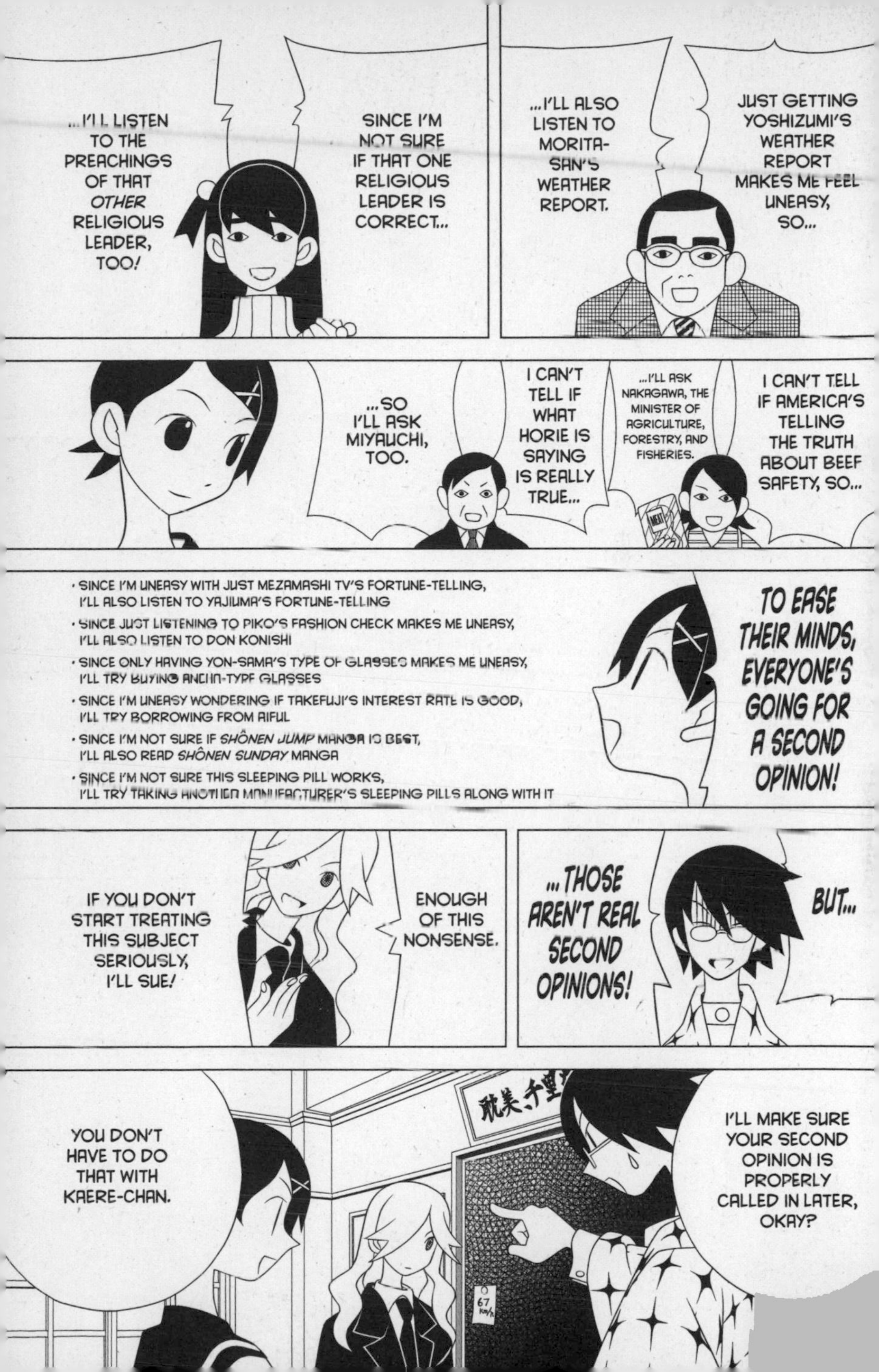
JUST GETTING YOSHIZUMI'S WEATHER REPORT MAKES ME FEEL UNEASY, SO...
...I'LL ALSO LISTEN TO MORITA-SAN'S WEATHER REPORT.
SINCE I'M NOT SURE IF THAT ONE RELIGIOUS LEADER IS CORRECT...
...I'LL LISTEN TO THE PREACHINGS OF THAT *OTHER* RELIGIOUS LEADER, TOO!
I CAN'T TELL IF AMERICA'S TELLING THE TRUTH ABOUT BEEF SAFETY, SO...
...I'LL ASK NAKAGAWA, THE MINISTER OF AGRICULTURE, FORESTRY, AND FISHERIES.
MEAT
I CAN'T TELL IF WHAT HORIE IS SAYING IS REALLY TRUE...
...SO I'LL ASK MIYAUCHI, TOO.
TO EASE THEIR MINDS, EVERYONE'S GOING FOR A SECOND OPINION!
• SINCE I'M UNEASY WITH JUST MEZAMASHI TV'S FORTUNE-TELLING, I'LL ALSO LISTEN TO YAJIUMA'S FORTUNE-TELLING
• SINCE JUST LISTENING TO PIKO'S FASHION CHECK MAKES ME UNEASY, I'LL ALSO LISTEN TO DON KONISHI
• SINCE ONLY HAVING YON-SAMA'S TYPE OF GLASSES MAKES ME UNEASY, I'LL TRY BUYING ANCHIN-TYPE GLASSES
• SINCE I'M UNEASY WONDERING IF TAKEFUJI'S INTEREST RATE IS GOOD, I'LL TRY BORROWING FROM AIFUL
• SINCE I'M NOT SURE IF *SHÔNEN JUMP* MANGA IS BEST, I'LL ALSO READ *SHÔNEN SUNDAY* MANGA
• SINCE I'M NOT SURE THIS SLEEPING PILL WORKS, I'LL TRY TAKING ANOTHER MANUFACTURER'S SLEEPING PILLS ALONG WITH IT
BUT...
...THOSE AREN'T REAL SECOND OPINIONS!
ENOUGH OF THIS NONSENSE.
IF YOU DON'T START TREATING THIS SUBJECT SERIOUSLY, I'LL SUE!
I'LL MAKE SURE YOUR SECOND OPINION IS PROPERLY CALLED IN LATER, OKAY?
YOU DON'T HAVE TO DO THAT WITH KAERE-CHAN.

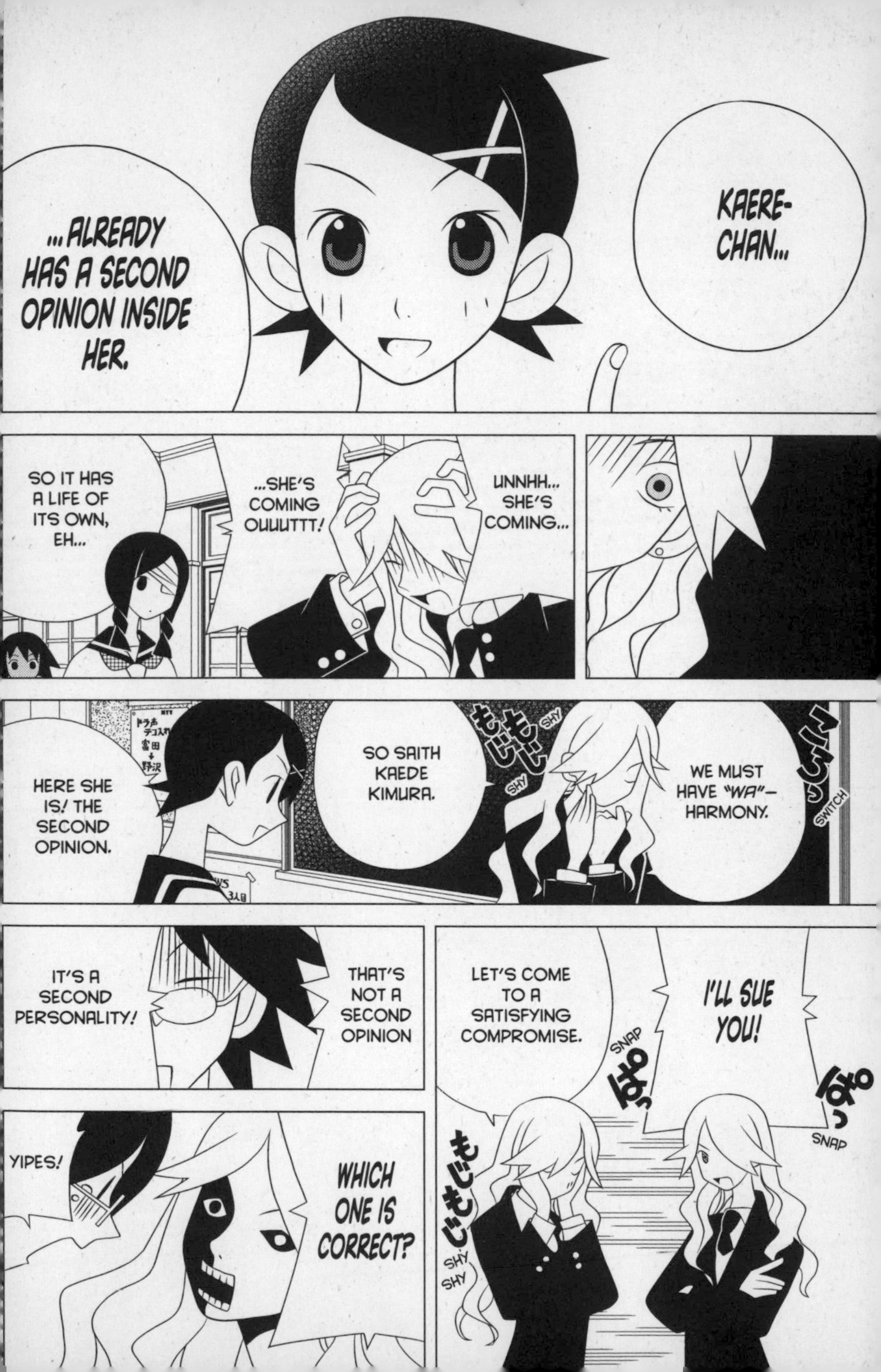
KAERE-CHAN...
...ALREADY HAS A SECOND OPINION INSIDE HER.
UNNHH... SHE'S COMING...
...SHE'S COMING OUUUTTT!
SO IT HAS A LIFE OF ITS OWN, EH...
SWITCH
WE MUST HAVE "WA"—HARMONY.
もじもじ
SHY
SHY
SO SAITH KAEDE KIMURA.
HERE SHE IS! THE SECOND OPINION.
I'LL SUE YOU!
ぽっ
SNAP
LET'S COME TO A SATISFYING COMPROMISE.
ぽっ
SNAP
もじもじ
SHY
SHY
THAT'S NOT A SECOND OPINION
IT'S A SECOND PERSONALITY!
WHICH ONE IS CORRECT?
YIPES!

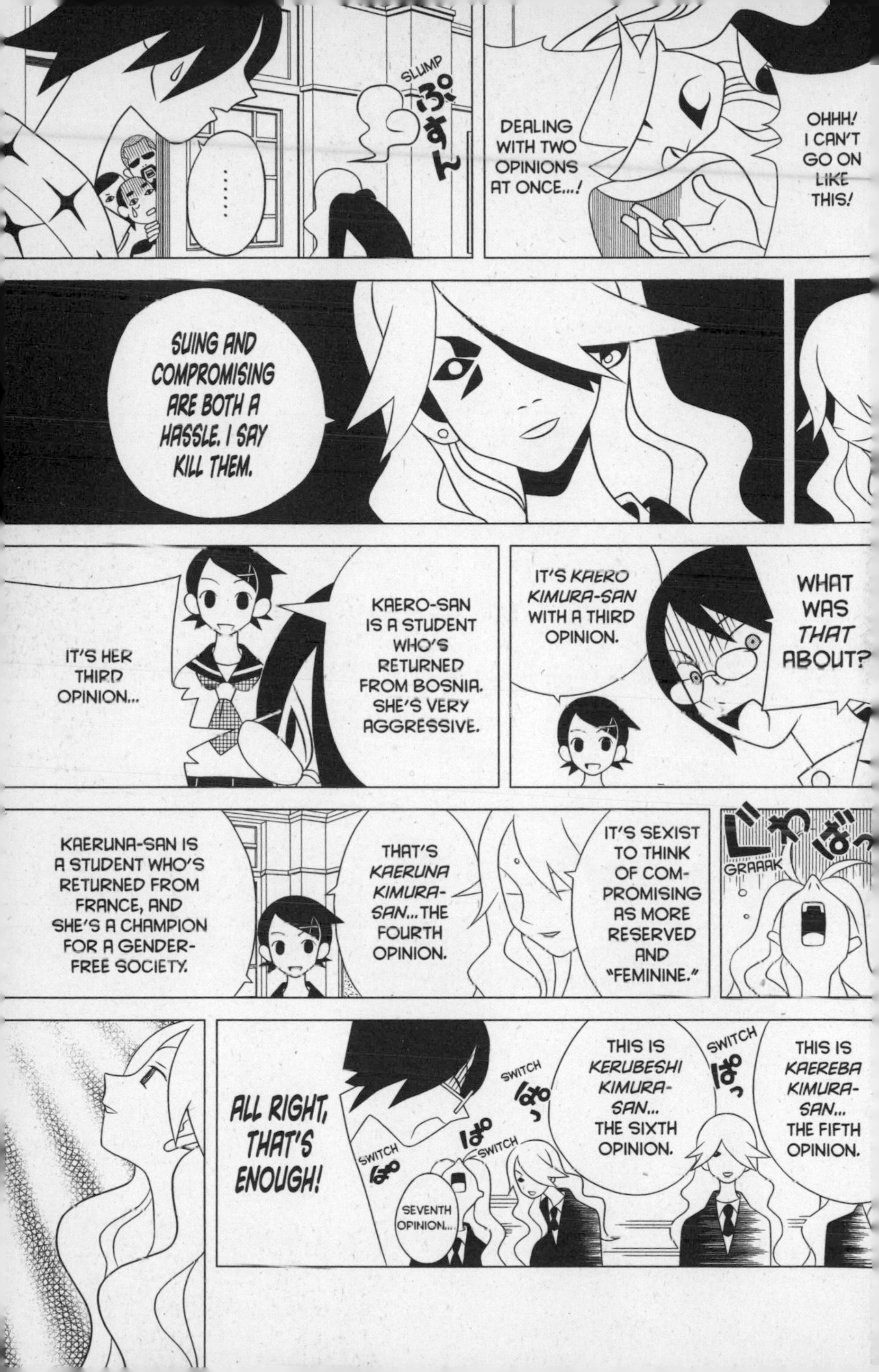
OHHH! I CAN'T GO ON LIKE THIS!
DEALING WITH TWO OPINIONS AT ONCE...!
SLUMP
ぷすん~
......
SUING AND COMPROMISING ARE BOTH A HASSLE. I SAY KILL THEM.
WHAT WAS *THAT* ABOUT?
IT'S *KAERO KIMURA-SAN* WITH A THIRD OPINION.
KAERO-SAN IS A STUDENT WHO'S RETURNED FROM BOSNIA. SHE'S VERY AGGRESSIVE.
IT'S HER THIRD OPINION...
GRAAAK
じゃばっ
IT'S SEXIST TO THINK OF COM-PROMISING AS MORE RESERVED AND "FEMININE."
THAT'S *KAERUNA KIMURA-SAN*... THE FOURTH OPINION.
KAERUNA-SAN IS A STUDENT WHO'S RETURNED FROM FRANCE, AND SHE'S A CHAMPION FOR A GENDER-FREE SOCIETY.
THIS IS *KAEREBA KIMURA-SAN*... THE FIFTH OPINION.
SWITCH
ぱっ
THIS IS *KERUBESHI KIMURA-SAN*... THE SIXTH OPINION.
SWITCH
ぱっ
ALL RIGHT, THAT'S ENOUGH!
SWITCH
ぱっ
SEVENTH OPINION...
SWITCH
ぱっ

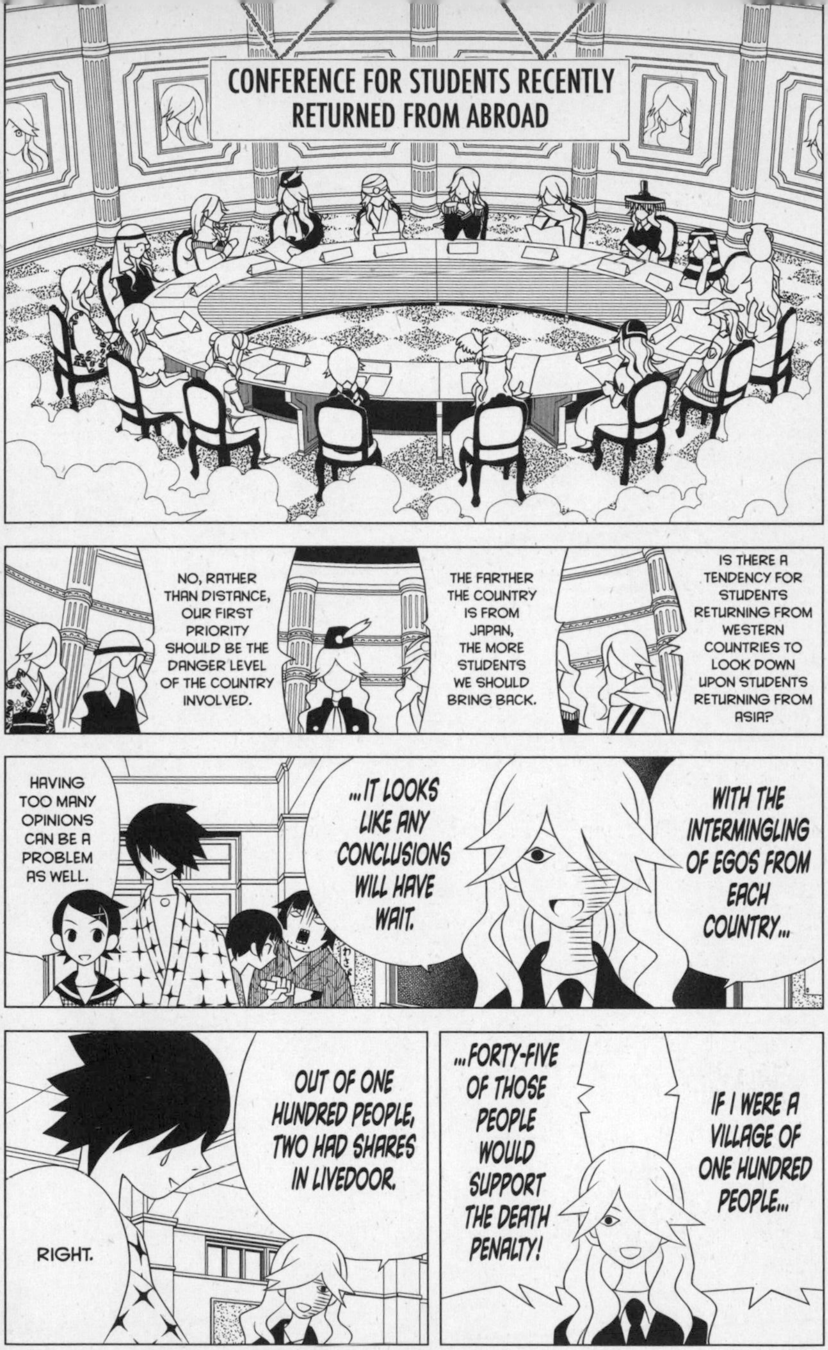
CONFERENCE FOR STUDENTS RECENTLY RETURNED FROM ABROAD
IS THERE A TENDENCY FOR STUDENTS RETURNING FROM WESTERN COUNTRIES TO LOOK DOWN UPON STUDENTS RETURNING FROM ASIA?
THE FARTHER THE COUNTRY IS FROM JAPAN, THE MORE STUDENTS WE SHOULD BRING BACK.
NO, RATHER THAN DISTANCE, OUR FIRST PRIORITY SHOULD BE THE DANGER LEVEL OF THE COUNTRY INVOLVED.
WITH THE INTERMINGLING OF EGOS FROM EACH COUNTRY...
...IT LOOKS LIKE ANY CONCLUSIONS WILL HAVE WAIT.
HAVING TOO MANY OPINIONS CAN BE A PROBLEM AS WELL.
IF I WERE A VILLAGE OF ONE HUNDRED PEOPLE...
...FORTY-FIVE OF THOSE PEOPLE WOULD SUPPORT THE DEATH PENALTY!
OUT OF ONE HUNDRED PEOPLE, TWO HAD SHARES IN LIVEDOOR.
RIGHT.

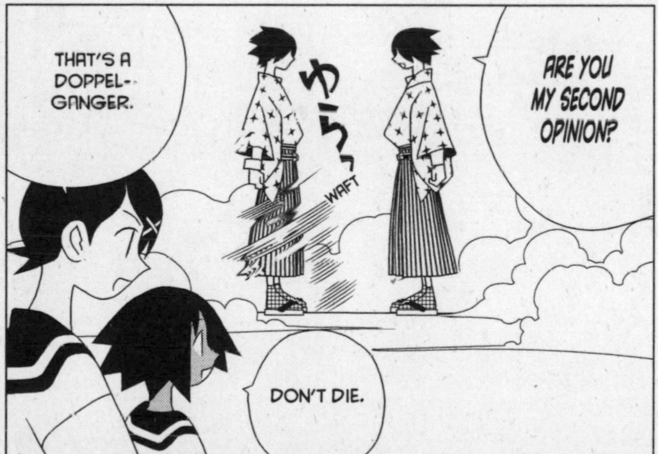
ARE YOU MY SECOND OPINION?
ゆらっ
WAFT
THAT'S A DOPPEL-GANGER.
DON'T DIE.

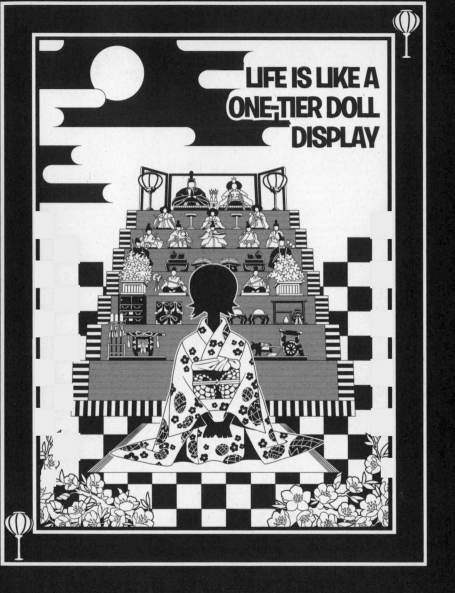

LIFE IS LIKE A ONE-TIER DOLL DISPLAY

CHAPTER 40

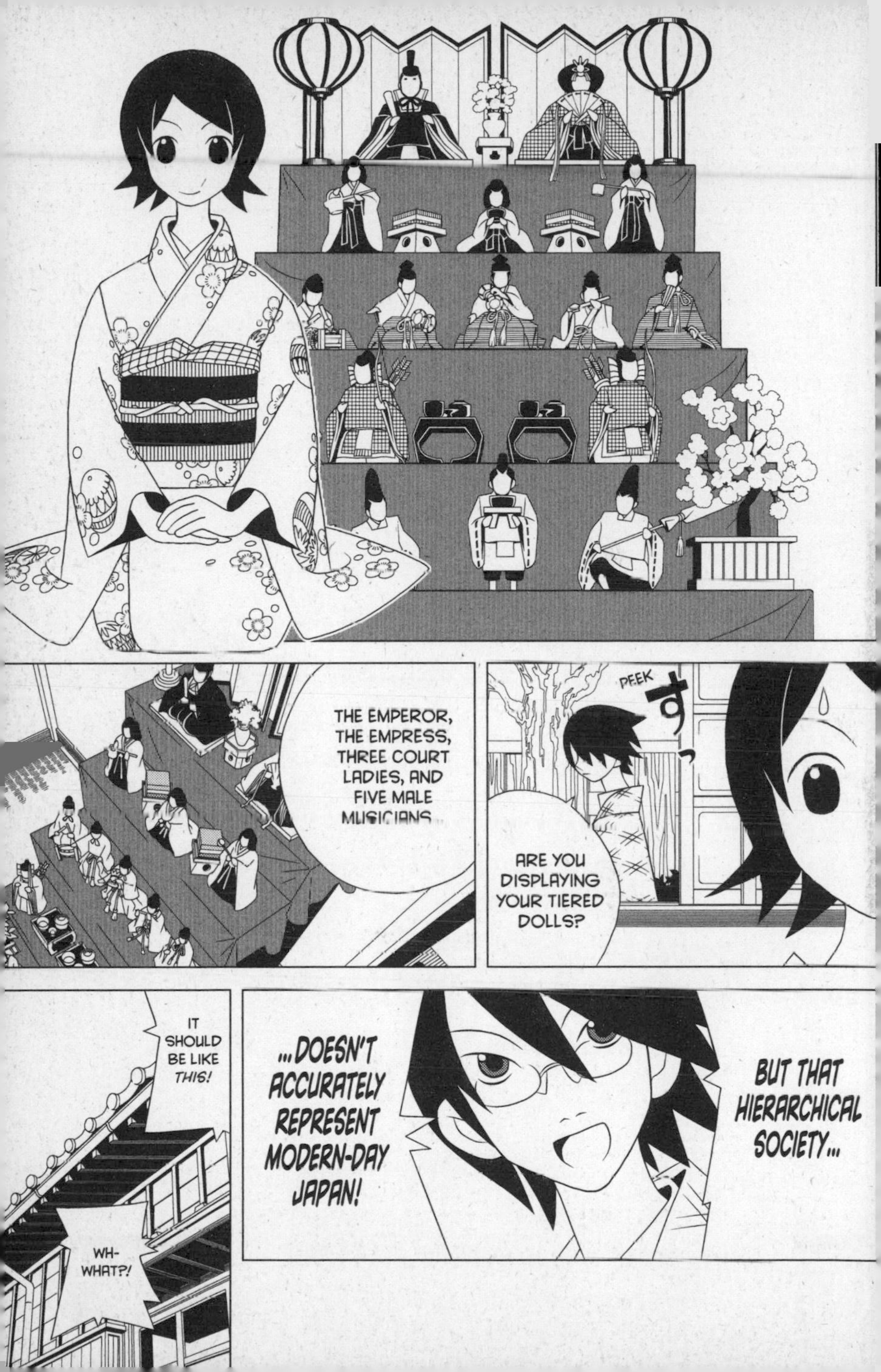
PEEK
す
ARE YOU DISPLAYING YOUR TIERED DOLLS?
THE EMPEROR, THE EMPRESS, THREE COURT LADIES, AND FIVE MALE MUSICIANS...
BUT THAT HIERARCHICAL SOCIETY...
...DOESN'T ACCURATELY REPRESENT MODERN-DAY JAPAN!
IT SHOULD BE LIKE *THIS!*
WH- WHAT?!

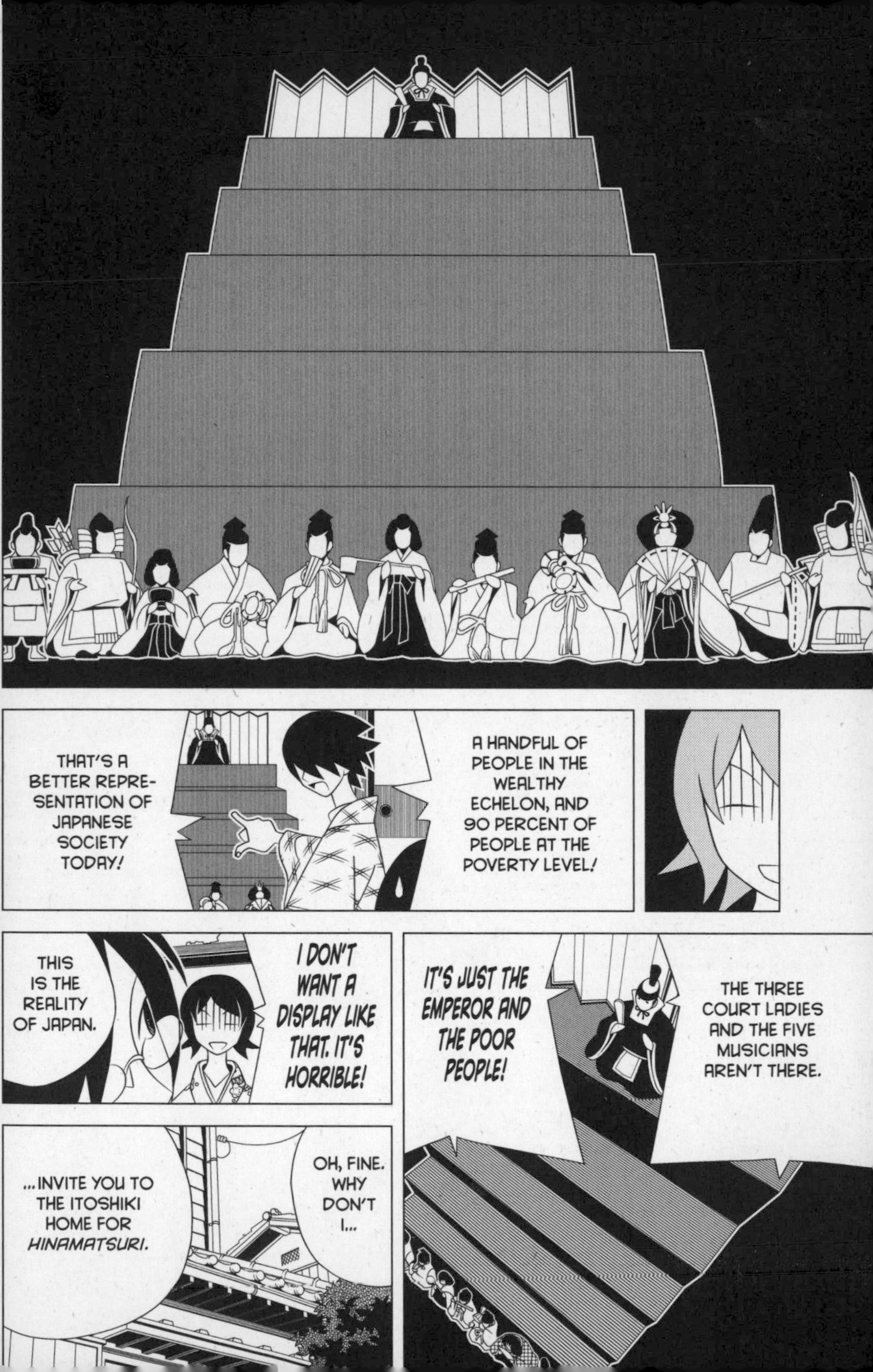
A HANDFUL OF PEOPLE IN THE WEALTHY ECHELON, AND 90 PERCENT OF PEOPLE AT THE POVERTY LEVEL!
THAT'S A BETTER REPRE-SENTATION OF JAPANESE SOCIETY TODAY!
THE THREE COURT LADIES AND THE FIVE MUSICIANS AREN'T THERE.
IT'S JUST THE EMPEROR AND THE POOR PEOPLE!
I DON'T WANT A DISPLAY LIKE THAT. IT'S HORRIBLE!
THIS IS THE REALITY OF JAPAN.
OH, FINE. WHY DON'T I...
...INVITE YOU TO THE ITOSHIKI HOME FOR *HINAMATSURI*.

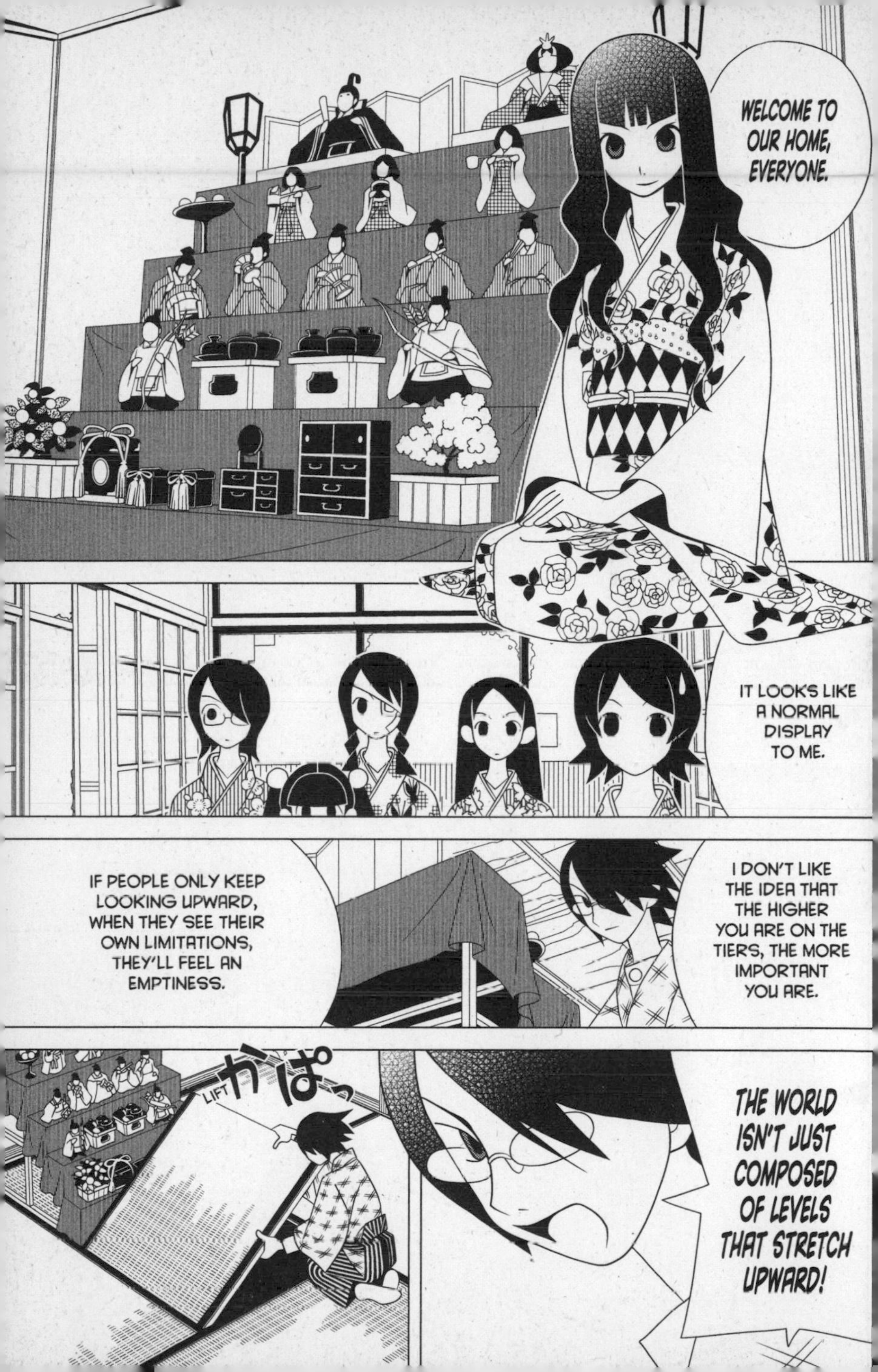
WELCOME TO OUR HOME, EVERYONE.
IT LOOKS LIKE A NORMAL DISPLAY TO ME.
I DON'T LIKE THE IDEA THAT THE HIGHER YOU ARE ON THE TIERS, THE MORE IMPORTANT YOU ARE.
IF PEOPLE ONLY KEEP LOOKING UPWARD, WHEN THEY SEE THEIR OWN LIMITATIONS, THEY'LL FEEL AN EMPTINESS.
THE WORLD ISN'T JUST COMPOSED OF LEVELS THAT STRETCH UPWARD!
LIFT かぱっ

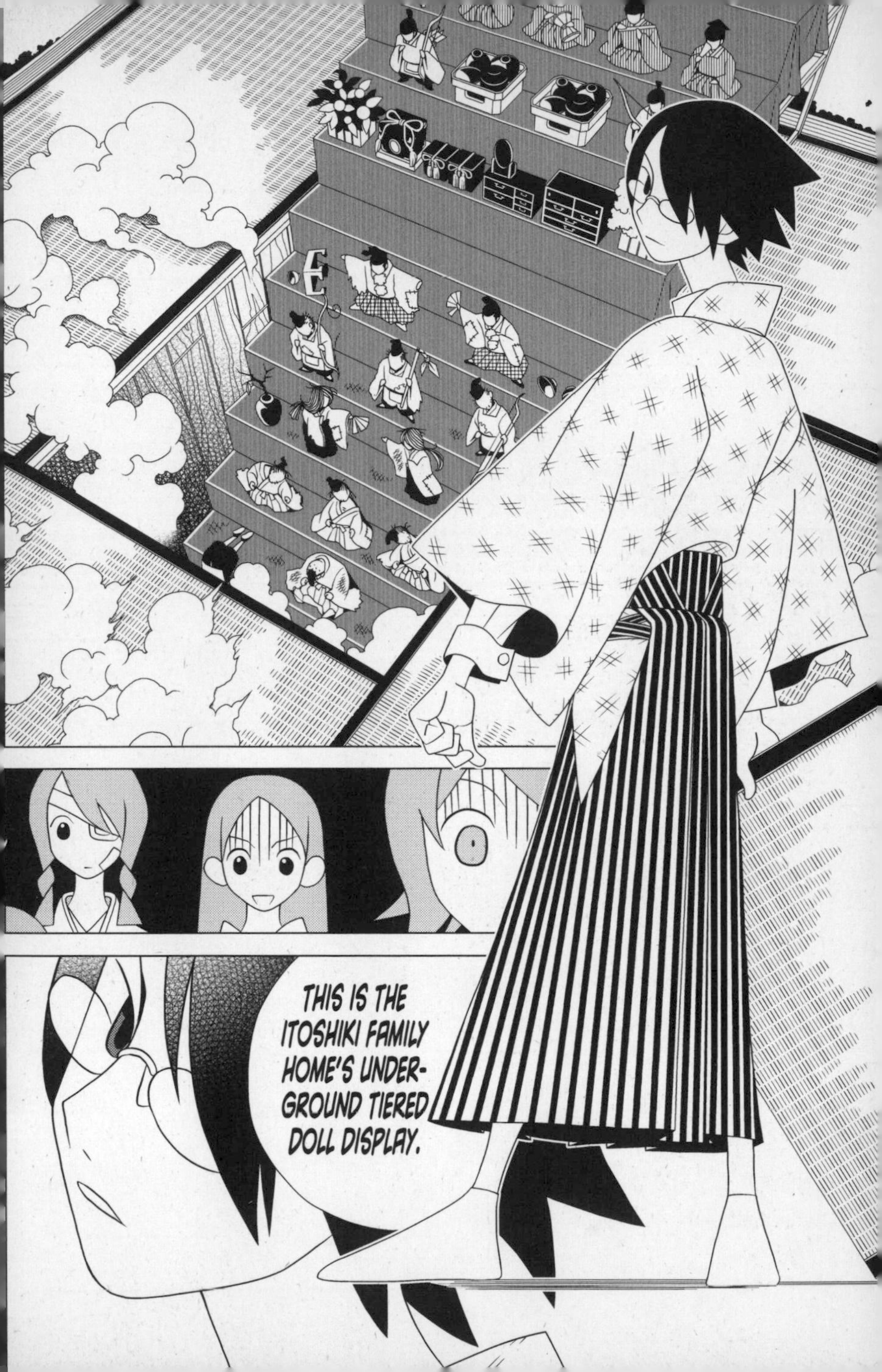
THIS IS THE ITOSHIKI FAMILY HOME'S UNDER-GROUND TIERED DOLL DISPLAY.

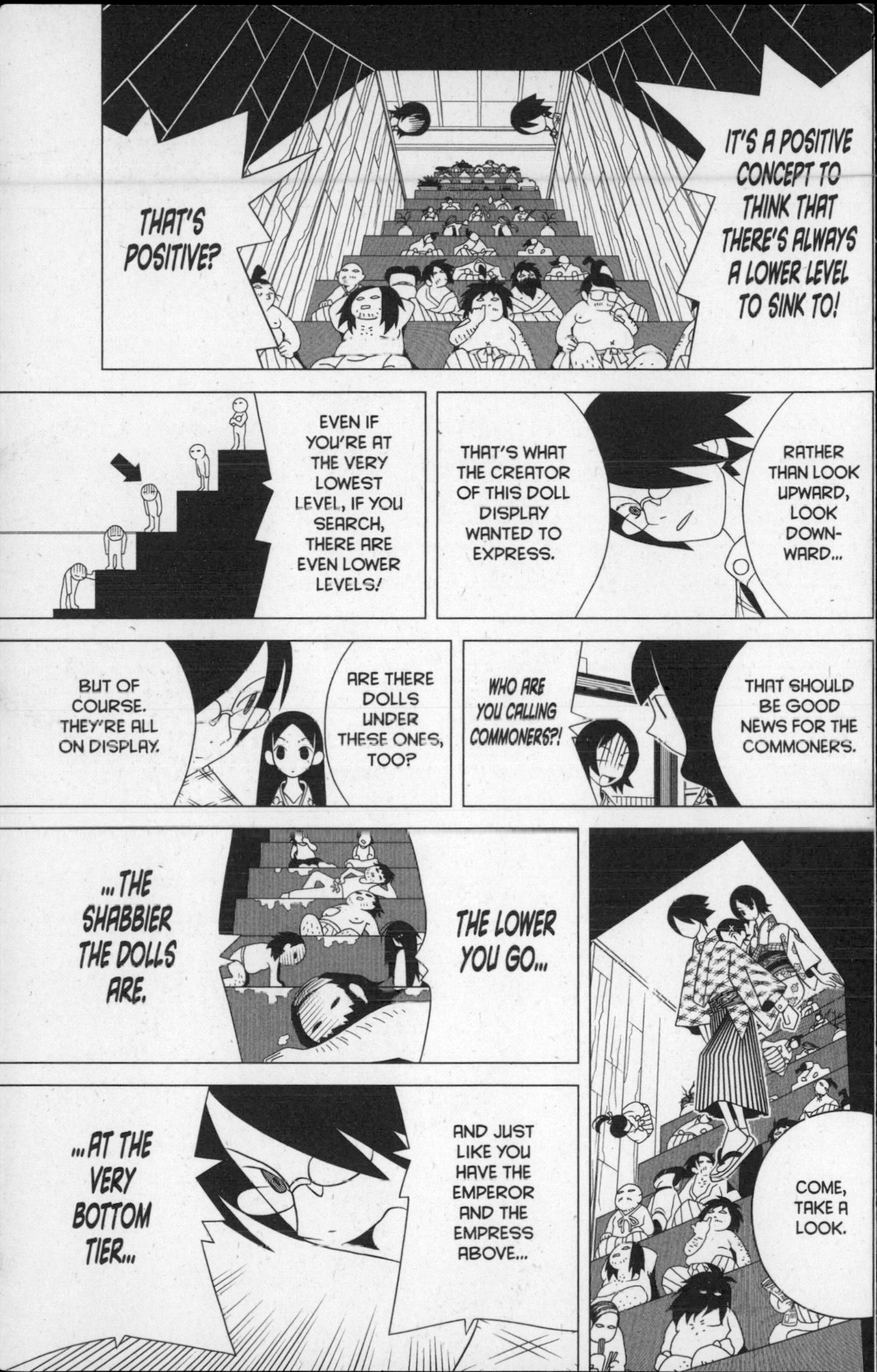
IT'S A POSITIVE CONCEPT TO THINK THAT THERE'S ALWAYS A LOWER LEVEL TO SINK TO!
THAT'S POSITIVE?
RATHER THAN LOOK UPWARD, LOOK DOWNWARD...
THAT'S WHAT THE CREATOR OF THIS DOLL DISPLAY WANTED TO EXPRESS.
EVEN IF YOU'RE AT THE VERY LOWEST LEVEL, IF YOU SEARCH, THERE ARE EVEN LOWER LEVELS!
THAT SHOULD BE GOOD NEWS FOR THE COMMONERS.
WHO ARE YOU CALLING COMMONERS?!
ARE THERE DOLLS UNDER THESE ONES, TOO?
BUT OF COURSE. THEY'RE ALL ON DISPLAY.
COME, TAKE A LOOK.
THE LOWER YOU GO...
...THE SHABBIER THE DOLLS ARE.
AND JUST LIKE YOU HAVE THE EMPEROR AND THE EMPRESS ABOVE...
...AT THE VERY BOTTOM TIER...

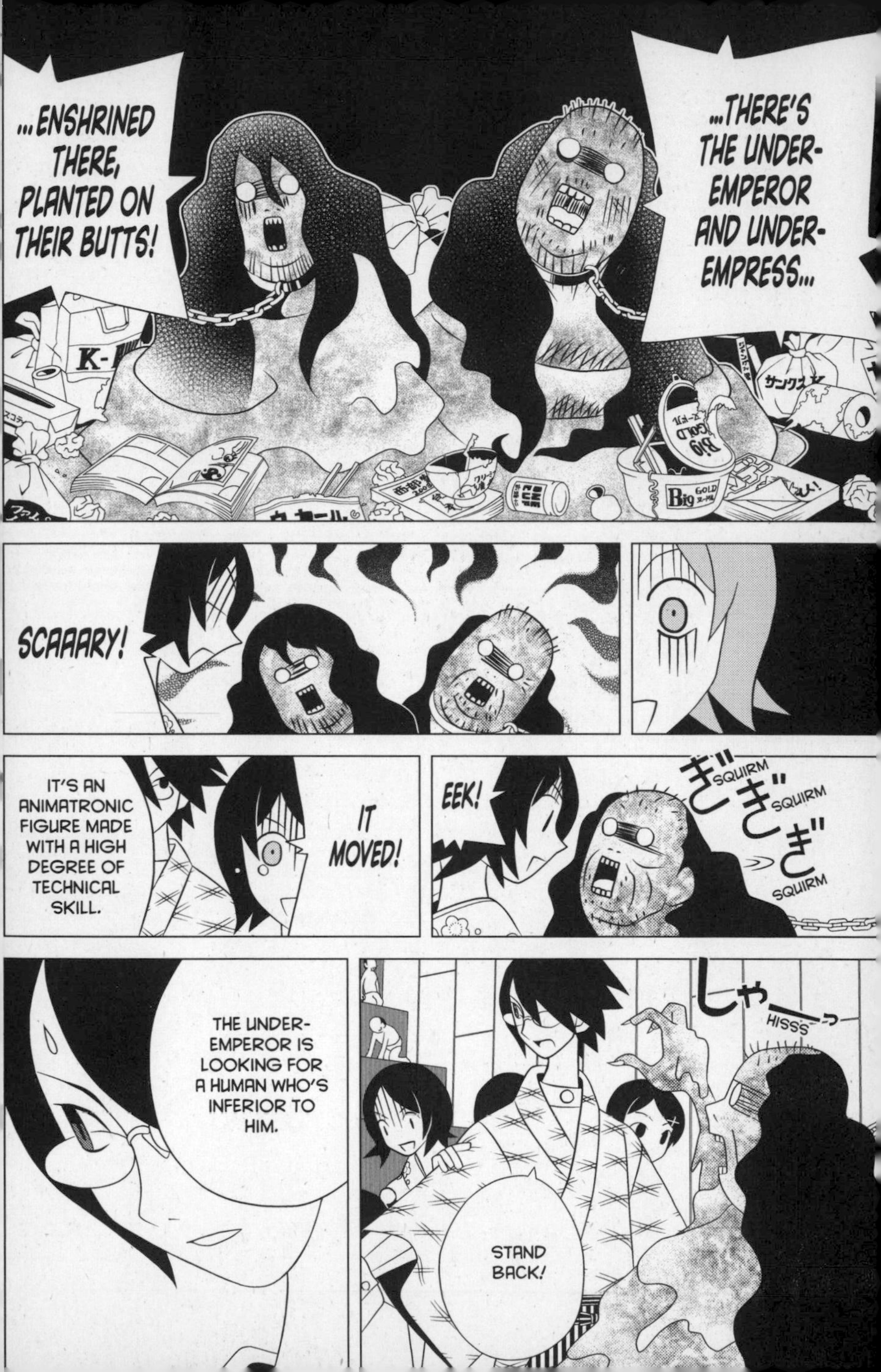
...THERE'S THE UNDER-EMPEROR AND UNDER-EMPRESS...
...ENSHRINED THERE, PLANTED ON THEIR BUTTS!
SCAAARY!
ぎ SQUIRM
ぎ SQUIRM
ぎ SQUIRM
EEK!
IT MOVED!
IT'S AN ANIMATRONIC FIGURE MADE WITH A HIGH DEGREE OF TECHNICAL SKILL.
しゃーっ HISSS
STAND BACK!
THE UNDER-EMPEROR IS LOOKING FOR A HUMAN WHO'S INFERIOR TO HIM.

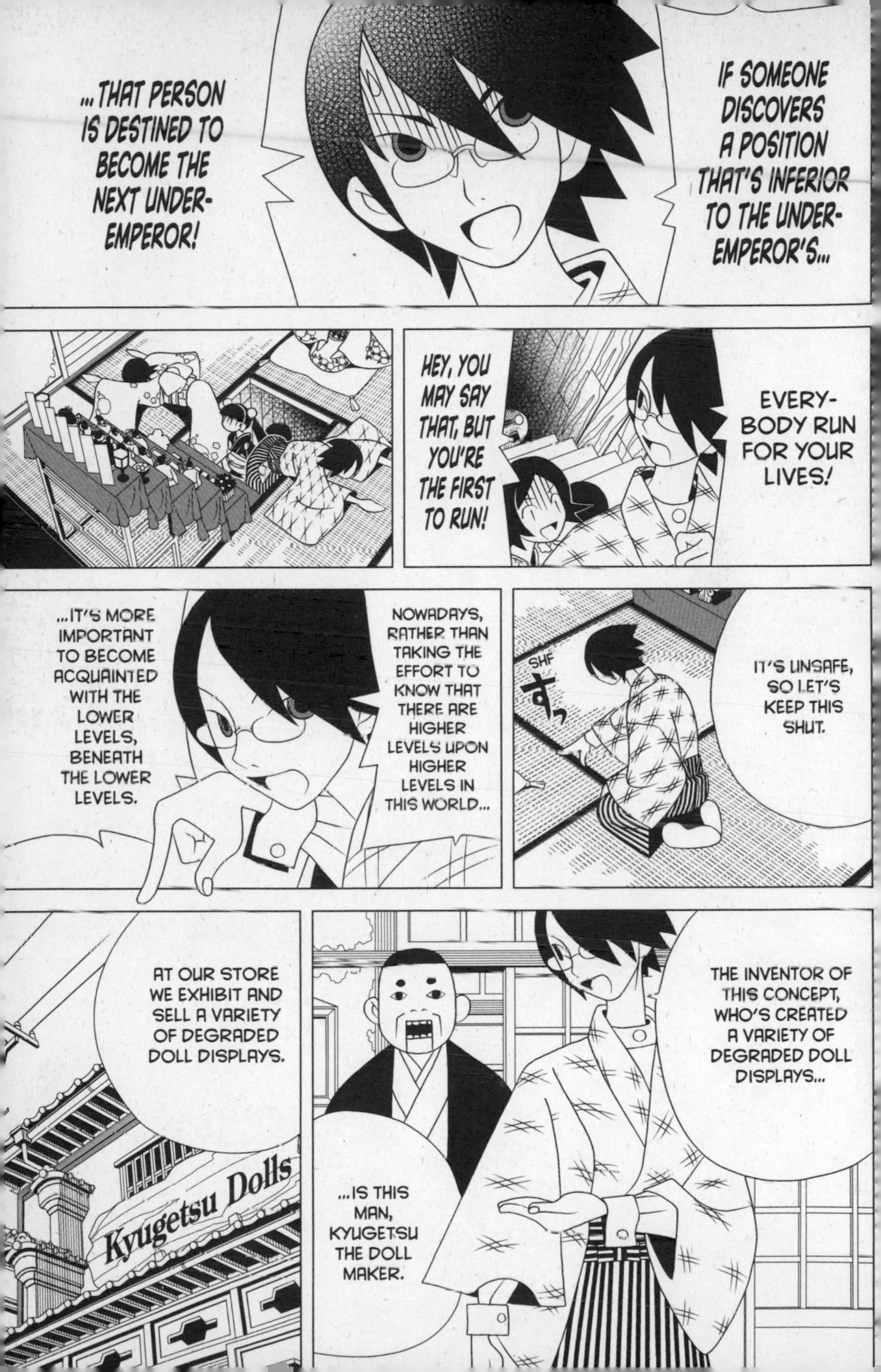
IF SOMEONE DISCOVERS A POSITION THAT'S INFERIOR TO THE UNDER-EMPEROR'S...
...THAT PERSON IS DESTINED TO BECOME THE NEXT UNDER-EMPEROR!
EVERY-BODY RUN FOR YOUR LIVES!
HEY, YOU MAY SAY THAT, BUT YOU'RE THE FIRST TO RUN!
IT'S UNSAFE, SO LET'S KEEP THIS SHUT.
SHF
すっ
NOWADAYS, RATHER THAN TAKING THE EFFORT TO KNOW THAT THERE ARE HIGHER LEVELS UPON HIGHER LEVELS IN THIS WORLD...
...IT'S MORE IMPORTANT TO BECOME ACQUAINTED WITH THE LOWER LEVELS, BENEATH THE LOWER LEVELS.
THE INVENTOR OF THIS CONCEPT, WHO'S CREATED A VARIETY OF DEGRADED DOLL DISPLAYS...
...IS THIS MAN, KYUGETSU THE DOLL MAKER.
AT OUR STORE WE EXHIBIT AND SELL A VARIETY OF DEGRADED DOLL DISPLAYS.
Kyugetsu Dolls

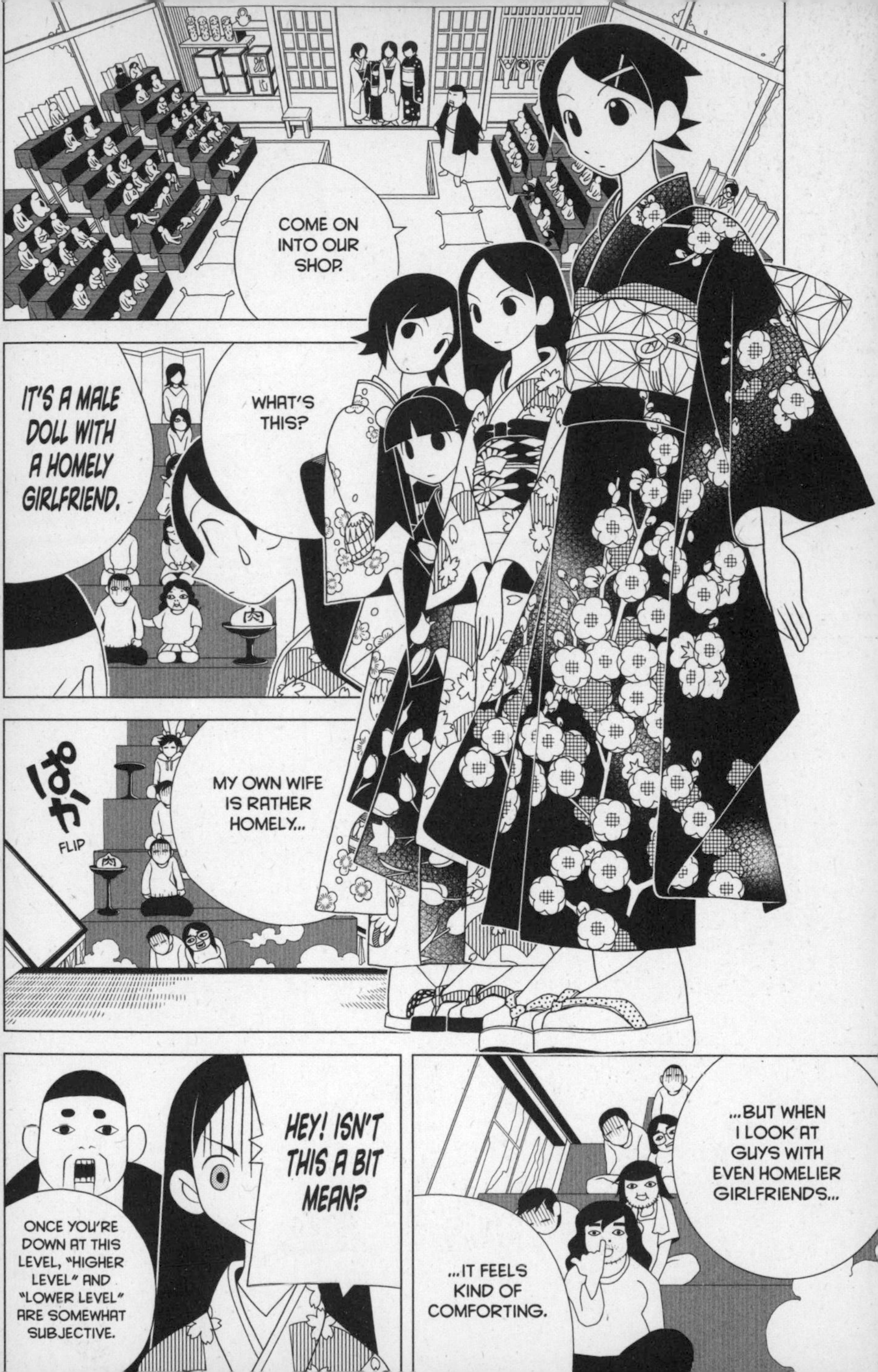
COME ON INTO OUR SHOP.
WHAT'S THIS?
IT'S A MALE DOLL WITH A HOMELY GIRLFRIEND.
MY OWN WIFE IS RATHER HOMELY...
ぱか
FLIP
...BUT WHEN I LOOK AT GUYS WITH EVEN HOMELIER GIRLFRIENDS...
...IT FEELS KIND OF COMFORTING.
HEY! ISN'T THIS A BIT MEAN?
ONCE YOU'RE DOWN AT THIS LEVEL, "HIGHER LEVEL" AND "LOWER LEVEL" ARE SOMEWHAT SUBJECTIVE.

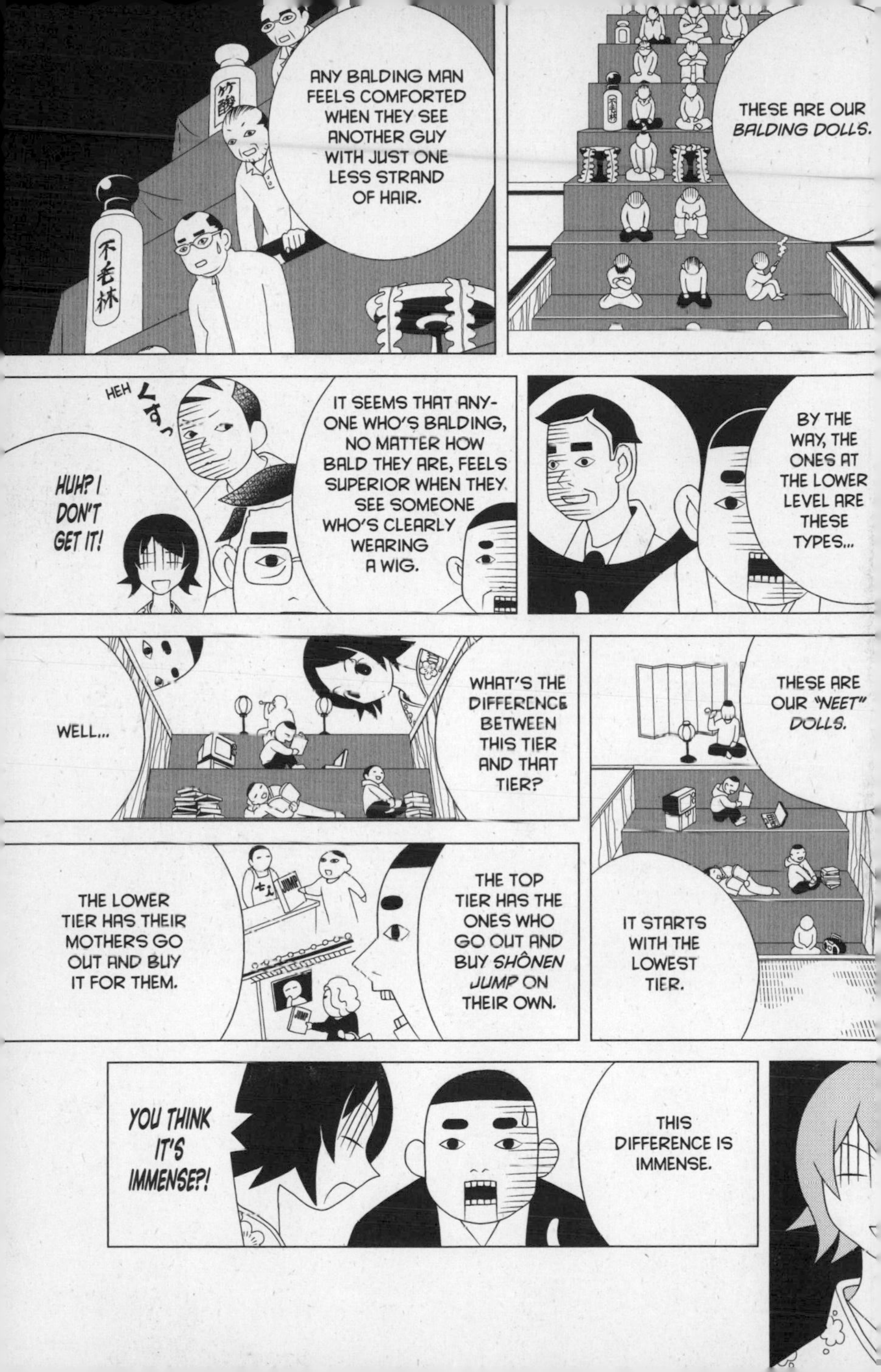
THESE ARE OUR *BALDING DOLLS.*
不毛林
ANY BALDING MAN FEELS COMFORTED WHEN THEY SEE ANOTHER GUY WITH JUST ONE LESS STRAND OF HAIR.
竹酸
不毛林
BY THE WAY, THE ONES AT THE LOWER LEVEL ARE THESE TYPES...
IT SEEMS THAT ANY-ONE WHO'S BALDING, NO MATTER HOW BALD THEY ARE, FEELS SUPERIOR WHEN THEY SEE SOMEONE WHO'S CLEARLY WEARING A WIG.
HEH くすっ
HUH? I DON'T GET IT!
THESE ARE OUR "NEET" DOLLS.
IT STARTS WITH THE LOWEST TIER.
WHAT'S THE DIFFERENCE BETWEEN THIS TIER AND THAT TIER?
WELL...
THE TOP TIER HAS THE ONES WHO GO OUT AND BUY *SHÔNEN JUMP* ON THEIR OWN.
JUMP
JUMP
THE LOWER TIER HAS THEIR MOTHERS GO OUT AND BUY IT FOR THEM.
THIS DIFFERENCE IS IMMENSE.
YOU THINK IT'S IMMENSE?!

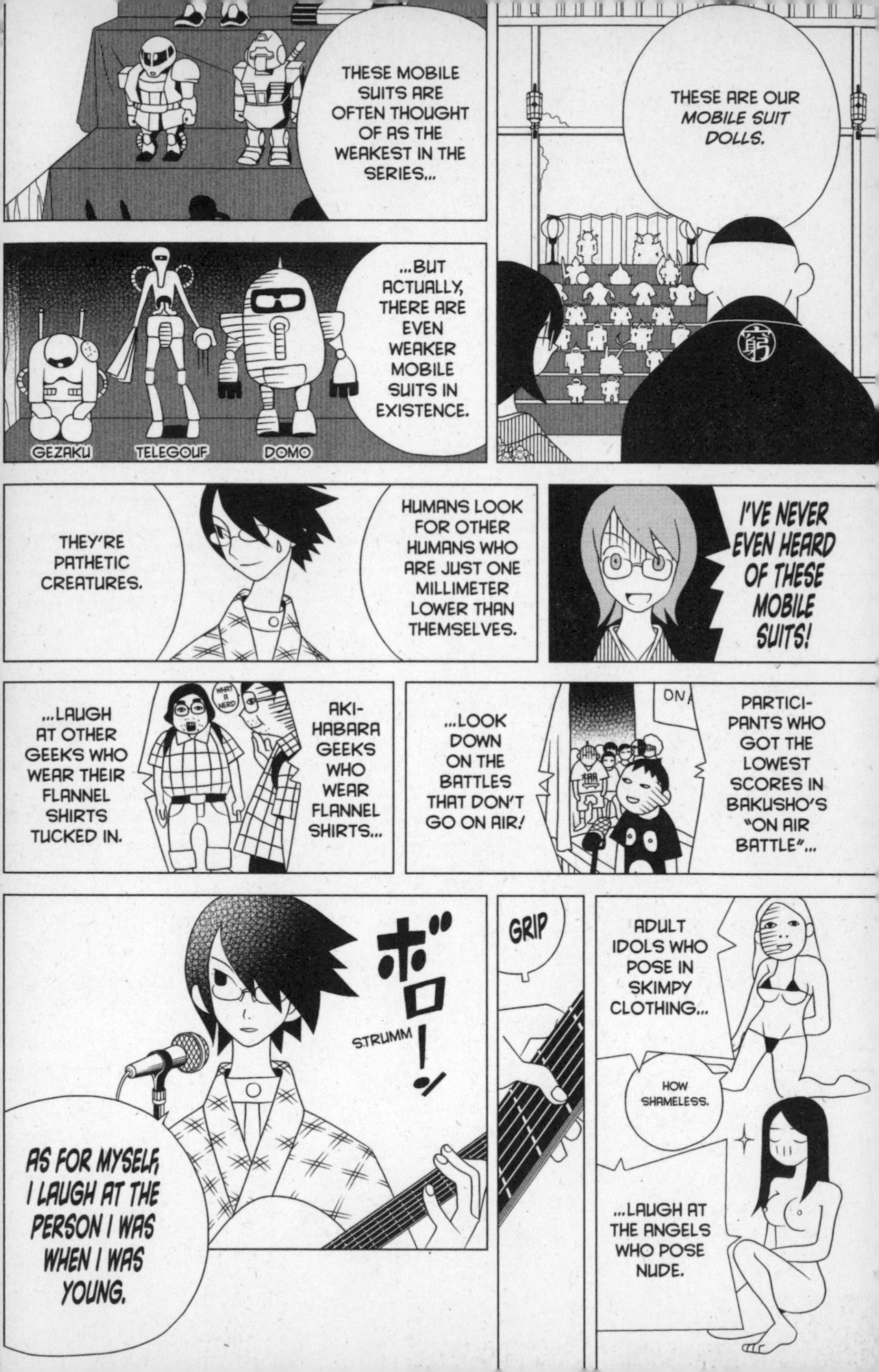
THESE ARE OUR *MOBILE SUIT* DOLLS.
THESE MOBILE SUITS ARE OFTEN THOUGHT OF AS THE WEAKEST IN THE SERIES...
...BUT ACTUALLY, THERE ARE EVEN WEAKER MOBILE SUITS IN EXISTENCE.
GEZAKU
TELEGOUF
DOMO
I'VE NEVER EVEN HEARD OF THESE MOBILE SUITS!
HUMANS LOOK FOR OTHER HUMANS WHO ARE JUST ONE MILLIMETER LOWER THAN THEMSELVES.
THEY'RE PATHETIC CREATURES.
PARTICI-PANTS WHO GOT THE LOWEST SCORES IN BAKUSHO'S "ON AIR BATTLE"...
ONA
...LOOK DOWN ON THE BATTLES THAT DON'T GO ON AIR!
AKI-HABARA GEEKS WHO WEAR FLANNEL SHIRTS...
WHAT A NERD
...LAUGH AT OTHER GEEKS WHO WEAR THEIR FLANNEL SHIRTS TUCKED IN.
ADULT IDOLS WHO POSE IN SKIMPY CLOTHING...
HOW SHAMELESS.
...LAUGH AT THE ANGELS WHO POSE NUDE.
GRIP
ボロー
STRUMM
AS FOR MYSELF, I LAUGH AT THE PERSON I WAS WHEN I WAS YOUNG.

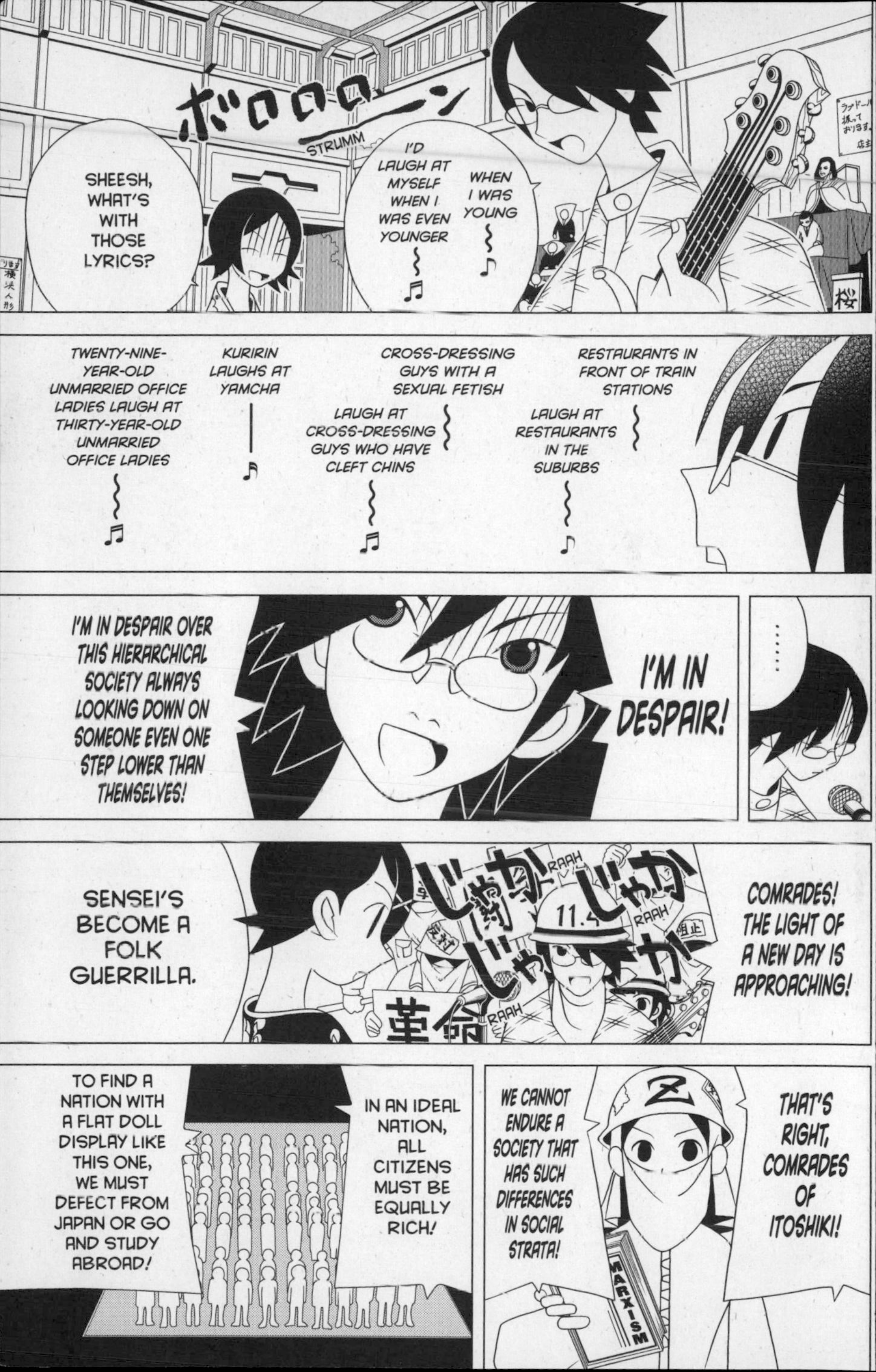
ボロロローン
STRUMM
WHEN I WAS YOUNG ~ ♪
I'D LAUGH AT MYSELF WHEN I WAS EVEN YOUNGER ~ ♫
SHEESH, WHAT'S WITH THOSE LYRICS?
桜
RESTAURANTS IN FRONT OF TRAIN STATIONS ~
LAUGH AT RESTAURANTS IN THE SUBURBS ~ ♪
CROSS-DRESSING GUYS WITH A SEXUAL FETISH ~
LAUGH AT CROSS-DRESSING GUYS WHO HAVE CLEFT CHINS ~ ♫
KURIRIN LAUGHS AT YAMCHA — ♬
TWENTY-NINE-YEAR-OLD UNMARRIED OFFICE LADIES LAUGH AT THIRTY-YEAR-OLD UNMARRIED OFFICE LADIES ~ ♫
......
I'M IN DESPAIR!
I'M IN DESPAIR OVER THIS HIERARCHICAL SOCIETY ALWAYS LOOKING DOWN ON SOMEONE EVEN ONE STEP LOWER THAN THEMSELVES!
COMRADES! THE LIGHT OF A NEW DAY IS APPROACHING!
じゃかじゃか
じゃかじゃか
RAAH
RAAH
11.4
革命
RAAH
SENSEI'S BECOME A FOLK GUERRILLA.
THAT'S RIGHT, COMRADES OF ITOSHIKI!
WE CANNOT ENDURE A SOCIETY THAT HAS SUCH DIFFERENCES IN SOCIAL STRATA!
MARXISM
IN AN IDEAL NATION, ALL CITIZENS MUST BE EQUALLY RICH!
TO FIND A NATION WITH A FLAT DOLL DISPLAY LIKE THIS ONE, WE MUST DEFECT FROM JAPAN OR GO AND STUDY ABROAD!

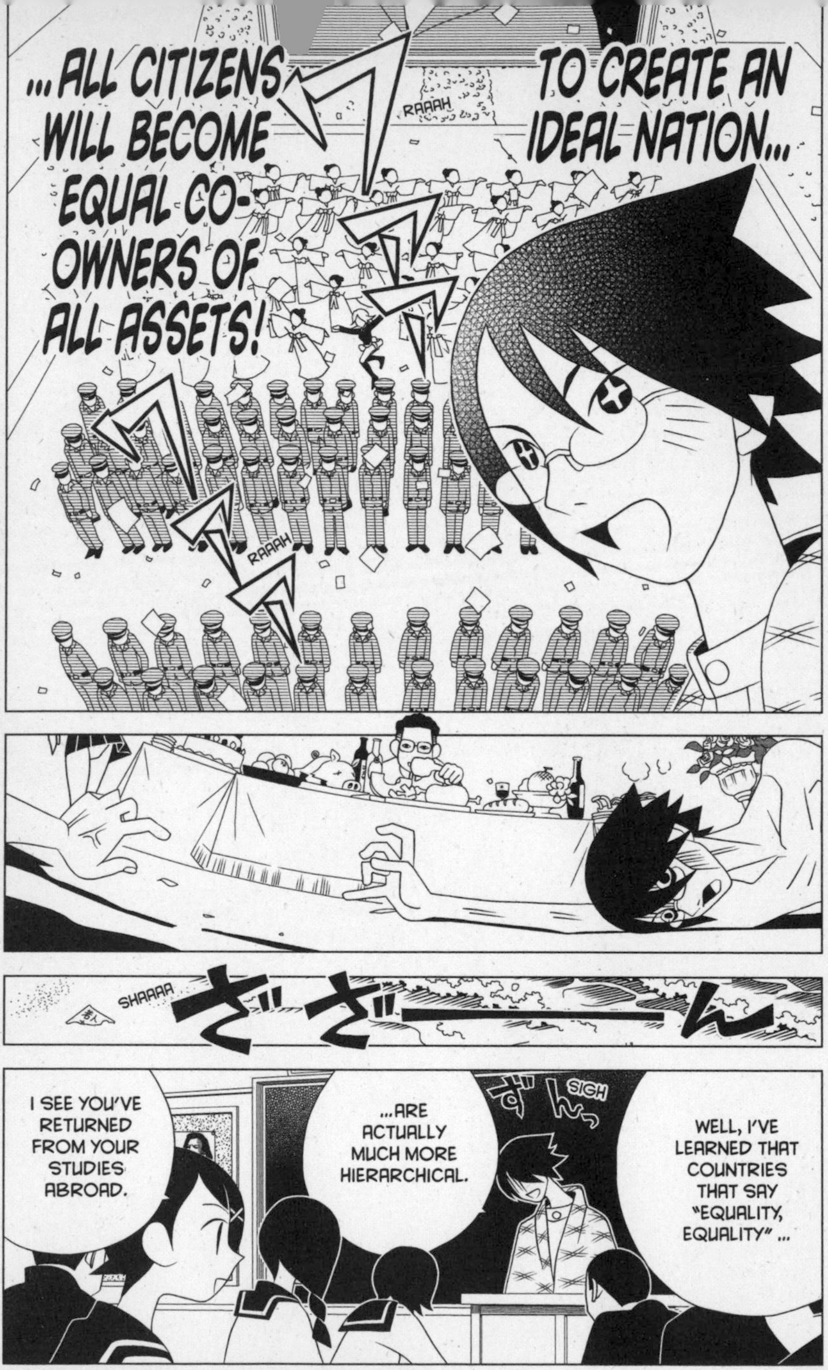
TO CREATE AN IDEAL NATION...
...ALL CITIZENS WILL BECOME EQUAL CO-OWNERS OF ALL ASSETS!
RAAAH
RAAAH
SHAAAA
ざざーーーん
WELL, I'VE LEARNED THAT COUNTRIES THAT SAY "EQUALITY, EQUALITY"...
ずんっ
SIGH
...ARE ACTUALLY MUCH MORE HIERARCHICAL.
I SEE YOU'VE RETURNED FROM YOUR STUDIES ABROAD.

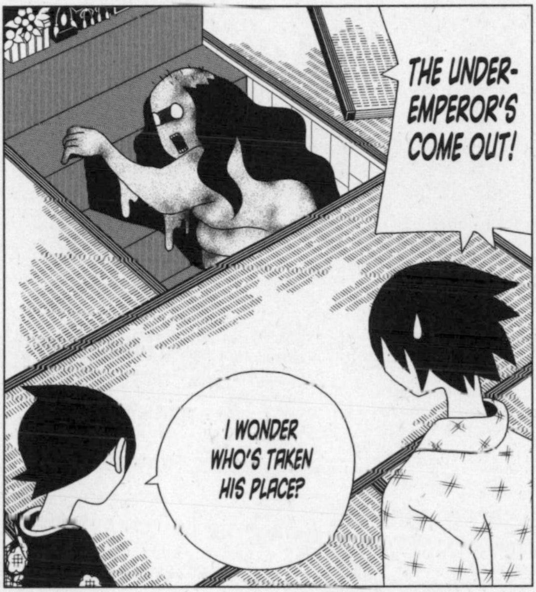
THE UNDER-EMPEROR'S COME OUT!
I WONDER WHO'S TAKEN HIS PLACE?

CURRENT CHARGES FROM THIS ISSUE

LETTER OF ACCUSATION

PLAINTIFF:
OCCUPATION: STUDENT
NAME: KAERE KIMURA

DEFENDANT:
OCCUPATION: STUDENT
NAME: KAGERO USUI

DATE: NOVEMBER 1
ATTN: CHIEF OF POLICE

- PURPOSE OF ACCUSATION
THE ACTS BY THE DEFENDANT AS STATED BELOW ARE CONSIDERED TO FALL UNDER CRIMINAL LAW, ARTICLE 176 (CRIME OF ATTEMPTED SEXUAL ASSAULT) AND THIS COMPLAINT IS MADE TO PURSUE SEVERE PUNISHMENT TO BE HANDED OUT TO THE DEFENDANT.

- FACTS OF THE ACCUSATION
AT ABOUT 11:00 A.M., WHILE I WAS PASSING BY ON A BICYCLE AND WAS LOOKING THE OTHER WAY, I WAS STRUCK FROM THE FRONT.

I TRIED WITH ALL MY MIGHT TO TRY TO AVOID A COLLISION WITH THE DEFENDANT BY CHANGING THE DIRECTION OF MY BIKE, BUT THE DEFENDANT PURPOSELY HINDERED MY PASSAGE AND ALLOWED MY BIKE TO BE OVERTURNED. FURTHERMORE, THE DEFENDANT, GENTLY AND YEARNINGLY, TOOK OUT AN EGGPLANT, GRASPED BOTH MY ANKLES, AND THEN COMMITTED AN INDECENT ACT BY PUTTING THAT EGGPLANT BETWEEN MY THIGHS AND [redacted] IT INTO ME.

THE AFOREMENTIONED ACT IS DEEMED TO FALL UNDER CRIMINAL LAW, ARTICLE 176 (CRIME OF ATTEMPTED SEXUAL ASSAULT) AND IN ORDER FOR THE DEFENDANT TO BE GIVEN STRICT PUNISHMENT, I HEREBY MAKE MY CHARGES.

DEMONSTRATION OF EVIDENCE
1. WITNESS: NOZOMU ITOSHIKI
2. WITNESS: MARIA TARO SEKIUCHI

PHYSICAL EVIDENCE
THE AFOREMENTIONED EGGPLANT (ONE)

LETTER OF ACCUSATION

PLAINTIFF:
OCCUPATION: STUDENT
NAME: KAERE KIMURA

DEFENDANT:
OCCUPATION: STUDENT
NAME: CHIRI KITSU

DATE: DECEMBER 24
ATTN: CHIEF OF POLICE

- PURPOSE OF ACCUSATION
THE ACTS BY THE DEFENDANT AS STATED BELOW ARE CONSIDERED TO FALL UNDER CRIMINAL LAW, ARTICLE 203 (CRIME OF ATTEMPTED MURDER) AND THIS COMPLAINT IS MADE TO PURSUE SEVERE PUNISHMENT TO BE HANDED OUT TO THE DEFENDANT.

- FACTS OF THE ACCUSATION
AT ABOUT 7:00 P.M., WHEN I WENT OUTSIDE TO VIEW THE CHRISTMAS ILLUMINATIONS, THE DEFENDANT APPROACHED ME, AND STRAIGHT OUT OF HER MOUTH CAME HER CANDID THOUGHT: "I'M JEALOUS OF YOUR MOST-BEAUTIFUL-IN-THE-WORLD FIGURE."

I FELT THAT PHYSICAL DANGER WAS IMMINENT, AND ATTEMPTED TO RUN AWAY FROM THE DEFENDANT. THEN THE DEFENDANT GRABBED MY LEFT ANKLE AND HUNG ME UPSIDE DOWN, EXPOSING MY PANTIES AND THUS COMMITTING AN INDECENT ACT. FURTHERMORE, SHE JUST LEFT ME HANGING THERE.

THE AFOREMENTIONED ACT IS DEEMED TO FALL UNDER CRIMINAL LAW, ARTICLE 203 (CRIME OF ATTEMPTED MURDER) AND IN ORDER FOR THE DEFENDANT TO BE GIVEN STRICT PUNISHMENT, I HEREBY MAKE MY CHARGES.

DEMONSTRATION OF EVIDENCE
1. WITNESS: RIN ITOSHIKI AND SEVERAL OTHER PERSONS
2. WITNESS: DOCTOR FROM THE UNIVERSITY HOSPITAL – MEDICAL CERTIFICATE PREPARED BY THE DOCTOR

ACCOMPANYING DOCUMENTS
THE AFOREMENTIONED MEDICAL CERTIFICATE – (ONE DOCUMENT)

ZETSUBOU ART GALLERY

ZETSUBOU CLASS NEWS

VOL. 3

The Best Zetsubou Fan Art for These Stories (That We Could Print...)

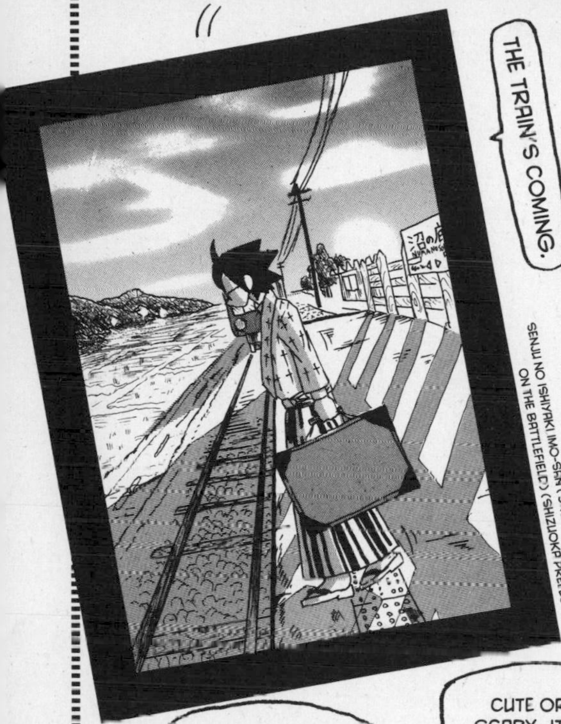

THE TRAIN'S COMING.

SENJU NO ISHIYAKI IMO-SAN (SWEET POTATO VENDOR ON THE BATTLEFIELD) (SHIZUOKA PREFECTURE)

IT TAKES GUTS TO TAKE THAT STEP FORWARD!

NICE CAMERA ANGLE (HEH).

CUTE OR SCARY—IT'S HARD TO TELL WITH THIS SKETCH.

LOSER DOG ZOMBIE-SAN (OSAKA)

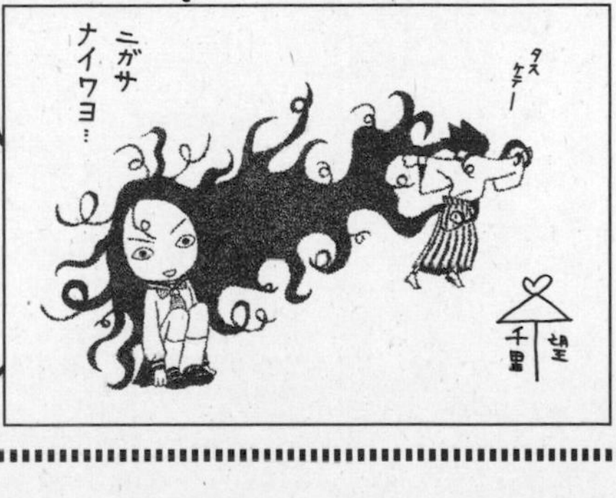
タスケテー
ニガサナイワヨ…
望
千里

DESIGN-WISE, I FEEL IT'S TASTEFUL. IT HAS A SUMMER FEEL TO IT.

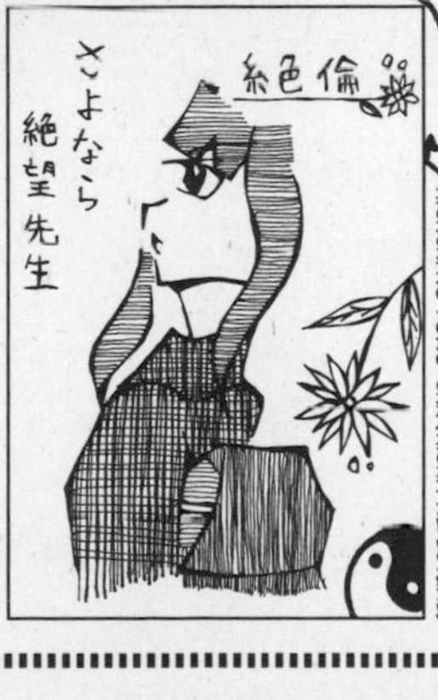
さよなら絶望先生
糸色倫

HISASHI NO YOKO-SAN (AICHI PREFECTURE)

YOU'VE CAPTURED MY FEELINGS FOR ME. →

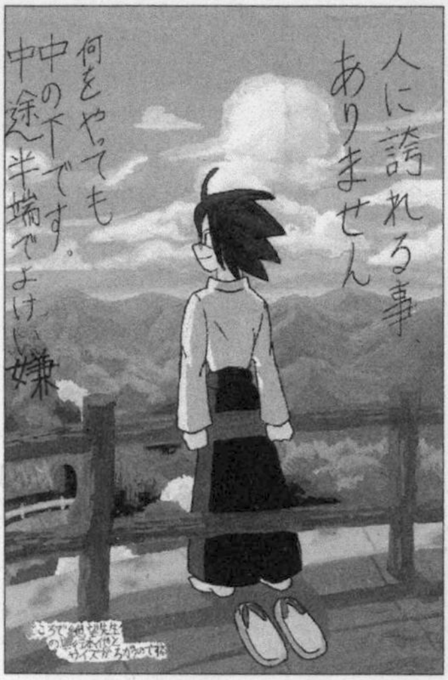
人に誇れる事ありません
何をやっても中の下です。中途半端でよけい嫌

KIIBO-SAN (FUKUI PREFECTURE)

I SUPPOSE THIS TYPE IS WHAT'S TRENDY NOW.

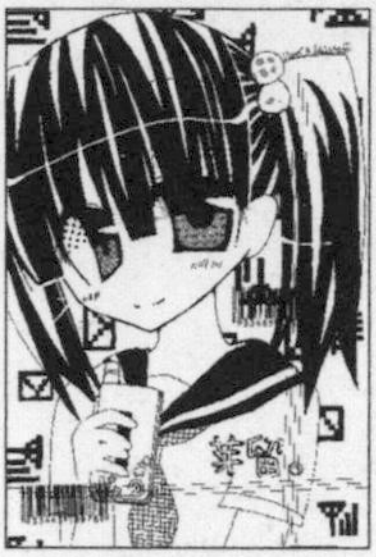

TSUKISHOKU KAMIYA-SAN
(MIE PREFECTURE)

THIS ONE LOOKS LIKE ME.

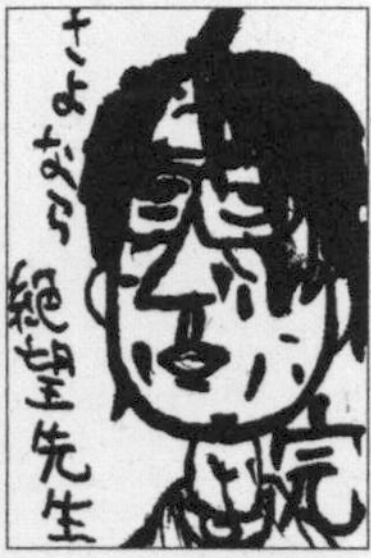
さよなら絶望先生

1993-SAN
(SAITAMA PREFECTURE)

SHE'S PROBABLY THINKING ABOUT GETTING BITTEN BY A DOG OR SOMETHING...

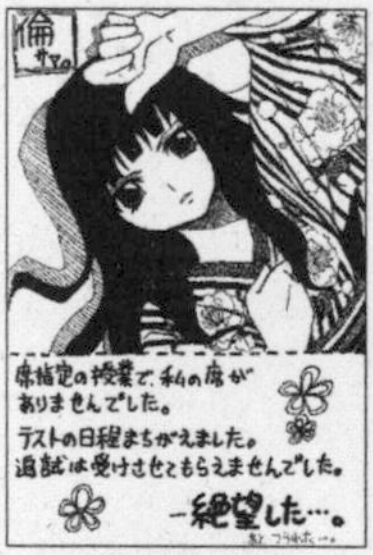
席指定の授業で、私の席がありませんでした。
テストの日程まちがえました。
追試は受けさせてもらえませんでした。
ー絶望した…。

KANCHAN-SAN (TOKYO)

THE GLASSES NEVER COME OFF.

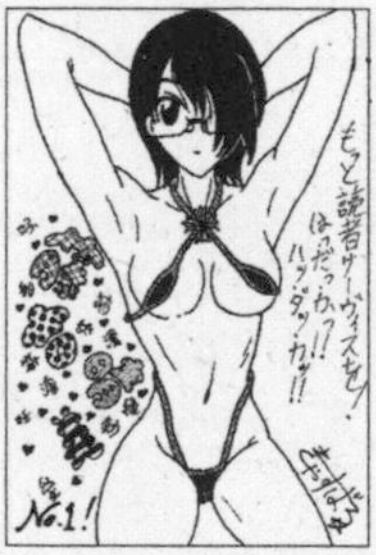
No.1!

CASVAL REM DEIKUN-SAN
(DAITO CITY)

WHO IS THIS? IS IT HIM? IS IT THAT DUDE?

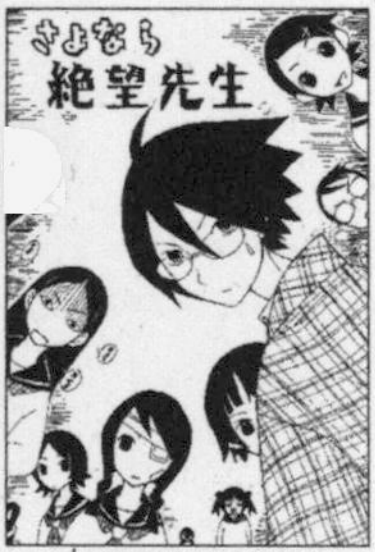
さよなら
絶望先生

EGUCHI KAZUHITO-SAN
(GUMMA PREFECTURE)

THAT WAS TO BE EXPECTED.

I WAS DECEIVED BY K. HAYASHI. →

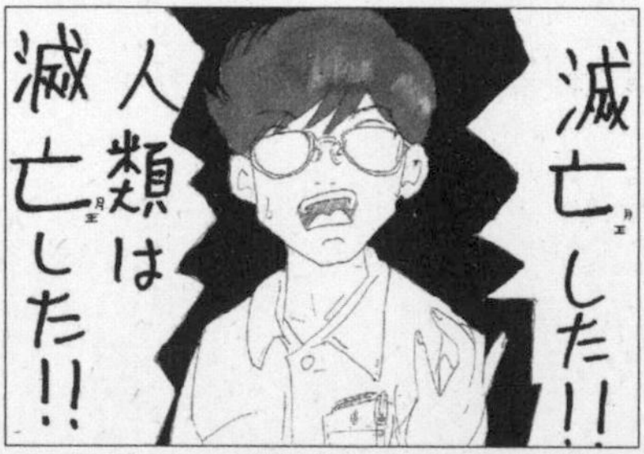
滅亡した!!
人類は滅亡した!!

DWINDLING SOLDIER KUROTOCHAN-SAN
(KUMAMOTO PREFECTURE)

IS THIS ABOUT ME? IS IT ABOUT YOU? →

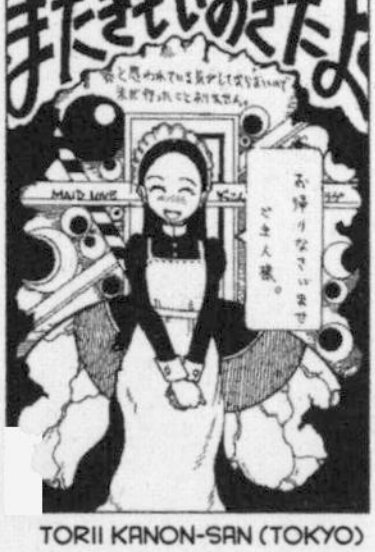
またきもいのきたよ

TORII KANON-SAN (TOKYO)

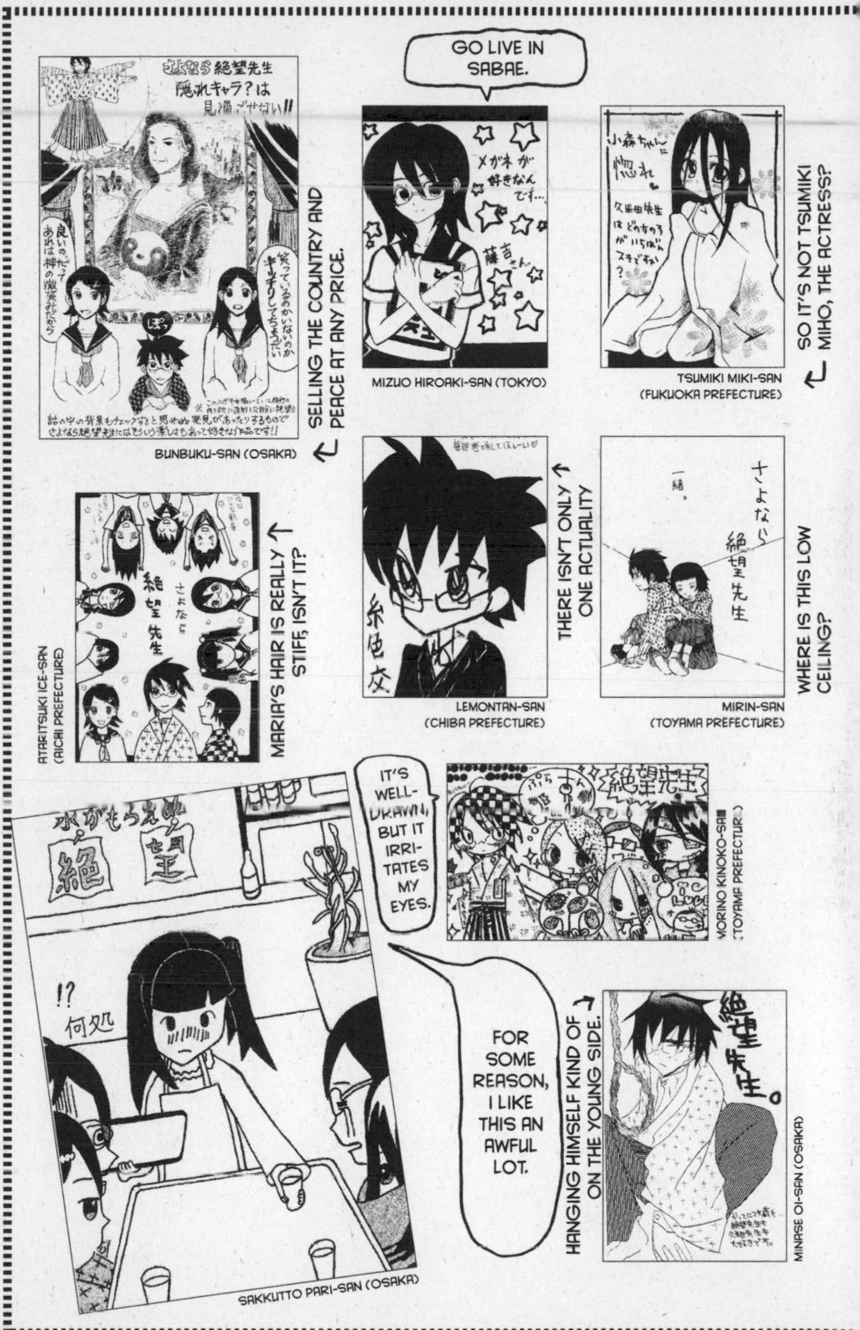
小森ちゃんに惚れ♥
TSUMIKI MIKI-SAN (FUKUOKA PREFECTURE)
SO IT'S NOT TSUMIKI MIHO, THE ACTRESS?
GO LIVE IN SABAE.
メガネが好きなんです...
藤吉さん
MIZUO HIROAKI-SAN (TOKYO)
さよなら絶望先生
隠れキャラ?は
見逃さない!!
BUNBUKU-SAN (OSAKA)
SELLING THE COUNTRY AND PEACE AT ANY PRICE.
さよなら絶望先生
一緒。
MIRIN-SAN (TOYAMA PREFECTURE)
WHERE IS THIS LOW CEILING?
糸色交
LEMONTAN-SAN (CHIBA PREFECTURE)
THERE ISN'T ONLY ONE ACTUALITY
さよなら絶望先生
ATARITSUKI ICE-SAN (AICHI PREFECTURE)
MARIA'S HAIR IS REALLY STIFF, ISN'T IT?
絶望先生。
MINASE OI-SAN (OSAKA)
HANGING HIMSELF KIND OF ON THE YOUNG SIDE.
絶望先生
MORINO KINOKO-SAN (TOYAMA PREFECTURE)
IT'S WELL-DRAWN, BUT IT IRRITATES MY EYES.
絶望
!? 何処
SAKKUTTO PARI-SAN (OSAKA)
FOR SOME REASON, I LIKE THIS AN AWFUL LOT.

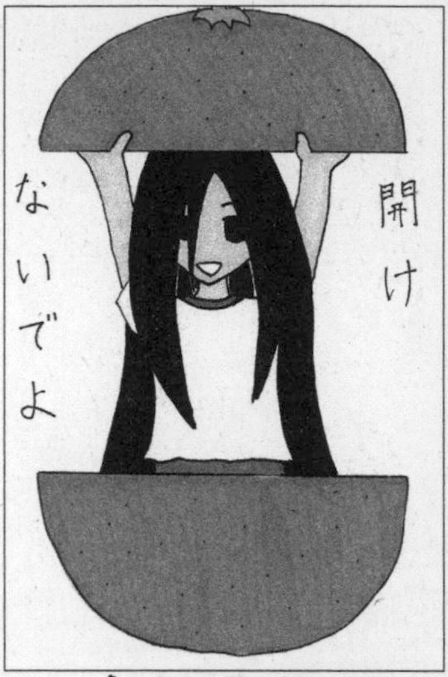
開けないでよ

TSUKIMI SO-SAN (EVENING PRIMROSE)
(CHIBA PREFECTURE)

BUT SHE'S CLEARLY OPENED IT HERSELF.

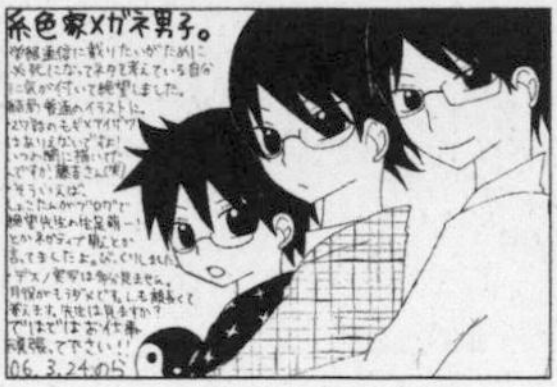
絲色家メガネ男子。
06.3.24

MERA-CHAN
(AKITA PREFECTURE)

THE BOOK CAME OUT ABOUT BECOMING GUYS IN SUITS...THAT'S RIGHT...KIND OF GOT CARRIED AWAY.

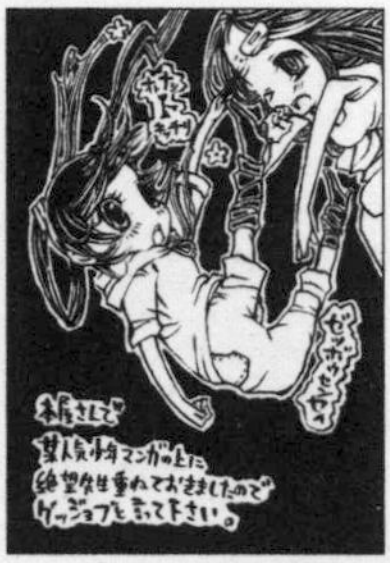

MITSUNORI-SAN
(IBARAGI PREFECTURE)

SEEM TO BE INTERTWINED IN A COMPLEX WAY.

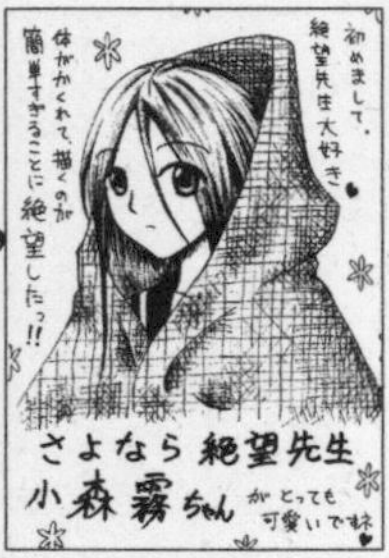
さよなら絶望先生
小森霧ちゃん が とっても可愛いですね

YUKIBANA-SAN (SNOW FLOWER)
(AICHI PREFECTURE)

DON'T TELL ME IT'S EASY TO DRAW A BODY THAT'S COVERED UP!!

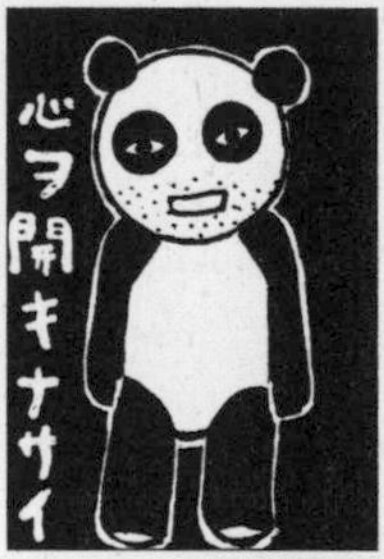
心ヲ開キナサイ

YAMINABE-SAN
(SHIMANE PREFECTURE)

I WOULDN'T OPEN IT FOR SOMETHING LIKE THAT.

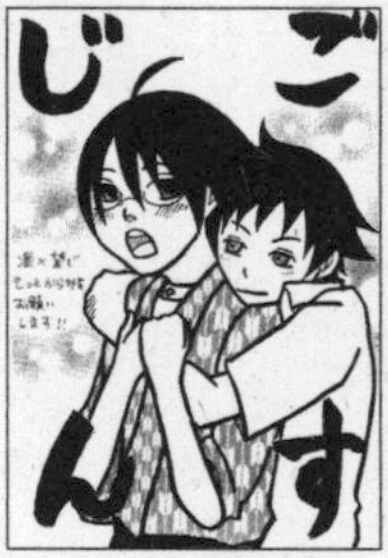

SWITCH HITTER-SAN
(AICHI PREFECTURE)

YOU BETTER NOT SAY "JIGONSU" (BUTTHOLE) TOO MUCH.

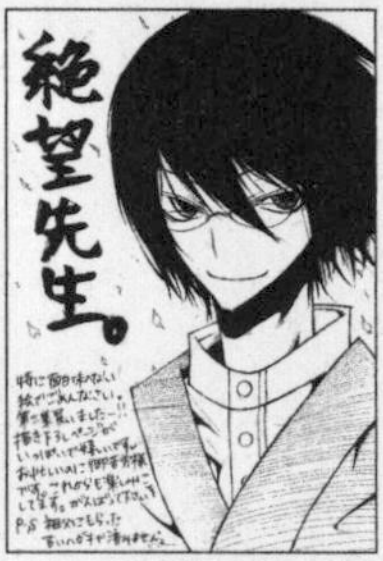
絶望先生。

TORO NORISUKE EMON
(TOCHIGI PREFECTURE)

THIS LOOKS COOLER THAN THE REAL ONE.

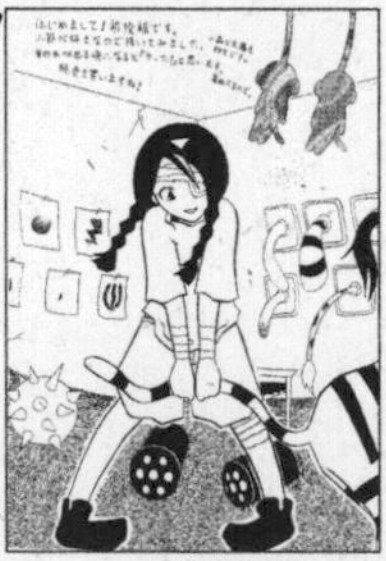

CHIKARAHITO-SAN
(CHIBA PREFECTURE)

IT'S HARD TO WRITE COMMENTS ABOUT PEOPLE WHO DO A REALLY GOOD JOB.

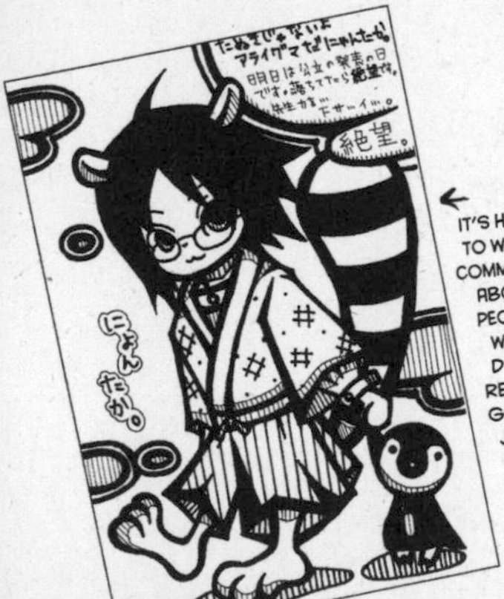
絶望。
にょんたか。

AZUZU-SAN
(GIFU PREFECTURE)

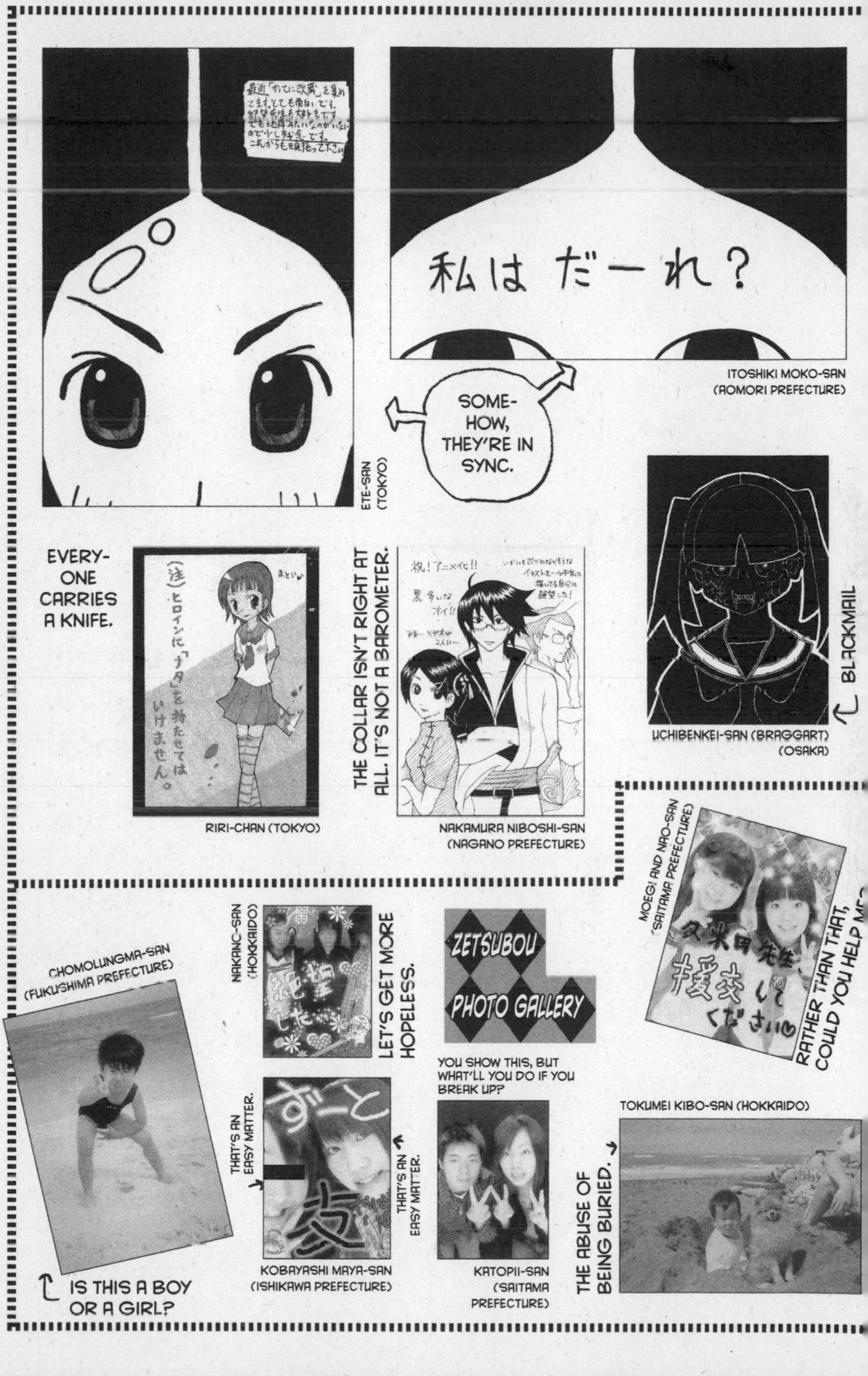
私は だーれ？
ITOSHIKI MOKO-SAN (AOMORI PREFECTURE)
SOME-HOW, THEY'RE IN SYNC.
ETE-SAN (TOKYO)
BLACKMAIL
UCHIBENKEI-SAN (BRAGGART) (OSAKA)
THE COLLAR ISN'T RIGHT AT ALL. IT'S NOT A BAROMETER.
祝！アニメ化!!
NAKAMURA NIBOSHI-SAN (NAGANO PREFECTURE)
EVERY-ONE CARRIES A KNIFE.
(注) ヒロインに「ナタ」を持たせてはいけません。
RIRI-CHAN (TOKYO)
MOEGI AND NAO-SAN (SAITAMA PREFECTURE)
久米田先生 援交して くださいね
RATHER THAN THAT, COULD YOU HELP ME?
ZETSUBOU PHOTO GALLERY
NAKANO-SAN (HOKKAIDO)
LET'S GET MORE HOPELESS.
CHOMOLUNGMA-SAN (FUKUSHIMA PREFECTURE)
IS THIS A BOY OR A GIRL?
ずーと
THAT'S AN EASY MATTER.
THAT'S AN EASY MATTER.
KOBAYASHI MAYA-SAN (ISHIKAWA PREFECTURE)
YOU SHOW THIS, BUT WHAT'LL YOU DO IF YOU BREAK UP?
KATOPII-SAN (SAITAMA PREFECTURE)
TOKUMEI KIBO-SAN (HOKKAIDO)
THE ABUSE OF BEING BURIED.

I COULD GET IN REAL HOT WATER HERE, SO I'LL TRY TO KEEP FROM COMMENTING.

ZETSUBOU RADIOWAVE BOX

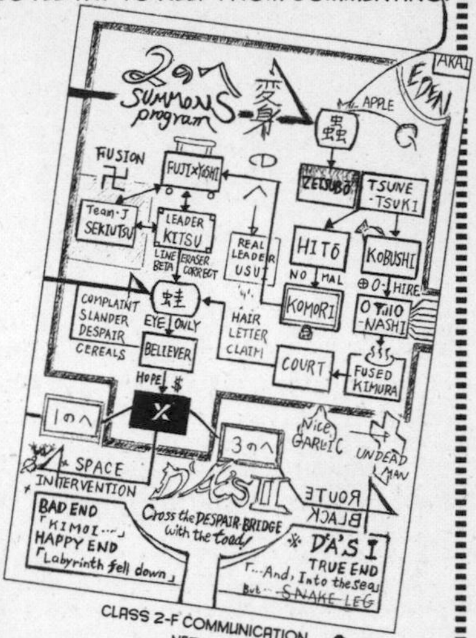

2のへ
SUMMONS program
FUSION
FUJI×YOSHI
ZETSUBO
TSUNE-TSUKI
Team J SEKIUTSU
LEADER KITSU
REAL LEADER USUI
HITO
KOBUSHI
COMPLAINT SLANDER DESPAIR CEREALS
EYE ONLY
BELIEVER
HAIR LETTER CLAIM
KOMORI
COURT
FUSED KIMURA
HOPE
1のへ
3のへ
SPACE INTERVENTION
Nice GARLIC
UNDEAD MAN
BAD END 「KIMOI…」
HAPPY END 「Labyrinth fell down」
Cross the DESPAIR BRIDGE with the toad
ROUTE BLACK
D'A'S I TRUE END 「…And, Into the sea」
APPLE
EDEN

CLASS 2-F COMMUNICATION NETWORK-SAN (?)

????

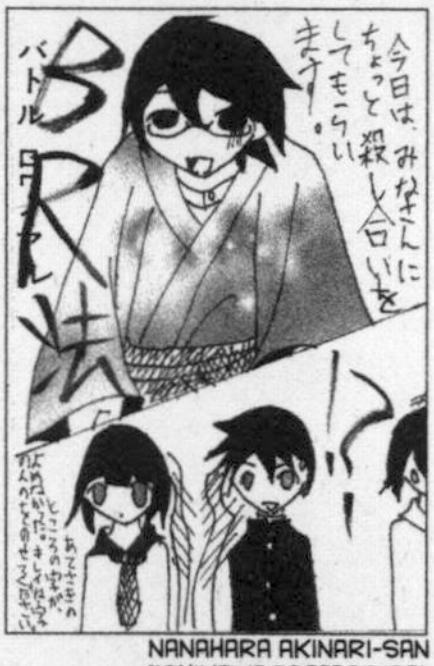

今日は、みなさんにちょっと殺し合いをしてもらいます。
BR法

NANAHARA AKINARI-SAN (ISHIKAWA PREFECTURE)

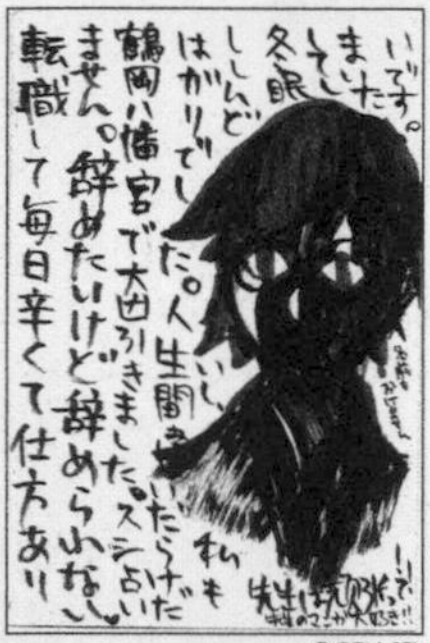

? SAN (?)

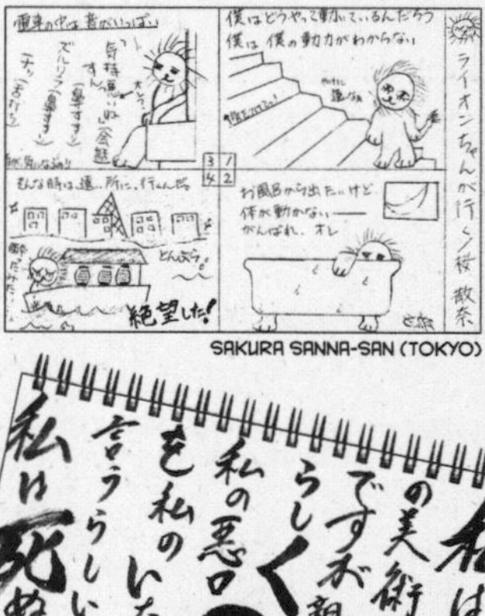

ライオンちゃんが行く 桜 散奈
僕はどうやって動いているんだろう
僕は僕の動力がわからない
お風呂から出た…けど 体が動かない—— がんばれ、オレ
絶望した!

SAKURA SANNA-SAN (TOKYO)

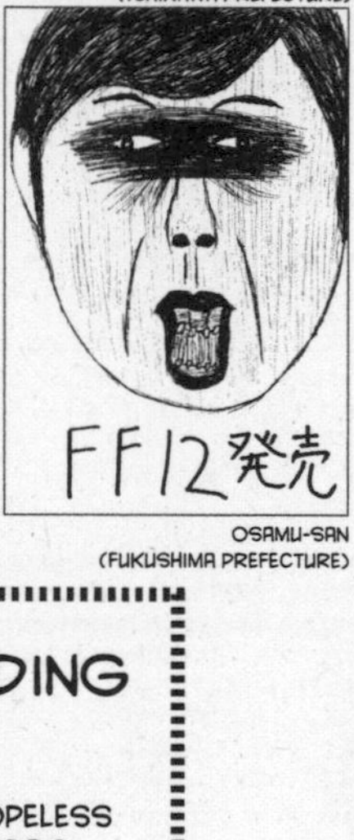

FF12発売

OSAMU-SAN (FUKUSHIMA PREFECTURE)

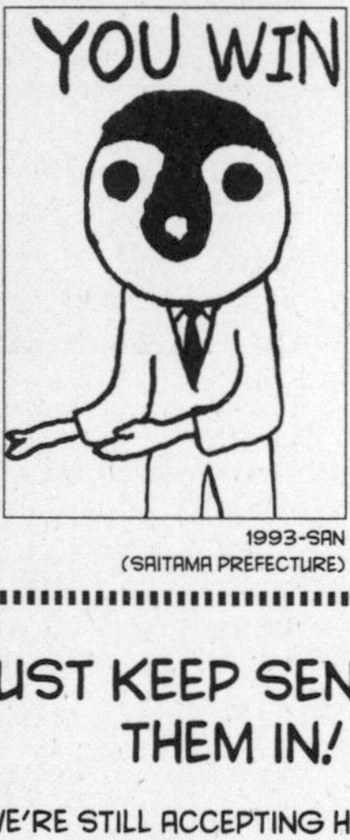

YOU WIN

1993-SAN (SAITAMA PREFECTURE)

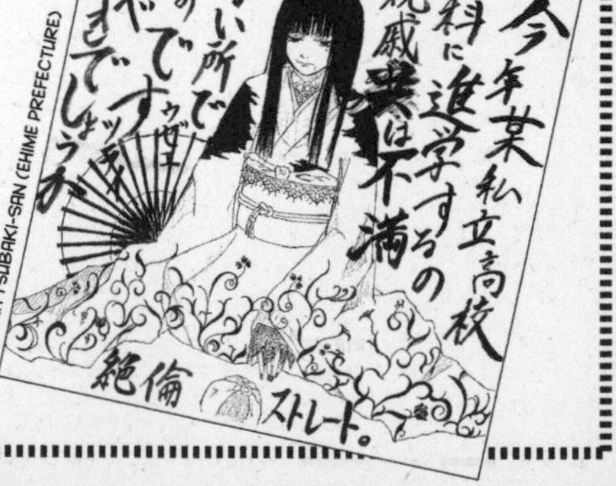

私は今年某私立高校の美術科に進学するのですが親戚一同は不満らしく私の悪口を私のいない所で言うらしいのです
ウザイッ
私は死ぬべきでしょうか
絶倫
ストレート。

YASHIMA TSUBAKI-SAN (EHIME PREFECTURE)

JUST KEEP SENDING THEM IN!

WE'RE STILL ACCEPTING HOPELESS ILLUSTRATIONS, POSTCARDS, PHOTOS, PRINT CLUB STICKERS, AND SO ON! READERS, KEEP SENDING YOUR HOPELESS THOUGHTS TO THIS CORNER.

SEND TO:

DELL REY MANGA
ATTN: ZETSUBOU ART
1745 BROADWAY
NEW YORK, NY 10019

PAPER BLOGS

FOREWORD | CUT OFF | CHRISTMAS

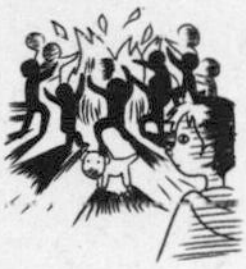

RIGHT BEFORE THE WORLD CUP, THE WORLD SURGES INTO A FRENZY OF EXCITEMENT. I LIKE SOCCER TOO, SO I'D LIKE TO GET ALL EXCITED, BUT FOR SOME REASON, WHEN EVERYONE AROUND ME IS EXCITED, I COOL OFF.

I'VE ALWAYS BEEN THAT WAY. WHENEVER THERE WERE FESTIVALS, I'D ALWAYS BE RIGHT OUTSIDE THE CIRCLE OF EXCITEMENT. I'D WANT TO BE IN THE CIRCLE, BUT I COULDN'T STAND IT, SO I'D STAY OUTSIDE. EVEN WHEN I WENT ON A CAMPING TRIP, I'D BE OUTSIDE THE CIRCLE, AND I'D STARE DISTANTLY AT THE CAMPFIRE FROM AFAR. WHEN I WENT TO KARAOKE, I'D STAY IN THE BATHROOM. I CAN'T GET ANY PLEASURE OUT OF FUNNY MANGA EITHER. WHEN I READ THEM, I'D BE TORMENTED BY AN INFERIORITY COMPLEX.

IT'S SUPPOSED TO BE ENJOYABLE, BUT IT'S NOT. I DON'T THINK I COULD EVER ENJOY ANYTHING. THE SECOND I THINK SOMETHING IS ENJOYABLE, IT CEASES TO BE.

BUT OF COURSE, IF SOMETHING IS UNINTERESTING, IT'S JUST UNINTERESTING.

LIFE IS ABOUT SUFFERING MISFORTUNES. LIFE, ITSELF, IS A PAIN.

FOREWORD | **CUT OFF** | CHRISTMAS

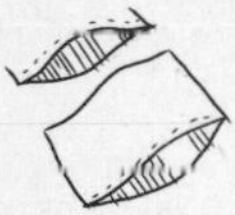

WHEN I THINK ABOUT IT, I'VE LIVED A LIFE IN WHICH I'VE OFTEN BEEN CUT OFF. WHEN I WAS IN ELEMENTARY SCHOOL AND WAS SUPPOSED TO BECOME PART OF A GROUP, I'D ALWAYS BE THE ONE LEFT OUT. I'M NOT INVITED TO CLASS REUNIONS EITHER.

I WASN'T INVITED TO WEDDINGS OF PEOPLE WHO I'D THOUGHT WERE CLOSE FRIENDS. RECENTLY, PEOPLE WHO USED TO READ ME WHEN I WROTE FOR *SHÔNEN SUNDAY* CUT ME OFF AS WELL. IF THIS CONTINUES, IN MY NEXT LIFE, I'LL BE THE HEMS ON A PAIR OF PANTS THAT GET CUT OFF. IT'S JUST TOO MISERABLE, SO I DECIDED TO THINK POSITIVELY, AND I CAME TO THIS CONCLUSION:

I'M PROBABLY NOT BEING CUT OFF, IT'S JUST THAT I'M NOT BEING NOTICED.

I'M CONFIDENT IN MY THEORY THAT I'M NOT BEING NOTICED. TAXIS DON'T STOP IF I RAISE MY HAND. SOMETIMES, AUTOMATIC DOORS AT CONVENIENCE STORES DON'T OPEN FOR ME. AT REVOLVING SUSHI RESTAURANTS, 80 PERCENT OF MY ORDERS ARE IGNORED. SOMEONE EVEN SAT ON MY LAP BY ACCIDENT ONCE. WHEN I CROSS AT PEDESTRIAN CROSSWALKS, CARS DRIVE RIGHT TOWARD ME AS IF I WASN'T THERE. I WAS WITH AN *ISHIKORO-BOSHI.*

IT'D SURE BE NICE IF TROUSER HEMS WERE USEFUL ONE DAY.

FOREWORD | CUT OFF | **CHRISTMAS**

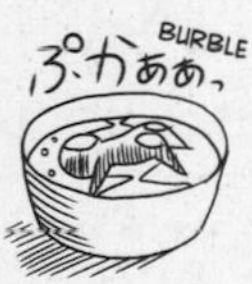
BURBLE
ぷかああ、

"YOU KNOW, THE SECOND YOU WERE BORN, YOU TRIED TO GET BACK IN."

MY MOTHER TOLD ME THIS HALF JOKINGLY.

I DON'T BELIEVE IT WAS A JOKE.

THERE'S NO WAY THAT I'D REMEMBER IT, BUT IF I WAS EVEN A LITTLE LIKE THE WAY I AM NOW, THE INSTANT I WAS BORN, I'D PROBABLY HAVE GRABBED MY UMBILICAL CORD AND HANGED MYSELF BY MY NECK. I'D PROBABLY HAVE PLANNED TO COMMIT SUICIDE BY DROWNING MYSELF IN MY FIRST BABY BATH.

I'D PROBABLY HAVE PLANNED TO COMMIT SUICIDE BY JUMPING OUT OF MY CRIB. I WANTED TO DIE FROM THE MOMENT I WAS BORN. THE SECRET TO MY SUCCESS IS NOW CLEAR.

ANYHOW, I CAN FORGIVE MY MOM FOR TELLING ME WHAT SHE DID, BUT THERE WAS ONE MORE TRUE STORY SHE TOLD ME THAT WAS A BIT MUCH.

"THE OBSTETRICIAN AND THE NURSE WHO BROUGHT YOU OUT COMMITTED DOUBLE SUICIDE BY DRIVING THEIR CAR INTO THE TSURUMI RIVER AFTER THEIR AFFAIR ENDED."

MOM, IT WASN'T NECESSARY TO TELL ME THAT, DON'T YOU THINK?

DEAD SPACE | NEW YEAR'S BOKES | FUKUBUKURO | TAKING ENTRANCE EXAMS

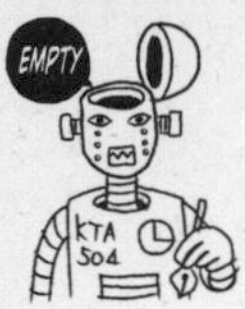
EMPTY
KTA
504

THE SETTING: KODANSHA'S SYSTEMS MANAGEMENT ROOM.

"THERE IS UNUSED SPACE IN THE BRAIN OF MANGA ROBOT KMT504. ORIGINALLY, THIS WAS SPACE RESERVED FOR TALENT, BUT MANGA ROBOT KMT504 IS A DEFECTIVE PRODUCT, SO IT SEEMS THAT PART WAS NEVER INSTALLED."

"WHAT'S A MANGA ROBOT WITHOUT TALENT? SEND IT BACK TO THE MANUFACTURER, SHOGAKUKAN!"

"WELL, THE KMT504 IS AN OLD MODEL; WE NO LONGER KNOW THE PEOPLE IN CHARGE, AND IT SEEMS ITS PARTS ARE NO LONGER BEING MANUFACTURED. PLUS, IT SEEMS THAT IT'LL COST MONEY TO RECALL IT."

"IT JUST CAN'T BE HELPED. WHY DON'T WE INSTALL OUR MOST ADVANCED OS—KIBAYASHI ENGINE XP, THE PRIDE OF OUR COMPANY—INTO IT?"

"NO, WE CAN'T. AFTER ALL, IT'S AN OLD MODEL, SO IT SEEMS THAT THE LATEST OS WON'T BE COMPATIBLE. PERHAPS WE COULD INSTALL FURONSON 95, BUT THERE ARE NO GUARANTEES. NONE OF THE PUBLISHING FIRMS ARE WILLING TO HANDLE THIS OLD MODEL ANY LONGER."

"ALL RIGHT, CONTACT THE GARBAGE DEPARTMENT."

"I GUESS I'M FINALLY TURNING INTO SCRAPS."

"RUN, 504, RUN."

"YOU'RE FJTKZ2160."

TO BE CONTINUED...

DEAD SPACE | **NEW YEAR'S BOKES** | FUKUBUKURO | TAKING ENTRANCE EXAMS

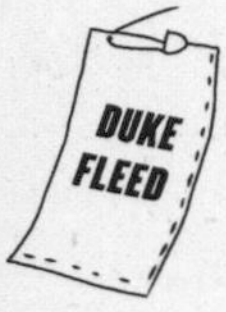
DUKE
FLEED

OF COURSE I HAD THE NEW YEAR'S *BOKES*, BUT I'M A *BOKE* ALL YEAR 'ROUND, SO IT DOESN'T REALLY NEED TO BE CALLED THE NEW YEAR'S *BOKES* SPECIFICALLY.

THE OTHER DAY, I FOUND MY FAVORITE MECHANICAL PENCIL IN MY FRIDGE. I OFTEN WEAR MY SHIRT INSIDE-OUT TO THE CONVENIENCE STORE. WHEN I GO TO TOWN TO DO SOME SHOPPING, I FORGET WHAT I'M SHOPPING FOR. WHEN I GO OUT, I HAVE TIMES WHEN I SUDDENLY DON'T KNOW WHERE I AM. I DON'T KNOW WHERE I STAND WITH *SHÔNEN MAGAZINE*.

WHERE AM I? AND WHERE AM I SUPPOSED TO GO? I'M A LOST CHILD OF MANGA. I'LL WANDER AROUND UNDER THE NAME "MAIGO HIROSHI," AKA "DUKE FLEED."

DEAD SPACE | NEW YEAR'S BOKES | **FUKUBUKURO** | TAKING ENTRANCE EXAMS

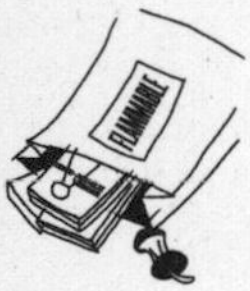

IF THERE WERE FUKUBUKURO FOR BOOKS, MY UNSOLD BOOKS WOULD BE IN 'EM.

THERE'S NO GOOD LUCK WITH LEFTOVERS. THERE'S JUST GARBAGE. SORRY THAT I'M GARBAGE.

AS AN AUTHOR, I'M A *GOMIMUSHI*, A GARBAGE BUG. I'M SORRY THAT GARBAGE IS PRODUCING GARBAGE. GARBAGE BUG KUMETA'S GARBAGE MANGA AWARD. LIKE KUMETA, THE GARBAGE BUG HAS GREEN IN ITS LEFTOVERS.

THE WORDS I'VE HEARD THE MOST OFTEN IN MY LIFE ARE, "IT CAME TO A BAD END."

THIS THOUGHT ALWAYS LINGERS.

EVERY WEEK I HARBOR REGRETS.

DEAD SPACE | NEW YEAR'S BOKES | FUKUBUKURO | **TAKING ENTRANCE EXAMS**

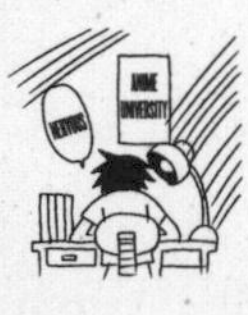

IN THIS LINE OF BUSINESS, EVERY WEEK SEEMS LIKE TAKING ENTRANCE EXAMS. EVERY WEEK, THERE ARE TESTS WITH SURVEYS. YOU MIGHT SAY I'M A STUDENT PREPARING FOR MY ENTRANCE EXAMS.

THE ONES GIVING ME THE GRADES ARE, OF COURSE, YOU, THE HONORABLE READERS. AS LONG AS I MAINTAIN A STANDARD SCORE OF 30, MY SERIES CAN GET PUBLISHED IN *SHÔNEN MAGAZINE*. WITH SUCH A LOW SCORE, I DEVELOPED ENTRANCE EXAM NEUROSIS. ON TOP OF BEING A STUDENT PREPARING FOR EXAMS, I'VE GOT ENTRANCE EXAM NEUROSIS, SO I NEED PEOPLE TO TREAT ME VERY GENTLY. IF MY MANUSCRIPT SEEMS LIKE IT'LL BE LATE, PLEASE HAVE A POLICE CAR ESCORT IT TO THE PRINTER FOR ME. PLEASE TRY NOT TO PAY ATTENTION TO THE PARTS THAT DON'T MAKE ANY SENSE. HOW MANY TESTS DO I HAVE TO TAKE TO PASS?

I'M NOW ON MY FIFTEENTH WAVE OF TESTS TO GET INTO ANIME UNIVERSITY.

EHOMAKI | VALENTINES | SECOND OPINION | DEGRADED DOLL DISPLAY

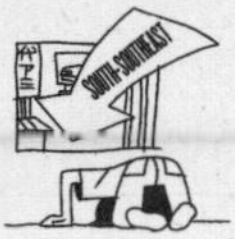
SOUTH-SOUTHEAST

OTHER PEOPLE MAY HAVE "LUCKY DIRECTIONS," BUT NOT ME. FOR THOSE OF US WITH GLOOMY HEARTS, THERE'S NOT A SINGLE LUCKY DEGREE OUT OF THE 360 DEGREES ON A COMPASS.

IF I GO NORTH, THERE'LL BE AN AVALANCHE.

IF I GO SOUTH, THERE'LL BE A TSUNAMI.

IF I GO EAST, THERE'LL BE A TORNADO.

IF I GO WEST, WHAT I'D THINK IS THE SETTING SUN WOULD BE A NUCLEAR TEST.

THAT'S 360 DEGREES OF CURSED ANGLES. IN TERMS OF HUMAN RELATIONSHIPS, I DON'T HAVE ANY FRIENDS ANYWHERE IN 360 DEGREES EITHER. IN THE MEANTIME, I'VE FACED *CHO*, THE LUCKY DIRECTION, AND PROSTRATED MYSELF.

EHOMAKI | **VALENTINES** | SECOND OPINION | DEGRADED DOLL DISPLAY

FW (21) RUTIN

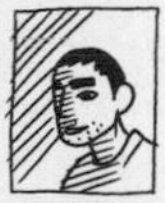

LEAVES THE OPPONENT'S DF BEHIND WITH A SIDE ATTACK

RECENTLY, THEY SAY THAT CHOCOLATES CONTAIN EFFECTIVE POLYPHENOLS AND ARE GOOD FOR OUR HEALTH. I DON'T KNOW WHETHER IT'S A SPECIAL HEALTH DRINK OR A FUNCTIONAL FOOD, AND FRANKLY, I DON'T KNOW WHAT IT'S ABOUT. WHAT IS THE CATECHIN IN TEA OR BCAA OR RUTIN? SO, I DECIDED TO JUST ARBITRARILY COME UP WITH DEFINITIONS FOR THESE WORDS.

POLYPHENOL →
AN ITALIAN PAINTER FROM THE MIDDLE AGES. HIS MASTERPIECE IS *A MAIDEN PILING BRICKS*.

RUTIN →
A PORTUGUESE SOCCER PLAYER. LEFT WINGER. THIS YEAR, HE'LL SUFFER FROM KNEE INJURIES.

BCAA →
A PROFESSIONAL SCHOOL FOR ANIME IN UTAH STATE, USA. IT'S SHORT FOR BRILLIANT CREATIVE ANIMATION ACADEMY.

CATECHIN →
THE MUSCLE BETWEEN YOUR SHOULDER AND YOUR HANDS.

EHOMAKI | VALENTINES | **SECOND OPINION** | DEGRADED DOLL DISPLAY

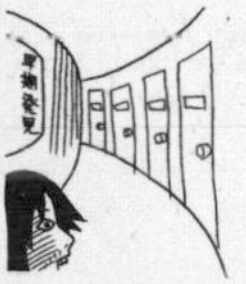

WITHOUT REALIZING IT, I FOUND MYSELF IN A LONG, LONG CORRIDOR. THERE WERE DOORS IN THE WALLS EVERY THREE METERS, AND IT CONTINUED ON INTO THE DISTANCE.

FIRST, I LOOKED AT THE NAME PLATE ON THE FIRST DOOR. IT SAID "ATTENDING PHYSICIAN."

WHEN I ENTERED, THE PHYSICIAN WAS READING MY MANGA AND SAID, "THIS IS BORING."

I REPLIED, "IS THAT SO? I THINK I'LL GET A SECOND OPINION."

SO SAYING, I LEFT THE ROOM. WHEN I LOOKED AT THE DOOR OF THE NEXT ROOM, IT SAID, "SECOND OPINION."

WHEN I ENTERED, THE "SECOND OPINION" DOCTOR WAS READING MY MANGA AND SAID, "THIS IS BORING."

I WENT THROUGH THE NEXT DOOR AND THE "SIDE OPINION" ALSO TOLD ME, "THIS IS BORING."

IN THE NEXT DOOR AND THE NEXT DOOR THEY SAID, "THIS IS BORING," "THIS IS BORING." EVEN THE FORTY-EIGHTH PERSON DIAGNOSED MY MANGA AS BORING.

NOW I'M IN FRONT OF THE FORTY-NINETH DOOR. HOW MANY DOORS DO I HAVE TO OPEN TO GET A DIFFERENT OPINION?

THE LONG, LONG CORRIDOR THAT CONTINUES FOR ETERNITY.

EHOMAKI | VALENTINES | SECOND OPINION | **DEGRADED DOLL DISPLAY**

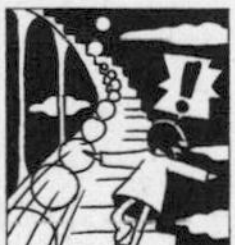

AT A CERTAIN POINT IN THEIR LIFE, PEOPLE REALIZE THAT THEY'RE AT THEIR MAXIMUM LEVEL AND THEY CAN'T GO ANY HIGHER. YOU NATURALLY REALIZE YOUR LIMITATIONS.

ABOUT SEVEN YEARS AGO, I REALIZED THAT THERE WASN'T ANOTHER LEVEL THAT I COULD GO UP TO. I HADN'T EVEN GONE UP MUCH, BUT I FELT SAD AND PAINED, THINKING I WAS GOING DOWNWARD. ANYONE WOULD THINK THEY'D RATHER STAY IN THE SAME PLACE FOREVER, RATHER THAN GO DOWNWARD. BUT IT DOESN'T WORK THAT WAY. THE DEMONS OF TIME ARE DEMOLISHING THE STEPS ALL AROUND YOU, CLOSING IN ON YOU, SO YOU HAVE NO CHOICE BUT TO RETREAT DOWNWARD.

FROM THIS POINT ON, IT'S WIN OR LOSE. SPECIFICALLY, IT'S ABOUT FINDING THE GENTLEST SLOPES TO GO DOWN FROM. FORTUNATELY, I'M NOT THAT HIGH UP, SO GOING DOWN IS EASY. IN THAT WAY, I SLOWLY HEAD DOWNWARD. WHAT'S GOING ON? IT'S EASY TO GO DOWN, BUT THERE'S THE UP STAIRCASE. GOD, I'M STILL CAPABLE. I CRY TEARS OF JOY. STRANGELY, IT'S EASY FOR ME TO CLIMB BACK UP THOSE STEPS. I CAN CLIMB. HEY MAN, I CAN CLIMB.

BUT HAPPINESS IS TRANSITORY. SUDDENLY THERE'S ANOTHER GUY NEXT TO ME RUNNING UPWARD. WHY? THE OLD MAN SITTING ON THE SIDE OF THE STAIRS TOLD ME:

"IT'S A HALLUCINATION, YOU SEE. IT HAPPENS A LOT, YOU KNOW THAT, DON'T YOU? IT'S AN ODD SLOPE WHERE CARS APPEAR TO SLIDE UPWARD. AS A MATTER OF FACT, THEY'RE REALLY GOING DOWN, AND SO ARE THE STAIRS."

I'M GETTING CLOSE TO SEEING GROUND LEVEL. GOOD-BYE.

WHAT'S NEXT FOR THESE TWO TALENTS?

YASUSHI HISAMOTO X OSAMU KOMETA

SPECIAL INTERVIEW!

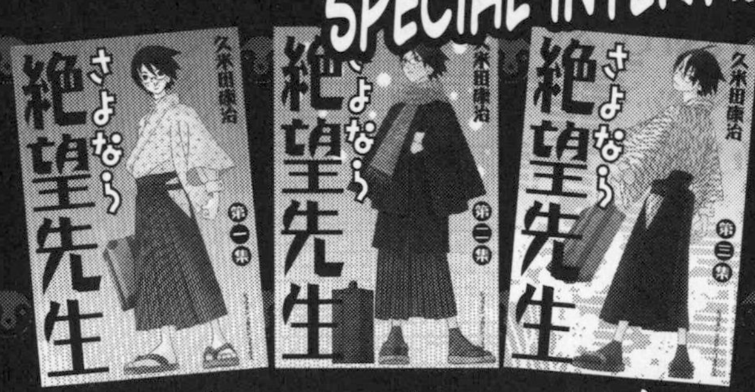

久米田康治
さよなら絶望先生
第一集
久米田康治
さよなら絶望先生
第二集
久米田康治
さよなら絶望先生
第三集

ONE ON ONE!

THESE TWO MANGA ARTISTS, WHO WORK TOGETHER UNDER THE PEN NAME KOJI KUMETA, DO A CANDID Q&A ABOUT THEIR LATEST SERIES.

OSAMU KOMETA
Born in Niigata Prefecture. In 1981, he debuted with *Great Snow River*. In 1986, *Guide to Tearooms in Outlying Islands*, *Shamisen Songs of Twisted Paper Strings* and *To You, a Mandala* were printed as indefinite serial publications. Following two years of recharging himself, his work *Deep Stagnation* is being serially published.

YASUSHI HISAMOTO
Born in Tokyo. In 1978, he debuted with *Funny Girl*. Serial publications were then begun with the same title. Currently, he's very busy with *Car-Navi (Detective) Navi* and others, as well as three serial publications.

DEEP STAGNATION BY OSAMU KOMETA

INTERVIEWER: I WANT TO THANK THE TWO OF YOU FOR TAKING THE TIME TO COME HERE DESPITE YOUR BUSY SCHEDULES.

HISAMOTO: LONG TIME, NO SEE.

KOMETA: LONG TIME, NO SEE.

INTERVIEWER: YOU'VE RESUMED WRITING AFTER DISAPPEARING FROM THE SCENE FOR TWO YEARS. I BELIEVE THAT IT'S BEEN A WHILE SINCE YOU'VE BEEN SEEN IN PUBLIC, BUT WHAT WERE YOU DOING DURING THOSE TWO YEARS?

KOMETA: ...

HISAMOTO: ...

INTERVIEWER: WELL THEN, LET ME ASK KOMETA-SENSEI ABOUT *DEEP STAGNATION*, HIS FIRST WORK SINCE HIS COMEBACK. CAN YOU TELL US, SENSEI, WHAT MAKES YOU SO ENTHUSIASTIC ABOUT THIS WORK?

KOMETA: ...(LONG SILENCE)...I SAW A DEAD PIGEON IN THE MOUNTAINS. AN OLD LOCAL MAN LOOKED AT IT AND SAID, "IT'S BEAUTIFUL." THAT'S WHY I DECIDED TO WRITE THIS STORY.

INTERVIEWER: A PIGEON, YOU SAY?

KOMETA: A PIGEON...I THINK I'VE SAID ENOUGH ABOUT THE STORY.

THERE'S A MODEL FOR THE ROLE OF THE ANTAGONIST

INTERVIEWER: NOW I HAVE SOME QUESTIONS FOR HISAMOTO-SENSEI. YOU WERE AWARDED THE KARUCHERATAN MANGA AWARD FOR *DETECTIVE CAR-NAVI*. WHAT DO YOU THINK MADE THIS MANGA SO POPULAR WITH READERS?

HISAMOTO: PERHAPS IT WAS THE SINGLE-MINDEDNESS OF THE LEAD CHARACTER. I THINK IT WAS POPULAR BECAUSE HE DIDN'T DEPEND ON HIS CAR NAVIGATION SYSTEM AND WORKED HARD TO SOLVE CASES IN A MOST HUMAN WAY. AND ANOTHER POINT WAS PROBABLY HAVING A MODERN-DAY CD NAVIGATION SYSTEM. AND THE SCENE WITH HIS MOTHER WAS VERY TOUCHING, TOO, DON'T YOU THINK?

INTERVIEWER: IN THE LATEST EPISODE WITH THE RIVAL HDD *DETECTIVE CAR-NAVI*, A GORILLA APPEARS. WHAT DID YOU MODEL IT AFTER?

HISAMOTO: IT'S JOE ODAGIRI.

INTERVIEWER: WHAT?!/ BUT IT'S A GORILLA.

HISAMOTO: RIGHT.

TEAMING UP AS "KOJI KUMETA"

INTERVIEWER: ER, WELL...MOVING ON TO THE NEXT QUESTION. THE TWO OF YOU HAVE TEAMED UP TO WORK ON *SAYONARA, ZETSUBOU-SENSEI*. WHICH ONE OF YOU DOES MOST OF THE WRITING?

HISAMOTO: HE DOES.

KOMETA: HE DOES.

HISAMOTO: DON'T TRY TO PIN THE BLAME ON SOMEONE ELSE!

KOMETA: SAME TO YOU!

(BOTH INTERVIEWEES GRAPPLE WITH EACH OTHER.)

INTERVIEWER: UM...LET'S MOVE ON TO THE NEXT QUESTION...

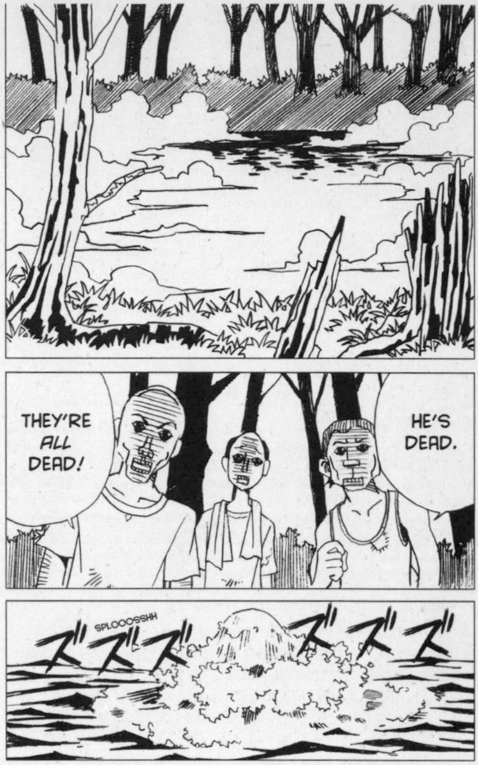
HE'S DEAD.
THEY'RE ALL DEAD!
SPLOOOSSHH
ズズズ
ズズズ

FROM *DEEP STAGNATION* BY OSAMU KOMETA

THE JOYS OF DISCOVERING INTERESTING MANGA

INTERVIEWER: WHAT'S THE MOST INTERESTING MANGA THAT YOU'VE READ RECENTLY?

HISAMOTO: FOR ME, IT'S MASAHIRO FUJITA-SENSEI'S *SEISHUN CHOCO-MINT CLUB*.

INTERVIEWER: ISN'T THAT THE MANGA WITH 251 GIRL CHARACTERS?

KOMETA: THEY'RE NOT ORDINARY HIGH SCHOOL GIRLS.

HISAMOTO: HE'S GOT TALENT.

KOMETA: YEAH, HE SURE DOES.

INTERVIEWER: KOMETA-SENSEI, DO YOU HAVE ANY FAVORITES?

KOMETA: TADASHI MURAEDA-SENSEI'S *DANCHI KURASHI* "LIFE IN A HOUSING COMPLEX."

HISAMOTO: THERE'S NOBODY WHO CAN DEPICT LIFE IN A HOUSING COMPLEX AS SKILLFULLY AS HIM.

KOMETA: IN CHAPTER 35, "MEASURES FOR WEDNESDAY GARBAGE DAY," THE PROCLAMATION OF AUTONOMY THAT DIDN'T REFLECT BACK UPON THE LOCAL GOVERNMENT LEADER'S SOLITARY LINEAGE, SEEMS TO HAVE MOVED A LOT OF READERS.

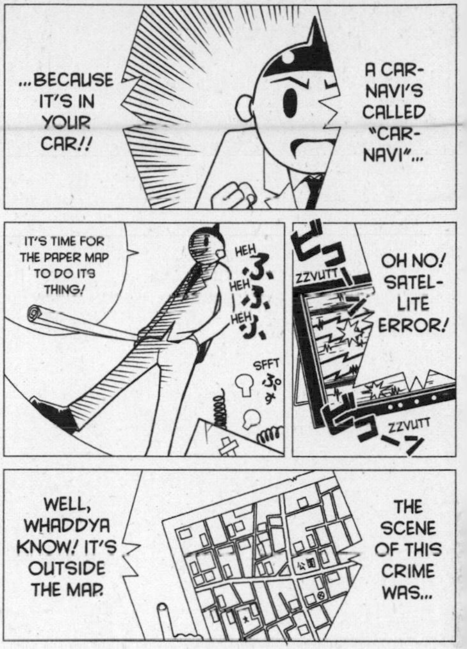
A CAR-NAVI'S CALLED "CAR-NAVI"...
...BECAUSE IT'S IN YOUR CAR!!
ZZVUTT
OH NO! SATELLITE ERROR!
ZZVUTT
IT'S TIME FOR THE PAPER MAP TO DO ITS THING!
HEH
HEH
HEH
SFFT
THE SCENE OF THIS CRIME WAS...
WELL, WHADDYA KNOW! IT'S OUTSIDE THE MAP.
FROM *CAR-NAVI DETECTIVE NAVI* BY YASUSHI HISAMOTO

WRITING STORIES ALONE, WRITING STORIES TOGETHER

INTERVIEWER: SO WHAT'S IT LIKE WHEN THE TWO OF YOU WRITE STORIES TOGETHER? WHAT KINDS OF THINGS HAPPEN?

KOMETA: ...

HISAMOTO: ...

INTERVIEWER: ...ALL RIGHT, LET'S MOVE ON TO THE NEXT QUESTION...

WE TAKE DAYS OFF PROPERLY

INTERVIEWER: THE TWO OF YOU MUST BE VERY BUSY, BUT WHAT DO YOU DO ON YOUR DAYS OFF?

HISAMOTO: I NEVER HAVE A FULL DAY OFF, SO THE MOST I DO IS PROBABLY WATCH A MOVIE.

INTERVIEWER: WHAT MOVIES HAVE YOU SEEN RECENTLY?

HISAMOTO: *THE BONCHI CODE*. THERE'S A HIDDEN CODE IN THE ROUTINES OF THE MANZAI COMEDY DUO "THE BONCHI" AND THE PROCESS OF SOLVING IT IS INTERESTING. BUT I WON'T TELL YOU ABOUT IT, BECAUSE IT'D GIVE AWAY THE STORY...

KOMETA: AH, I HAVEN'T SEEN IT YET.

INTERVIEWER: AND WHAT ABOUT YOU, KOMETA-SENSEI?

KOMETA: LATELY I'VE BEEN GOING TO A LOT OF SEMINARS. LISTEN, YOU! ATTAINING SUPREME PERFECT ENLIGHTENMENT MEANS "THERE'S NO ENLIGHTENMENT BETTER THAN THIS."

INTERVIEWER: GOT IT. LET'S MOVE ON TO THE NEXT QUESTION.

DESK MOTTOS

INTERVIEWER: WE'RE GETTING TO THE END OF THE INTERVIEW, BUT CAN I HAVE THE TWO OF YOU TELL ME WHAT YOU HAVE AS THE MOTTO ON YOUR DESK?

KOMETA: "AN OLD WARHORSE MAY BE STABLED, YET IT STILL LONGS TO GALLOP A THOUSAND *LI*."

HISAMOTO: FOR ME, IT'S "ALL IS VANITY."

INTERVIEWER: THANK YOU SO MUCH FOR BEING HERE TODAY.

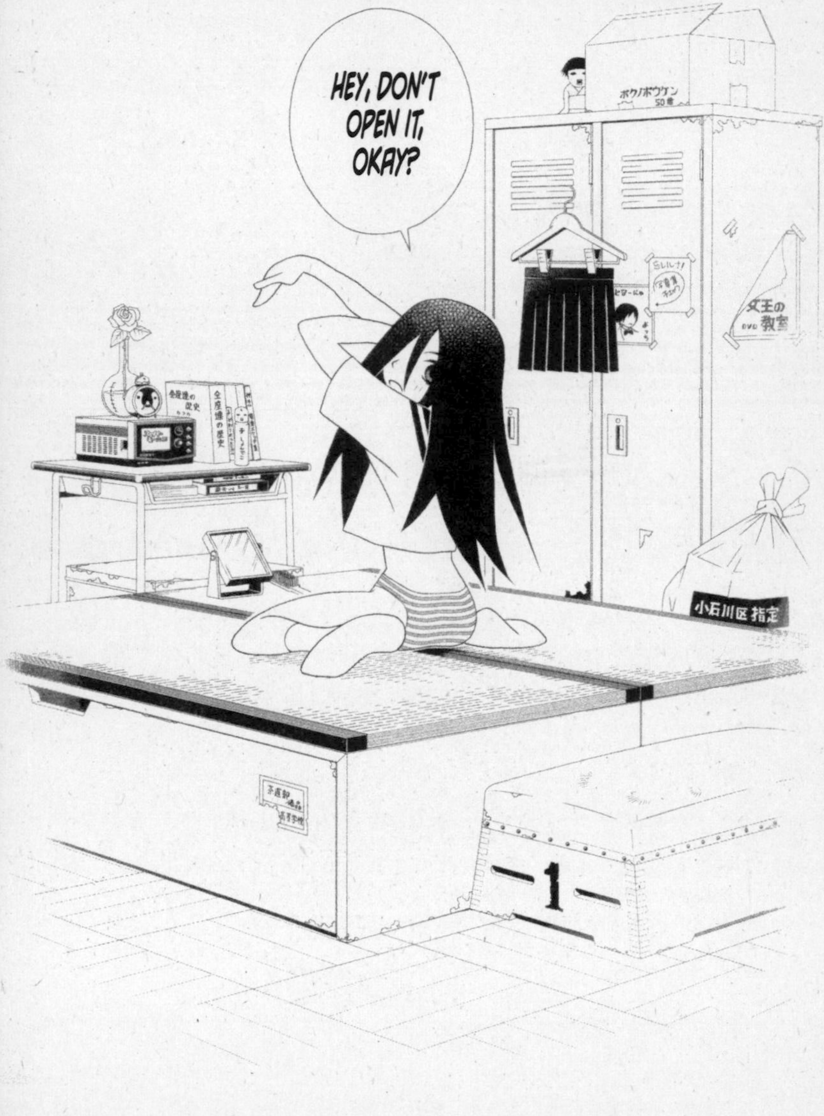
HEY, DON'T OPEN IT, OKAY?
ボクノボウケン
小石川区指定

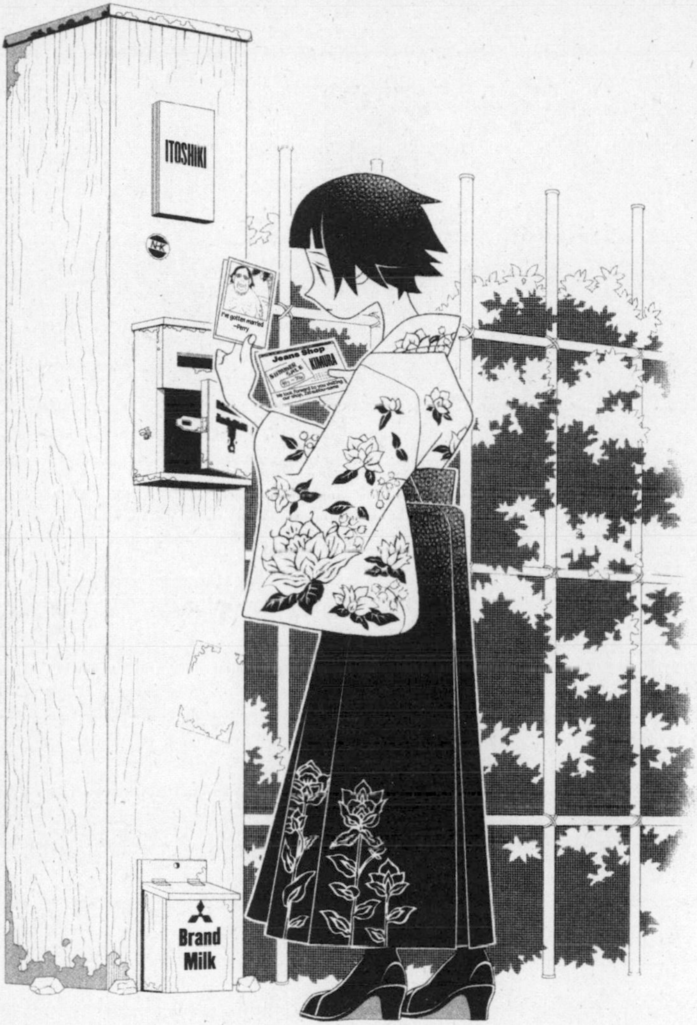
ITOSHIKI
I've gotten married
—Perry
Jeans Shop
SUMMER SALE
KIMURA
Brand
Milk

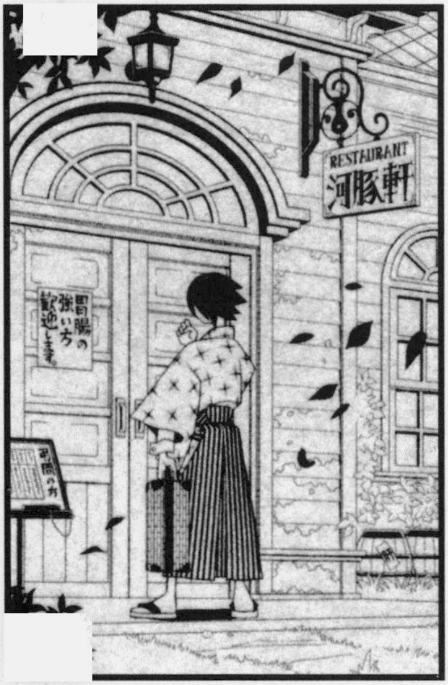
RESTAURANT
河豚軒
胃腸の強い方歓迎します。

ZETSUBOU LITERARY COMPILATION

THE RESTAURANT OF MANY CONDOLENCE CALLS

RESTAURANT "FUGU HOUSE"

"PLEASE UNDERSTAND THAT THIS RESTAURANT RECEIVES MANY CONDOLENCE CALLS."

"THE DECEASED CHEF MUST HAVE HAD A LOT OF FRIENDS WHILE HE WAS ALIVE."

"WELL, YOU KNOW, HE PREPARED *FUGU* (BLOWFISH) DISHES WITHOUT A LICENSE, SO IT'S NOT THAT THERE ARE LOTS OF FOLKS COMING TO OFFER CONDOLENCES FOR *HIM*. IT'S MORE LIKE THEY'RE OFFERING CONDOLENCES FOR THE DECEASED CUSTOMERS."

"OH NO...!" SHUDDER, SHUDDER, SHUDDER. THE TWO BEGIN TO SOB.

"PLEASE BURY YOURSELVES IN SAND HERE, AND DETOXIFY YOURSELVES.
THE AMBULANCE WON'T TAKE ANY LONGER THAN FIFTEEN MINUTES."

Translation Notes

Japanese is a tricky language for most Westerners, and translation is often more art than science. In the case of a text-dense manga like *Sayonara, Zetsubou-sensei*, it's a delicate art indeed. Although most of the jokes are universal, Koji Kumeta is famous for filling his manga with references to Japanese politics, entertainment, *otaku* culture, religion, and sports. Unless you're a true Japanophile, it's difficult to understand it all without some serious background knowledge of current events at the time the manga was running. Kumeta also uses references to foreign literature and politics, so even Japanese readers probably don't get all the humor. For your reading pleasure, here are notes on some of the more obscure references and difficult-to-translate jokes in *Sayonara, Zetsubou-sensei*.

General Notes

Sayonara, Zetsubou-sensei (title)

The title *Sayonara, Zetsubou-sensei* literally translates to "Goodbye, Mr. Despair." It's a possible reference to James Hilton's 1934 novel of a beloved teacher, *Goodbye, Mr. Chips* (known in Japan as *Chips-sensei, Sayonara*). The Del Rey edition preserves the original Japanese title, with "The Power of Negative Thinking" as a subtitle to express Itoshiki's philosophy. (The English subtitle is itself a reference to Norman Vincent Peale's 1952 self-help book *The Power of Positive Thinking*.)

Signs

Koji Kumeta's highly detailed and realistic renderings of modern Japanese life present one special challenge to the letterer. Kumeta fills his panels with all the ephemera of everyday life—street signs, product labels, magazine covers, newspaper pages, and so on. It's difficult to replace this text with English lettering without interfering with the integrity of the original illustrations. Out of respect for Kumeta's unique artwork, many signs have retained their original Japanese lettering.

Page Notes

Assorted references, page iv

Higashi-Jûjo ("East Jûjo") is the name of a railway station and the surrounding neighborhood in Tokyo's Kita ward. *Daisakkai* (literally, "great deadly sphere") is an extremely unlucky, "deadly" period of one's life according to the astrological system *rokusei senjutsu* ("six-star astrology"), while *Tenchûsatsu* (literally, "deadly within heaven") is an unlucky sign according to *sanmeigaku*, another form of fortune-telling based on birth date and the *kanji* in one's name.

Assorted references, page 3

Hikikomori is a Japanese term for individuals who have chosen to withdraw from society and not leave their homes. The word comes from the verb *hikikomoru*, which means "stay indoors" or "be confined indoors." It is considered a serious social problem in Japan. "Coupling" is a Japanese term for coming up with imaginary pairings between fictional characters. The equivalent English slang term is "shipping."

The Throwaway Bronze, page 4

Sayonara, Zetsubou-sensei's chapter titles are usually references to Japanese fiction, generally classics from the prewar period, in keeping with Zetsubou-sensei's old-fashioned clothes and tastes. This particular title is a pun on the novel *The Bronze Christ* by Nagayo Yoshiro (1888–1961). In Japanese, "the throwaway bronze" is *Seido no Kirisute* and "the bronze christ" is *Seido no Kirisuto*.

New Year's cards, page 5

In Japan, there is a tradition of sending New Year's postcards, called *nengajo*, to your friends, relatives, and business associates. The average family sends and receives more than a hundred *nengajo*, all of which are delivered promptly on January 1, through an amazing feat of the Japanese post office.

Cut me off, page 6

This chapter is full of puns based on the Japanese verb *kiri*, which meants "to cut, sever, or break off." It's part of the noun *ashikiri* ("cutoff") and is also used in the same sense that "discard" is used in English.

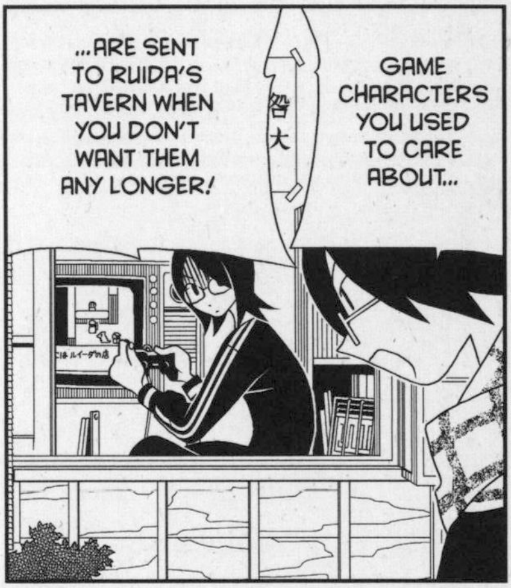
GAME CHARACTERS YOU USED TO CARE ABOUT...
...ARE SENT TO RUIDA'S TAVERN WHEN YOU DON'T WANT THEM ANY LONGER!

Ruida's Tavern, page 7

Ruida's Tavern (*Ruida no Sakaba*) is a location where unwanted party members are kept in the untranslated 1995 Super Famicom game *Dragon Quest 6*.

Assorted references, page 8

The "*Shônen Magazine* Editorial Cut-Off Meeting" refers to *Weekly Shônen Magazine*, where *Zetsubou-sensei* is printed in Japan. Over the year 2006, the magazine's page count went down, although it's unclear whether the editorial staff was quite so gleeful about it as depicted here. The National Center Test is the annual standardized admissions test used by public and some private universities in Japan.

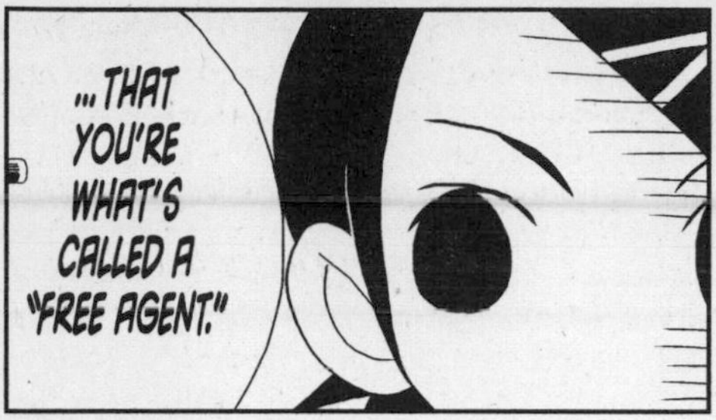
...THAT YOU'RE WHAT'S CALLED A "FREE AGENT."

Free agent, page 9

In the original Japanese, the term "free agent" is abbreviated "F.A."

Assorted references, page 10

JL is short for J-League, the top soccer league in Japan. Junichiro Koizumi (1942–) was the prime minister of Japan from 2001 to 2006, despite some opposition from within his own party, the Liberal Democratic Party. (He's also referenced on pages 60 and 95.) Colonel Muska is a character in Hayao Miyazaki's 1986 animated film, *Laputa: The Castle in the Sky*. The Roppongi Hills complex is a skyscraper business megacomplex opened in Tokyo in 2003 (see also the reference on page 40).

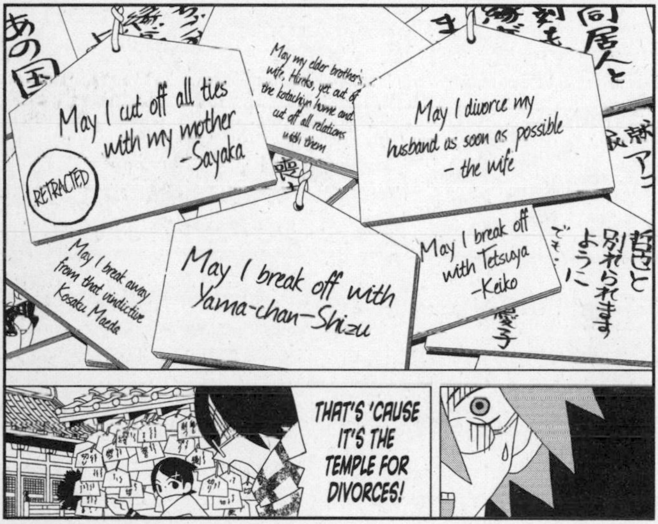
May I divorce my husband as soon as possible - the wife
別れられます
ように
May I break off with Tetsuya -Keiko
May my elder brother's wife, Hiroko, get out of the kotachiyo home and cut off all relations with them
May I cut off all ties with my mother -Sayaka
RETRACTED
May I break off with Yama-chan-Shizu
May I break away from that vindictive Kosaku Maeda
THAT'S 'CAUSE IT'S THE TEMPLE FOR DIVORCES!

Temple for Divorces, page 14

An *engiri tera* ("dissolution/divorce temple") is a temple that is traditionally used as a sanctuary for runaway wives seeking divorces. The various wishes written in the first panel are references to Japanese pop culture, such as the marriage between music producer/songwriter Tetsuya Komura (1958–) and singer Keiko Yamada (1972–), and the often troubled relationship between J-pop star Sayaka Kanda (1986–) and her mother, singer-songwriter Seiko Matsuda (1962–). *Kotachiyo* is the nickname for a Fuji TV program.

I'm Sorry for Being Born on November 4th, page 18

This title is a reference to Osamu Dazai's 1937 novel, *Nijusseiki Kishu* ("A Standard-Bearer of the 20th Century"), in which the protagonist says, "I'm sorry for being born."

Famous people, page 24

The list of people with birthdays around November 4 includes anime director/screenwriter Yoshiyuki Tomino, *Golgo 13* manga creator Takao Saito, and many other celebrities.

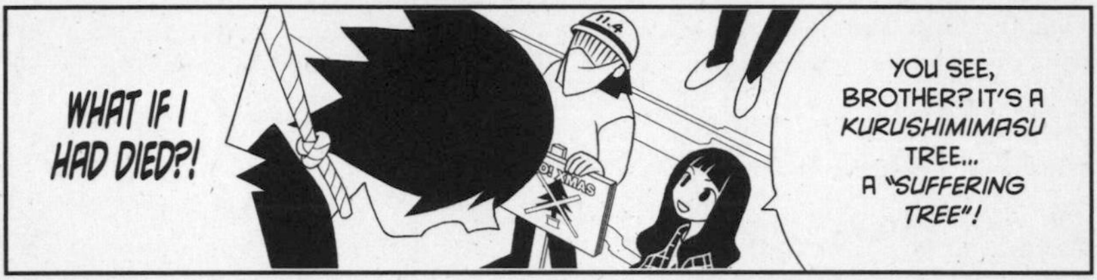
YOU SEE, BROTHER? IT'S A *KURUSHIMIMASU* TREE... A "*SUFFERING TREE*"!
WHAT IF I HAD DIED?!

Kurushimimasu tree, page 26

"Kurushimimasu Tree" sounds a lot like Christmas tree, which is pronounced "Kurisumasu Tsurii." *Kurushimimasu* literally means "you will suffer." *Tsuri* sounds like the English "tree" but can also be read as "hanging."

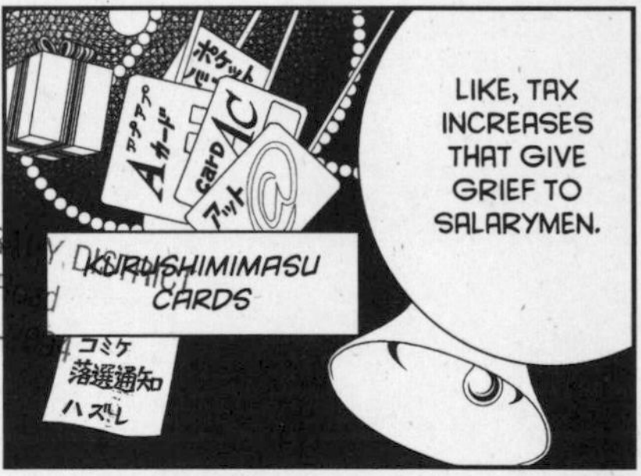
LIKE, TAX INCREASES THAT GIVE GRIEF TO SALARYMEN.
KURUSHIMIMASU CARDS
コミケ 落選通知 ハズレ

Kurushimimasu cards, page 26

The cards are takeoffs on actual consumer finance bank cards.

Assorted references, page 27

Cocco (1977–) is a J-pop singer whose 1997 single "Countdown" is apparently not held in high esteem by Koji Kumeta. "Eating your brain" refers to Hannibal Lecter, the fictional cannibal mastermind of Thomas Harris's novels *Red Dragon*, *The Silence of the Lambs*, and *Hannibal*. NEET stands for "Not currently engaged in Employment, Education, or Training." It's usually used to refer to adult losers who still live with their parents. (See also the reference on page 141.)

Fish scale, page 28

This is a reference to a Japanese saying, *me kara uroko ga ochiru* ("fish scales fall from the eyes"). It means that a person is suddenly "brought to their senses," i.e., awakened to the truth of something.

Dictator's switch, page 29

The *dokusaisha switch* ("dictator's switch") is one of the many strange and marvelous tools used by the title character of the manga and anime *Doraemon*. By using the switch, *Doraemon* can make people disappear leaving no traces of their former existence.

Assorted references, page 30

In addition to people, the tree is decorated with various things that cause suffering (such as childbirth, company "restructuring," which usually entails people getting laid off, etc.). Hidetsugu Aneha (1957–) is a former Japanese architect sentenced to five years in prison for falsifying data on earthquake safety. While he was in the public eye, he also received a lot of media attention to the style of his glasses (see pages 41 and 127).

How Do I Organize This One Space?, page 32

This title is a reference to Sakae Tsuboi's 1952 novel, *Nijushi no Hitomi* ("Twenty-Four Eyes"), in which the main character, a primary school teacher meeting her class for the first time, thinks, "How do I evade these twenty-four eyes?"

Book *obi*, page 35

Obi, which literally means the decorative sash worn around the waist of a kimono, is also used to mean a narrow band that goes around the dust jackets of Japanese books (including manga). They are meant to be disposable and usually contain blurbs and promotional text.

OR THE HOLE IN A *CHIKUWA!*

Chikuwa, page 40

A *chikuwa* (literally, "fish ring") is a food shaped like a hollow tube, but is meant to look like a stick of bamboo. It's made from fish paste, egg whites, and seasonings. It's a delicious and cheap food source.

Assorted references, page 40

The Yomiuri Giants is Japan's oldest professional baseball team. "No. 4 representing Japan" refers to Japan's team in the 2006 World Baseball Classic tournament; the first choice for the No. 4 batter, Hideki Matsui, declined, although the role was later filled by Nobuhiko Matsunaka. "The West's graded list is tops" is an obscure sumo reference. "Egawa's one empty day" is a reference to former pitcher and now baseball analyst Suguru Egawa (1955–). "The sea of trees" refers to Aokigahara, the dense woodland around Mt. Fuji, which is infamous throughout Japan as a popular spot for suicides.

Kefu no Ryori, page 41

Kefu no Ryori is a pun on *Kyo no Ryori* ("Today's Cooking"), a TV show on NHK.

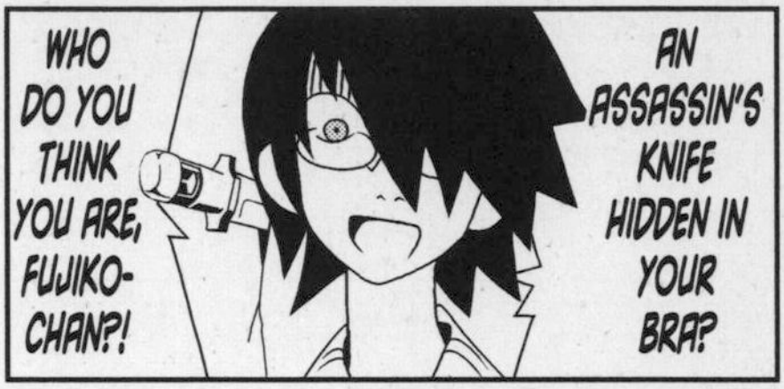
AN ASSASSIN'S KNIFE HIDDEN IN YOUR BRA?
WHO DO YOU THINK YOU ARE, FUJIKO-CHAN?!

Fujiko-chan, page 42

Fujiko Mine, aka Fujiko-chan, is a femme fatale from Monkey Punch's classic manga/anime series *Lupin III*. She's known for hiding weapons within her spacious cleavage.

Duo x Heero, page 47

Fujiyoshi's consternation is due to the fact that her *dôjinshi* (self-published comics) have been left out for the garbage collectors. Based on the cover, it's a *yaoi* (guy-on-guy) pairing of Duo Maxwell and Heero Yuy from the 1995 anime series *Mobile Suit Gundam Wing*.

Well, 'Tis Better to Be a Couple Than to Be by Oneself, page 48

This title is a reference to a line in Sakunosuke Oda's 1940 novel, *Meoto Zenzai* ("Bravo for the Couple").

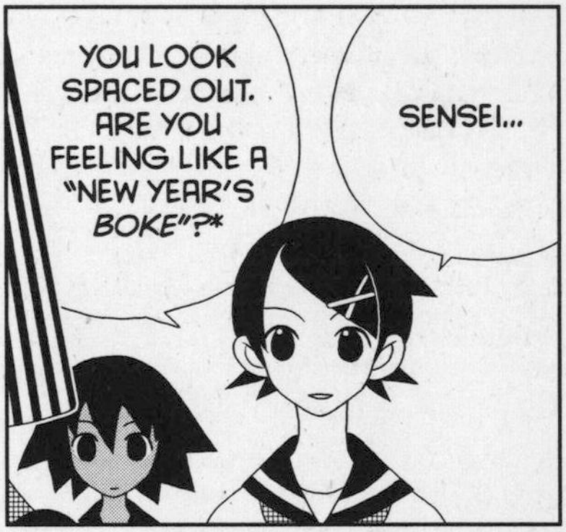
SENSEI...
YOU LOOK SPACED OUT. ARE YOU FEELING LIKE A "NEW YEAR'S *BOKE*"?*

Tsukkomi-boke, page 49

This chapter involves a play on words from Japanese *manzai* comedy, a form of stand-up comedy usually involving two performers—a funny man (*boke*), who says off-the-wall or obtuse things, and a straight man (*tsukkomi*), who reacts with exasperation and berates or slaps the *boke*. The term *boke* comes from the verb *bokeru*, which carries the meaning of "senility" or "airheadedness," while the term *tsukkomi* literally means "a powerful attack," "butting in," or generally inserting or forcing yourself into a situation. *Shogatsu Boke* ("New Year's Boke") is a slang term used to describe people who are "out of it" at the beginning of the New Year (presumably from all the holidays, partying, hustle-bustle, etc.). Misinterpreting the meaning of *tsukkomi* and *boke*, Maria takes it upon herself to go around slapping and correcting all the different kinds of *bokes* in Japan.

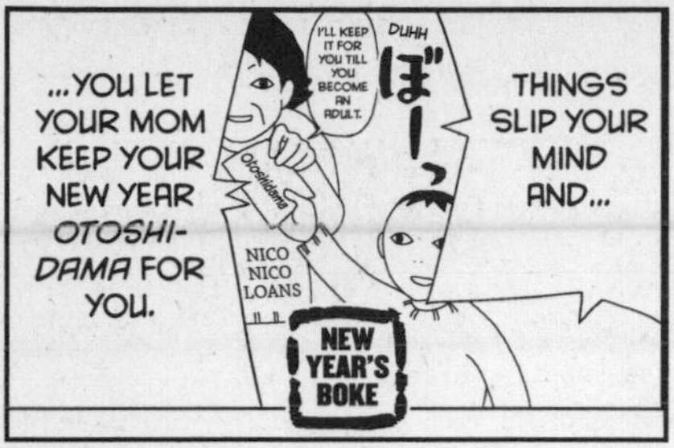
THINGS SLIP YOUR MIND AND...
DUHH
ぼーっ
I'LL KEEP IT FOR YOU TILL YOU BECOME AN ADULT.
...YOU LET YOUR MOM KEEP YOUR NEW YEAR OTOSHIDAMA FOR YOU.
Otoshidama
NICO NICO LOANS
NEW YEAR'S BOKE

Otoshidama, page 53

Otoshidama is the pocket money given out to children on New Year's Day. The money is put into a pretty little envelope made especially for the occasion.

Writing with a brush and ink, page 53

Kakizome is the Japanese custom of practicing calligraphy at the beginning of the New Year (usually when sending New Year's cards—see the notes for page 5). In the original Japanese, Zetsubou-sensei makes an embarrassing misspelling, hence the English translation "Happy New Yar."

Assorted references, page 53

"Receiving fees" refers to the Japanese law that each household with a working television must pay monthly fees to NHK, Japan's national public broadcasting system. However, there is no penalty for not paying, so many (possibly most) people don't pay anything, and the system is sort of a national joke. Autobacs is a chain retailer of automotive parts and accessories. The Print Gocco is a self-contained compact color printer invented in 1977, used for do-it-yourself screen printing. Very popular in Japan in their heyday, they were discontinued in 2008 due to competition from home computers and printers. "Bought a white band" refers to the white "awareness bracelets" sold for charity by the "Make Poverty History" campaign. Hikomaro (1966–) is a Japanese comedian and TV talent. Akiko Yada (1978–) is a Japanese actress who suffered from a scandal in 2006 when the paparazzi took suggestive photos of her on a Hawaiian vacation with "bad boy" actor/musician Manabu Oshio (1978–). Her image was tarnished and she lost several big ad contracts (see also the reference on page 111).

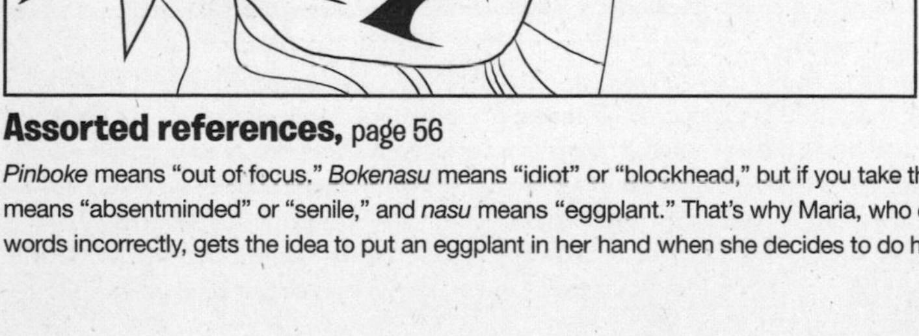
YOU BOKENASU!

Assorted references, page 56

Pinboke means "out of focus." *Bokenasu* means "idiot" or "blockhead," but if you take the word apart, *boke* means "absentminded" or "senile," and *nasu* means "eggplant." That's why Maria, who often interprets words incorrectly, gets the idea to put an eggplant in her hand when she decides to do her tsukommi.

Assorted references, page 57

Ai Hamanaka is the title character of Tozen Ujiie's frequently dirty gag manga *Shojo Daisei Kateikyoshi Hamanaka Ai* ("Ai Hamanaka, Adult Home Tutor Girl"), which ran in *Weekly Shônen Magazine*, the same magazine where *Sayonara, Zetsubou-sensei* appears. Rin Yuriko, "natural *boke*," is a parody of the idol/model Yuko Ogura (1983–), who is famous for affecting a ditzy, innocent, "cute and dumb" look.

Peace bokes, page 59

Heiwa Boke ("Peace Boke," or "Peace Stupor") is a term that has been used by hawkish Japanese politicians to describe Japanese people who (in keeping with Japan's pacifistic postwar constitution) believe that Japan should not have a true standing army or engage in military activity overseas. The building in panel 6 is the National Diet Building, where the main business of the Japanese government is conducted.

Assorted references, page 60

The "Kyushu Kinkai Gas Fields" are a veiled reference to the Higashi Shinakai (East China Sea) Natural Gas Fields, which lie beneath the ocean floor between Okinawa and China. Japan and China have disputed the ownership of the gas resources. Dr. Mashirito is a mad scientist in Akira Toriyama's 1980–1984 gag manga *Dr. Slump*. Former Japanese prime minister Junichiro Koizumi really did ride a Segway when President Bush gave him one as a gift in 2005. "Playing *Boke*" was originally written in Japanese as *otoboke* ("playing dumb").

I've Always Called That Person a Leftover, page 62

This title is a reference to a line in Natsume Soseki's 1914 novel, *Kokoro* ("Heart"). The original line reads "I've always called that person 'sensei.'"

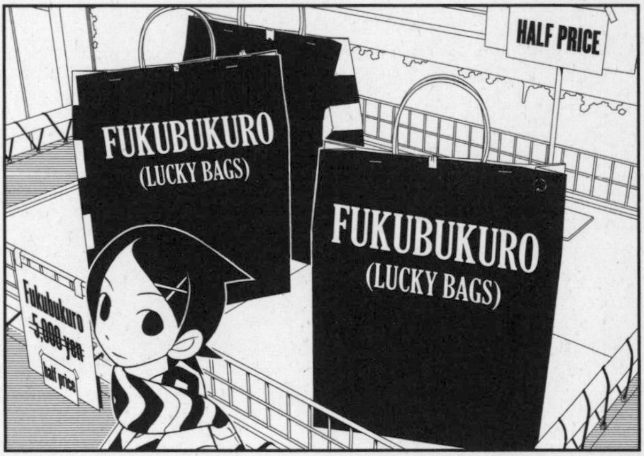
HALF PRICE
FUKUBUKURO
(LUCKY BAGS)
FUKUBUKURO
(LUCKY BAGS)
Fukubukuro
5,000 yen
half price

Fukubukuro, page 63

The word means "lucky bag." It's a Japanese New Year's Day custom for retailers to fill shopping bags with unknown, random contents and sell them for a big discount. Originally, it was a great way for merchants to get rid of excess merchandise, but nowadays, there are some seriously good *fukubukuro* available. *Fukubukuro* are available from all different types of retailers, who fill the bags according to what they specialize in, sometimes with rather iffy contents.

Cicciolina, page 69

Cicciolina, aka Ilona Staller (1951–), is a Hungarian-born Italian porn star and politician.

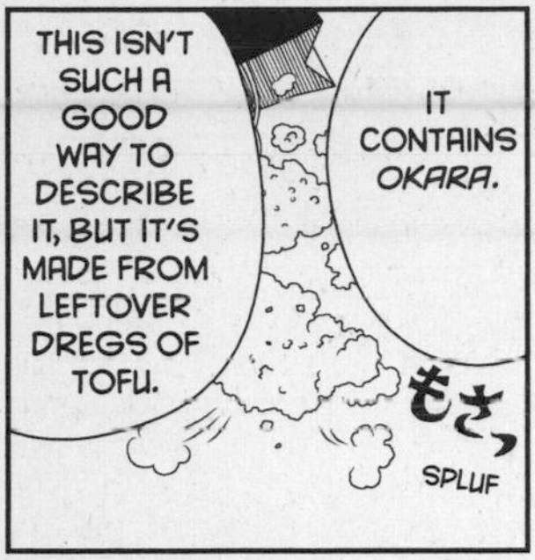
IT CONTAINS OKARA.
THIS ISN'T SUCH A GOOD WAY TO DESCRIBE IT, BUT IT'S MADE FROM LEFTOVER DREGS OF TOFU.
もさっ
SPLUF

Okara**,** page 69

This is a byproduct of making soy milk. It's rich in protein and calcium and is really tasty, and healthy when mixed with other ingredients. It's also used extensively as animal feed.

Assorted references, page 71

The Orix BlueWave was a Japanese pro baseball team owned by the Orix Group. In 2004 it was merged with the Orix Kintetsu Buffaloes to form the Orix Buffaloes. Hisashi Iwakuma (1981–) did not want to pitch for the new merged team, so he was released from his contract and signed with the Tohoko Rakuten Golden Eagles. "Dog heads" refers to Chinese restaurants in Japan that allegedly serve dog meat and to an incident in which a food importer threw an unsold dog's head into a river. He was caught and gave the excuse that he thought it would be good "carp food," hence Maria's comment. The chocolate bars refer to the confectionary company Lotte, a major sponsor of the Japan Skating Federation. They often use skaters in their advertisements and are said to even have a say in the Federation's selection process for skaters (see page 101). The "Osaka City Government" refers to Osaka's infamous deficits, wasteful public spending, and pork-barrel projects. "Embroidery included" refers to an incident in which government personnel used public funds to buy suits, adding some embroidery to justify the purchase by calling the suits "uniforms." "Teikyo Electric Power Company" is a play on the real-life Tokyo Electric Power Company.

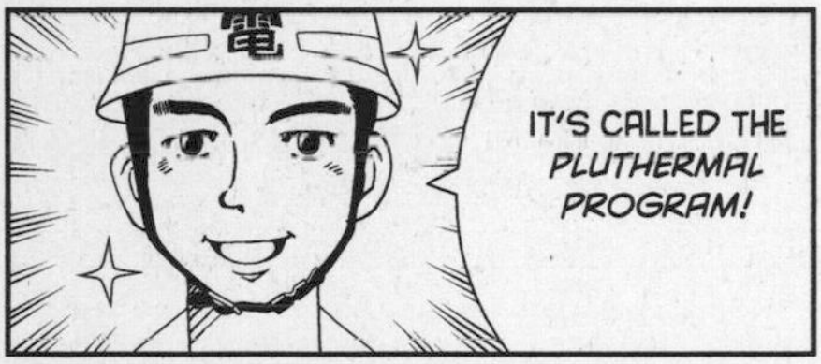
電
IT'S CALLED THE PLUTHERMAL PROGRAM!

Pluthermal program, page 72

"Pluthermal" is a Japanese word made of the English words "plutonium" and "thermal." It's a word invented by the Japanese government and electric utilities to describe a plan to use a new fuel in Japanese nuclear power plants (as described by the spokesperson on page 72).

THIS IS A PLASTIC SURGERY FUKUBUKURO.
THERE ARE LEFT-OVERS IN HERE.
UENO CLINIC

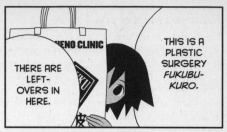

Plastic surgery *fukubukuro*, page 73

This joke refers to the Ueno Clinic, a popular clinic specializing in circumcisions, a fairly common form of cosmetic surgery among Japanese adult men. Therefore, the "leftovers" from their surgeries would be...

Tsugaru Correspondence School, page 76

This title is a reference to Osamu Dazai's 1994 novel, *Tsugaru*.

Hanten, page 81

A *hanten* is a short jacket usually worn over a kimono.

Assorted tests, page 82

In contrast to the very serious tests listed on page 81, the tests listed here are generally frivolous or of dubious merit. The Hakatakko Certification Test is a test given by the Japanese Culture Kentei Association to promote interest in regional culture. The Nahamage Qualification Trials is a test given to promote tourism in Japan's Oga peninsula. Based on the local custom in which *namahage* (demons or bogeymen) visit people's homes on New Year's Eve looking for "bad children" to scare, the test trains people to dress up and play the role of *namahage*. The Akashi Tako (octopus) Test is a test given in the major fishing port Akashi City, in which people are judged on their knowledge of the fishing industry, fishing culture, and the ability to test the freshness of fish and octopus. The Fabre Exams, named after entomologist Jean-Henri Fabre (1823–1911) and administered by the Japan Association Henri Fabre NPO, test one's knowledge of insects.

I'VE GOT TO BE-COME A STUDENT AGAIN!
AHA! THERE'S A MOUNTAIN OF EXAMS I CAN GET QUALIFICA-TIONS FOR!
PRACTICE AND LEARN

Assorted references, page 83

"Practice and Learn" is written in Japanese as *Keiko to Manabu*, the title of a continuing-education magazine that provides information on various courses, schools, and qualifications. However, Kumeta uses it as a pun on the name of the playboy actor Manabu Oshio (1978–), who has gone out with many different women, including women named Keiko, Megumi Yokoyama, Natsumi Abe, Akiko Yada (see notes for page 53), etc. The Time Schedule Qualifying Test is a test on how to save time on train and transportation schedules by finding the fastest routes.

Assorted references, page 88

The Sanzu River, or "River of Three Crossings," is a river that the dead must cross in Japanese Buddhist tradition, similar to the River Styx. One common way of committing suicide in Japan is to burn charcoal briquets in an enclosed space and suffocate on the smoke.

Ah, silence..., page 90

Ah, Mugon... ("Ah, silence") is a reference to Victor Hugo's 1862 novel, *Les Miserables*, originally translated in Japanese under the title *Aamujô* ("Ah, cruelty").

AH, IT'S *SETSUBUN* ALREADY.

Setsubun, page 91

This festival is celebrated on February 3. One of the main rituals is the "*mamemaki* ceremony" (literally, bean-throwing ceremony) to drive away the evil spirits. People scatter soybeans out the door while shouting, "Demons out!" and soybeans are thrown in while saying, "Good luck in!" Roasted soybeans are also eaten as a good-luck snack. Another ritual related to Setsubun, *ehomaki*, is described on page 92.

Things that shouldn't have been said, page 93

The quotes are references to unwise comments made by various Japanese media figures.

Anatahan Island, page 95

This refers to a famous incident in which a dozen Japanese merchant seamen were shipwrecked on the barren volcanic island of Anatahan in 1944. They found a man and a woman living there alone. By the time they were rescued in 1951, five men had died in fights over the woman. The story became the basis of a 1953 movie, *The Saga of Anatahan*.

BY USING A *FUTOMAKI* ROLL, YOU DON'T HAVE TO TALK ABOUT THINGS YOU DON'T WANT TO.
• THE HAPPENING AT ANATAHAN ISLAND
• THE SALES IN JAPAN FOR THE XBOX 360
• GAY OR STRAIGHT?
• REAL INTENTIONS TOWARD OTHER COUNTRIES

Real intentions toward other countries, page 95

The head on the left looks suspiciously like former Japanese prime minister Junichiro Koizumi (see notes for page 10).

CLAIRVOYANCE

Clairvoyance, page 99

When Kafuka uses the word "clairvoyance" after Chiri starts magically seeing things beyond her realm, Usui snidely remarks, "I bet you set up this whole scary scene just so you could make that pun!" In Japanese, *senrigan* ("clairvoyance") is written with three characters that can also be read as *Chirigan* ("Chiri's eyes"). It's all because the *kanji* for "thousand" can be read as either *sen* or *chi*. A similar *sen/chi* pun appears in the name of the heroine of Hayao Miyazaki's anime *Spirited Away*.

Assorted references, page 101

"T.A." is short for Ami Tokito (1987–), a former child actor and J-pop idol. She is often photographed wearing glasses. "The anchorwoman" is Yuko Aoki, a Japanese TV announcer who, in 2006, was rumored to be living with a married TV producer. "What's inside the soup" refers to a plotline involving drugged soup in Yûsei Matsui's 2005 manga *Majin Tantei Nôgami Neuro* (*Demon Detective Neuro Nôgami*). The "person who knows how to read the Poneglyph language" is the historian Nico Robin in the manga *One Piece*. "Princess Knight" (literally, *Ribon no Kishi*, "Knight of Ribbons") is a reference to Osamu Tezuka's classic manga of the same name, about a princess who disguises herself as a boy.

RATHER THAN USE AN *EHOMAKI*, WHICH IS KIND OF SHORT-SIGHTED...
...MAYBE IT'D BE BETTER TO USE A ROLLED UP *MAKI-SU* SO I CAN PLUG UP YOUR MOUTH FOREVER...CLEAN AND PRECISE.

Maki-su, page 102

A *maki-su* is a small bamboo or reed mat used to roll sushi.

Chocolates Returned Without Hesitation, page 104

This title is a reference to *Oshiminiaku Ai wa Ubau* ("Love Robs Without Hesitation"), a novel by Takeo Arishima (1878–1923). This chapter refers to Japanese Valentine's Day customs; on Valentine's Day, girls are supposed to give chocolates to guys they like, and on March 14 ("White Day"), guys are supposed to return the favor with gifts for the girls, such as white chocolate. Evidently, though, a lot can happen in the one-month waiting period.

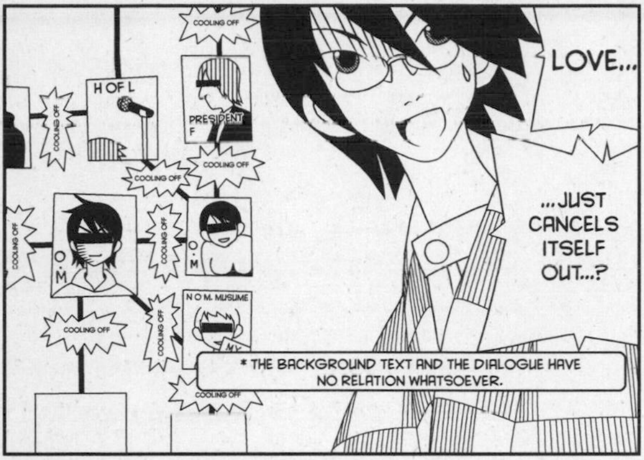
LOVE...
...JUST CANCELS ITSELF OUT...?
* THE BACKGROUND TEXT AND THE DIALOGUE HAVE NO RELATION WHATSOEVER.
COOLING OFF
H OF L
PRESIDENT F
O.M
O.M
N O M. MUSUME

Love just cancels itself out, page 109

The diagram in the lower left is a twisted web of Japanese celebrities who've had affairs with one another, including Manabu Oshio (the male O.M.), Megumi Okina (the female O.M.), Natsumi Abe of the J-pop group Morning Musume, and Susumu Fujita (president/CEO of the online ad agency CyberAgent, Inc.).

Assorted references, page 110

"Revival of the beef bowl" refers to the problems of the Yoshinoya Beef Bowl restaurant chain, which lost popularity following the mad cow disease scare in 2006 (see also page 127) "Embyronic stem cells" refers to the 2005–2006 controversy surrounding the Korean biotechnologist Hwang Woo-Suk (1953–), whose breakthroughs in stem cell research were later found to be a hoax. *Yutori Kyoiku* ("relaxed education") is a 2002 education initiative aimed at reducing stress in students and giving them more outlets for self-expression by shortening the Japanese school week from six days to five days (see page 113), reducing workload, and offering more electives. Some people blame it for a decline in Japanese academic abilities. "Hanshin" refers to the Hanshin Electric Railway Co., owners of the Hanshin Tigers baseball team. There were plans to list Hanshin on the Japanese stock exchange, but they were canceled when fans protested. Masahiro Kawai (1964–) is a former Japanese baseball player and now coach. Hayao Miyazaki (1941–) is a famous Japanese animator who "retired" in 1997 from his company Studio Ghibli, only to break his retirement several times to work on new films. "610,000 yen" refers to a 2005 incident when Mizuho Securities Co. made a data error in a stock sell order, entering a client's order to "sell one share of J-Com Co. at 610,000 yen" as "sell 610,000 shares at 1 yen each." Mizuho Securities lost 40 billion yen due to the mistake. Bobby Ologun is a Nigerian K-1 wrestler who became a popular TV personality in Japan, despite a scandal when it was discovered that he had lied about his age (claiming to be born in 1973, when actually, according to his driver's license, he was born in 1966). The Chubu Centrair International Airport was opened in Japan in 2005, despite criticism of the made-up name "Centrair." "Permission to join Keidanren" refers to the *Nippon Kaidanren* (Japan Business Federation). The IT corporation LiveDoor tried to join the Keidanren, but their attempt was cut short when LiveDoor was accused of securities fraud in one of Japan's biggest corporate criminal cases of 2006. "Alliances between TV stations and IT companies" refers to the planned business alliance between LiveDoor and Fuji TV, which was canceled for the same reason.

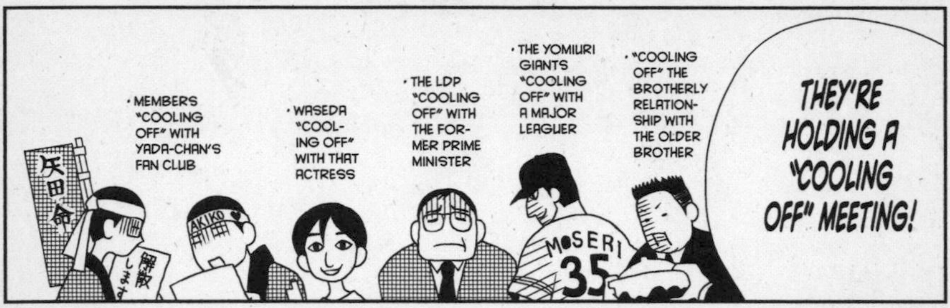
THEY'RE HOLDING A "COOLING OFF" MEETING!
• "COOLING OFF" THE BROTHERLY RELATION-SHIP WITH THE OLDER BROTHER
• THE YOMIURI GIANTS "COOLING OFF" WITH A MAJOR LEAGUER
• THE LDP "COOLING OFF" WITH THE FOR-MER PRIME MINISTER
• WASEDA "COOL-ING OFF" WITH THAT ACTRESS
• MEMBERS "COOLING OFF" WITH YADA-CHAN'S FAN CLUB
MOSERI
35
AKIKO
矢田命
解散します

Assorted references, page 111

"Cooling off the brotherly relationship" refers to the public dispute between two popular sumo wrestlers, brothers Takanohana and Wakanohana, as to who was going to take over the honorable role of "chief mourner" at the funeral of their sumo wrestler father in 2005.

Assorted references, page 112

It's hard to quit the motorcycle gang lifestyle, particularly in Japan. Nobuhiko Matsunaka (1973–) is a Japanese baseball player who, in 2006, signed a seven-year contract with the Fukuoka SoftBank Hawks. Paman, aka Perman, is a reluctant superhero in the classic manga *Paman* by Fujiko F. Fujio. "Buying brand names" refers to the phenomenon of people who buy expensive brand items, use them for a while, and then sell them at pawnshops to get money to buy the next hot brand item. Due to pushy salespeople, it's notoriously difficult to cancel a newspaper subscription in Japan. ODA stands for "Official Development Assistance," a category of development aid provided to poor countries by rich ones (not only by Japan). Kappa Ebisen is a popular Japanese snack food (a sort of shrimp-flavored crackers) that had a famous advertising slogan *Yamerarenai, tomaranai* ("Can't quit, can't stop").

The Story of Jiro, page 118

"The Story of Jiro" (*Jiro Monogatari*) is the name of a novel by Kojin Shimomura (1884–1955).

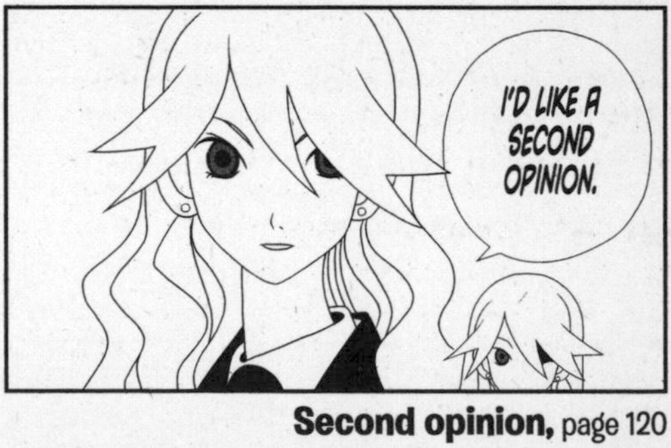
I'D LIKE A SECOND OPINION.

Second opinion, page 120

Throughout this chapter, the term "second opinion" is used in English in the original Japanese edition. It's an English loan word, which is why the characters go out of their way to define it on page 121.

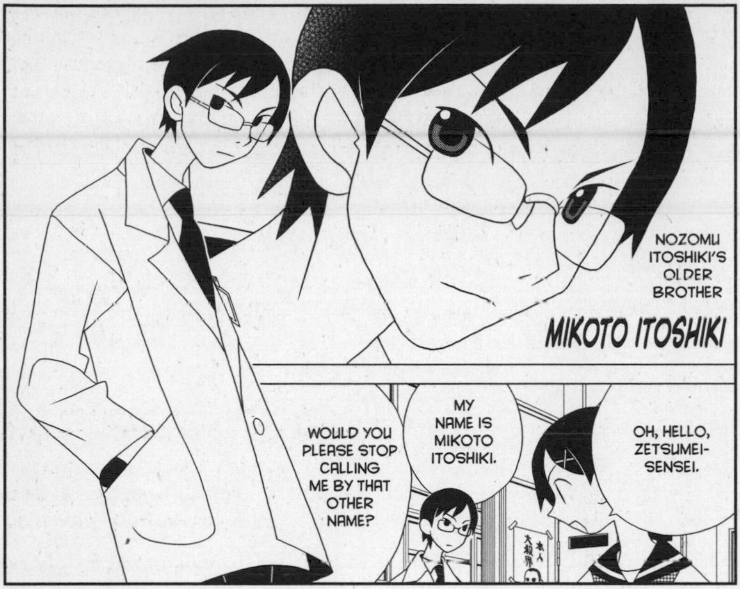
NOZOMU ITOSHIKI'S OLDER BROTHER
MIKOTO ITOSHIKI
OH, HELLO, ZETSUMEI-SENSEI.
MY NAME IS MIKOTO ITOSHIKI.
WOULD YOU PLEASE STOP CALLING ME BY THAT OTHER NAME?

Zetsumei-sensei, page 121

Like his younger brother, Nozomu, whose name can be misread as *zetsubou* ("despair"), school doctor Mikoto Itoshiki has a name with an unfortunate double meaning. His name can be misread as *zetsumei*, which means "to die," hence the nickname "Dr. Death."

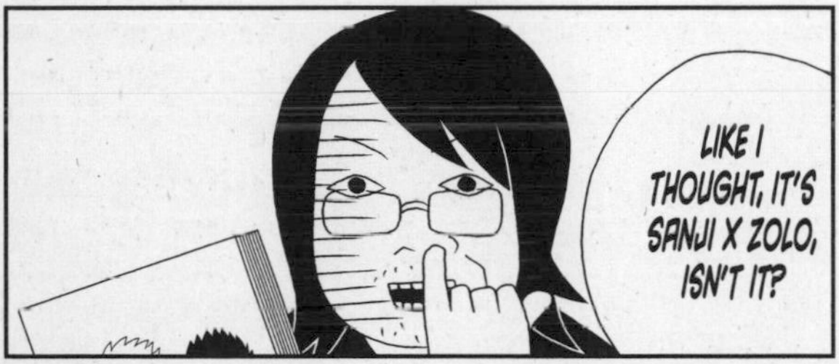
LIKE I THOUGHT, IT'S SANJI X ZOLO, ISN'T IT?

Sanji x Zolo, page 125

Sanji and Zolo are characters from the manga *One Piece*.

Assorted references, page 126

The Japan Teachers Union, founded in 1947, is Japan's oldest and largest union of teachers and school staff. Arthur Antunes Coimbra (1953–), aka Zico, is a former Brazilian soccer player and coach. He coached the Japanese national team from 2002 to 2006, and is known in Japan as *soccer no kamisama* ("the god of soccer"). Hidetoshi Nakata (1977–) is a famous Japanese soccer player. ("Nakata-shi" is a very formal, respectful way of saying his name.) The "Kitasenju Club" is the name of a *hitotsuma* ("someone else's wife") club, i.e., a gentleman's club with an adultery theme.

Assorted references, page 127

Yoshizumi Ishihara and Masamitsu Morita are TV weather reporters. Takafumi Horie (1972–) is a Japanese entrepreneur who founded the Internet portal LiveDoor (see notes for page 110). When LiveDoor was investigated for securities fraud in 2006, Horie resigned as CEO but was indicted on charges. Ryoji Miyauchi was LiveDoor's former CFO, and was also indicted. *Mezamishi TV* and *Yajiuma* are Japanese news/infotainment shows that run in competing time slots every weekday morning; both have fortune-telling segments. Piko and Don Konishi are competing TV fashion commentators. Bae Yong Joon (1972–) is a popular South Korean actor who often wears trendy glasses, although Hidetsugu Aneha (see page 30) also had an interesting style. Takefuji and Aiful are Japanese consumer finance companies.

Life Is Like a One-Tier Doll Display, page 132

This title is a reference to the 1927 novel *Aru Aho no Issho* ("A Fool's Life") by Ryunosuke Akutagawa. This chapter in general refers to the Japanese custom of *Hinamatsuri* ("Girl's Day"), a holiday on March 3, in which people display traditional dolls on a tiered display.

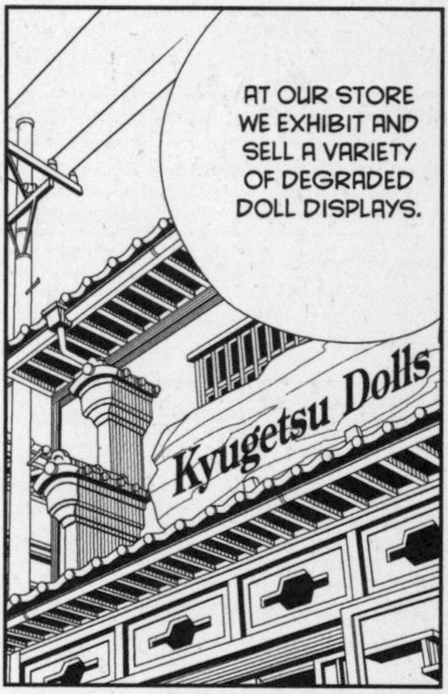
AT OUR STORE WE EXHIBIT AND SELL A VARIETY OF DEGRADED DOLL DISPLAYS.
Kyugetsu Dolls

Kyugetsu, page 139

Kyugetsu is a traditional Japanese doll store that's been in business since 1830. However, the Kyugetsu store in this story is spelled with different *kanji* that, although pronounced the same, mean "suffering month" or "destitute month."

THESE MOBILE SUITS ARE OFTEN THOUGHT OF AS THE WEAKEST IN THE SERIES...
...BUT ACTUALLY, THERE ARE EVEN WEAKER MOBILE SUITS IN EXISTENCE.
DOMO
TELEGOUF
GEZAKU

Assorted references, page 142

Panels 2 and 3 display an assortment of extremely obscure (and weak) mecha from the *Mobile Suit Gundam* anime and model franchise. *Bakusho On-Air Battle*, launched in 1999, is a TV show in which young comedians compete for laughs on-air (alone, in skits, or in *manzai* pairs).

RESTAURANTS IN FRONT OF TRAIN STATIONS
LAUGH AT RESTAURANTS IN THE SUBURBS
CROSSDRESSING GUYS WITH A SEXUAL FETISH
LAUGH AT CROSSDRESSING GUYS WHO HAVE CLEFT CHINS
KURIRIN LAUGHS AT YAMCHA
TWENTY-NINE-YEAR-OLD UNMARRIED OFFICE LADIES LAUGH AT THIRTY-YEAR-OLD UNMARRIED OFFICE LADIES

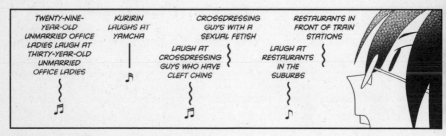

"Kuririn Laughs at Yamcha," page 143

Kuririn is one of the weaker characters in Akira Toriyama's 1984–1995 martial arts manga *Dragon Ball*. Yamcha, however, is even weaker.

Ishhikoro boshi, page 147

The *ishikoro boshi* (*ishikoro* hat) is a gadget in the manga *Doraemon* that causes the wearer to go unnoticed by everyone.

Duke Fleed, page 148

Duke Fleed is the name of the hero in the 1975 sci-fi mecha-anime *UFO Robo Grandizer*. The last survivor of his doomed planet, he escapes to earth and pretends to be a normal human with a human name, although it's not "Hiroshi Maigo."

A thousand *li,* page 153

Li is a Chinese unit of measurement equal to approximately 2.5 miles.

The Restaurant of Many Condolence Calls, page 162

This is a reference to the novel *The Restaurant of Many Orders* by Kenji Miyazawa (1896–1933).

BY CLAMP

Watanuki Kimihiro is haunted by visions. When he finds himself irresistibly drawn into a shop owned by Yûko, a mysterious witch, he is offered the chance to rid himself of the spirits that plague him. He accepts, but soon realizes that he's just been tricked into working for the shop to pay off the cost of Yûko's services! But this isn't any ordinary kind of shop . . . In this shop, Yûko grants wishes to those in need. But they must have the strength of will not only to truly understand their need, but to give up something incredibly precious in return.

Ages: 13+

Special extras in each volume! Read them all!

STORY BY KEN AKAMATSU
ART BY TAKUYA FUJIMA

BASED ON THE POPULAR ANIME!

Negi Springfield is only ten years old, but he's already a powerful wizard. After graduating from his magic school in England, the prodigy is given an unusual assignment: teach English at an all-girl school in Japan. Now Negi has to find a way to deal with his thirty-one totally gorgeous (and completely overaffectionate) students—without using magic! Based on the *Negima!* anime, this is a fresh take on the beloved *Negima!* story.

Available anywhere books or comics are sold!

PUMPKIN SCISSORS

RYOTARO IWANAGA

AFTER THE WAR. BEFORE THE PEACE.

Years of bitter war have devastated the Empire. Disease and privation ravage the land. Marauding bandits prey on the innocent.

To aid reconstruction, the Empire has formed Imperial Army State Section III, a.k.a. the Pumpkin Scissors, an elite unit dedicated to protecting the people.

They are the last best hope for a beleaguered nation. But will they be enough?

Special extras in each volume! Read them all!

VISIT WWW.DELREYMANGA.COM TO:
- Read sample pages
- View release date calendars for upcoming volumes
- Sign up for Del Rey's free manga e-newsletter
- Find out the latest about new Del Rey Manga series

RATING OT AGES 16+

DEL REY MANGA

The Otaku's Choice™

TOMARE! STOP

You're going the wrong way!

MANGA IS A COMPLETELY DIFFERENT TYPE OF READING EXPERIENCE.

TO START AT THE **BEGINNING**,
GO TO THE **END**!

That's right!

Authentic manga is read the traditional Japanese way—from right to left, exactly the *opposite* of how American books are read. It's easy to follow: Just go to the other end of the book and read each page—and each panel—from right side to left side, starting at the top right. Now you're experiencing manga as it was meant to be!